D1161115

The Book of
LEVITICUS

by

GORDON J. WENHAM

WILLIAM B. EERDMANS PUBLISHING COMPANY
GRAND RAPIDS, MICHIGAN

Reprinted, March 1988

Library of Congress Cataloging in Publication Data

Bible. O. T. Leviticus. Wenham, 1979.
    The book of Leviticus.

    (The New International Commentary on the Old
Testament: v. 3)
        Includes index.
        1. Bible. O. T. Leviticus—Commentaries.
I. Wenham, Gordon J. II. Title. III. Series.
BS1253   1979   222'.13'077   79-99
ISBN 0-8028-2353-X

TO LYNNE

AUTHOR'S PREFACE

Leviticus used to be the first book that Jewish children studied in the synagogue. In the modern Church it tends to be the last part of the Bible anyone looks at seriously. This neglect is understandable, since Leviticus is largely concerned with subjects that seem incomprehensible and irrelevant to contemporary man. Rituals for sacrifice and regulations concerning uncleanness appear to have nothing to say to men living in the closing years of the twentieth century. "You shall love your neighbor as yourself" (Lev. 19:18) is the only memorable maxim in what is to many an otherwise dull book. In practice then, though not of course in theory, Leviticus is treated as though it does not really belong to the canon of sacred Scripture.

This attitude is reflected in some modern commentaries, which view Leviticus as little more than a record of one stage in Israel's religious development without any permanent spiritual value. Other commentators have gone to the opposite extreme in an attempt to christianize Leviticus. By means of allegorical interpretation every detail of the law is made to prefigure some aspect of Christ's work and ministry. Though this approach is less popular today than it was in the early church, it still has its adherents.

The approach favored in this commentary takes with equal seriousness both the plain original meaning of the text and its abiding theological value. The primary duty of every commentator is to elucidate what the author of the book meant and to recover what the earliest readers understood it to mean. But Christian commentators are bound to go further and say what the sacred text has to teach the church today, remembering Paul's words that "whatever was written in former times was written for our learning" (Rom. 15:4). I am tempted to describe this approach as the classic Protestant approach, since one of the best early commentaries along these lines is

vii

John Calvin's *Commentaries on the Four Last Books of Moses*. But in more recent times the Catholic writer R. North in his study of Lev. 25 has provided the finest example of an attempt to expound the plain historical meaning of Leviticus and its enduring theological message.[1]

The process of biblical interpretation is never ending. Every commentator builds on the insights of his predecessors, sometimes endorsing, sometimes correcting their views. But alongside the ordinary commentaries I have found great value in three other types of approach. First, there are studies of OT ritual and sacrifice which compare and contrast biblical customs with the practices of other peoples of the ancient Near East.[2] These help to clarify the distinctive features of biblical religion. Second, there are the works of social anthropologists,[3] whose sensitivity to the significance of ritual has produced valuable suggestions about the meaning of its symbolism, replacing the intuitive guesses of earlier exegetes by empirically based interpretation. Third, the methods of the new literary criticism[4] with its concern for structure, key words, repetition, and summaries, can be of great value in bringing out the author's special interests and making exegesis more objective. Using these new exegetical tools this commentary aims to update the interpretations in the older commentaries and make clear what the text meant in its original context.

In pursuit of the second aim, to bring out "the abiding theological value" of Leviticus, I have included at the end of each chapter or at some other appropriate place a discussion of the relationship of the section to the NT and to Christianity. In these discussions the reader's attention is drawn to passages in the NT which make use of ideas, words, or rituals drawn from the relevant chapter in Leviticus. It came as a surprise to discover how pervasive are Levitical ideas in the NT. The Introduction also includes two sec-

---

1. R. North, *Sociology of the Biblical Jubilee* (Rome: Pontifical Biblical Institute, 1954).
2. E.g., B. A. Levine, *In the Presence of the Lord* (Leiden: Brill, 1974); J. Milgrom, *Studies in Levitical Terminology* (Berkeley: University of California, 1970) and *Cult and Conscience* (Leiden: Brill, 1976).
3. E.g., M. Douglas, *Purity and Danger* (London: Routledge and Kegan Paul, 1966) and *Implicit Meanings* (London: Routledge, 1975); E. R. Leach, *Culture and Communication* (London: Cambridge UP, 1976).
4. E.g., S. E. McEvenue, *The Narrative Style of the Priestly Writer* (Rome: Biblical Institute Press, 1971). The new literary criticism should not be confused with the old source criticism.

tions dealing with the relationship between the OT law and the NT gospel.[5]

One omission may be noted. Modern commentaries often devote a great deal of space to source and historical criticism of Leviticus. Detailed discussion of these issues has been deliberately eschewed in this commentary. It seemed more important to establish the plain meaning of the text and its theological message than to pursue conjectures about how the book was written. These critical debates have their place, but when they are allowed to dominate a commentary they can turn an intrinsically interesting part of the Bible into a desert more arid than Sinai. I have preferred to restrict this sort of discussion to the Introduction (see below—"Sources," "Date and Authorship"). There the main positions are set out so that the reader may appreciate the arguments for himself and follow them up if he wants to.

Finally I should like to thank all those who have helped me in the composition of the commentary: particularly the general editor, Professor R. K. Harrison, for his original invitation to write on Leviticus and his subsequent helpful advice; the publishers Routledge and Kegan Paul, for permission to quote from M. Douglas, *Purity and Danger;* my colleague Professor D. W. Gooding, for his guidance on various points; Mr. D. J. Davies of Nottingham University, for allowing me to read the typescript of his article "An Interpretation of Sacrifice in Leviticus" before its publication in *ZAW* 89 (1977); Miss G. Totten of the Baptist Union of Ireland, for typing the manuscript; my parents, for checking it; Mr. D. G. Deboys and Mrs. H. McConville for proofreading; and my wife Lynne for her constant support and encouragement.

GORDON J. WENHAM

---

5. See below, "The Theology of Leviticus" and "Leviticus and the Christian."

CONTENTS

ABBREVIATIONS

ANET	*Ancient Near Eastern Texts*[2]
AT	Ancien/Altes Testament
AV	Authorized (King James) Version
BASOR	*Bulletin of the American Schools of Oriental Research*
BDB	Brown-Driver-Briggs, *A Hebrew and English Lexicon of the OT*
BTB	*Biblical Theology Bulletin*
BZAW	*Beihefte zur Zeitschrift für die Alttestamentliche Wissenschaft*
CAD	*Chicago Assyrian Dictionary*
CBQ	*Catholic Biblical Quarterly*
DJD	*Discoveries in the Judaean Desert*
EQ	*Evangelical Quarterly*
ExpT	*Expository Times*
GK	Gesenius-Kautsch, *Hebrew Grammar*
HL	Hittite Laws
HTR	*Harvard Theological Review*
HUCA	*Hebrew Union College Annual*
IDBS	*The Interpreter's Dictionary of the Bible,* Supplementary Volume, 1977
IEJ	*Israel Exploration Journal*
JAOS	*Journal of the American Oriental Society*
JBL	*Journal of Biblical Literature*
JNES	*Journal of Near Eastern Studies*
JQR	*Jewish Quarterly Review*
JSS	*Journal of Semitic Studies*
LE	Laws of Eshnunna
LH	Laws of Hammurabi
LXX	Septuagint
MAL	Middle Assyrian Laws
MT	Masoretic Text
NEB	New English Bible
OTS	*Oudtestamentische Studiën*
PEQ	*Palestine Exploration Quarterly*

ABBREVIATIONS

RB	*Revue Biblique*
RSV	Revised Standard Version
SP	Samaritan Pentateuch
TB	*Tyndale Bulletin*
TDOT	*Theological Dictionary of the OT*
TEV	Today's English Version (*Good News for Modern Man*)
THWAT	*Theologisches Handwörterbuch zum AT*
UF	*Ugarit-Forschungen*
VT	*Vetus Testamentum*
VTE	Vassal-Treaties of Esarhaddon
VTS	*Supplements to Vetus Testamentum*
ZAW	*Zeitschrift für die Alttestamentliche Wissenschaft*

The Book of
LEVITICUS

INTRODUCTION

I. TITLE AND CONTENTS

The first word of the book serves as its Hebrew title, *wayyiqrā'*, "and he called." The English title Leviticus is borrowed from the Latin Vulgate translation, which in turn had adapted it from the Septuagint, the early Greek version of the Pentateuch.

Leviticus is a fairly appropriate title for the book for it deals largely with priestly matters, and the priests were drawn from the tribe of Levi. Thus chs. 1–7 deal with sacrifice, chs. 8–10 with the institution of the high-priesthood, chs. 11–15 with the rules of uncleanness administered by the priests, and so on.

It would be wrong, however, to describe Leviticus simply as a manual for priests. It is equally, if not more, concerned with the part the laity should play in worship. Many of the regulations explain what the layman should sacrifice. They tell him when to go to the sanctuary, what to bring, and what he may expect the priest to do when he arrives. Most of the laws apply to all Israel: only a few sections specifically concern the priests alone, e.g., chs. 21–22. The lay orientation of the legislation is particularly noticeable in ch. 23, where the whole emphasis lies on the days that must be observed as days of sabbath rest. This contrasts with Num. 28–29, which is a calendar for priests specifying what sacrifices must be offered at which festival.

II. THE STRUCTURE OF LEVITICUS

The material in Leviticus is for the most part clearly and logically arranged. This is immediately apparent from a summary of its contents.

3

I. Laws on Sacrifice (1:1–7:38)
  A. Instructions for the Laity (1:1–5:26 [Eng. 6:7])
    1. The burnt offering (ch. 1)
    2. The cereal offering (ch. 2)
    3. The peace offering (ch. 3)
    4. The purification offering (4:1–5:13)
    5. The reparation offering (5:14–26 [Eng. 6:7])
  B. Instructions for the Priests (6:1 [Eng. 8]–7:38)
    1. The burnt offering (6:1–6 [Eng. 8–13])
    2. The cereal offering (6:7–11 [Eng. 14–18])
    3. The priest's cereal offering (6:12–16 [Eng. 19–23])
    4. The purification offering (6:17–23 [Eng. 24–30])
    5. The reparation offering (7:1–10)
    6. The peace offering (7:11–36)
    7. Summary (7:37–38)
II. Institution of the Priesthood (8:1–10:20)
  A. Ordination of Aaron and his Sons (ch. 8)
  B. Aaron's First Sacrifices (ch. 9)
  C. Judgment on Nadab and Abihu (ch. 10)
III. Uncleanness and its Treatment (11:1–16:34)
  A. Unclean Animals (ch. 11)
  B. Uncleanness of Childbirth (ch. 12)
  C. Unclean Diseases (ch. 13)
  D. Cleansing of Diseases (ch. 14)
  E. Unclean Discharges (ch. 15)
  F. Purification of the Tabernacle from Uncleanness (ch. 16)
IV. Prescriptions for Practical Holiness (17:1–27:34)
  A. Basic Principles about Sacrifice and Food (ch. 17)
  B. Basic Principles of Sexual Behavior (ch. 18)
  C. Principles of Neighborliness (ch. 19)
  D. Capital and Other Grave Crimes (ch. 20)
  E. Rules for Priests (ch. 21)
  F. Rules about Eating Sacrifices (ch. 22)
  G. Religious Festivals (ch. 23)
  H. Rules for the Tabernacle (24:1–9)
  I. A Case of Blasphemy (24:10–23)
  J. Sabbatical and Jubilee Years (ch. 25)
  K. Exhortation to Obey the Law: Blessing and Curse (ch. 26)
  L. Redemption of Votive Gifts (ch. 27)

The overall logic of the arrangement is particularly clear in chs. 1–16. First of all, the different kinds of sacrifice are explained in

4

chs. 1–7, since they are presupposed in the rituals described in the following sections. Three different kinds of sacrifice are involved in the ordination and installation of the priests (chs. 8–10). Sacrifices are also necessary in the purificatory rites described in chs. 14–16.

To offer sacrifice a priesthood is necessary. Therefore the ordination of the first priests is described in the second main section, chs. 8–10.

The occasions for sacrifice form the subject of the third main section (chs. 11–16). Many things, e.g., certain animals, diseases, and bodily discharges as well as moral failures can make a man unclean and necessitate the offering of sacrifice as part of the cleansing process. These faults affect not only the individual, but the tabernacle itself, the seat of God's presence among his people. If this is polluted, Israel's holy redeemer can no longer dwell among them and their *raison d'être* is destroyed. This section therefore concludes fittingly with a description of the great day of atonement ceremonies when the tabernacle was purged of all its defilements.

Under the Sinai Covenant Israel had been called to become "a kingdom of priests and a holy nation" (Exod. 19:6). The first sixteen chapters of Leviticus focus almost exclusively on Israel's priestly responsibilities. By preserving her purity these laws enable her to remain in contact with God and witness to his presence in the world. The closing chapters of the book focus on the demand for national holiness: "You must be holy: for I the Lord your God am holy" (Lev. 19:2). This and similar formulas are used repeatedly throughout chs. 18–26 to emphasize that Israel has been redeemed to be God's holy people, and serve to bring together laws on a variety of subjects whose interrelationship is not always obvious. This collection of laws concludes in typical oriental fashion with a series of blessings on the nation if she keeps the law and threats if she does not. Ch. 27 seems to be a sort of appendix.

One striking feature of the Levitical laws is so obvious that it can be overlooked. At the beginning of nearly every chapter, and often several times within a chapter, it says, "The Lord spoke to Moses." In other words, all the laws are set within a narrative framework. According to the author they were revealed to Moses during Israel's wilderness wanderings to meet specific problems that arose at that time. This historical setting accounts for some features of the book that seem out of place if the book were arranged in a purely logical fashion. For example, the instructions to the priests in ch. 10 are placed in their present position because they were given

then, and the same motive may account for the law on blasphemy in
ch. 24. The people knew that it was wrong "to take God's name in
vain" (Exod. 20:7), but did not know how to punish those who did.
This episode explains how God disclosed that stoning was the appropriate penalty.

The laws were thus intended to meet immediate pressing
problems. The point is made specifically in the cases just discussed,
but the same idea underlies the arrangement of the other groups of
law. Leviticus is part of the Pentateuch. It is preceded by Exodus
and followed by Numbers and therefore cannot be looked at in
isolation. Exodus told how God brought Israel out of Egypt, and
made a covenant with them at Sinai that they should be his people
and that he should be their God. The book of Exodus concluded with
the erection of the tabernacle and God appearing in glory there, a
sign that he would be with them wherever they went (Exod. 40:34–
38).

A church building needs services and ministers as well as
God's presence, so it is natural that the sequel to Exodus should
begin by describing the worship in the tabernacle (Lev. 1–17). The
succeeding chapters are equally apt within the historical framework
of the Pentateuch. Israel's goal was Canaan, not the wilderness, and
indeed until the disastrous episode of the spies (Num. 13–14) the
Israelites expected to enter the promised land very shortly. Guidance as to the conduct befitting a holy people was therefore wel-
come at this stage of their development. Many of the laws in
chs. 18–27 could only apply to a sedentary agricultural community,
not to wandering nomads.

The actual quantity of narrative in Leviticus is very small.
Apart from the introductory formulas it is confined to chs. 8–10 and
24. Yet it is essential to recognize that all the laws are set within this
historical frame if their arrangement is to be appreciated.

III. THE SOURCES OF LEVITICUS

As we have seen, Leviticus is a well-organized book. Each topic
naturally succeeds the one before. But the author did not impose a
uniform literary style on the book: the laws are not always cast in the
same pattern. Words or turns of phrase characteristic of one section
do not always appear in another section, even though both sections
may deal with similar topics. In this respect Leviticus more closely

resembles the laws of Eshnunna with their variations in style between different sections than the laws of Hammurabi, which are drafted in an artificial and uniform style. Using such criteria as opening and closing formulas, the following groups of laws may be distinguished within Leviticus.

(1)	Chs. 1–3	key word	"food-offerings"
(2)	Chs. 4–5 (Eng. 6:7)	key word	"he will be forgiven"
(3)	Chs. 6 (Eng. 6:8)–17	opening formula	"this is (the law of)"
(4)	Chs. 18–26	regular formula	"I am the Lord (your God)"
(5)	Ch. 27	key word	"valuation"

This analysis of the material differs from the usual analysis of Leviticus. This ascribes the whole book to the priestly source (P), which in turn used earlier collections of law. Scholars generally hold that only the narrative sections (chs. 8–10, 16) come from P itself. The other sections were originally independent and have been worked over to give them a priestly slant and style. The earlier collections consisted of chs. 1–7, chs. 11–15, chs. 17–26 (the Holiness Code), and ch. 27.

The standard critical analysis just explained seems vulnerable at two points. First, it fails to recognize that the recurring opening phrase "this is" (these are) links together chs. 6–17. Indeed 17:2, "This is the thing which the Lord has commanded," is identical with 8:5. It is wrong to propose the existence of different sources merely on the basis that some sections are narrative, others legal. All Leviticus is law within a narrative framework. Second, it is doubtful whether ch. 17 belongs with the following chapters as part of the Holiness Code. Long ago Hoffmann[1] pointed out that ch. 17 seems to belong with what precedes it, not with what follows. Much more recently Kilian pointed out that Lev. 17 is quite distinct from the rest of the Holiness Code.[2]

The tentativeness of all attempts to discover sources in Leviticus must be underlined. Even if one admits their presence it does not necessarily follow that they ever circulated independently of each other. Analyses which purport to distinguish between an original source and the work of later redactors should be treated

---

1. Hoffmann I, p. 469.
2. R. Kilian, *Literarkritische und Formgeschichtliche Untersuchung des Heiligkeitsgesetzes* (Bonn: Hanstein, 1963), pp. 176ff.

more warily still. We do not know enough about the development of Hebrew language, law, and religion to make the elaborate analyses offered in some works anything more than conjectures.[3]

IV. AUTHORSHIP AND DATE

Everywhere Leviticus claims to record what God revealed to Moses; nowhere does it ever state that Moses wrote down what he heard. The book's lack of explicitness about its literary origin is one reason for the great diversity of views among modern scholars. Traditionalists hold that Leviticus is one of the earliest parts of the OT, dating from the time of Moses. The majority critical view puts its composition nearly a thousand years later, after the return from exile. A third view, associated with some Israeli scholars, dates Leviticus much earlier, though not as early as Moses. The issue is highly complex: it really involves the question of the composition of the whole Pentateuch. Here there is only space to set out very briefly the arguments for and against the different views as far as they concern Leviticus.

1. The Traditional View[4]

This is the view that Leviticus was compiled by Moses himself, or at least that the material in the book, if not its final shape, goes back to Moses.

Four main arguments are used to support it. First, the book always presupposes that the laws were given to Moses in the wilderness. Time and again we are told, "The Lord spoke to Moses." The wilderness setting is not merely referred to in the introduction to each group of laws, it is often alluded to in the laws themselves. The sacrifices are offered in the tabernacle, not in the temple (chs. 1–17); lepers must live outside the camp, not outside the city (13:46);

---

3. C. S. Lewis wisely cautioned biblical critics against putting too much faith in the results of critical analysis. "The 'assured results of modern criticism', as to the way in which an old book was written are 'assured', we may conclude, only because the men who knew the facts are dead and can't blow the gaff." C. S. Lewis, *Fern-seed and Elephants* (Glasgow: Fontana, 1975), p. 117. T. Jacobsen's literary analysis of the *Sumerian King List* (Chicago: 1939) succeeded because he had sufficient inscriptions to date changes in Sumerian grammar. Were OT scholars in the same position with Hebrew their critical analyses would command more respect.
4. See bibliography under Bonar, Calvin, Gispen, Harrison, Hertz, Hoffmann, Keil, Külling.

17:1-9 presupposes that every Israelite is within easy reach of the tabernacle. Where laws would apply only to a settled people, they are generally prefaced by a statement that God is bringing Israel into the land of Canaan where they would become applicable (14:34; 18:3; 23:10; 25:2).

Second, traditional commentators assert there is nothing in Leviticus that could not date from the Mosaic period. Elaborate rituals and sacrificial systems are attested in the ancient Near East long before the time of Moses. The normal critical view that these institutions are a late feature of Israelite religion is contrary to what is known about the religious practices in neighboring contemporary cultures.

The third argument often advanced in favor of a Mosaic date for Leviticus is that the book is unsuited to the needs of the post-exilic age. For example, although Lev. 18 and 20 deal at length with the question of marriage, nothing is said about intermarriage with Canaanites, the burning issue in Ezra and Nehemiah's time (Ezra 9-10; Neh. 13:23ff.). While Leviticus magnifies the office of high priest, the priests of Nehemiah's day seem to have been opposed to reform (Neh. 13). The tithe laws[5] seem to presuppose a ratio of ten Levites to one priest, yet from Ezra 8:15 we discover that after the exile there was a great shortage of Levites; the lists (Ezra 2:36ff.; Neh. 7:39ff.) suggest a ratio of twelve priests to one Levite among the returning exiles.

Finally, the book of Ezekiel quotes or alludes to Leviticus many times[6] (e.g., Lev. 10:10//Ezek. 22:26; Lev. 18:5//Ezek. 20:11; Lev. 26//Ezek. 34). This does not of course prove a Mosaic date for Leviticus, merely that it was an old work, the laws of which were binding on Israel because they enshrined the covenant between God and his people.

2. The Standard Critical View[7]

The postexilic origin of the priestly work (P) (Leviticus and parts of Genesis, Exodus, and Numbers) has become such an axiom of biblical scholarship that few modern commentaries or OT introduc-

---

5. Num. 18:26ff. Scholars of all persuasions agree that this material is of the same general period as Leviticus.
6. See Hoffmann I, p. 478; II, pp. 3f., 81f., 319f., 359-361, 384-86 for full lists of parallels.
7. See bibliography under Baentsch, Bertholet, Clements, Eissfeldt, Elliger, Fohrer, Kaiser, Kilian, Kornfeld, Maarsingh, Noth, Porter, Reventlow, Snaith, Wellhausen.

tions set out in detail the arguments in favor of this position. One has to turn to J. Wellhausen's *Prolegomena to the History of Israel* (1878) for the classic exposition of why P is believed to be the latest of the Pentateuchal sources.[8]

According to Wellhausen one can trace a development in Israel's religious life and practice. In the earliest days worship was simple, free, and spontaneous. It gradually became more hidebound by law and custom, until eventually it reached a stage of rigid ritualistic legalism. With the growing emphasis on form and ritual went an increase in the power and privileges of the priesthood. P and the books of Chronicles represent the endpoint of this religious evolution.

These trends can be discerned in several different areas of religious life. First, there is the question of the place of worship. In the days of Samuel there was freedom to sacrifice wherever one chose (e.g., 1 Sam. 16:2). King Josiah, however, limited all sacrifice to the temple in Jerusalem (2 K. 23; cf. Deut. 12). Leviticus (e.g., 17:1–9) simply assumes that all sacrifices must be offered in the tabernacle. According to most critical scholars the tabernacle and the cult described in Leviticus are projections into the Mosaic past of the temple in Jerusalem. That Leviticus just takes it for granted that all sacrifice will take place in the tabernacle, i.e., the temple, and does need to underline the point, shows that Josiah's centralization measures had been universally accepted, having taken place a long time before P was written.

The trend toward ritualism is obvious in the history of sacrifice. In early times sacrifice was a joyful fellowship meal (Judg. 13:16ff.). In Leviticus sacrifice has become an elaborate priestly function whose prime purpose was the atonement of sin.

In the great national festivals the flexibility of the early period subsequently gave way to a rigid timetable. The feasts of unleavened bread, weeks, and booths were originally harvest festivals. In early times each tribe celebrated them at times that suited the state of crops in their area. Later when all worship was centralized in Jerusalem it was necessary to give a fixed date so that the whole nation could keep the festivals together. This is what is presupposed in Lev. 23.

Over the years the priestly hierarchy became more highly developed and richer. In early times a priest was not even necessary

8. S. R. Külling, *Zur Datierung der "Genesis-P-Stücke"* (Kampen: Kok, 1964), gives the most thorough review of the arguments for and against the late date of P.

to offer sacrifice. By postexilic times priests were not only indispensable, but there were great differentiations within the priesthood, with Levites, priests, and high priest. Leviticus with its stress on the importance of the high priest betrays its late origin. In early times gifts to the priests were optional, or at least unregulated by law. Gradually the priests extended their rights. In Leviticus they insist on being given tithes, firstfruits, and many parts of the sacrifices. According to Wellhausen this was a late development.

One final argument in favor of a late date for P rests on the difference between the books of Chronicles and Kings. Kings, probably written about 550 B.C., says little about the worship in Jerusalem. But Chronicles, possibly written two centuries later than Kings, describes a very elaborate cult with many features akin to P. This similarity between P and Chronicles, it is claimed, proves the late date of P.

Since Wellhausen, many details of the above scheme have been modified; but the general picture has remained unaltered in most textbooks: Israel's religion evolved from the simple, flexible, liberal Protestantism attested in the books of Judges and Samuel into the legalistic ritualism akin to medieval Catholicism that is found in the postexilic priestly code. It is, however, admitted by those who accept this general position that while P (and therefore Leviticus) was not finally edited until the late fifth century B.C., it does at some points reflect the practices of the preexilic temple.

3. A Mediating Position[9]

A third view mediates between the traditional view and the standard critical view of Leviticus by maintaining that P is preexilic, but not Mosaic. This view owes its contemporary standing mainly to the advocacy of Y. Kaufmann, though it was much more common in the nineteenth century before Wellhausen's *Prolegomena* was published.

Kaufmann challenged the basic assumptions of the standard view, observing that "Fixity in times and rites and absence of 'natural spontaneity' characterize the festivals of ancient Babylonia, Egypt, and all known early civilizations. . . . These elements are . . . no indication of lateness."[10] Wellhausen assumed that Israelite society developed from a fairly secular one into one preoccupied with

9. See bibliography under Hurvitz, Kaufmann, Speiser, Weinfeld.
10. Y. Kaufmann, *The Religion of Israel* (London: Allen and Unwin, 1961), p. 178.

holiness and religion. Usually societies tend to become more secular with time,[11] and this, it is argued, would indicate that the priestly source is earlier than Deuteronomy, often dated to the seventh century B.C.

Kaufmann and his school have advanced more specific grounds for believing in the antiquity of P. Their arguments fall into three main types. First, the language, laws, and institutions of P do not fit with what else is known of the postexilic age. Chronicles, Ezra, and Nehemiah were written after the exile, Ezekiel during the exile. Their cultic vocabulary shares a number of terms with post-biblical Hebrew. But quite different terms are used in P. The only feasible explanation seems to be that P comes from a different, earlier period.[12] Similarly, some of the legal terminology in Leviticus was not understood in postexilic times, yet it finds parallels in second-millennium Mesopotamian law. This also points to an early date for Leviticus.[13] Other sacral institutions mentioned in P, e.g., animal tithes, the anointing of the high priest, the Urim and Thummim, did not exist in the era of the second temple. This is very strange if we suppose P was composed at this time.

The second point to note is that Deuteronomy and Joshua quote Leviticus and other P passages, but not vice versa. This is quite understandable if P was written before Deuteronomy, but not the other way around.[14]

The third reason for holding to the antiquity of P is that its notions of holiness and war, and its laws on sacrifice and blood, closely resemble those mentioned in the books of Judges and Samuel.[15] For example, Lev. 26:31 mentions a multiplicity of sanctuaries where sacrifices are offered. Lev. 17:2ff., which insists that all animals must be slaughtered in the sanctuary, could only apply to the wilderness period. If it had been intended for the settlement situation, it would have prevented most of the population

---

11. M. Weinfeld, *Deuteronomy and the Deuteronomic School* (Oxford: Clarendon, 1972), p. 179 n. 1.
12. A. Hurvitz, "The Evidence of Language in Dating the Priestly Code," *RB* 81 (1974), pp. 24–57.
13. E. A. Speiser, "Leviticus and the Critics," in *Oriental and Biblical Studies* (Philadelphia: University of Pennsylvania, 1967), pp. 123–142.
14. Weinfeld, *Deuteronomy*, pp. 180f.
15. This argument is put forward by Kaufmann and Weinfeld. It receives independent support from M. Douglas (*Implicit Meanings*, pp. 315f.), who says that on anthropological grounds she would date Leviticus early if it were not for the critical consensus dating it late.

from ever eating meat, unless there were numerous legitimate sanctuaries equivalent to the tabernacle scattered through the land. The ban on eating blood (Lev. 17:10ff.) is referred to in 1 Sam. 14:33–34.

In the commentary on the text I have tried to avoid making my exegesis dependent on any particular critical position. Each of three main positions has its own difficulties, and it would be rash to attempt to decide between them here. Despite the broad scholarly consensus, it does seem to me that a postexilic date for Leviticus is difficult to maintain in face of the abundant quotations in Ezekiel and of the linguistic evidence that P's vocabulary does not resemble that of late biblical Hebrew. A much earlier date is required by the evidence.

V. THE HEBREW TEXT OF LEVITICUS

The Hebrew text used for the translation contained in this commentary is the Masoretic Text (MT), which is the text found in the great majority of Hebrew manuscripts after the tenth century A.D.[16] This was the standard text used in the Jewish synagogue. The Samaritans preserved a slightly different Hebrew version of the first five books of the OT, the Samaritan Pentateuch (SP). Like the MT it is found complete only in medieval manuscripts. From early days the Christian Church relied on a Greek translation of the OT called the Septuagint (LXX). Though the translation of the Pentateuch was made in the third century B.C., the earliest complete manuscripts of the LXX date from the fourth century A.D. Other translations include the Peshitta (Syriac), the Targums (Aramaic), and the Vulgate (Latin), but they are less important for the textual criticism of the Pentateuch than the MT, SP, and LXX.

For many years it has been accepted that for most of the OT the MT preserves the best text: that is, it is closest to the original and fewer mistakes have been made in copying it than in transcribing the other versions. Translations or versions such as the LXX and SP need to be considered only where the MT presents obvious difficulty. This faith in the value of the MT of the Pentateuch has been

---

16. The most recent critical edition of Leviticus is *Biblia Hebraica Stuttgartensia* (Stuttgart: Württembergische Bibelanstalt, 1973).

vindicated by recent manuscript discoveries and studies of the LXX and SP.[17]

Among the Dead Sea Scrolls discovered since 1947, nine Hebrew manuscripts of Leviticus have been found,[18] two manuscripts of the LXX of Leviticus,[19] and one early targum.[20] As yet only a few of these manuscripts have been fully published, and they are just fragments, often containing a few words from a few verses. Nevertheless their antiquity makes them of extreme value to the textual critic. They push back our knowledge of the Hebrew text some 1100 years, from A.D. 1000 to about 100 B.C. They show that the MT type of text as well as texts akin to the SP and LXX were already in existence in pre-Christian times. The differences between these versions are not in the first instance the result of the way they were copied in the first millennium A.D. but are based on much earlier textual traditions. This gives the textual critic more confidence in using the standard editions of the MT, SP, LXX and so on to reconstruct the primitive Hebrew.

D. N. Freedman[21] has analyzed the Leviticus manuscript from Cave 11. He notes that it diverges from the MT, SP, and LXX at certain points, but none of its special readings is superior to the other versions. The editors of the other Qumran fragments point out that the fragment from Cave 1 is of the MT type, while those from Caves 2 and 6 have readings in common with SP and LXX.[22]

The relative merits of different texts cannot be assessed on the basis of a few isolated readings such as are preserved in the Qumran fragments. These manuscript fragments must be seen in the context of a broader textual grouping, such as the MT, SP, and LXX text type. When this is done the MT text of the Pentateuch is seen to

17. For a balanced survey of recent developments in OT textual criticism see S. Talmon, "The OT Text," in *The Cambridge History of the Bible* I (ed. P. R. Ackroyd and C. F. Evans) (Cambridge UP, 1970), pp. 159–199. On the LXX see S. Jellicoe, *The Septuagint and Modern Study* (Oxford: Clarendon, 1968); E. Tov and R. A. Kraft, *IDBS* pp. 807–815; and D. W. Gooding, *The Account of the Tabernacle* (Cambridge UP, 1959). On the SP see J. D. Purvis, *The Samaritan Pentateuch and the Origin of the Samaritan Sect* (Cambridge: Harvard UP, 1968), and B. K. Waltke, "The Samaritan Pentateuch and the Text of the OT," in *New Perspectives on the OT* (ed. J. B. Payne) (Waco: Word Books, 1970), pp. 212–239.
18. Total number of manuscripts mentioned by P. W. Skehan, *Jerome Bible Commentary* II (R. E. Brown et al., ed. (London: Geoffrey Chapman, 1968), p. 564.
19. Preliminary publication by P. W. Skehan in *VTS* 4 (1957), pp. 157–160.
20. *DJD* VI, pp. 86–89, 92f.
21. "Variant Readings in the Leviticus Scroll from Qumran Cave 11," *CBQ* 36 (1974), pp. 525–534.
22. *DJD* I, pp. 51–53; *DJD* III, pp. 56f., 106.

be superior to both the SP and the LXX, even when the latter share common readings against the MT. For example, in 1:6 SP and LXX both use the plural implying that the priests chop up the burnt offering, whereas the MT by using the singular suggests this was the worshipper's task. This could be a witness to different sacrificial customs, or to a different understanding of the law. This sort of variant is typical of the differences between the MT on the one hand and the LXX and SP on the other; for the most part they are slight changes or small additions intended to clarify the meaning.

One explanation of the distinctive features of the diverse textual traditions is that they developed in different geographical centers, the proto-MT possibly in Babylon, while the SP and LXX are both ultimately of Palestinian provenance. The original text from which the proto-MT and old Palestinian texts developed was presumably written even earlier in Palestine. It may be, however, that the divergences between the different textual traditions are due to factors other than geography. Nonetheless, what has been established is that for the Pentateuch the MT must be much closer to the original text than the SP and LXX. The MT has more archaic orthography, morphology, and syntax than the "Old Palestinian" text (SP and LXX). Indeed it has been argued that the "Old Palestinian" text is a fifth-century B.C. modernization of the original Hebrew text, a modernization that the MT has largely escaped. Such a view of the Pentateuch's textual history inevitably implies an earlier date for its original composition than generally espoused by critical scholars.[23]

For these reasons our translation adheres closely to the MT. Where I have departed from the MT I have drawn attention to it in the footnotes, though some trivial differences, such as the omission of a copula or definite article, which are not noticeable in translation are not mentioned.[24]

VI. THE THEOLOGY OF LEVITICUS

Leviticus is a book of laws set within a narrative framework, and it may therefore seem odd to talk about its theology. But the biblical

---

23. See the preceding section; for a fuller discussion of these points see Waltke, "The Samaritan Pentateuch," pp. 232ff.
24. The commentaries of Elliger and Gispen give more detailed discussions of the textual variants.

writers believed, and the Church has always accepted, that they were writing more than history. They were recording God's word to his people. Leviticus is therefore more than a description of past historical events and more than a collection of dated laws. It tells us about God's character and will, which found expression in his dealings with Israel and in the laws he gave them. Those who believe that God the Lord "is the same yesterday and today and for ever" may look to the book's theology for insights that are still valid and relevant.

The theology of Leviticus can hardly be discussed in isolation from that of the other books of the Pentateuch, particularly of those most closely related to it, the books of Exodus and Numbers. When these books are read in conjunction with Leviticus, some of the theological presuppositions of the latter stand out the more clearly. For instance Exodus describes the making of the Sinai Covenant and the erection of the tabernacle: both these institutions are fundamental to the theology of Leviticus. In an attempt to clarify some of the most important themes in the book we shall look at its theology under four main headings: the presence of God, holiness, the role of sacrifice, and the Sinai Covenant.

1. The Presence of God

God is always present with Israel in a real way. On occasion his presence becomes both visible and tangible. This idea is expressed times without number in Leviticus. The enduring presence of God is one of the theological presuppositions running through the whole book.

God is preeminently present in worship. The laws on sacrifice say repeatedly that the ceremonies take place "before the Lord"; the food offerings make "a soothing aroma for the Lord" (e.g., 1:9, 13, 17; 2:9; 3:5). In offering sacrifice the priests approach the Lord (16:1; 21:17). It is therefore of supreme importance for them to obey strictly God's instructions when performing their duties (8:9, 13, 17, 21, 29, 36, etc.). Death was a real possibility where priests acted on their own initiative (8:35; 10:2, 6, 7, 9; 16:2, 13). In one sense God was ever present with his people (Exod. 33:14ff.; 40:36–38), for he spoke regularly to Moses from the tabernacle (1:1; 4:1, etc.; cf. Exod. 29:42). But on special occasions the divine glory appeared in cloud and fire, so that all the people could recognize his coming. The initial law-giving at Sinai, the erection of the tabernacle, the ordination of the priesthood (Exod. 19; 40:34ff.; Lev. 9:23–24) were all marked in this spectacular fashion. So too were the judgments on Aaron's sons, the whole nation, and on Korah and his supporters (Lev. 10:2; Num. 14:10ff.; 16:19ff.).

God is present not only in worship, but at all times, even in the mundane duties of life. Leviticus knows of nothing that is beyond God's control or concern. The whole of man's life must be lived out in the presence of God. The recurring refrain in the later chapters, "I am the Lord your God" (e.g., 18:2ff.; 19:3–4, 10; 20:7), reminds the people of Israel that every aspect of their life—religion (chs. 21–24), sex (chs. 18 and 20), relations with neighbors (chs. 19, 25)—is of concern to their covenant redeemer. The behavior of each member of the covenant people must mirror that of God himself (20:7). The fear of God should prompt men to undertake good deeds they might otherwise neglect, such as help for the blind, the deaf, the elderly, and the poor. Though such people may have no redress against unfair treatment, God is aware of their plight and cares what his people do to them (19:14, 32; 25:17, 36, 43). They are warned that if they neglect his law, he will set his face against them. Individuals can expect to be cut off, that is suffer premature death (17:9–10; 18:29; 20:5–6, etc.), while the nation will endure the horrible consequences set out in ch. 26 (vv. 14–45).

Leviticus distinguishes between the permanent presence of God with his people, a presence which is to regulate their whole way of life, and his visible presence in glory which was obvious on special occasions. The book similarly distinguishes between his general presence within the camp of Israel and his localized presence above the ark within the tent of meeting. This tent of meeting ('ōhel mô'ēḏ, literally "tent of appointment," "rendezvous tent") was divided into two parts, the inner "holy of holies" housing the ark, and the outer section, the holy place. Outside the tent of meeting was the main altar for sacrifice. Because God dwelt in the tent of meeting, the sacrifices carried out before it on the altar are described as being performed "before the Lord" (e.g., 1:5, 11, etc.). It was because of the divine presence in the holy of holies that the high priest was allowed to enter it only once a year after performing the elaborate rituals described in ch. 16. It was from the tent of meeting that God spoke to Moses (1:1), and it was over the tent that God appeared in cloud and fire signifying his dwelling within it (Exod. 40:34–38).

According to Exod. 29:43–45 God's real and visible presence in the tabernacle was at the heart of the covenant. "There I will meet

with the people of Israel, and it shall be sanctified by my glory. . . .
And I will dwell among the people of Israel, and will be their God."
After the covenant was broken by the manufacture of the golden calf
Moses pleaded with God to renew his covenant: "If thy presence
will not go with me, do not carry us up from here" (Exod. 33:15). All
human efforts are in vain without divine aid. The same point is made
several times in Lev. 26. If the Israelites disobey the law, God will
walk contrary to them (vv. 21, 24, 28, 41). But if they obey, they can
expect to enjoy the highest of all divine blessings, his personal
presence. "I shall walk among you and become your God, and you
will become my people" (v. 12). All that was initially promised in
the Sinai Covenant (Exod. 19:5–6) will then prove true in reality.

For the NT Christian, God's presence was made known in the
incarnation. Alluding to the OT description of the tabernacle John
wrote "the Word became flesh and tabernacled among us . . .; we
have beheld his glory" (John 1:14). For Paul every Christian is a
walking shrine, a temple for the Holy Spirit in which God is to be
glorified (1 Cor. 6:19–20). Like the OT tabernacle the Christian
enjoys the permanent presence of the Spirit, but just as the old
shrine enjoyed a special manifestation of God's glory from time to
time, so the Christian should be filled with the Spirit and display
God's glory to the world (cf. Acts 6:15; 7:55–56; 2 Cor. 3;
Eph. 5:18).

2. Holiness

"Be holy, for I am holy" (11:44–45; 19:2; 20:26) could be termed the
motto of Leviticus. Certainly "holy," "clean," "unclean" and cognate words are among the most common in the book.[25] Yet their
precise significance is elusive. In this section, an attempt is made to
define them more precisely.

The priests were instructed "to distinguish between the holy
and the common, and between the unclean and the clean" (10:10). In
this verse a double contrast is made between "holy" and "common" on the one hand, and "clean" and "unclean" on the other.
"Holy" is therefore the opposite of "common," just as "clean" is

---

25. "Holy" (*qādôsh*) and its cognate terms, e.g., "sanctify," "holiness," occur 152
times in Leviticus (about 20 percent of the total occurrences in the OT). "Unclean"
(*ṭāmē'*) and its cognates occur 132 times (more than 50 percent of the total OT
occurrences). "Clean" (*ṭāhôr*) and related terms occur 74 times (35 percent of the
total). "Profane" (*ḥillēl*) occurs 14 times in Leviticus out of 66 references in the OT.
Statistics are from *THWAT* I, pp. 571, 647, 665; II, p. 593.

the opposite of "unclean." Ch. 11 divides the animal kingdom into two groups, those that are clean and those that are unclean. Similarly the following chapters (12–15) detail which illnesses make someone unclean and which leave him clean. "Common" (*ḥōl*) is likewise the reverse of "holy" (*qādôsh*), just as to "profane" (*ḥillēl*) is the converse of to "sanctify" (*qiddēsh*). In Hebrew thinking everything was either clean or unclean, holy or common. But what exactly constituted holiness and uncleanness? How do the different concepts relate to each other? Can something be holy and unclean at the same time? To clarify the following exposition I shall present a summary of my conclusions before defining in more detail what the different terms mean.

Everything that is not holy is common. Common things divide into two groups, the clean and the unclean. Clean things become holy, when they are sanctified. But unclean objects cannot be sanctified. Clean things can be made unclean, if they are polluted. Finally, holy items may be defiled and become common, even polluted, and therefore unclean. The relationship between these terms is set out in the following diagrams.

The diagrams can be combined as follows:-

$$\leftarrow \text{sanctify} \leftarrow \quad \leftarrow \text{cleanse} \leftarrow$$

holy   clean   unclean

$$\rightarrow \text{profane} \rightarrow \quad \rightarrow \text{pollute} \rightarrow$$

It is perhaps because "common" is a category between the two extremes of holiness and uncleanness that it is mentioned only once, in Lev. 10:10.

From this chart it is evident that cleanness is a state intermediate between holiness and uncleanness. Cleanness is the normal condition of most things and persons. Sanctification can elevate the clean into the holy, while pollution degrades the clean into the unclean. The unclean and the holy are two states which must never come in contact with each other. If for example an unclean person eats holy food, i.e., part of a sacrificial animal, he will be cut off (7:20–21; 22:3). Holy people such as priests and Nazirites should not pollute themselves by coming in contact with corpses, which are by definition unclean (21:2ff., 11–12; Num. 6:6–8). Should a Nazirite accidentally touch a corpse and become unclean, he must offer various sacrifices to cleanse himself from the uncleanness and start his period of consecration all over again (Num. 6:9–12).

This and many other examples show that uncleanness may be transmitted from some unclean things by contact (e.g., 11:39–40; 14:36; 15:4ff., etc.). Similarly some holy objects make everything that touches them holy (Exod. 29:37; 30:29; Lev. 6:11 [Eng. 18], 20 [27]). But cleanness is not conveyed to other things. Cleanness is the ground state; holiness and uncleanness are variations from the norm of cleanness.

The basic meaning of cleanness is purity. For example, "clean," i.e., pure, gold was required for plating the ark and other items of tabernacle furniture (Exod. 25:11, 24, etc.). That cleanness basically means purity is shown by the frequent use of water to purify unclean persons and things (Lev. 11:25, 28; 14:8–9, etc.). Once fire was specified as an alternative means of purification (Num. 31:23). But cleanness is a broader concept than purity. It approximates to our notion of normality. Many of the diagnostic tests for skin diseases in Lev. 13 conclude with the remark, "he is clean" (vv. 13, 17, 39). As the passages make clear, this does not mean the person concerned is not suffering from some complaint, merely that it was thought unimportant and not to be worried about. As a modern doctor might say, "it is normal." Similarly the clean animals are those that travel in a manner appropriate to their class, in a normal way. Fishes with scales and fins are clean, but those without these normal aids to propulsion are unclean (11:9–11). The idea of normality underlies 21:17–23, where any priest with a physical deformity is forbidden to minister at the altar. Admittedly these priests are not said to be unclean, but as I shall argue below the notion of normality has very wide ramifications in Levitical theology.

Uncleanness is the converse of cleanness. Anything that is not clean (ṭāhôr) is unclean (ṭāmē'). Unlike cleanness, though, uncleanness is contagious and incompatible with holiness. Things may be unclean in themselves (e.g., some animals, ch. 11) (this might be termed permanent uncleanness), or what is intrinsically clean may become temporarily unclean. Temporary uncleanness may result from contact with corpses, childbirth, disease, discharges (chs. 11–15), and various sins including illicit sexual intercourse (ch. 18) and murder (Num. 35:33). All these different types of uncleanness are regarded as in some way abnormal, or at least not quite usual. The greater the deviation from the norm the greater is the degree of uncleanness and the difficulty in cleansing.

Permanent uncleanness cannot be altered and is not contagious, so no rites are prescribed to cure it. Unclean animals do not pass on their uncleanness to others: they simply cannot be eaten. Paradoxically, temporary uncleanness is taken more seriously. Some types of this uncleanness are contagious and may be passed on to others (e.g., 15:19ff.). All types of temporary uncleanness require cleansing. Those who neglect to undergo the appropriate decontamination procedures endanger themselves and the whole community (Num. 19:13, 20).

Different degrees of uncleanness require different cleansing rituals. For example the slight uncleanness consequent on marital intercourse requires the couple to wash and wait till the evening for the uncleanness to clear. Menstrual discharge results in an uncleanness lasting seven days. But unnatural discharges from the sexual organs cause uncleanness that lasts for seven days after the discharge ceases and require washing and sacrifice to cleanse the person (ch. 15). Similarly those healed of unclean skin diseases have to wash, wait seven days, and offer sacrifice (ch. 14).

Some persistent skin diseases cause uncleanness and the sufferer is therefore expelled from the camp for the duration of his illness (13:45–46). Theology, not hygiene, is the reason for this provision. The unclean and the holy must not meet (7:20–21; 22:3). The camp of Israel is holy, and in the middle of it stood the tabernacle, seat of God's most holy presence. For this reason Num. 5:2–3 insists, "Put out of the camp everyone suffering from a serious skin disease, everyone having a discharge, and everyone that is unclean through contact with the dead . . . that they may not pollute their camp, in the midst of which I dwell." Neglect of these purity rules pollutes the tabernacle and leads to the death of the offender (Num. 19:13, 20). The day of atonement ceremonies were designed to cleanse the tabernacle from the uncleanness that it contracted owing to people's negligence in purifying themselves (15:31; 16:16, 19).

This insistence on purification of the unclean is a corollary of the idea that Israel, the camp, and especially the tabernacle are holy.

21

Contact between uncleanness and holiness is disastrous. They are utterly distinct in theory, and must be kept equally distinct in practice, lest divine judgment fall.

Holiness characterizes God himself and all that belongs to him: "Be holy, for I am holy" (11:44–45; 19:2; 20:26). God's name, which expresses his character, is holy (20:3; 22:2, 32). His name is profaned (desanctified) by idolatry, swearing falsely, and other sins (18:21; 19:12; 20:3; 21:6; 22:2). God demonstrates his holiness in judging sin (10:3; Num. 20:13). But apart from these remarks there is no explanation of what God's holiness is in itself. Holiness is intrinsic to God's character.

Anyone or anything given to God becomes holy. For example, the fruit of a newly planted fruit tree is not to be eaten for three years: the fruit of the fourth year is "a holy praise offering to the Lord" (19:24). Only in the fifth year can the owner enjoy the fruit himself. Similarly the priests' portions of the sacrifices are holy. The tabernacle and its equipment are holy (Exod. 40:9; 29:36; 30:29). So too are the sabbath and the other religious festivals (Lev. 23).

A person dedicated to the service of God is holy. Preeminently holy in this sense are the priests (Exod. 29:1; 39:30; Lev. 21:6ff.). Similarly the Levites were given wholly to the Lord in place of the first-born Israelites who had been sanctified. This dedication involves separation from uncleanness, as the case of the Nazirite makes clear: "he shall not go near a dead body. . . . All the days of his separation he is holy to the Lord" (Num. 6:6–8). In a more general sense all Israel is called out from the nations to serve God and is therefore holy (Exod. 19:5–6; cf. Lev. 20:26).

Uncleanness results from natural causes (e.g., disease) or human actions (e.g., sin), but holiness is not simply acquired by ritual action or moral behavior. Leviticus stresses that there are two aspects to sanctification, a divine act and human actions. God sanctifies and man also sanctifies. Only those people whom God calls to be holy can become holy in reality. "The man whom the Lord chooses shall be the holy one" (Num. 16:7). The divine side to sanctification is expressed in the frequent refrain "I am the Lord your sanctifier" (Lev. 20:8; 21:8, 15, 23; 22:9, 16, 32). Sometimes the divine part in sanctification and the human side are mentioned together: "You must sanctify him . . . for I the Lord sanctify you" (Lev. 21:8). Another example is in the fourth commandment: "Remember the sabbath day to sanctify it. . . . and the Lord sanctified it" (Exod. 20:8, 11).

Usually, however, the main emphasis of the book is on the human contribution to sanctification, what man has to do to make something holy. In some cases such as the offering of property or animals to the sanctuary, no special rituals are laid down according to Lev. 27, though sacrifice accompanied the gifts mentioned in Num. 7. In the more important cases such as the altar, the priesthood, and the tabernacle, sanctification was expressed by anointing the holy thing with oil and offering various sacrifices (Exod. 29:1–36; 40:9; cf. Lev. 8–9). When the whole nation was made holy through the covenant at Sinai, they had to cleanse themselves from uncleanness (Exod. 19:10–15), offer sacrifice, and promise to obey the law (Exod. 24:3–8). Keeping the law is indeed one of the most important duties of the people of Israel if they are to demonstrate holiness (Lev. 19:2ff.; 20:7ff.; Num. 15:39–40). To disobey God is profanity worthy of death (Exod. 31:14; Num. 20:12).

This survey of the use of the terms for holiness, cleanness, and uncleanness has demonstrated the importance of these ideas for understanding Leviticus. I have suggested that cleanness is the natural state of most creatures. Holiness is a state of grace to which men are called by God, and it is attained through obeying the law and carrying out rituals such as sacrifice. Uncleanness is a substandard condition to which men descend through bodily processes and sin. Every Israelite had a duty to seek release from uncleanness through washing and sacrifice, because uncleanness was quite incompatible with the holiness of the covenant people.

M. Douglas has tried to discover the deep underlying principles that unite these concepts of holiness and cleanness. She argues that holy means more than separation to divine service. It means wholeness and completeness.

> Much of Leviticus is taken up with stating the physical perfection that is required of things presented in the temple and of persons approaching it. The animals offered in sacrifice must be without blemish, women must be purified after childbirth, lepers should be separated and ritually cleansed before being allowed to approach it once they are cured. All bodily discharges are defiling and disqualify for approach to the temple. Priests may only come into contact with death when their own close kin die. But the high-priest must never have contact with death.[26]

She quotes Lev. 21:17–21, listing imperfections that bar one from

26. Douglas, *Purity and Danger*, p. 51.

acting as a priest, and summarizes: "In other words, he must be perfect as a man, if he is to be a priest."[27]

Other precepts develop the idea of wholeness in another direction. The metaphors of the physical body and of the new undertaking relate to the perfection and completeness of the individual and his work. Other precepts extend holiness to species and categories. Hybrids and other confusions are abominated.

18:23. "And you shall not lie with any beast and defile yourself with it, neither shall any woman give herself to a beast to lie with it: it is perversion."

The word "perversion" is a significant mistranslation of the rare Hebrew word *tebhel*, which has as its meaning mixing or confusion. The same theme is taken up in Leviticus 19:19.

"You shall keep my statutes. You shall not let your cattle breed with a different kind; you shall not sow your field with two kinds of seed; nor shall there come upon you a garment of cloth made of two kinds of stuff."

All these injunctions are prefaced by the general command:

"Be holy, for I am holy."

We can conclude that holiness is exemplified by completeness. Holiness requires that individuals shall conform to the class to which they belong. And holiness requires that different classes of things shall not be confused.

Another set of precepts refines on this last point. Holiness means keeping distinct the categories of creation. It therefore involves correct definition, discrimination and order. Under this head all the rules of sexual morality exemplify the holy. Incest and adultery (Lev. 18:6–20) are against holiness, in the simple sense of right order. Morality does not conflict with holiness, but holiness is more a matter of separating that which should be separated than of protecting the rights of husbands and brothers.

Then follows in chapter 19 another list of actions which are contrary to holiness. Developing the idea of holiness as order, not confusion, this list upholds rectitude and straight-dealing as holy, and contradiction and double-dealing as against holiness. Theft, lying, false witness, cheating in weights and measures, all kinds of dissembling such as speaking ill of the deaf (and presumably smiling to their face), hating your brother in your heart (while presumably speaking kindly to him), these are clearly contradictions between what seems and what is.[28]

This idea of wholeness or normality as the notion implicitly

27. *Ibid.*
28. *Ibid.*, pp. 53f.

assumed to be essential to holiness and cleanness is the key determining the divisions of the animal kingdom according to Douglas.[29]

New Testament theology makes full use of the idea of holiness. All Christians are holy, "saints" in most English translations.
That is, they have been called by God to be his people just as ancient
Israel had been (Col. 1:2; 1 Pet. 1:2; 2:9–10; cf. Exod. 19:5–6). But
this state of holiness must find expression in holy living (Col. 1:22;
1 Pet. 1:15). Sanctification is expressed through obedience to the
standard of teaching (Rom. 6:17–19), just as in Leviticus through
obedience to the law. Peter urges his readers to make the motto of
Leviticus their own: "Be holy, for I am holy" (1 Pet. 1:16). The
imitation of God is a theme that unites the ethics of Old and New
Testaments (cf. Matt. 5:48; 1 Cor. 11:1).

3. The Role of Sacrifice

"Under the law almost everything is purified with blood, and without the shedding of blood there is no forgiveness of sins"
(Heb. 9:22). The author of Hebrews had in mind the rites described
in Exodus and Numbers as well as those in Leviticus; but Leviticus
is particularly concerned with sacrifice, devoting its first seventeen
chapters to explaining the occasions for and the correct procedures
to be followed in sacrifice. The specific significance of the different
kinds of sacrifice will be dealt with at appropriate points in the
commentary. Here broader issues will be considered: the role of
sacrifice in general and its relationship to sin and uncleanness.

In the last hundred years various theories about the significance of OT sacrifice have been advanced. To review them all would
be inappropriate here.[30] My aim is more modest. Taking as a starting
point the most recent discussions,[31] I shall try to explain the basic
principles of OT sacrifice insofar as the Pentateuch makes them
plain.

According to D. J. Davies, Israelite sacrifice was concerned
with restoring the relationships between God and Israel, and between different members of the nation. The Sinai Covenant had
created a fellowship characterized by life and order, harmony between God and man and between man and man. Outside the covenant and its institutions was the realm of death and disorder from

29. This is more fully discussed below. See comments on ch. 11.
30. For a trenchant critique of some early discussions see D. J. Davies, "An Interpretation of Sacrifice in Leviticus," *ZAW* 89 (1977), pp. 387–399.
31. See Davies, *ibid.*, and E. R. Leach, *Culture and Communication*, pp. 81–93.

which Israel had been redeemed. Anything that disturbed this order, e.g., death, disease, or sin, was a potential threat to the whole community, and sacrifice was the principal means for remedying the disruption and restoring harmony into the community. Different types of disruptions were corrected by different kinds of sacrifice.

This analysis has much to commend it. But it only partially comes to terms with the concepts of Leviticus. In Leviticus sacrifice, or more precisely sacrificial blood, is regularly associated with cleansing and sanctification. For example the hallowing of the altar and the priests is effected through anointing with oil and sacrificial blood (Exod. 29:36–37; Lev. 8:11–15, 23–30). The man who recovered from a skin disease was anointed with blood to cleanse him from ritual uncleanness (Lev. 14:6ff.). The various purification and reparation offerings detailed in chs. 4–5 are all appointed to deal with the uncleanness associated with sin. All these sacrifices reached their annual climax in the day of atonement ceremonies, when each part of the tabernacle was smeared with blood "to cleanse it and sanctify it from the uncleannesses of the Israelites" (16:19).

According to Leviticus, then, sacrificial blood is necessary to cleanse and sanctify. Sacrifice can undo the effects of sin and human infirmity. Sin and disease lead to profanation of the holy and pollution of the clean. Sacrifice can reverse this process. We may elaborate the chart used in the previous section.

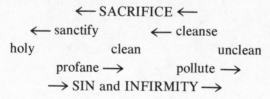

We saw that contact between the holy and the unclean results in death. Sacrifice, by cleansing the unclean, makes such contact possible. The holy God can meet with sinful man. Many of the rituals described in Exodus, Leviticus, and Numbers illustrate this point. For example, at the ordination of Aaron, blood of the ordination ram was smeared on Aaron and his sons and the rest was thrown on the altar (Lev. 8:22–24). A similar procedure was followed when the covenant was sealed with the elders of Israel: when they had agreed to the terms of the covenant, half the sacrificial blood was thrown over them and the rest over the altar

(Exod. 24:6-8). Through ordination Aaron was sanctified to the priesthood. Through the covenant Israel was made a kingdom of priests and a holy nation (Exod. 19:6). The priesthood of Israel meant that the nation was in a unique relationship to God, able to draw near to him and mediate his presence to the world. It is tempting to regard the rituals prescribed for the "leper" (Lev. 14) as a recapitulation of the process by which Israel had been made holy. As a result of disease he had become unclean and excluded from the covenant community. After his healing, hyssop was used to sprinkle blood over him (14:6-7). This may echo the passover ritual (cf. Exod. 12:22). The second stage in resanctifying a "leper" involved a real sacrifice and further blood smearing. Similar rites accompanied the ordination of Aaron and the ratification of the Sinai Covenant (cf. Lev. 8:22-24 and Exod. 24:6-8). At Sinai the whole nation had become holy. If later, as the result of sin, an individual member of Israel became unclean, he had to reenact the processes of sanctification. He had to be born again into the community by blood and water (cf. John 3).

Above it was argued that sanctification presupposed a divine call to holiness. Holiness was not acquired merely by obeying the law or undergoing some ritual (e.g., Num. 16:5). The laws on sacrifice go further still. They assert not only that sacrifice must be in accordance with God's will for it to be effective in the first place, but that it is God himself who gives the desired result of holiness or cleanness. Many of the laws conclude with the remark, "the priest shall make atonement for him and he will be forgiven" (or be clean) (e.g., 4:20, 26, 31; 12:7, 8). The addition "he will be forgiven" (clean) is significant. Mere performance of the rite by the priest is inadequate. God is the one who grants forgiveness and cleansing.[32]

Where uncleanness caused by sin was left unatoned for by sacrifice, deaths were liable to occur. Indeed the Pentateuch records a number of incidents where the enormity of the sin led to instant judgment, so that it was impossible to offer a sacrifice quickly enough to avert disaster (Exod. 32:25-35; Lev. 10; Num. 25). It may not be coincidence that on such occasions, when God's wrath was demonstrated in the death of some of the guilty, no sacrifices are mentioned to renew the holiness of the rest of the people. Where a man died there was no need for animals to be sacrificed as well (Num. 25:6-13; cf. 17:1-15 [Eng. 16:36-50]).

32. See B. A. Levine, *In the Presence of the Lord*, pp. 65f.

Another indication that the death of the animal in some way substituted for the death of the guilty person is provided by the verb "to make atonement" (*kipper*), which regularly describes what the priest does in sacrifice. However, despite its frequent occurrence, its etymology and its meaning are uncertain. One possible derivation is from the Akkadian verb *kuppuru*, "to cleanse" or "wipe." This fits those contexts where the altar or the sanctuary is the direct object of the verb and the action involved smearing the altar with blood (Lev. 16:33).

Alternatively *kipper*, "to make atonement," may be derived from the Hebrew word *kōper*, meaning "ransom price." A *kōper* is the money a man condemned to death can pay to escape the death penalty (Exod. 21:30; Prov. 6:35). *Kipper*, "to make atonement," could then be literally translated, "to pay a ransom (for one's life)." In certain passages where various monetary payments are said to make atonement, to pay a ransom would seem to be a much more appropriate rendering than "to cleanse" (e.g., Exod. 30:15; Num. 31:50). Such an understanding is compatible with most of the passages that speak of sacrifice "making atonement" for someone. Through the animal's death and the subsequent rituals men are ransomed from the death that their sin and uncleanness merit.

There were at least three parties involved in every sacrifice: God, the priest, and the worshipper. We have already seen that Leviticus insists that sacrifice must be offered in response to God's call, not on one's own initiative, if it is to be effective in making men holy (cf. Lev. 10). It also points out that correct performance of the atonement rituals by the priest is not enough by itself. God must grant forgiveness and cleansing. It makes one final point concerning the attitude of the worshipper. In the case of unintentional sin, remorse and sacrifice are sufficient for atonement. But where the sin was "high-handed," i.e., deliberate, reparation and public confession were necessary prerequisites to sacrificial atonement[33] (ch. 5 [Eng. 5:1–6:7]; cf. Num. 15:27–30).

John the Baptist, our Lord himself, Paul, Peter, and the writer of Hebrews are among those in the NT who make use of the idea that Christ's death was a sacrifice which atoned for sin. Unlike the sacrifices in Leviticus the crucifixion was unlimited in its scope and required no repetition. "Jesus Christ the righteous . . . is the propitiation for our sins, and not for ours only but also for the sins of

---

33. See below on ch. 5; also J. Milgrom, *Cult and Conscience*, pp. 104ff.

the whole world" (1 John 2:1–2). "He has appeared once for all at the end of the age to put away sin by the sacrifice of himself" (Heb. 9:26). But like the OT sacrifices, there must be a divine call to the individual and a response of faith and repentance if any man is to enjoy the effects of Christ's atonement (cf. Eph. 1–2).

4. The Sinai Covenant

In sharp contrast to the terms for sacrifice and holiness, the covenant is mentioned rarely in Leviticus. In fact it is mentioned only ten times altogether, of which eight occurrences are in ch. 26.[34] But though the word for covenant (*berît*) is rare, covenantal ideas pervade the whole book. Like the presence of God with Israel, the covenant is one of the fundamental presuppositions informing the theology of Leviticus.

Leviticus is the sequel to Exodus. At the heart of Exodus (chs. 19ff.) is the Sinai Covenant. All that follows in Exodus is a working out of the covenant. Ch. 32 describes the first time Israel ruptured the covenant by worshipping the golden calf. Chs. 33ff. describe the renewal of the covenant. The laws were written down a second time and the tabernacle was built, so that the covenant promise that God should dwell among his people might be fulfilled. Leviticus explains how covenant worship should be conducted (chs. 1–17), then how the covenant people should behave (18–25), and closes with a section of blessings and curses, entirely appropriate to a covenant document (ch. 26). Indeed the last verse of this chapter connects all that precedes with Sinai, where the covenant was concluded. "These are the rules, judgments, and laws which the Lord put between himself and the Israelites in Mount Sinai by the hand of Moses" (26:46).

Recent studies[35] have shed much light on the form of the OT covenant. It bears a marked resemblance to the form used in other Near Eastern texts for drawing up treaties and collections of law. This is entirely appropriate, for the Sinai Covenant[36] was at once a treaty between God and Israel and laws imposed on the nation.

---

34. 2:13; 24:8; 26:9, 15, 25, 42 (3x), 44, 45.
35. Basic treatments in K. Baltzer, *The Covenant Formulary* (Oxford: Blackwell, 1971); D. J. McCarthy, *Treaty and Covenant* (Rome: Biblical Institute Press, 1963); and with particular reference to Deuteronomy see M. Weinfeld, *Deuteronomy and the Deuteronomic School*, pp. 59ff.; J. A. Thompson, *Deuteronomy* (London: IVP, 1974), pp. 14ff.; P. C. Craigie, *The Book of Deuteronomy* (Grand Rapids: Eerdmans, 1976), pp. 20ff.
36. The Hebrew word *berît* means both covenant and treaty.

Six main parts have been distinguished in the Near Eastern covenant/treaty form.

(1) Title naming the suzerain, the author of the treaty: Exod. 20:1, "I am the Lord your God." Each time Leviticus repeats these solemn words, Israel is reminded of the way God first spoke to the whole nation assembled on the slopes of Mount Sinai.

(2) Historical prologue explaining the background to the conclusion of the treaty. Hittite treaties typically stress the kindness of the Hittite king in his dealings with his vassal and draw attention to the vassal's perversity and rebelliousness. The Decalog was introduced by a short historical introduction reminding Israel of their redemption: "who brought you out of the land of Egypt, out of the house of bondage" (Exod. 20:2). In Deuteronomy the first eleven chapters reflect on the grace of God shown to Israel in the past and serve as a historical prologue. Leviticus in contrast has but short reminders of the Exodus deliverance (e.g., 11:45; 18:3; 19:34, 36; 22:33). They are particularly apposite in the case of the jubilee laws, which were designed to prevent permanent enslavement of the poor (25:38, 42).

(3) The centerpiece of every treaty was the stipulations section. In collections of law, such as Hammurabi's, the laws formed the central section. The same holds for the biblical collections of law. In the treaties a basic stipulation of total fidelity to the suzerain may be distinguished from the more detailed stipulations covering specific problems. In this terminology "Be holy" could be described as the basic stipulation of Leviticus. The other laws explain what this means in different situations.

(4). The document clause. Treaties and legal collections often mention how and where the text of the treaty was written down, and the importance of reading it regularly. This element is present in the biblical covenant texts too (Exod. 24:4, 12; 32:15–16; 34:1–4; Deut. 27:2–8; 31:11–12, 24ff.).

(5) Blessings and curses. Those who keep the laws or treaty stipulations are promised prosperity, while those who spurn them are warned of the terrible punishments the gods will inflict. Lev. 26 and Deut. 28 are excellent examples of this; indeed many of the blessings and curses in these chapters find close parallels in other Near Eastern sources.

(6) God list. A list of gods who witness the treaty usually concludes a treaty. But this feature is missing from Mesopotamian legal collections and, for obvious theological reasons, from OT covenant passages.

The covenant/treaty background of Pentateuchal law high-lights three important features of the laws. First, the law was given in a context of grace. In the treaty form the stipulations came after the historical prologue. This was analogous to the historical situa-tion: God gave his law to Israel after they had been redeemed from Egypt, not as a means for securing their redemption. God's call to Israel to be his holy people preceded the revelation of the law at Sinai, but only obedience could make holiness a living reality. In Leviticus, whenever the exodus from Egypt is mentioned it is al-ways as a motive for keeping the law (e.g., 11:45; 18:3; 23:43). The OT believer was to treat others as God had treated him: "love the resident alien as yourself, because you were resident aliens in the land of Egypt" (19:34).

Second, though Israel had been saved from Egyptian bondage and called to be God's people, this did not mean they were free to do as they pleased. The very reverse was the case. As a holy nation they had to keep themselves pure from sin and uncleanness lest God's wrath break out against them. The covenant texts express the same notion in the blessings and curses that are found in Lev. 26 and Deut. 28. There the nation is reminded that all God's promises, of good harvests, peace, and his own presence, will be theirs if they observe his commandments. But if they forget his word and go their own way, they will experience all those things that men fear most: sickness, drought, death of children, famine, enemy occupation, and deportation to foreign lands. Leviticus stresses that if such a fate befalls Israel, it will not be in spite of the covenant but because of it. God himself will punish his disobedient people: "I personally shall defy you, and shall strike you seven times for your sins" (26:24, 28). In the words of the prophet Amos, "You only have I known of all the families of the earth, *therefore* I will punish you for all your in-iquities" (Amos 3:2).

The third point to note about the covenant is its eternity. In the covenant God pledged himself to Israel forever, and Israel was expected to reciprocate by offering back her eternal allegiance to her sovereign redeemer. The purpose of the horrifying curses in Lev. 26 was to make Israel turn back from her evil ways and listen to God (26:18, 21, 23, 27). But they are assured that however long it takes for them to come to their right mind and confess their sin, God will be ready to reinstate them when they do change their ways (26:40–41). Even if they do not turn back, they will not be deserted by their God, though they may suffer continued exile from their land (26:44). The reason for God's faithfulness is his promise to the patriarchs,

31

Abraham, Isaac, and Jacob (26:42, 45; cf. Exod. 32:11-14; Deut. 4:30-31; 30:1-10; Isa. 49:15; Jer. 31:36). Divine blessing depends on obedience, but disobedience will not result in total rejection, just continued divine judgment.

The prophets looked forward to a new covenant under which the law would be written in men's hearts instead of on stone as the Sinai Covenant had been. The NT affirms that this covenant was inaugurated by Christ's death, which saved his people from the bondage of sin. The new covenant like the old covenant displays God's grace to sinful man. The new covenant is like the old in that members of both are expected to obey the law: "If you love me, you will keep my commandments" (John 14:15). Finally, the new covenant also offers an assurance of God's eternal faithfulness to his people: "I give them eternal life, and no one shall snatch them out of my hand" (John 10:28).

VII. LEVITICUS AND THE CHRISTIAN

Each section on the theology of Leviticus, and most chapters of the commentary, conclude with a paragraph or two relating the laws in Leviticus to the NT. Here I shall try to spell out the principles underlying these comments.[37] The problem of relating the OT to the difficulties of the modern Church is not peculiar to Leviticus, so where it seems appropriate, examples from other parts of the Pentateuch are included.

Christians customarily divide the OT law into three parts: the moral, e.g., the ten commandments, the civil, i.e., the legislation for OT society, and the ceremonial, i.e., the sacrificial and ritual laws. Many, despite Paul's teaching that "all Scripture is inspired and profitable" (2 Tim. 3:16), assert that only the moral law binds the Christian. This position faces three main difficulties. First, the NT does not seem to distinguish between the different types of law in this way. Second, it is difficult to draw the line between moral precepts and other law. Is the sabbath a moral law or a ceremonial one? Third, much of the civil legislation is grounded on moral judgments, often expressed in the ten commandments. Though the three-fold division of the law is in my view arbitrary and artificial, it

---

37. A fuller and better statement of the same approach is to be found in J. Bright, *The Authority of the OT* (Grand Rapids: Baker, 1975).

does provide a convenient framework for our discussion, in which a slightly different approach will be advocated.

As far as basic principles of behavior are concerned the OT and NT are in broad agreement. "You shall love the Lord your God with all your heart, and with all your soul, and with all your mind, and with all your strength. You shall love your neighbor as yourself" (Mark 12:30–31; Deut. 6:5; Lev. 19:18). With this double quotation from Deuteronomy and Leviticus Jesus drew out the quintessence of OT law and gave it his own seal of approval. The ten commandments are often quoted by the NT. Peter quotes the Levitical injunction to holiness (1 Pet. 1:16). The examples could be multiplied to show that the NT advocates the same standard of personal morality as the OT. This is to be expected, since the God of the OT is the God of the NT. The people of God are supposed to imitate God. If Leviticus summons men to "be holy, for I am holy," our Lord urges us: "You, therefore, must be perfect as your heavenly Father is perfect" (Matt. 5:48). It is evident that the personal ethics of both testaments are similar.

One may go farther. The theological setting of the ethical imperatives is similar in both testaments. In both the OT and NT, law forms part of the covenant relationship between God and his people. Although this has already been alluded to (see VI.4 above), it is so important that it deserves further elaboration.

Three clear parallels may be drawn between the OT view of the covenant and the NT teaching on law and grace. It is true that in the NT it is hard to find covenant terminology and structures, but that does not mean that the principles enshrined in the OT covenant have disappeared. In the teaching of Jesus and Paul the covenant has come down to the level of basic presuppositions. Though as a rule they do not talk about the covenant, their assumptions about the relationship of grace and law show that their teachings are governed by the principles inherent in the OT covenant.

First and foremost the OT covenants were arrangements of divine grace. God called Abraham. He brought Israel out of Egypt. He chose David. In every case God took the initiative in saving his people and created a relationship of fellowship between himself and them. In the NT our Lord came to seek and to save that which was lost and to call sinners to repentance. "While we were yet sinners Christ died for us" (Rom. 5:8).

Second, the covenants involved law. Abraham was told to "walk before me and be perfect" (Gen. 17:1). The covenants created a fellowship between God and man; the Davidic covenant is compared to the relationship between father and son (2 Sam. 7:14). Man is expected to respond to God's grace. But how? This is the role of the law. The law explains how men are to imitate God. The NT insists that the law is not a means to salvation, but a response to salvation. The disciple is not merely to observe the letter of the commandment. His righteousness must exceed that of the scribes and Pharisees. He must be perfect as his heavenly Father is perfect (Matt. 5:17–48).

Finally the covenant involved blessing and curse. If Israel obeyed the law, she was told to expect greater and greater prosperity. If she was disobedient, her suffering would be terrible. David was warned that if his son committed iniquity, "I will chasten him with the rods of men" (2 Sam. 7:14). The same themes reappear in the NT. Those who seek God's kingdom and his righteousness are assured they will not be short of food and clothing (Matt. 6:25–33). But those who refuse to forgive others will forfeit their own forgiveness (Matt. 18:23–35). Paul remarks that some Christians' efforts will be rewarded, but the work of others will be destroyed by fire, though they themselves will be saved (1 Cor. 3:10–15). He compares the experience of Israel in the wilderness to that of the Corinthian church. Many Israelites died in the wilderness for indulging in immorality. The same fate will befall the Corinthians if they do not repent. Indeed some have suffered already (1 Cor. 10:1–11:32).

It seems fair to say that the NT not only accepts the moral law of the OT, but reiterates the basic theology of the covenant of which the law forms a part. If the NT stresses much more strongly the grace of God, this is because Christ's incarnation and death displayed God's mercy more strikingly than even the exodus from Egypt.

Besides moral laws such as "you shall love your neighbor as yourself" (19:18) Leviticus contains a number of laws that are sometimes described as civil legislation, e.g., laws about farming (e.g., 19:9–10, 19, 23–25) and rules fixing the death penalty for certain offenses (e.g., 20:9–16). This type of law is quoted less frequently in the NT than the simple moral imperatives, but when quoted it is treated as equally authoritative (e.g., 1 Cor. 9:9 quoting Deut. 25:4 and Mark 7:10 citing Lev. 20:9). The arbitrariness of the distinction between moral and civil law is reinforced by the arrangement of the material in Leviticus. Love of neighbor immediately precedes a prohibition on mixed breeding; the holiness motto comes just before the law on executing unruly children

(19:18–19; 20:7–9). Instead of distinguishing between moral and civil laws, it would be better to say that some injunctions are broad and generally applicable to most societies, while others are more specific and directed at the particular social problems of ancient Israel. In this commentary the following position is assumed: the principles underlying the OT are valid and authoritative for the Christian, but the particular applications found in the OT may not be. The moral principles are the same today, but insofar as our situation often differs from the OT setting, the application of the principles in our society may well be different too.

Some examples may clarify the problem. According to Deut. 22:8, "When you build a new house, you shall make a parapet for your roof, that you may not bring the guilt of blood upon your house, if anyone fall from it." The principle underlying this law is obvious: the Israelite must take precautions so that his friends and neighbors do not suffer fatal accidents. This house-building regulation could be regarded as an application of the sixth commandment, "You shall not kill." In the Near East, where flat-roofed houses are common and may be used for sleeping and sunbathing, it was a sensible precaution to have parapets to prevent people falling off. But unless our houses have flat roofs used for similar purposes, there is little point in surrounding them with parapets. That is not to say we can learn nothing from this law or that it has no authority for us. It does. It tells the Christian to think about the danger points in his home. To ignore them is to break the sixth commandment by omission, if not by commission. Safety measures are more than humane: they are the will of God.

Many other laws in the Pentateuch can be regarded as applications of the Decalog to specific situations. The ten commandments express pure principles in very broad terms without detailed application. They are not laws for judges to administer. Human judges could never enforce the tenth commandment, for example. Rather the ten commandments enshrine the religious and moral principles that should inspire and guide every aspect of Israel's national life.

Some of the laws in Leviticus are written with judges in mind. They prescribe what penalty is appropriate when the Decalog has been broken. For example, idolatry, blasphemy, dishonoring parents, and adultery were punished with the death penalty. Such punishment (20:2; 24:10–23; 20:9; 20:10) underlined the gravity of these offenses. But theft, for example, was dealt with much more leniently (Lev. 5:20–26 [Eng. 6:1–7]). It is a feature of biblical law that it treats offenses against property more leniently than was customary in the ancient Near East, while offenses against life and religion were dealt with more severely.[38]

The moral and religious principles underlying OT legislation include the ten commandments, but there are other principles as well. Again I would argue that it is the underlying principles that should bind the Christian, not the specific applications found in the OT. For example a recurrent theme in biblical law is that the weakest members of society should be specially protected. The poor, the orphan and widow, the clergy (Levites), and the immigrant (resident alien) are often singled out for special treatment. Lev. 19:9–10 says: "When you reap the harvest of your land, do not go right up to the corner of your field to reap and do not gather up the gleanings of your harvest. . . . Leave them for the poor and for the resident alien: I am the Lord your God."

It is misguided to try to apply this law directly to our society. It does not mean that efficient combine harvesters that gather up every stalk of grain are contrary to the will of God.[39] The aim of this law is very clear, namely, to allow the landless poor to collect some free food. Inefficient combines are of no benefit to the poor in our society, who usually live in city centers far from the harvest fields. But though this law is inapplicable literally in modern societies, the principles underlying it should still challenge Christian men to devise the most effective means that can help the poor of our age. It is not the task of the commentator to say which means should be adopted, e.g., food subsidies or welfare benefits, but simply to emphasize that Christian politicians and voters have a duty to support good schemes to help the needy. The jubilee laws in Lev. 25 again offer very relevant comment on issues of wealth and poverty.

Finally we come to the question of the ceremonial law. Very detailed comments on the uncleanness regulations and the sacrificial rituals are to be found in the epistle to the Hebrews. The great argument of that writer is that Christ fulfilled all the ideals enshrined in the OT law. His high-priesthood is superior to Aaron's. His sacrifice is more effective in purging sin than the blood of bulls and goats. Unlike the OT rites it need never be repeated, since it has secured the forgiveness of sins once and for all. In one sense then

38. M. Greenberg, "Some Postulates of Biblical Criminal Law," *Y. Kaufmann Jubilee Volume* (ed. M. Haran; Jerusalem: Magnes, 1960), pp. 5–28; E. M. Good, "Capital Punishment and its Alternatives in Ancient Near Eastern Law," *Stanford Law Review* 19 (1967), pp. 947–977.

39. So J. V. Taylor, *Enough Is Enough* (London: SCM, 1975), pp. 50f.

the whole ceremonial law in Leviticus is obsolete for the Christian. We are interested in the sacrifice of Christ, not in animal sacrifice. But in another sense the Levitical rituals are still of immense relevance. It was in terms of these sacrifices that Jesus himself and the early church understood his atoning death. Leviticus provided the theological models for their understanding. If we wish to walk in our Lord's steps and think his thoughts after him, we must attempt to understand the sacrificial system of Leviticus. It was established by the same God who sent his Son to die for us; and in rediscovering the principles of OT worship written there, we may learn something of the way we should approach a holy God.

VIII. SELECT BIBLIOGRAPHY

A. COMMENTARIES

These are cited in the footnotes by the author's name alone.

B. Baentsch, *Exodus, Leviticus, Numeri* (Handkommentar zum AT) (Göttingen: 1903).

A. Bertholet, *Leviticus* (Kurzer Handkommentar zum AT) (Tübingen: Mohr, 1901).

A. A. Bonar, *A Commentary on Leviticus* (London: Banner of Truth, 1966 reprint of 1861).

J. Calvin, *Commentaries on the Four Last Books of Moses* (Grand Rapids: Eerdmans, reprint of 1852 translation).

H. Cazelles, *Le Lévitique²* (Bible de Jérusalem) (Paris: du Cerf, 1958).

R. E. Clements, "Leviticus," in *The Broadman Bible Commentary* II (C. J. Allen, ed.) (London: Marshall, Morgan and Scott, 1970).

F. C. Cook (ed.), *Speaker's Commentary* 1.2 (London: Murray, 1871).

A. Dillmann, *Exodus und Leviticus²* (Kurzgefasstes exegetisches Handbuch zum AT) (Leipzig: Hirzel, 1880).

B. D. Eerdmans, *Das Buch Leviticus* (Giessen: Töpelmann, 1912).

K. Elliger, *Leviticus* (Handbuch zum AT) (Tübingen: Mohr, 1966).

C. R. Erdman, *The Book of Leviticus* (New York: Revell, 1951).

W. H. Gispen, *Het Boek Leviticus* (Commentaar op het OT) (Kampen: Kok, 1950).

P. Heinisch, *Das Buch Leviticus* (Die heilige Schrift des AT) (Bonn: Hanstein, 1935).

J. H. Hertz, *Leviticus* (The Pentateuch and Haftorahs) (London: Oxford UP, 1932).

D. Hoffmann, *Das Buch Leviticus* I-II (Berlin: Poppelauer, 1905–6).

C. F. Keil, *The Pentateuch* II (Biblical Commentary on the OT) (Grand Rapids: Eerdmans, reprint).

W. Kornfeld, *Das Buch Leviticus* (Kleinkommentare zur Heiligen Schrift) (Düsseldorf: Patmos, 1972).

B. Maarsingh, *Leviticus* (De Prediking van het OT) (Nijkerk: Callenbach, 1974).

N. Micklem, "The Book of Leviticus," in *The Interpreter's Bible* II (G. A. Buttrick, ed.) (New York: Abingdon, 1953).

J. Milgrom, "The Book of Leviticus," in *The Interpreter's One Volume Commentary on the Bible* (C. M. Laymon, ed.) (Nashville: Abingdon, 1971).

M. Noth, *Leviticus* (OT Library) (London: SCM, 1965).

J. R. Porter, *Leviticus* (Cambridge Bible Commentary) (Cambridge: University Press, 1976).

Rashi, *Pentateuch with Rashi's Commentary* (translated by M. Rosenbaum and A. M. Silbermann) (New York: Hebrew Publishing Company).

J. L. Saalschütz, *Das Mosaische Recht*² (Berlin: Heymann, 1853) (1974 reprint).

N. H. Snaith, *Leviticus and Numbers* (New Century Bible) (London: Nelson, 1967).

B. GENERAL AND INTRODUCTORY

Books

K. Baltzer, *The Covenant Formulary* (Oxford: Blackwell, 1971).

D. Baly, *The Geography of the Bible* (London: Lutterworth, 1957).

J. Bright, *The Authority of the OT* (London: SCM, 1967).

M. Douglas, *Purity and Danger* (London: Routledge and Kegan Paul, 1966).

Idem, *Natural Symbols* (London: Barrie and Rockliff, 1970).

Idem, *Implicit Meanings* (London: Routledge and Kegan Paul, 1975).

O. Eissfeldt, *The OT: An Introduction* (Oxford: Blackwell, 1965).

G. Fohrer, *Introduction to the OT* (Nashville: Abingdon, 1968).

R. K. Harrison, *Introduction to the OT* (Grand Rapids: Eerdmans, 1969; London: Tyndale, 1970).

O. Kaiser, *Introduction to the OT* (Oxford: Blackwell, 1975).

Y. Kaufmann, *The Religion of Israel* (London: Allen and Unwin, 1961).

C. F. Keil, *Manual of Biblical Archaeology* I-II (Edinburgh: Clark, 1887–88).

R. Kilian, *Literarkritische und formgeschichtliche Untersuchung des Heiligkeitsgesetzes* (Bonn: Hanstein, 1963).

S. R. Külling, *Zur Datierung der "Genesis–P–Stücke"* (Kampen: Kok, 1964).

E. R. Leach, *Culture and Communication* (Cambridge: University Press, 1976).

D. J. McCarthy, *Treaty and Covenant* (Rome: Pontifical Biblical Institute, 1963).

S. E. McEvenue, *The Narrative Style of the Priestly Writer* (Rome: Biblical Institute Press, 1971).

C. L. Meyers, *The Tabernacle Menorah; a Synthetic Study of a Symbol from the Biblical Cult* (Missoula: Scholars Press, 1976).

J. Milgrom, *Studies in Levitical Terminology* I (Berkeley: University of California, 1970).

J. Neusner, *The Idea of Purity in Ancient Judaism* (Leiden: Brill, 1973).

M. Noth, *The Laws in the Pentateuch and Other Studies* (Edinburgh: Oliver and Boyd, 1966).

Idem, *A History of Pentateuchal Traditions* (Englewood Cliffs: Prentice-Hall, 1972).

G. von Rad, *Die Priesterschrift im Hexateuch literarisch untersucht und theologisch gewertet* (Stuttgart: Kohlhammer, 1934).

R. Rendtorff, *Die Gesetze in der Priesterschrift*[2] (Göttingen: Vandenhoeck and Ruprecht, 1963).

H. G. Reventlow, *Das Heiligkeitsgesetz formgeschichtlich untersucht* (Neukirchen: 1961).

E. A. Speiser, *Oriental and Biblical Studies* (Philadelphia: University of Pennsylvania, 1967).

V. W. Turner, *The Ritual Process* (London: Routledge and Kegan Paul, 1969).

R. de Vaux, *Ancient Israel* (London: Darton, Longman and Todd, 1961).

M. Weinfeld, *Deuteronomy and the Deuteronomic School* (Oxford: Clarendon, 1972).

J. Wellhausen, *Prolegomena to the History of Ancient Israel* (Cleveland: Meridian, 1957 reprint of 1885 edition).

Articles

W. Brueggemann, "The Kerygma of the Priestly Writers," *ZAW* 84 (1972), pp. 397–413.

W. Dommershausen, "Heiligkeit, ein alttestamentlichen Sozialprinzip?" *Tübingener Theologische Quartalschrift* 148 (1968), pp. 153–166.

G. R. Driver, "Three Technical Terms in the Pentateuch," *JSS* 1 (1956), pp. 97–105.

D. N. Freedman, "Variant Readings in the Leviticus Scroll from Qumran Cave 11," *CBQ* 36 (1974), pp. 525–534.

A. Hurvitz, "The Usage of *šēš* and *bûṣ* in the Bible and its Implication for the Date of P," *HTR* 60 (1967), pp. 117–121.

Idem, "Linguistic Observations on the Biblical Usage of the Priestly Term '*ēdāh*" (Hebrew), *Tarbiz* 40 (1971), pp. 261–67.

Idem, "The Evidence of Language in Dating the Priestly Code," *RB* 81 (1974), pp. 24–57.

J. I. Packer, "What did the Cross Achieve?" *TB* 25 (1974), pp. 3–45.

P. W. Skehan, "The Qumran Manuscripts and Textual Criticism," *VTS* 4 (1957), pp. 148–160.

J. G. Vink, "The Date and Origin of the Priestly Code in the OT," *OTS* 15 (1969), pp. 1–144.

B. K. Waltke, "The Samaritan Pentateuch and the Text of the OT," in *New Perspectives on the OT* (J. B. Payne, ed.) (Waco: Word, 1970), pp. 212–239.

G. J. Wenham, "History and the OT," in *History, Criticism and Faith* (C. Brown, ed.) (Leicester: IVP, 1977), pp. 13–75.

C. CHAPTERS 1–7

Books

G. B. Gray, *Sacrifice in the OT* (Oxford: Clarendon, 1925).

A. R. W. Green, *The Role of Human Sacrifice in the Ancient Near East* (Missoula: Scholars Press, 1975).

B. A. Levine, *In the Presence of the Lord* (Leiden: Brill, 1974).

S. Lyonnet and L. Sabourin, *Sin, Redemption and Sacrifice* (Rome: Pontifical Biblical Institute, 1970).

J. Milgrom, *Cult and Conscience: The 'Asham' and the Priestly Doctrine of Repentance* (Leiden: Brill, 1976).

L. Moraldi, *Espiazione sacrificale e riti espiatori nell' ambiente biblico e nell' Antico Testamento* (Rome: Pontifical Biblical Institute, 1956).

R. Rendtorff, *Studien zur Geschichte des Opfers im alten Israel* (Neukirchen: 1967).

R. Schmid, *Das Bundesopfer in Israel* (Munich: Kösel, 1964).

R. J. Thompson, *Penitence and Sacrifice in Early Israel outside the Levitical Law* (Leiden: Brill, 1963).

R. de Vaux, *Studies in OT Sacrifice* (Cardiff: University of Wales, 1964).

Articles

A. van den Branden, "Lev. 1–7 et le tarif de Marseilles, CIS I, 165," *Revista degli Studi Orientali* 40 (1965), pp. 107–130.

D. J. Davies, "An Interpretation of Sacrifice in Leviticus," *ZAW* 89 (1977), pp. 387–399.

L. R. Fisher, "A New Ritual Calendar from Ugarit," *HTR* 60 (1970), pp. 485–501.

P. Garnet, "Atonement Constructions in the OT and the Qumran Scrolls," *EQ* 46 (1974), pp. 131–163.

A. de Gugliemo, "Sacrifice in the Ugaritic Texts," *CBQ* 17 (1955), pp. 76–96.

J. Heller, "Die Symbolik des Fettes im AT," *VT* 20 (1970), pp. 106–108.

D. R. Hillers, "Ugaritic *šnpt* 'Wave Offering,'" *BASOR* 198 (1970), p. 42; *BASOR* 200 (1970), p. 18.

J. Hoftijzer, "Das sogenannte Feueropfer," *VTS* 16 (1967), pp. 114–134.

B. A. Levine, "Ugaritic Descriptive Rituals," *JCS* 17 (1963), pp. 105–111.

Idem, "The Descriptive Tabernacle Texts of the Pentateuch," *JAOS* 85 (1965), pp. 307–318.

Idem, and W. W. Hallo, "Offerings to the Temple Gates at Ur," *HUCA* 38 (1967), pp. 17–58.

D. J. McCarthy, "The Symbolism of Blood and Sacrifice," *JBL* 88 (1969), pp. 166–176.

J. Milgrom, "The Function of the *Ḥaṭṭā't* Sacrifice" (Hebrew), *Tarbiz* 40 (1970), pp. 1–8.

Idem, "Sin-Offering or Purification-Offering," *VT* 21 (1971), pp. 237–39.

Idem, "The Alleged Wave-Offering in Israel and in the Ancient Near East," *IEJ* 22 (1972), pp. 33–38.

Idem, "*shôq hattᵉrûmāh*: A Chapter in Cultic History" (Hebrew), *Tarbiz* 42 (1972), pp. 1–11.

Idem, "Two Kinds of *Ḥaṭṭā't*," *VT* 26 (1976), pp. 333–37.

Idem, "Israel's Sanctuary: The Priestly 'Picture of Dorian Gray,' " *RB* 83 (1976), pp. 390–99.

Idem, "Atonement in the OT," *IDBS*, pp. 78–82.

Idem, "Sacrifices and Offerings, OT," *IDBS*, pp. 763–771.

J. C. de Moor, "The Peace Offering in Ugarit and Israel," *Schrift en uitleg (W. H. Gispen FS)* (Kampen: Kok, 1970), pp. 112–17.

R. Péter, "L'imposition des mains dans l'A.T.," *VT* 27 (1977), pp. 48–55.

A. F. Rainey, "The Order of Sacrifice in OT Ritual Texts," *Biblica* 51 (1970), pp. 485–498.

Idem, "Sacrifice and Offerings," *The Zondervan Pictorial Encyclopedia of the Bible* 5 (M. C. Tenney, ed.) (Grand Rapids: Zondervan, 1975), pp. 194–211.

L. Rost, "Erwägungen zum israelitischen Brandopfer," *BZAW* 77 (1958), pp. 177–183.

Idem, "Der Leberlappen," *ZAW* 79 (1967), pp. 35–41.

N. H. Snaith, "Sacrifices in the OT," *VT* 7 (1957), pp. 308–317.

Idem, "The Sin Offering and the Guilt Offering," *VT* 15 (1965), pp. 73–80.

W. B. Stevenson, "Hebrew Olah and Zebach Sacrifices," in *Festschrift A. Bertholet* (Tübingen: 1950), pp. 488–497.

D. M. L. Urie, "Sacrifice among the West Semites," *PEQ* 81 (1949), pp. 67–82.

A. Vincent, "Les rites du balancement (tenoûphâh) et du prélèvement (teroûmâh) dans le sacrifice de communion de l'A.T.," *Mélanges Syriens offerts à R. Dussaud* I (Paris: Geuthner, 1939), pp. 267–272.

D. CHAPTERS 8–10

Articles

R. Gradwohl, "Das 'fremde Feuer' von Nadab und Abihu," *ZAW* 75 (1963), pp. 288–296.

M. Haran, "The Uses of Incense in the Ancient Israelite Ritual," *VT* 10 (1960), pp. 113–129.

J. C. H. Laughlin, "The 'Strange Fire' of Nadab and Abihu," *JBL* 95 (1976), pp. 559–565.

E. CHAPTER 11

Books

G. Bare, *Plants and Animals of the Bible* (United Bible Societies: 1969).

G. S. Cansdale, *Animals of Bible Lands* (Exeter: Paternoster, 1970).

D. Schapiro, *L'Hygiene alimentaire des Juifs devant la science moderne* (Paris: Erelji, 1930).

F. J. Simoons, *Eat not this Flesh: Food Avoidances in the Old World* (Madison: University of Wisconsin, 1961).

Articles

G. R. Driver, "Birds in the OT," *PEQ* 87 (1955), pp. 5–20.

W. H. Gispen, "The Distinction between Clean and Unclean," *OTS* 5 (1948), pp. 190–96.

A. Jirku, "Lev. 11:29–33 im Lichte der Ugarit-Forschung," *ZAW* 84 (1972), p. 348.

L. Khalifé, "Etude sur l'histoire rédactionelle de deux textes parallèles: Lev. 11 et Deut. 14:1–21," *Melto* 2 (1966), pp. 57–72.

J. Milgrom, "The Biblical Diet Laws as an Ethical System," *Interpretation* 17 (1963), pp. 288–301.

W. L. Moran, "The Literary Connection between Lev. 11:13–19 and Deut. 14:12–18," *CBQ* 28 (1966), pp. 271–77.

R. de Vaux, "Les sacrifices de porcs en Palestine et dans l'Ancient Orient," *BZAW* 77 (1958), pp. 250–265.

G. J. Wenham, "The Theology of Unclean Food," *EQ* [forthcoming].

F. CHAPTERS 12–15

Books

S. G. Browne, *Leprosy in the Bible* (London: Christian Medical Fellowship, 1970).

C. J. Vos, *Women in OT Worship* (Delft: Judels and Brinkman, 1968).

Articles

E. V. Hulse, "The Nature of Biblical 'Leprosy' and the Use of Alternative Medical Terms in Modern Translations of the Bible," *PEQ* 107 (1975), pp. 87–105.

D. I. Macht, "A Scientific Appreciation of Lev. 12:1–5," *JBL* 52 (1933), pp. 253–260.

R. R. Wilcox, "Venereal Disease in the Bible," *British Journal of Venereal Disease* 25 (1949), 28–33.

G. CHAPTER 16

Articles

D. Ashbel, "The Goat sent to Azazel" (Hebrew), *Beth Miqra* 11 (1965), pp. 89–102.

C. L. Feinberg, "The Scapegoat of Lev. 16," *Bibliotheca Sacra* 115 (1958), pp. 320–333.

M. Haran, "The Complex of Ritual Acts Performed inside the Tabernacle," *Scripta Hierosolymitana* 8 (1961), pp. 272–302.

S. H. Langdon, "The Scape-Goat in Babylonian Religion," *ExpT* 24 (1912–13), pp. 9–13.

J. Milgrom, "Day of Atonement," *Encyclopedia Judaica* 5, pp. 1384–87.

H. CHAPTERS 17–27

Books

L. M. Epstein, *Marriage Laws in the Bible and the Talmud* (Cambridge: Harvard, 1942).

R. Fox, *Kinship and Marriage* (Harmondsworth: Penguin, 1967).

B. S. Jackson, *Theft in Early Jewish Law* (Oxford: Clarendon, 1972).

Idem, *Essays in Jewish and Comparative Legal History* (Leiden: Brill, 1975).

I. Mendelsohn, *Slavery in the Ancient Near East* (New York: Oxford UP, 1949).

J. Murray, *Principles of Conduct* (Grand Rapids: Eerdmans, 1957; London: Tyndale, 1957).

R. North, *Sociology of the Biblical Jubilee* (Rome: Pontifical Biblical Institute, 1954).

S. M. Paul, *Studies in the Book of the Covenant in the Light of Cuneiform and Biblical Law* (Leiden: Brill, 1970).

A. C. J. Phillips, *Ancient Israel's Criminal Law* (Oxford: Blackwell, 1970).

Articles

H. H. Cohn, "The Penology of the Talmud," *Israel Law Review* 5 (1970), pp. 53–74.

J. J. Finkelstein, "Sex Offences in Sumerian Laws," *JAOS* 86 (1966), pp. 355–372.

Idem, "Some New *Misharum* Material and its Implications," in *Studies in Honor of B. Landsberger* (Chicago: University Press, 1965), pp. 233–246.

Idem, "The Goring Ox," *Temple Law Quarterly* 46 (1973), pp. 169–290.

E. J. Fisher, "Cultic Prostitution in the Ancient Near East? A Reassessment," *BTB* 6 (1976), pp. 225–236.

H. Gamoran, "The Biblical Law against Loans on Interest," *JNES* 30 (1971), pp. 127–134.

E. M. Good, "Capital Punishment and its Alternatives in Ancient Near Eastern Law," *Stanford Law Review* 19 (1967), pp. 947–977.

M. Greenberg, "Some Postulates of Biblical Criminal Law," in *Y. Kaufmann Jubilee Volume* (Jerusalem: Magnes, 1960), pp. 5–28.

M. Haran, "The Passover Sacrifice," *VTS* 23 (1972), pp. 86–116.

J. B. Hennessey, "Excavation of a Late Bronze Age Temple at Amman," *PEQ* 98 (1966), pp. 155–162.

S. B. Hoenig, "Sabbatical Years and the Year of Jubilee," *JQR* 59 (1969), pp. 222–236.

H. A. Hoffner, Jr., "2nd Millennium Antecedents to the Hebrew *'ôḇ*," *JBL* 86 (1967), pp. 385–401.

Idem, "Incest, Sodomy and Bestiality in the Ancient Near East," *Orient and Occident: Essays for C. H. Gordon* (Neukirchen: 1973), pp. 81–90.

F. L. Horton, "Form and Structure in Laws Relating to Women: Lev. 18:6–18," *SBL 1973 Seminar Papers*, pp. 20–33.

W. Krebs, "Zur kultischen Kohabitation mit Tieren im alten Orient," *Forschungen und Fortschritte* 37 (1963), pp. 19–21.

S. E. Loewenstamm, "*M/Tarbit* and *Neshek*," *JBL* 88 (1969), pp. 78–80.

R. P. Maloney, "Usury and Restrictions on Interest-Taking in the Ancient Near East," *CBQ* 36 (1974), pp. 1–20.

J. Milgrom, "A Prolegomenon to Lev. 17:11," *JBL* 90 (1971), pp. 149–156.

N. H. Snaith, "The Cult of Molech," *VT* 16 (1966), pp. 123f.

G. J. Wenham, "*Betûlāh*: A Girl of Marriageable Age," *VT* 22 (1972), pp. 326–348.

Idem, "The Biblical View of Marriage and Divorce: 1—The Cultural Background," *Third Way* 1:20 (20 October, 1977), pp. 3–5.

Idem, "The Biblical View of Marriage and Divorce: 2—Old Testament Teaching," *Third Way* 1:21 (3 November, 1977), pp. 7–9.

Idem, "The Restoration of Marriage Reconsidered," *JJS* 30 (1979), pp. 36–40.

Idem, "Leviticus 27:2–8 and the Price of Slaves," *ZAW* 90 (1978), pp. 264f.

R. Westbrook, "Jubilee Laws," "Redemption of Land," *Israel Law Review* 6 (1971), pp. 209–226, 367–375.

D. J. Wiseman, "The Laws of Hammurabi Again," *JSS* 7 (1962), pp. 161–172.

Idem, "Law and Order in OT Times," *Vox Evangelica* 8 (1973), pp. 5–21.

TEXT AND COMMENTARY

I. LAWS ON SACRIFICE (1:1–7:38)

A. INSTRUCTIONS FOR THE LAITY (1:1–5:26 [6:7])

The Structure of Leviticus 1–3

Leviticus opens with instructions about how the three commonest types of OT sacrifice are to be performed. Ch. 1 deals with burnt offerings, ch. 2 with cereal offerings, and ch. 3 with peace offerings. They are grouped together because all these sacrifices constitute "food offerings for the Lord which have a soothing aroma." This phrase, sometimes abbreviated, concludes each paragraph.

After an introduction to the whole section (1:1–2) come nine paragraphs of detailed directives, three paragraphs for each of the three kinds of sacrifice. Each time the most valuable sacrifice is handled first, and then the less valuable.

chapter 1 burnt offerings		*chapter 2* cereal offerings		*chapter 3* peace offerings	
3–9	cattle	1–3	uncooked	1–5	cattle
10–13	sheep or goats	4–10	cooked	6–11	sheep
14–17	birds	11–16	miscellaneous	12–17	goats

It has been suggested that the order of the material in these chapters of Leviticus is dictated by didactic considerations: the rules about the different sacrifices have been arranged in a logical fashion in order to make them easier to memorize.[1] Other points of similarity and difference are touched on in the detailed analysis of each chapter.

---

1. A. F. Rainey, "The Order of Sacrifices in OT Ritual Texts," *Biblica* 51 (1970), pp. 485–498, esp. p. 487.

THE BOOK OF LEVITICUS

1. THE BURNT OFFERING (CH. 1)

1 *The Lord called to Moses and spoke to him from the tent of meeting as follows:*

2 *"Speak to the Israelites and say to them, If any man among you offers an offering to the Lord, you must make your offering of domestic animals either from the herd or from the flock.*

3 *If his burnt offering comes from the herd, he must offer a perfect male animal. He must bring it to the entrance of the tent of meeting, so that the Lord may accept him.*

4 *Then he must lay his hand on the head of the burnt offering, so that it may be accepted on his behalf to make atonement for him.*

5 *Then he must kill the bull before the Lord and the sons of Aaron, the priests, must offer the blood and splash it over the altar which is at the entrance of the tent of meeting.*

6 *Then he must skin the burnt offering and chop it into pieces.*

7 *Then the sons of Aaron, the priests, must light a fire on the altar, lay wood on the fire,*

8 *and lay the pieces of the animal, including the head and the fat, on top of the firewood on the altar.*

9 *But he must wash its intestines and hind legs in water and the priest must burn the whole lot as a burnt offering, a food offering for the Lord which has a soothing aroma.*

10 *If his burnt offering comes from the flock, from the sheep or the goats, he must offer a perfect male animal.*

11 *He must kill it on the north side of the altar before the Lord, and then the sons of Aaron, the priests, must splash its blood over the altar.*

12 *Then he must chop it into pieces, and the priest must lay them, including the head and the fat, on top of the firewood on the altar.*

13 *But he must wash its intestines and hind legs with water, and then the priest must offer the whole lot and burn it as a burnt offering. It is a food offering for the Lord which has a soothing aroma.*

14 *If his burnt offering for the Lord consists of birds, he must offer either doves or pigeons as his offering.*

15 *The priest must bring it to the altar, wring its head off and burn it on the altar and let its blood drain down the side of the altar.*

16 *Then he must remove the crop with its contents and throw it on the east side of the altar in the ash pit.*

17 *Then he must split it open by the wings without tearing it apart, and the priest must burn it on the altar on top of the firewood. It is a burnt offering, a food offering for the Lord which has a soothing aroma."*

The Structure of Leviticus 1

1–2 Introduction
3–9 Burnt offerings of cattle
10–13 Burnt offerings of sheep and goats
14–17 Burnt offerings of birds

48

The structure of this chapter is clear. It begins by defining the general case, "If (*kî*) any man among you . . ." (v. 2). Then three subordinate cases are handled in three longer paragraphs, each introduced by "if" (*'im*) (vv. 3–9, 10–13, 14–17). The phraseology in each sub-case follows a consistent pattern. They all begin, "If his burnt offering (for the Lord) comes from. . . ." They all close with "a burnt offering, it is a food offering for the Lord which has a soothing aroma."

The first case is dealt with in the most detail. The two subsequent ones are explained more briefly. But in all three the law makes clear exactly what the worshipper does and what the priest does. The worshipper brings the animal, kills it, skins it or guts it, and chops it up. The priest sprinkles the blood on the altar and places the dismembered carcass on the fire.

Introduction

1 *The Lord called to Moses*. This slightly unusual expression emphasizes the solemnity and importance of the revelation that is about to follow. *Called* (*qārā'*) is often used when a child is given a name. "Abram called the name of his son . . . Ishmael" (Gen. 16:15). Basically "to call" means to speak in a loud clear voice. "The 'leper' . . . must call out, 'Unclean, unclean' " (Lev. 13:45). When God reveals himself in the OT he more often "speaks" and "says" rather than "calls." Here, however, he calls to Moses and this hints at the significance of what is coming. Sacrifice is the heart of Israel's worship, and therefore the regulations on sacrifice which are about to be announced are most important.

From the tent of meeting. This phrase and the form of the opening verb "called" remind us that Leviticus is the sequel to Exodus. Exodus ended with the erection of the tabernacle and God appearing in a cloud over the tent of meeting, the tent at the center of the tabernacle housing the ark and other sacred furniture (Exod. 40:16–38). It is important to recognize that the laws in Leviticus form part of a historical narrative. They are recorded to show how Israel became the nation it did. They show what was involved in being called to be the people of God. They illustrate how God's covenant purpose to make them "a kingdom of priests and a holy nation" (Exod. 19:6) was worked out in an all-embracing system of religious services and social law.

The laws about sacrifice are included at this point to explain the sacrifices and ceremonies mentioned at Aaron's ordination (chs. 8–9). Then come many more laws intended to help the people become pure and holy, to teach them to distinguish between clean and unclean (chs. 11–16). Time and again it is mentioned that God spoke to Moses, and that Moses then passed on God's instructions to the people. In 24:10ff. we learn of a man cursing God, and the judgment of God on his sin being declared through Moses to the people. This little incident epitomizes the whole of Leviticus. Though at first glance the book looks like an accumulation of laws, this impression is inaccurate. Leviticus is really part of the great history of Israel's journey from Egypt to the promised land. The law-giving was one of the most important events in this story.

In interpreting Leviticus, and especially in seeking to apply it to the modern situation, the historical context of the laws should be borne in mind. They are not timeless universal precepts such as are found in the book of Proverbs. The laws of Leviticus were revealed to the covenant nation at a particular phase of their history. They were designed to mold Israel into a holy people in a particular historical environment. Though God's holiness is unchanging, its expression may vary from age to age.

2 *Speak to the Israelites*. With these words Moses is told to resume his characteristic role as mediator between God and the people. Exodus emphasizes Moses' special position as the prophet who declares God's will to men and as intercessor when they sin. From the burning bush (Exod. 3), to the plagues (Exod. 7–12), the law given at Sinai (Exod. 19ff.), and the golden calf episode (Exod. 32–34), Moses carries out his role of mediator. Num. 12:6ff. likens him to God's confidential servant, while Deut. 18:15ff. tells Israel to await another prophet like Moses.

An offering (qorbān). The term[2] used here is a general one covering all the sacrifices that an individual Israelite could offer, burnt offerings, peace offerings, purification offerings, and so on. The following laws deal with offerings made by private persons. The public national sacrifices offered each day and at the festivals are listed in Num. 28–29. But here it is a question of a personal act of devotion or atonement. Sacrifices had to be offered if a man sinned, or became defiled in some way (Lev. 4–5; 12–15). They could also be presented to mark other significant occasions, e.g., the fulfilment

2. This term *qorbān* occurs in the NT (Mark 7:11), where Jesus condemns a legal device of the Pharisees who avoided supporting their parents by dedicating property to God.

of a vow (Num. 6:9ff.), Aaron's ordination (Lev. 8–9), childbirth (Lev. 12). In fact every meal at which meat was eaten had a sacrificial character, and the animal had to be presented in the tabernacle before it could be eaten (Lev. 17).

You must make your offering (lit. "You shall offer your offering"). The Hebrew imperfect often has an imperative force in legal passages, which is best conveyed by English "shall" or "must."

Of domestic animals. Hebrew *bᵉhēmāh* usually refers to domestic as opposed to wild animals, for which the common term is *ḥayyāh*. Often *bᵉhēmāh* denotes larger domestic animals, hence RSV "cattle"; but as this passage makes plain, it also covers smaller animals such as sheep and goats. Sacrifice was at the heart of OT worship. An essential ingredient of sacrifice was that it had to be costly. As David said, "I will not offer burnt offering to the Lord my God which cost me nothing" (2 Sam. 24:24). The same sentiment underlies the remark that the offering should be *from the herd or from the flock,* which meant in practice young bulls, sheep, and goats. The sacrifices were to be of domestic animals, not wild animals or game. According to Deut. 14:5 game could be eaten if correctly slaughtered, but not offered as sacrifice, since it cost nothing. Furthermore, only perfect animals were acceptable in worship (Lev. 1:3, 10; 22:18ff.). Only the best is good enough for God. The prophet Malachi later told those who offered second-rate animals that they were despising the Lord's name and polluting his table: " 'You sniff at me,' says the Lord of hosts; 'You bring what has been taken by violence or is lame or sick, and this you bring as your offering. Shall I accept that from your hand?' says the Lord" (Mal. 1:7, 13).

In the overfed West we can easily fail to realize what was involved in offering an unblemished animal in sacrifice. Meat was a rare luxury in OT times for all but the very rich (cf. Nathan's parable, 2 Sam. 12:1–6). Yet even we might blanch if we saw a whole lamb or bull go up in smoke as a burnt offering. How much greater pangs must a poor Israelite have felt.

The Burnt Offering

3–17 The burnt offering heads the list of sacrifices in chs. 1–5, though from other passages we discover that when different sacrifices were presented at the same time, purification offerings were offered before burnt offerings (e.g., Lev. 9; Num. 6:11ff.; 2 Chr. 29:20–30). The reason for describing the burnt offering first is that it was the commonest of all the sacrifices, performed every morning and evening, and more frequently on holy days. It is followed by instructions for cereal offerings and peace offerings (chs. 2–3), because they are like the burnt offering in being "food offerings" producing "a soothing aroma for the Lord" (1:9, 13, 17; 2:2, 9, 16; 3:5, 16). This makes it plausible to suppose that the sacrifices in chs. 1–5 are arranged according to their various theological concepts, so that it is easier to remember their distinctive features. It may be that they were grouped in this way to help the priests learn their tasks.[3] To clarify the significance of these strange ceremonies, each sacrifice will be expounded under various subheadings instead of verse by verse.

The Sacrificial Animals

Various animals were permitted for burnt offerings. For private offerings, bulls, sheep, goats, or even pigeons and turtledoves were allowed. As a rule the sacrificial victim had to be a perfect male specimen, though this is not insisted on with birds. For official services one-year-old male lambs were the commonest victim, though on some occasions rams or young bulls were preferred (Num. 28–29).

The Rite

The characteristic feature of the burnt offering was that the whole animal (apart from its skin, Lev. 7:8, or crop, 1:16) was burned on the altar. The Hebrew term for *burnt offering, 'ōlāh*, probably means "ascending," i.e., to God in the smoke (cf. Judg. 13:20). But before the animal was burned, various other things had to be done to it.

First of all the animal was brought by its owner into the outer court of the tabernacle or temple, *to the entrance of the tent of meeting* (v. 3). This was the tent which housed the ark and other sacred furniture (Exod. 37). Outside the tent was found the large altar for burnt offerings, 7'6" (2.2 meters) square and 4'6" (1.3 meters)

---

3. So A. F. Rainey, *Biblica* 51 (1970), pp. 486f.

high, which is described in Exod. 27:1–8. It was here that the various ceremonies took place.

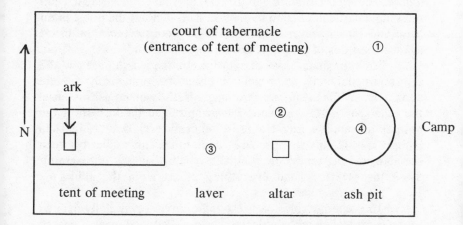

When he reached "the entrance of the tent of meeting," the worshipper laid his hand on the animal's head (see ① on diagram; v. 4). Leviticus mentions only the act, but it is very unlikely that it was all done in silence. Most probably the worshipper explained at this point why he was bringing the sacrifice; e.g., childbirth, healing, or uncleanness (chs. 12, 14, 15). He may even have recited or sung a psalm. Several psalms mention burnt offerings (20:4 [Eng. 3]; 40:7 [6]; 50:8; 51:18 [16], 21 [19]; 66:13, 15). Psalms 40, 51, and 66 could well have been sung by the worshipper himself, whereas Pss. 20 and 50 would have been more appropriate as the priest's reply. Certainly the priest must also have said something to assure the worshipper that his sacrifice was *accepted* (v. 4).

Then the worshipper had to *kill* the animal himself, on the north side of the altar (see ② on diagram; vv. 5, 11). In the daily sacrifice of course the priest would have killed the animal himself. The word for killing (*shāḥaṭ*) the animal is a special term usually saved for sacrificial slaughter in the OT. In postbiblical Hebrew the word denotes a specific method of ritual killing which ensured that all the blood was drained out of the animal's body. Since from earliest times Israel was forbidden to eat flesh with blood in it (Gen. 9:4; Lev. 17:10ff.; 1 Sam. 14:32ff.), it probably has the same meaning here. In the burnt offering the blood had to be collected in a basin by the priests as it poured out of the dying animal. They then were to *offer the blood* to God. What was involved in "offering the blood" is not made clear in this passage. The term used here (*qārab*, Hiphil) is a general one. In 1:13; 3:9, 14; 7:3, 33; 8:18 it again refers to a particular action in the sacrifice. Perhaps the priest lifted it up and said a prayer. Then the priest would *splash*[4] the blood against the sides of the altar, not on top of it.

Then the animal was chopped up by the worshipper and the priest burned it bit by bit on top of the altar, beginning with the head and the fat. While the priest was doing this, the worshipper prepared the other parts. He washed the *hind legs*[5] and the viscera of the animal to remove any traces of excreta (cf. Deut. 23:13–15 [Eng. 12–14]). This was probably done in the large laver between the altar and the tent of meeting (Exod. 40:7, see ③ on diagram). Then the priest burned everything, apart from the skin (see Lev. 7:8), on the altar.

The separate roles of priest and offerer are carefully defined in the laws dealing with cattle and sheep. The worshipper prepared the animal for the sacrifice, by killing it, skinning it, washing the dirty parts, and chopping it up. The priest on the other hand had to catch the blood and sprinkle it over the altar, and then put the pieces of meat on the altar fire. Such a distribution of duties was hardly feasible when a small bird was offered. This time the priest did nearly everything. All the worshippper had to do was to remove *the crop with its contents*,[6] put these bits in the ashpit (see ④ on diagram), and *split* the bird open, presumably to help it burn (vv. 16f.). Removing "the crop with its contents" parallels washing the viscera and back legs of the larger animals (vv. 9, 13). The law is concerned that the clean and holy priest be kept from pollution. Therefore the worshipper must undertake the messier tasks associated with sacrifice.

---

4. *Splash (zāraq)* is used of pouring liquids or powders from a container (Exod. 24:6, 8), sometimes with a view to dispersing them (e.g., Ezek. 10:2).

5. *Kerā'ayim: hind legs* (so TEV and Snaith, p. 31) clearly denotes the back legs of hopping insects in 11:21. The same sense is likely here, since the hind legs are more likely to be soiled by excreta. But the rarity of the term makes this uncertain. LXX understood "feet," and this idea is followed by NEB "shins."

6. *Contents (nōtsāh)* occurs only here in the OT, and its meaning is therefore uncertain. It may be an alternative way of spelling *nôtsāh*, which means "feathers" (so the Greek and Vulgate and some modern commentators, e.g., RSV; Elliger, pp. 26f.). However, the Targums and Peshitta and the majority of modern commentators prefer to translate it "contents." The word may be derived from *yātsā'*, "to go out."

The Purpose of the Burnt Offering

Using a little imagination every reader of the OT soon realizes that these ancient sacrifices were very moving occasions. They make modern church services seem tame and dull by comparison. The ancient worshipper did not just listen to the minister and sing a few hymns. He was actively involved in the worship. He had to choose an unblemished animal from his own flock, bring it to the sanctuary, kill it and dismember it with his own hands, then watch it go up in smoke before his very eyes. He was convinced that something very significant was achieved through these acts and knew that his relationship with God was profoundly affected by this sacrifice. Yet because they understood the purpose of the burnt offering so well, the men of ancient Israel have left this most common OT sacrifice largely without explanation. This chapter of Leviticus is like an extract from a prayer book from which the prayers have been omitted, leaving just the rubrics, i.e., the instructions for the conduct of the service. It is in the prayers that the purpose of a ritual becomes clear; by themselves rubrics tend to be ambiguous. There are a few cryptic hints in this chapter about the purpose of the sacrifice, but in themselves they are insufficient to answer our questions. After considering the evidence of this chapter, we shall therefore turn to other passages in an attempt to elucidate the function of the burnt offering.

The first point to note is that the victim must be *a perfect male animal* (vv. 3, 10). This requirement underlines the importance of the burnt offering. For some kinds of peace offerings slightly blemished animals could be offered, but this was never allowed in the case of a burnt offering (22:23). *Male* animals were also regarded as more valuable than females. For example, in the case of purification offerings a ruler had to bring a he-goat, but an ordinary person was expected to offer only a she-goat (4:22–31). Except for the burnt offering and reparation offerings, animals of either sex could be offered: the limitation to male animals shows the high status of these two sacrifices.

So that the Lord may accept him (v. 3); *that it may be accepted on his behalf*[7] (v. 4). In these phrases the general aim of the sacrifice is indicated. It is that the offerer may be *accepted* (*rātsāh*) by God. Peace with God is the goal of sacrifice. Leviticus lays down

7. Verse 4b may also be translated "and it will be accepted for him to make atonement for him." However, *waw* + perfect may express purpose (GK 165a) (cf. Lev. 14:36), and a final sense is appropriate here (cf. v. 3b) (Hoffmann I, p. 123).

several rules, the infringement of which will mean that a sacrifice
will not be accepted (7:18; 22:23, 25, 27). The psalmists often pray
for God to accept his people, that is, to hear their prayers and bless
them (Ps. 40:14 [Eng. 13]; 77:8 [7]; 85:2 [1]). Conversely one of the
most serious threats in the prophetic writings is that God will not
accept their sacrifices (Jer. 14:12; Hos. 8:13; Amos 5:22).

The idea that sacrifice pleases God is expressed in the phrase
characteristic of Lev. 1–3, *a food offering*[8] *for the Lord which has a
soothing aroma* (e.g., 1:9, 13, 17). The Hebrew word order makes it
clear that the sacrificial aroma soothes the Lord, not man. The idea
is expressed at its starkest and simplest in the flood story. Before the
flood, "the Lord saw that . . . every imagination of man's heart was
only evil continually" (Gen. 6:5). So he decided to destroy mankind.
After the flood Noah offered a sacrifice. "And when the Lord
smelled the soothing aroma the Lord thought, 'I will never again
curse the ground because of man, for the imagination of man's heart
is evil from his youth' " (Gen. 8:21). Though man was unchanged in
his sinfulness, God's attitude to man altered, thanks to the burnt
offering. This is not an isolated example. The idea that man is always
in danger of angering God runs through the whole Pentateuch.
Fierce judgments and sudden death stud its pages. Sacrifice is the
appointed means whereby peaceful coexistence between a holy God
and sinful man becomes a possibility.[9]

---

8. Heb. *'ishsheh*. The meaning of this term is obscure. The traditional translation has
been "fire offering," deriving it from *'ēsh*, "fire." This view is still accepted by de
Vaux, *Studies*, p. 31 and Snaith, p. 32. The difficulty with this view is that *'ishsheh*
refers not only to sacrifices which are burned in whole or in part on the altar, but to
the portions of sacrifices eaten by the priests (2:3, 10; 7:30, 35) and to the bread of the
Presence (24:7, 9). For this reason other proposals have been made. Elliger, p. 35,
following an earlier suggestion of Wetzstein, derives it from *'ānash* and thinks it
means a gift to create friendly relations between God and man. A third possibility is
that it is connected with Ugaritic *'itt*, a word of uncertain meaning according to
J. Hoftijzer, "Das sogenannte Feueropfer," *VTS* 16 (1967), pp. 114–134. This explanation has been accepted by Maarsingh, p. 22, and G. R. Driver, *Ugaritica* 6 (1969),
pp. 181–84, who translates *'itt* as "generous, rich gift." A fourth suggestion due to
Cazelles, p. 13, derives *'ishsheh* from Akkadian *eshsheshu*. He suggests that it means
food offered to Yahweh, hence "food offering" of the NEB, TEV, and our translation.
The derivation looks probable, since *eshsheshu* festivals were a regular feature of
Mesopotamian religion from the 3rd to the 1st millennium B.C. The sacrifices offered on
these occasions were called *eshsheshu* offerings and cover roughly the same range
of materials as Heb. *'ishsheh*. But *CAD* E, pp. 371–73, offers no translation of
eshsheshu, and if Hebrew *'ishsheh* means the same as *eshsheshu* it should also be left
untranslated. Only one observation really favors "food offering" as a rendering of
'ishsheh: in several places (3:11, 16; 21:6, 21) it seems to be explained by adding
alongside it the more common term *leḥem*, "bread, food."
9. See Introduction VI.3, "The Role of Sacrifice."

To make atonement for him (v. 4). This is the clearest clue to the purpose of the burnt offering to be found in the Levitical law. It atones for the worshipper's sins. Yet many commentators play down the atoning value of the burnt offering. Since the purification (sin) offering (Lev. 4) and the reparation (guilt) offering (Lev. 5) are those that atone for sin, some other meaning is ascribed to the burnt offering. According to Keil the burnt offering expresses "complete surrender to the Lord. . . , consecration . . . to a course of life pleasing to God."[10] In similar vein de Vaux says it is "an act of homage, expressed by a gift."[11]

Others[12] more correctly insist that the burnt offering does make atonement, though in a slightly different way from the purification and reparation offerings. Whereas the purification offering is concerned with cleansing the different parts of the tabernacle from the uncleanness caused by sin,[13] the burnt offering makes atonement for sin in a more general sense.[14] The atoning value of the burnt offering is also hinted at in Lev. 14:20 and 16:24 and even more explicitly outside the law. In Gen. 8:21 God's attitude to man is reversed by the burnt offering. Instead of a flood there is a promise that the harvests will not fail, and a covenant is made with future generations that the earth will never again be destroyed by a universal flood. Thus the burnt offering does not remove sin or change man's sinful nature, but it makes fellowship between sinful man and a holy God possible. It propitiates God's wrath against sin. The idea that the burnt offering appeases God's anger is expressed in many other passages. If a commandment was broken unwittingly, it was necessary to offer a burnt offering along with other sacrifices (Num. 15:24). David's decision to take a census brought a plague upon all Israel and many died. It stopped when David offered burnt offerings and peace offerings (2 Sam. 24:25; cf. 1 Chr. 21:26). Job offered burnt offerings every week for each of his seven sons, "for Job said, 'It may be that my sons have sinned' " (Job 1:5). After Job's ordeal was over his friends were told to offer a burnt offering for themselves, so that God would not deal with them according to

10. Keil, *Biblical Archaeology* I, p. 317.
11. De Vaux, *Studies*, p. 37. Similar views are expressed by Gispen, p. 47; A. F. Rainey, "Sacrifice and Offerings," *Zondervan Pictorial Encyclopedia of the Bible* 5 (Grand Rapids: 1975), pp. 205f. Levine, *Presence of the Lord*, pp. 22–27, argues that the burnt offering is simply an invitation to God to join in a peace offering.
12. E.g., Clements, p. 11; Dillmann, pp. 391f.
13. See below on ch. 4.
14. See Milgrom, *Encyclopedia Miqrait* 7 (1976), p. 243.

their folly (42:8). Finally 2 Chr. 29:7–8, describing the neglect of divine worship by Ahaz, mentions that the burnt offerings were not offered, "Therefore the wrath of the Lord came on Judah and Jerusalem." On the basis of these passages we conclude that one function of the burnt offering was to prevent God's displeasure at man's sin from being turned into punishment. Because man's very nature is sinful, there is always friction between him and his maker. For this reason Job felt obliged to offer burnt offerings for his sons every week. It seems likely that similar ideas underlie the institution of the burnt offering in Num. 28.

Other texts do suggest that the burnt offering involved more than atonement. It could be offered as an act of obedience or thanksgiving. Gen. 22 tells how Abraham was told to sacrifice his son Isaac as a burnt offering. In the biblical story this forms the supreme test of Abraham's faith in God's promise that his children would inherit the land of Canaan. Faced with a divine command that appeared to nullify the promise, Abraham had to decide whether to obey, lose his son, and see his hopes dashed, or to salvage what he could by disobedience. As the story indicates, he obeyed and at the critical moment his son was saved and his own faith was vindicated. This is the main theological thrust of the story. Yet the exegete may ask why a burnt offering was the chosen means to test Abraham's obedience. Other ways of verifying Abraham's devotion could be suggested. Perhaps the burnt offering was chosen because it was a service in which the worshipper bore witness to his faith in God and his willingness to obey his commandments. In Exod. 18:11–12 Jethro acknowledged that "the Lord is greater than all gods"; then he offered a burnt offering and sacrifices. Similarly, after the people had accepted the terms of the Sinai Covenant, Moses offered burnt offerings and peace offerings (Exod. 24:3–8). In 1 K. 18:38–39, when divine fire fell and consumed the burnt offering, the people shouted out, "The Lord, he is God." In 1 Sam. 15:22 and Ps. 40:7 [Eng. 6] sacrifice and obedience are contrasted with the implication that sacrifice ought to express obedience; sacrifice without obedience is an empty ritual. If affirmation of faith and obedience are underlying motives for bringing a burnt offering, it is very appropriate that it should be offered as a thanksgiving for deliverance, as a freewill offering, or when a vow is fulfilled (Num. 6:14; 15:3; Ps. 50; 66:13–15). The worshipper has proved God's faithfulness in his life and wishes now to express his faith publicly.

This motive could underlie the prescription that after

childbirth, healing, or bodily pollution a person must offer purification offerings and burnt offerings (Lev. 12:6; 14:13, 19, etc.; 15:15, 30). Thanksgiving on these occasions would not be out of place (cf. 1 Sam. 1:24–2:11). However, if it is right to regard the sin offering as a means of purifying the sanctuary from the pollutions of sin, it could well be that the burnt offering is intended to free the worshipper from the consequences of sin, to protect him from God's wrath. To the modern mind it seems strange that skin diseases and childbirth should have been looked on as defiling, rendering someone liable to divine displeasure. Yet this is a pervasive theme in the Levitical legislation. Only the pure are fit for God. We shall see when we look at the food laws that only animals that fall into certain clear categories may be sacrificed and eaten. Those that cross the category boundaries are forbidden. Similarly priests with deformities may not officiate in the sanctuary. Plowmen may not use a mixed team of plow-animals or mix their crops. There is thus running through the legislation a concern to preserve the purity of the natural order. Disorder symbolizes sin. Wherever disorder is manifested, man is reminded of the sin which perpetually disrupts creation (Gen. 3:14ff.). When man is reminded of sin, whether by disease or childbirth or by his own obvious fault, he has to offer a burnt offering, the sacrifice that makes divine and human coexistence possible.

The burnt offering, then, makes atonement for man. It was pointed out in the introduction that *to make atonement* (*kipper*) has two different meanings in Hebrew, "to wipe clean" or "to pay a ransom."[15] Which meaning is more appropriate in the case of the burnt offering?

In those rituals where *kipper* means "to wipe clean" or "to cleanse" it is clear that the blood is the cleansing agent that has to be applied carefully to the polluted object, e.g., the horns of the altar (4:25) or the mercy seat (16:14). This is not the case with the burnt offering. The blood is simply caught and thrown over the altar. The focus of attention is the animal's burning carcass and the soothing aroma thereby produced. In the burnt offering there is no sign of any attempt at cleansing the worshipper, priest, or altar. Can the burnt offering instead be regarded as a ransom payment for the worshipper? It appears that it can, if seen in its wider OT context.

15. A third meaning "to cover," from Arabic *kappara,* was once favored by many scholars. This has little to commend it, though Snaith, p. 30, and more circumspectly, F. Maass, *THWAT* I, p. 843, prefer it.

In modern usage a ransom tends to mean the sum paid to terrorists to free innocent hostages. It often involves buying off an outrageous and illegal act. But in the OT the payment of a ransom was a very humane act. It allowed a guilty person to be punished with a lesser penalty than he deserved. If a man owned a dangerous ox and he allowed it to run amok and someone was killed, the owner was liable to the death penalty. But the court could decide to save his life if he paid a ransom (Exod. 21:30). In the case of adultery the aggrieved husband was entitled to exact the death penalty; he could put to death his faithless wife and her lover (Lev. 20:10). He might choose to spare his wife and her lover, however, if the latter paid compensation, literally "ransom" (Prov. 6:35). This permission to substitute a ransom for the maximum penalty was common in ancient Near Eastern law, but in the case of premeditated murder the OT explicitly excluded it.

"You shall accept no ransom for the life of a murderer . . . but he shall be put to death. . . . No atonement can be made for the land (lit. "no ransom can be paid"), for the blood that is shed in it, except by the blood of him who shed it" (Num. 35:31, 33).

Another passage that clearly uses the verb "to make atonement" in the sense "pay a ransom" is 2 Sam. 21:3–6. The nation of Israel was suffering from famine and learned that it was the consequence of Saul's unatoned sin. So David asked, "How shall I make expiation?" (lit. "What shall I pay as a ransom?"). The Gibeonites reply, "It is not a matter of silver or gold . . . but let seven of Saul's sons be given to us, so that we may hang them up before the Lord." David wanted to pay a ransom, but in this case the Gibeonites insisted that some of Saul's family should be put to death to atone for Saul's sins.

In this passage the idea of ransom has become broader. The death of some of Saul's relatives saved the rest of the family and the whole nation. In Num. 25:13 Phinehas is said to have made atonement (paid a ransom) for the people of Israel. He did this by slaying one of the guilty Israelites, thereby halting the plague that was sweeping the nation. Similarly by offering incense Aaron made atonement and stopped the plague that would have destroyed Israel after the sin of Korah, Dathan, and Abiram (Num. 16–17). The Levites by their service made atonement for Israel. Every first-born Israelite was in theory consecrated to God, because the first-born had been spared the final plague in Egypt. But the Levites took over this role from the first-born; they were substituted for them. They have been likened to a lightning rod, whereby God's wrath was turned away from the whole people and concentrated on them.[16] They in turn offered bulls to make atonement for themselves to divert God's wrath onto the animal (Num. 8:5ff.). Finally, Moses offered to make atonement for Israel's great sin of making the golden calf. In his prayer he asked God to forgive their sin or "blot me out of your book." This is another case of one man sacrificing himself so that the nation should go free. But Moses' prayer was rejected "and the Lord sent a plague upon the people" (Exod. 32:30-35).

In nonsacrificial texts *kipper* means to pay a ransom, so that a guilty person does not suffer the death penalty demanded by the law or God's holiness in particular situations. The ransom itself can be money, or the suffering of some other person, or even of animals who take the place of men (Num. 8:10-12). This seems to be what Lev. 17:11 has in view. "I have given the blood to make atonement (lit. "to ransom") for your lives, for the blood makes atonement (ransoms) at the price of a life."[17] It is this interpretation that seems to fit the burnt offering best. God in his mercy allowed sinful man to offer a ransom payment for sins, so that he escaped the death penalty that his iniquities merit. As ransoms are wont to be, the burnt offering was a high price to pay. Unblemished rams and bulls were even more expensive then than they are today.

This interpretation is confirmed by one feature of the ritual that has not been discussed so far: *he must lay his hand on the head of the burnt offering* (v. 4). *Lay* is perhaps a rather weak translation of the Hebrew (*śāmak*); "press" might be preferable (cf. Isa. 59:16; Ezek. 24:2; 30:6; Amos 5:19). The worshipper was not just to touch the animal; he was to lean on it. This action forms part of many sacrifices (cf. 3:2, 8, 13; 4:4, 15, 24; 16:21). Here its importance is specially emphasized by the context. It is the imposition of the man's hands that makes the sacrifice acceptable as an atonement (vv. 3 and 4).

One reason for emphasizing this part of the action is that it was at this point that the worshipper said his prayer. The laying on of hands is associated with praying in Lev. 16:21 (cf. Deut. 21:6-9) as well as in later Jewish tradition. This is an important theological principle. Sacrifice without prayer is useless. All a man's powers must be active in divine worship, heart and mouth as well as hands

16. J. Milgrom, *Studies*, p. 31.
17. For further discussion see below on ch. 17 and Levine, *Presence of the Lord*, pp. 67ff.

and feet. Mere ceremonial or church attendance is inadequate by itself. They must be accompanied by heartfelt prayer and praise.

Another reason for the imposition of hands was that it established a close relationship between the worshipper and the offering. It is uncertain exactly what relationship is expressed through the act. Some see the imposition of hands as a statement of ownership: "this is my animal that is being sacrificed," carrying with it the implication that the benefits of the sacrifice should accrue to the worshipper.[18] This is so self-evident that it hardly seems necessary to express such a sentiment in a specific act. Two other interpretations have more to commend them. The laying on of hands may indicate that the animal is taking the place of the worshipper. The worshipper is offering himself to God through the sacrificial victim. "The plain implication is that, in some metaphysical sense, the victim is a vicarious substitution for the donor himself."[19] Or alternatively the laying on of hands transfers the worshipper's sins symbolically to the animal.[20] Both these meanings seem to be attested in Scripture. By laying hands on the Levites, the Israelites appointed them to serve in place of the first-born (Num. 8:10; cf. 3:40–51). Similarly Moses laid hands on Joshua, thereby conferring authority on him to act in his place as his successor (Num. 27:18, 23; Deut. 34:9). But on the day of atonement Aaron had to place his hands on the scapegoat and confess over it "all the iniquities of the Israelites . . . and he must place them on the head of the goat and drive it into the wilderness" (Lev. 16:21). Similarly in 24:14 those who heard the blasphemer had to lay their hands on him to transfer their sin (of hearing the blasphemy) onto the man who was to be punished for his own sin and theirs.[21]

It does not seem necessary to decide between these explanations. Both fit in well with sacrifices making atonement, i.e., the animal serving as a ransom for the life of man. One may regard the animal either as dying in the worshipper's place as his substitute, or as receiving the death penalty because of the sin transferred to it by the laying on of hands.

Outside the Law the burnt offering is mentioned with relative infrequency, but particularly informative are the references to sacrifice in the Psalms. It seems likely that psalms were often said or

18. E.g., Clements, p. 10; de Vaux, *Studies,* p. 28; R. Péter, *VT* 27 (1977), p. 52.
19. E. R. Leach, *Culture and Communication,* p. 89.
20. E.g., Gispen, pp. 38f.; Keil, pp. 283f.
21. So Gispen, p. 38.

sung during the sacrifices, and can therefore give us a glimpse of the theology underlying these services. The burnt offering is mentioned in Ps. 20:4 [Eng. 3]; 40:7 [6]; 50:8; 51:21[19]; 66:15. The burnt offering was the main sacrifice of every morning and evening, so it is possible that Pss. 4 and 5, which mention sacrifices at these times, were also used in the service for the burnt offering.

Primarily the burnt offering brought reconciliation between God and man; but it also expressed faith in God and obedience to his law and could be offered in fulfilment of a vow. These themes are alluded to in the Psalms. In Ps. 51:18–19 [Eng. 16–17] a burnt offering is said to be worthless if it is not accompanied by a broken and a contrite spirit.[22] In Pss. 4, 5, 40, 50, and 66, confessions of faith, protestations of obedience, and fulfilling vows all intermingle and intertwine. In all these psalms there is constantly expressed the conviction that God answers the prayers of those who pray and sacrifice in the right way (cf., e.g., Ps. 20).

Summary of the Burnt Offering in the OT

The burnt offering was the commonest of all the OT sacrifices. Its main function was to atone for man's sin by propitiating God's wrath. In the immolation of the animal, most commonly a lamb, God's judgment against human sin was symbolized and the animal suffered in man's place. The worshipper acknowledged his guilt and responsibility for his sins by pressing his hand on the animal's head and confessing his sin. The lamb was accepted as the ransom price for the guilty man. The daily use of the sacrifice in the worship of the temple and tabernacle was a constant reminder of man's sinfulness and God's holiness. So were its occasional usages after sickness, childbirth, and vows. In bringing a sacrifice a man acknowledged his sinfulness and guilt. He also publicly confessed his faith in the Lord, his thankfulness for past blessing, and his resolve to live according to God's holy will all the days of his life.

The NT and the Burnt Offering

The burnt offering is mentioned explicitly in only two passages in the NT (Mark 12:33; Heb. 10:6–8), both of which are quotations from, or paraphrases of, the OT. On other occasions the presentation of burnt offerings is implied, but not explicitly recorded (Luke 2:24; cf.

22. For a discussion of this passage see the commentaries, esp. A. A. Anderson, *Psalms* I (New Century Bible, Oliphants, 1972), pp. 400f.

Lev. 12:6; Luke 17:14; cf. Lev. 14:2ff.; Acts 21:26; cf. Num. 6:14).

These passing references do not do justice to the importance of the burnt offering in NT theology. It is one of a number of images used to describe the self-sacrifice of Christ on the cross. Jesus said he came "to give his life as a ransom for many" (Mark 10:45). In language borrowed from Leviticus, Paul says, "Walk in love as Christ loved us and gave himself up for us, a fragrant offering and sacrifice to God" (Eph. 5:2). Peter too echoes the OT: "You were ransomed . . . with the precious blood of Christ, like that of a lamb without blemish or spot" (1 Pet. 1:18–19). Heb. 7:27 mentions the daily sacrifices the OT priests had to offer, but Christ offered one sacrifice "once for all when he offered up himself."

The idea that Jesus was the one true burnt offering that takes away the sin of the world probably goes back to Jesus himself.[23] In early Jewish discussions of the burnt offering one occasion stands out as specially significant: the sacrifice of Isaac. For some Jews at least it was Isaac's willingness to be sacrificed that really secured atonement for sins. The daily burnt offering and the passover lambs were reminders to God of Isaac's self-giving, and it was because of his merits that the later sacrifices were accepted by God. In the Gospels we can see that Jesus takes the place given to Isaac in Jewish theology. At his baptism the voice from heaven cries, "This is my beloved Son, with whom I am well pleased" (Matt. 3:17; cf. Mark 1:11; Luke 3:22), an amalgam of phrases from Gen. 22:16 and Isa. 42:1. Similarly John the Baptist hails Jesus as "the Lamb of God who takes away the sin of the world" (John 1:29). Whether John was referring to the passover lamb or the lamb of the burnt offering makes little difference, for both were seen as reminders of the greatest atoning sacrifice, that of Isaac. In NT theology Jesus takes the role of Isaac while God the Father takes the role of Abraham. Such thinking underlies such well-known passages as John 3:16, "For God so loved the world that he gave his only-begotten Son," and Rom. 8:32, "He who did not spare his own Son but gave him up for us all, will he not also give us all things with him?"

The NT uses the image of the burnt offering in a quite different way as well. Christian service, in church and in the community, is compared to sacrifice: "Through him let us continually offer up a

23. G. Vermes, *Scripture and Tradition in Judaism* (Leiden: Brill, 1961), pp. 193–227.

sacrifice of praise to God. . . . Do not neglect to do good and to share what you have, for such sacrifices are pleasing to God" (Heb. 13:15–16; cf. Phil. 4:18; 1 Pet. 2:5). In that the only burnt offering that can atone for sin has been made by Christ, Christians no longer have to bring their lambs to the altar to receive forgiveness of sins. But bringing a sacrifice involved praising God for his grace and declaring one's intention to love God and keep his commandments. Now that animal sacrifice is obsolete, praise and good works by themselves constitute the proper sacrifices expected of a Christian.

The Christian Significance of the Burnt Offering

With the death of Christ the only sufficient "burnt offering" was offered once and for all, and therefore the animal sacrifices which foreshadowed Christ's sacrifice were made obsolete. Christians therefore have no need to offer burnt offerings for the atonement of their sins. The shedding of Christ's blood was the payment of the perfect ransom price. He has borne the Father's wrath for us, just as the bulls and lambs in the OT did, so that sinful men can, despite their sin, enjoy the presence of God and have their prayers answered.

The laws in Leviticus remind us then of Christ's death and what he has done for us. They also remind us of the serious consequences of sin and its pervasiveness. Sin can only be atoned for by death. The worshipper might well feel very much deprived when he had paid for a choice lamb to be sacrificed. But it reminded him that the animal was a ransom, a substitute payment instead of his own life. "For the wages of sin is death." God in his mercy provided a cheap alternative in OT times—a lamb. In NT times a free pardon is available. "The gift of God is eternal life in Christ Jesus our Lord" (Rom. 6:23).

The burnt offering had to be offered daily to atone for sins. The Christian too is aware of the need for daily forgiveness. As the worshipper had to confess his sins and declare his intention to walk in God's ways when he presented his animal, so must the Christian. In the words of 1 John 1:7–9, "If we walk in the light . . . we have fellowship with one another, and the blood of Jesus his Son cleanses us from all sin. . . . If we confess our sins, he is faithful and just and will forgive our sins and cleanse us from all unrighteousness." The burnt offering was the first offering of the day in normal worship.

65

This reminds us that forgiveness of sins is the prerequisite of true worship. Only those whose sins are forgiven can enjoy God's fellowship and praise him from their hearts.

The pattern of OT sacrifices may thus provide a pattern of truly Christian worship. Worship should begin with confession of sins, a claiming of Christ's forgiveness, and a total rededication to God's service, before going on to praise and petition.

2. THE CEREAL OFFERING (CH. 2)

1 *"If anyone offers a cereal offering to the Lord, his offering must be of fine flour and he must pour oil on it and put incense on it.*

2 *He must then bring it to the sons of Aaron, the priests, and must take a handful of the flour and oil as well as all the incense, and the priest must burn it on the altar as a memorial portion, a food offering for the Lord which has a soothing aroma.*

3 *But the rest of the cereal offering belongs to Aaron and his sons; it is a most holy portion of the Lord's food offerings.*

4 *If you offer a cereal offering baked in an oven, it may consist of thin cakes of unleavened flour mixed with oil or unleavened wafers coated with oil.*

5 *If your offering is cooked on a griddle, it must be made into a cake of unleavened bread mixed with oil.*

6 *You must crumble it into pieces and pour oil on it: it is a cereal offering.*

7 *If your cereal offering is cooked in a pan, it must be made with flour and oil.*

8 *Then you must bring the cereal offering made of these ingredients to the Lord and offer it to the priest, and he must bring it to the altar.*

9 *Then the priest must take from the cereal offering its memorial portion and burn it on the altar, a food offering for the Lord which has a soothing aroma.*

10 *But the rest of the cereal offering belongs to Aaron and his sons; it is a most holy portion from the Lord's food offerings.*

11 *None of your cereal offerings to the Lord may be made with yeast. You may not burn any yeast or honey as a food offering for the Lord.*

12 *You may present them as an offering of the firstfruits to the Lord, but they must not be offered upon the altar to make a soothing aroma.*

13 *You must salt every cereal offering. The salt of your God's covenant must never be missing from your cereal offering. All your offerings must be salted.*

14 *But if you make a cereal offering to the Lord of the first crops, you must make your offering of roast grain or ground meal.*

15 *You must add oil to it and place incense on it: it is a cereal offering.*

16 *Then the priest must burn the memorial portion consisting of some meal, some oil, and all the incense, as a food offering for the Lord."*

The Structure of Leviticus 2

The chapter divides into three paragraphs:

1–3   Cereal offerings of uncooked grain
4–10   Cooked cereal offerings
11–16 Miscellaneous rules about cereal offerings

The first two paragraphs are similarly structured. Each opens with "If anyone (you) offer a cereal offering" and closes with "a food-offering . . . from the Lord's food-offerings" (vv. 2–3, 9–10). As in ch.. 1, the law makes clear what the offerer must do and what the priest's duties were. The second paragraph deals with three different types of cooked cereal offering. The first case is introduced with "if" (*kî*) (v. 4), the sub-cases with "if" (*'im*) (vv. 5, 7; cf. ch. 1).

The third paragraph deals with a number of rules governing the use of all types of cereal offerings. Its subject matter means that it is structured differently from the first two paragraphs, with the exception of the last verse (v. 16), which imitates vv. 2 and 9 quite closely.

The Cereal Offering

The official daily burnt offering was always followed by the cereal offering (Num. 28). The burnt and cereal offerings are often mentioned together in the historical books (Josh. 22:23, 29; Judg. 13:19, 23; 1 K. 8:64; 2 K. 16:13, 15). It is therefore natural that the cereal offering should be described immediately after the burnt offering in Leviticus. It is also one of three sacrifices (the burnt offering, Lev. 1, and the peace offering, Lev. 3, are the others) that produce a "soothing aroma to the Lord" (1:9, 17; 2:2, 9, 12; 3:5, 16).

It is unlike the burnt and peace offering, however, in that it is not an animal sacrifice, but a cereal offering. It is also unlike the burnt offering in that only a handful of the sacrifice was burned in the fire, the rest being given to the priests to eat, whereas in the burnt offering everything except the skin was burned. The completely different way in which the ingredients of the sacrifice were used makes unlikely the suggestion of rabbinic commentators that the cereal offering was the burnt offering of the very poor. Though the cereal offering is described immediately after the burnt offering, this does not mean it was offered only in conjunction with the burnt offering. It could be offered on its own, for example when the firstfruits of harvest were brought to the sanctuary (2:14; cf. Deut. 26).

The Materials of the Cereal Offering

Flour and oil were the principal ingredients of the cereal offering. The flour could be cooked or uncooked. Three different ways of cooking the bread are detailed. It could be *baked in an oven* (v. 4), or *cooked on a griddle* (a flat plate used like a frying pan but with very little oil) (v. 5), or *cooked in a pan*, i.e., fried (v. 7). At harvest time a special kind of cereal offering was encouraged, *of roast grain or ground meal* (v. 14). *Salt* had to be added to every cereal offering: this point is specially stressed, being put three different ways in v. 13. A pinch of *incense*[1] was also usually added to cereal offerings (vv. 2, 15–16). But yeast and honey were prohibited (v. 11; cf. Exod. 23:18; 34:25).

The Rite

The offerer first of all prepared the cereals. If it was fine flour or roast new grain he mixed it with oil and added a little incense (vv. 1–2, 14–15). If it was a cooked offering, he baked the flour without yeast, broke up the wafers, and sprinkled them with oil (vv. 4ff.). This was then presented to the priest[2] who took a handful of the mixture and all the incense and burned it as *a memorial portion*.[3] The rest of the offering was given to the priests to eat

1. Elliger's suggestion that incense was not used in Israelite worship until the age of Jeremiah (p. 45) is disproved by the discovery of incense burners from much earlier times. See R. Amiran, *Ancient Pottery of the Holy Land* (Jerusalem: Massada, 1969), pp. 302–306.

2. *And he must bring to the altar* (v. 8). Because it was a priestly prerogative to approach the altar, it is generally assumed that "he" refers to the priest. But since the priest is the explicit subject of v. 9, it may be that the implied subject of "bring" in v. 8 is the worshipper. (Cf. the alternation between the unnamed worshipper and the priest in ch. 1.) If the former interpretation is adopted, it is best to take *w⁽ᵉ⁾higgîshāh* as final, "that he may bring" (cf. 1:4) with Hoffmann I, p. 149; Elliger, p. 39.

3. *Memorial portion* (*'azkārāh*) is a technical term used in Lev. 2:2, 9, 16; 5:12; 6:8(15); 24:7; Num. 5:26. It is a difficult term to find an exact English equivalent for. It is derived from the verb *zākar*, "to remember." Hence the traditional rendering "memorial" (AV) or "memorial portion" (RSV). G. R. Driver, *JSS* 1 (1956), p. 100, preferred to translate it "token," which he understood in the following sense: "It is the sign whereby the worshipper is reminded or taught that the whole offering is in fact owed to God but that He is pleased to accept only a part of it as a 'token' while remitting the burning of the rest of it on the altar so that it may be otherwise consumed." This translation has been adopted by the NEB and TEV. I think Driver's explanation of the term is correct, but I doubt whether "token" conveys the idea any better than "memorial portion."

within the sanctuary: this is implied by v. 3, *it is a most holy portion of the Lord's food offerings* (cf. 6:7-11 [Eng. 14-18]).

The Meaning of the Cereal Offering

Leviticus 2 gives us few clues as to what the cereal offering was thought to achieve in divine/human relationships, or what the worshipper's purpose was in presenting it. The Hebrew word for *cereal offering* is *minḥāh*. In Leviticus this is a technical term for cereal offerings as defined in this chapter. But elsewhere its meaning is much broader. It may refer to animal sacrifices as well as cereal offerings; for example, both Cain's and Abel's offerings are called *minḥāh*, though Abel's consisted of animals and Cain's of cereals. Other references to *minḥāh* in nontechnical passages may well refer to animal sacrifices as well as cereal offerings (1 Sam. 2:17, 29; 26:19).

In nonreligious usage *minḥāh* often means "tribute," the money paid by a vassal king to his overlord as a mark of his continuing good will and faithfulness (Judg. 3:15, 17-18; 2 Sam. 8:6; 1 K. 5:1 [Eng. 4:21]; 10:25; 2 K. 17:3, etc.). It may simply mean "a present," though it frequently suggests that the giver is afraid of the recipient and that he is seeking to ingratiate himself by means of the gift. Thus Jacob sends a *minḥāh* to his brother Esau (Gen. 32:19ff. [18ff.]) and later to his son Joseph, prime minister of Egypt (Gen. 43:11, 15, 25-26) (cf. also 2 K. 8:7-9).

There seems very little difficulty in transferring these secular meanings of *minḥāh* into the religious sphere. The cereal offering is a kind of tribute from the faithful worshipper to his divine overlord. When a treaty was made, the conquered nations were expected to bring their tribute to the great king. Israel too was bound by a covenant with God, and therefore had a responsibility to express her fidelity by bringing her cereal offerings. These helped to keep her in good standing before God. This is alluded to in the phrase *a food offering for the Lord which has a soothing aroma* (2:2, 9, 16). On the meaning of this see the commentary on ch. 1.

Usually the cereal offering was presented in conjunction with other sacrifices, and this makes it hard to discover the exact purpose of the rite from the occasions on which it was used. Verse 14 suggests that one appropriate occasion for presenting a cereal offering was the harvest festival, when the firstfruits were brought to the altar. According to Deut. 26 the worshipper at such a service had to acknowledge God's covenant mercies toward him in bringing him into the promised land, and declare that he had faithfully kept the law of the firstfruits. In his prayer the worshipper put into words what bringing an offering of the firstfruits signified: he was loyal to the great lord of the covenant and his offering was in effect a tribute to him. He was returning to God some of his agricultural produce in an act of thanksgiving which acknowledged God's goodness to him. The Lord "brought us into this place and gave us this land, a land flowing with milk and honey. And behold, now I bring the first of the fruit of the ground, which thou, O Lord, hast given me" (Deut. 26:9–10).

The other occasion where a cereal offering had to be presented unaccompanied by other sacrifices was very different. If a man suspected his wife of adultery, but could not prove it, he could bring her to the priest, who pronounced various curses over her and made her drink bitter waters to see whether she was guilty or not. In the course of this ceremony a cereal offering of barley meal was presented. However, no oil or frankincense was used in the offering, "for it is a cereal offering of jealousy, a cereal offering of remembrance, bringing iniquity to remembrance (or declaring guilt)" (Num. 5:15). In this case the offering does not seem to be much more than a payment to the priest for administering the jealousy ritual.

The omission of the oil and frankincense from this type of cereal offering, however, prompts the further question as to the significance, if any, of individual elements in the ritual. Since we are not told explicitly, we can only make suggestions. It may be that the *oil* and *incense* make the offering richer and more desirable, therefore more pleasing to God. Oil and frankincense are also omitted from the poor man's purification offering in Lev. 5:11. Keil suggests that the reason in this case is that a man needing atonement for sin "was not allowed to add oil and incense, as symbols of the Spirit and praise of God, to the sacrifice with which he sought the forgiveness of sin."[4] It is true that oil is sometimes associated with the Spirit in the OT (1 Sam. 10:1, 9ff.; 16:13); elsewhere oil is associated with joy (Isa. 61:3; Ps. 45: 8 [7]; cf. 2 Sam. 14:2). "Oil and perfume make the heart glad" (Prov. 27:9). It could be that oil and frankincense were not used for the purification offering and the ritual with the suspected adulteress because they were not joyful occasions.

4. Keil, p. 313.

Finally the prohibition of *yeast* and *honey* from the cereal offering is to be noted. The use of leaven was forbidden at the passover (Exod. 12:15; 13:3, 7) and with sacrifices (Exod. 23:18; 34:25). Yet the loaves of firstfruits (Lev. 23:17, 20) were leavened, and honey was also included in the firstfruits offered in Hezekiah's time (2 Chr. 31:5). No rationale for the ban on the use of yeast in sacrifice is provided in the Bible. Most commentators reckon that yeast and honey were prohibited because they cause fermentation. This they believe was unacceptable because it suggested corruption.[5] Another explanation is that yeast is a living organism and only dead things could be burned on the altar in sacrifice.

Salt on the other hand was necessary in every sacrifice. This point is made very emphatically in v. 13, so presumably its symbolic value was important. Generally the use of salt is seen as the counterpart to the prohibition of yeast. "Salt prevents putrefaction while leaven and honey produce it."[6] True as this observation is, there is little evidence that it was the symbolism intended here. It could indicate that the sacrifice was dedicated to God[7] (Judg. 9:45; 2 K. 2:20-22). Most probably *the salt of your God's covenant* (v. 13) gives the clue to the symbolism. It suggests that the salt symbolized the covenant. Greeks and Arabs are known to have eaten salt together when they concluded covenants. In the OT salt is connected with covenants on two occasions, and in both a covenant of salt means an eternal covenant (Num. 18:19; 2 Chr. 13:5). Salt was something that could not be destroyed by fire or time or any other means in antiquity. To add salt to the offering was a reminder that the worshipper was in an eternal covenant relationship with his God. This meant that God would never forsake him, and also that the worshipper had a perpetual duty to uphold and keep the covenant law.

The cereal offering then was a gift by the worshipper to God. It normally followed the burnt offering. God having granted forgiveness of sins through the burnt offering, the worshipper responded by giving to God some of the produce of his hands in cereal offering. It was an act of dedication and consecration to God as Savior and covenant King. It expressed not only thankfulness but obedience and a willingness to keep the law. Like the burnt offering, the cereal offering was a sacrifice that was repeated often in a worshipper's life-

5. So Keil, p. 295; Hertz, p. 16.
6. Hertz, p. 16.
7. Porter, p. 27.

time. Man's sinful nature requires that he repeatedly seek divine forgiveness and that he renew his dedication to God and his covenant vows.

The cereal offering also served a practical purpose—of providing the priests with their staple foodstuffs. The priests and the Levites had no land of their own and were entirely dependent on the people's good will. The Levites relied on the tithes, but the priests relied on the sacrificial offerings, and particularly on the cereal offering, as it was the most frequent of the sacrifices which went to the priests. The priests in their turn gave a part of their income to God, by burning a handful of the cereal offering on the altar as a "memorial portion" (vv. 2, 9, 16).

The NT and the Cereal Offering

The Septuagint translation of cereal offering (*thysía*) is the common word for sacrifice in the NT. So some of the NT passages referring to "sacrifice" could be references to the cereal offering. There is no specific reference to anyone bringing a cereal offering in the NT, but those occasions which required a burnt offering usually demanded a cereal offering as well. Presumably we should understand the presentation of a cereal offering in Luke 17:11–14 and Acts 21:22–26.

The cereal offering symbolized the dedication of a man's life and work to God. He brought his normal food to the priest, and he declared his willingness to keep the law. These attitudes should also be true of the Christian: Paul urged the Romans "to present your bodies as a living sacrifice, holy and acceptable to God, which is your spiritual worship. Do not be conformed to this world but be transformed by the renewal of your mind, that you may prove what is the will of God, what is good and acceptable and perfect" (Rom. 12:1–2). In a similar vein the writer to the Hebrews says, "Through him then let us continually offer up a sacrifice of praise to God, that is, the fruit of lips that acknowledge his name. Do not neglect to do good and to share what you have, for such sacrifices are pleasing to God" (13:15–16). In ancient Israel the cereal offering was presented morning and evening; "the time of the cereal offering" (1 K. 18:36; 2 K. 3:20) referred to a specific time of day. A Christian is called to be as regular and diligent in rededicating himself to Christ's service as the men of ancient Israel.

The cereal offering also provided the priests with their main source of income. Christian laity are responsible for ensuring that their ministers and clergy receive proper provision. "Do you not know that those who are employed in the temple service get their food from the temple, and those who serve at the altar share in the sacrificial offerings? In the same way, the Lord commanded that those who proclaim the gospel should get their living by the gospel" (1 Cor. 9:13–14). Paul justifies the payment of ministers by appealing to the practice of the OT and to the teaching of Christ—"the Lord commanded." He seems to be referring to Jesus' remark in Luke 10:7 that "the laborer deserves his wages." Church people could well ponder the NT teaching on this subject, for few ministers have Paul's forthrightness when it comes to their own remuneration. According to Jesus and Paul the minister is entitled to be paid for his preaching. He should receive enough to cover his housing, his food and drink (Luke 10:7; 1 Cor. 9:4). He should receive an allowance for his wife, if he is married (1 Cor. 9:5). In fact he should be paid on the same basis as other workers—soldiers, farmers, and shepherds being the examples Paul cites (1 Cor. 9:7).

3. THE PEACE OFFERING (CH. 3)

1 *If his offering is a peace offering of cattle, he must offer before the Lord a perfect male or female animal.*

2 *He must lay his hand on the head of the offering and kill it in the entrance of the tent of meeting. Then the sons of Aaron, the priests, must splash the blood over the altar.*

3 *Then he must offer as a food offering for the Lord from the peace offering all the fat covering the intestines,*

4 *the kidneys and the fat that is on them at the loins, and he must also set aside the long lobe of the liver near the kidneys.*

5 *Then the sons of Aaron must burn these pieces on the altar on top of the burnt offering on the fire and wood. It is a food offering for the Lord with a soothing aroma.*

6 *If his peace offering for the Lord comes from the flock, he must offer a perfect male or female animal.*

7 *If he offers a lamb, he must offer it before the Lord,*

8 *lay his hand on the head of his offering and kill it before the tent of meeting. Then the sons of Aaron must splash its blood over the altar.*

9 *Then he must offer a food offering to the Lord from the peace offering: he must set aside its fat, the whole tail cut off close to the backbone, all the fat covering the intestines,*

10 *the kidneys and the fat that is on them at the loins, and the long lobe of the liver near the kidneys.*

11 *Then the priest must burn these pieces on the altar as food, as a food offering for the Lord.*

12 *If his offering is a goat, he must offer it before the Lord,*

13 *lay his hand on its head, and kill it before the tent of meeting. Then the sons of Aaron must splash its blood over the altar.*

14 *Then he must offer some of his offering as a food offering to the Lord. He must set aside all the fat covering the intestines,*

15 *the kidneys and the fat that is on them at the loins, and the long lobe of the liver near the kidneys.*

16 *Then the priest must burn these pieces on the altar as food, as a food offering with a soothing aroma: all fat is the Lord's.*

17 *This is a permanent rule for your descendants wherever you dwell: You must never eat any fat or blood.*

The Structure of Leviticus 3

Like chs. 1 and 2 this chapter falls into three paragraphs.

    1–5   Peace offerings of cattle
    6–11   Peace offerings of sheep
  12–17 Peace offerings of goats

Each paragraph follows the same pattern. Almost identical formulas occur in all of them. They open with, "If his peace offering is of . . . he must offer a perfect male or female animal." Then the different tasks of offerer and priest are specified. The worshipper kills and cuts up the animal, while the priest splashes the blood on the altar and burns specified parts of the carcass. Each paragraph closes with the words, "a food offering for the Lord." In the third paragraph this closing formula is somewhat expanded (vv. 16–17) to explain why the fat is to be burned rather than eaten. The statement (v. 17) "This is a permanent rule for your descendants . . ." is used a number of times in Leviticus to underline particularly important religious principles. Structurally it serves as a link between various groups of law within the book (cf. 7:36; 10:9; 16:29, 34; 17:7; 23:14, 21, 31, 41; 24:3).

The Peace Offering

The peace offering follows the burnt offering and the cereal offering, because like them it is one of the offerings that are burned to produce a *soothing aroma for the Lord* (3:5, 16; cf. 1:9; 2:2, etc.). But in other respects it is very different from the previous offerings. The peace offering was an optional sacrifice, which a man could bring when he felt like it. Lev. 7:12ff. gives three possible reasons for bringing it: as a confession offering, as a free-will offering, or to fulfil a vow. It did not form part of the regular daily offerings in the temple,[1] whereas the burnt and cereal offerings were brought every morning and evening. The other principal difference between this sacrifice and the others was that the worshipper was allowed to eat part of the animal himself. In the burnt offering the whole animal was burned, and in the cereal offering all but the memorial handful was eaten by the priest. In the peace offering some of the animal was burned, some was eaten by the priests, and the rest was returned to the worshipper for his own consumption. The peace offering was therefore a festive meal eaten in or near the sanctuary. Although it is this aspect of the offering that naturally attracts most attention in the historical books of the OT, Leviticus says very little about it, being more concerned with the preliminary rituals and the priests' duties on these occasions.

The Sacrificial Animals

For the peace offering the same animals, cattle, sheep, and goats, were used as in the burnt offering, except for birds, presumably because they were too small to make a worthwhile meal. Female as well as male animals could be used in the peace offering. For the burnt offering only males were acceptable. The use of female animals in the peace offering shows that this was regarded as a less important sacrifice than the burnt offering.

The Rite

The worshipper brought his animal to *the entrance of the tent of meeting*, vv. 1–2, 7–8, 12–13 (see diagram, p. 53). Then he had to *lay his hand on the head* of the animal (vv. 2, 8, 13), thereby identifying himself with the animal or transferring his guilt to it. At this point in the ceremony he probably explained why he was offering the sacrifice, e.g., that he had come to thank God for his prayer being answered, or his vow being fulfilled. Then he had to *kill* (*shāḥaṭ*, cf. 1:5) the animal, and the priest would *splash its blood over the altar*. The animal was now skinned and cut up. This is not stated in ch. 3 but must be assumed on the analogy of the burnt offering.

Up to this point the ceremony was identical to that of the burnt offering. From now on the ritual was quite different. Instead of the whole animal being burned on the altar, only the *kidneys*, the *fat*

---

1. Only at Pentecost was the peace offering officially demanded (23:19).

covering the intestines and *the long lobe of the liver,*[2] and in the case of the fat-tailed sheep, the fat of the *tail* (v. 9) were burned on the altar as *a food offering to the Lord* (vv. 5, 11, cf. above). In addition to the skin, which was the priests' perquisite from the burnt offering, the priest was also given the breast of the animal and the right thigh (7:31ff.).

The ceremony concluded with the worshipper and his friends or family joining in a sacred meal to eat up the rest of the meat. In the words of Deut. 12:7, "You shall eat before the Lord your God, and you shall rejoice, you and your households, in all that you undertake, in which the Lord your God has blessed you." Leviticus gives very few details about the meal itself. 7:20 stipulates that all participants must be in a state of ritual purity. 7:15–16 states that the meat should be eaten up on the same day, if it is a confession sacrifice, and by the following day if it is for other purposes.

The Purpose of the Peace Offering

For many years scholars have debated the function of the peace offering. Even today there is no consensus about the most appropriate way to translate the Hebrew term *sheʿlāmîm*, often rendered *peace offering*. Recent suggestions include "shared offering" or "fellowship offering."[3] This is simply a guess based on the nature of the party after the sacrifice, when the worshipper and his friends ate the meat together.

Other suggested interpretations depend on finding a suitable etymology for *sheʿlāmîm*. Since *shlm* is a common root with a wide variety of meanings, this does not narrow the field much. *Shālēm*, "be complete," is the basis of the suggestion that *sheʿlāmîm* means "concluding sacrifice."[4] It also is the basis of the rendering "cove-

---

2. The translation of *yōṭeret* is uncertain (AV "caul," RSV "appendage," NEB *long lobe*). With L. Rost, "Der Leberlappen," *ZAW* 79 (1967), pp. 35–41, I have tentatively adopted the last rendering, as it appears to be the interpretation of the earliest versions, i.e., the LXX and the targums. The *lobus caudatus* is a finger-like projection from the liver.

Why it should be singled out for burning is also unclear. Hoffmann I, p. 166, suggests it was regarded as one of the choicest parts of the animal (cf. TEV, "the best part of the liver"). Rost, pp. 39f., that it was to avoid its use in extispicy.

The following phrase *near* ('*al*) *the kidneys* is also problematic. Hoffmann I, p. 164, and Elliger, p. 47, say it refers to the place where this part of the liver is cut away, whereas NEB, RSV, and Rost, pp. 37f., suppose '*al* means "with."

3. E.g., Snaith, p. 37, NEB, and TEV.

4. Clements, p. 14; Rendtorff, *Studien zur Geschichte des Opfers im alten Israel* (Neukirchen: 1967), p. 133.

nant sacrifice."[5] In offering this sacrifice the worshipper demonstrated his "complete" fidelity to the Lord of the covenant. Certainly it was offered on a number of occasions when the covenant was being ratified or renewed, but "covenant sacrifice" seems to read too much into the term. In a sense all the sacrifices were designed to celebrate and uphold the covenant[6] between God and his people. Furthermore the peace offering was an optional sacrifice, unlike the other sacrifices, and certainly a sacrifice designed to sustain the covenant relationship would have formed a regular part of the cult and would not have been left to the initiative of pious individuals.

Another suggestion[7] connects Heb. *sheˡāmîm* with Akk. *shulmānu*, "a gift." But in a sense all sacrifices are gifts to God, and therefore this idea hardly advances our understanding of this particular sacrifice.

Much more probable is the view that Heb. *sheˡāmîm* is the same as Ugar. *šhlmm*.[8] In the Ugaritic texts, North Canaanite texts dating from about 1400 B.C., quite close to the Mosaic period, a pair of sacrifices are mentioned, burnt offerings (*šrp*) and *šlmm*. In the Bible burnt offerings are often paired with peace offerings (e.g., 1 Sam. 13:9; 1 K. 9:25). Indeed in our text the peace offering is offered "on top of the burnt offering" (v. 5), which implies they were offered one after the other. Unfortunately we cannot be sure what the Ugaritic term *šlmm* meant, possibly "gifts offered . . . to obtain peace."[9] We are therefore forced back to the OT to examine it for clues.

The traditional rendering "peace offering" connects *sheˡāmîm* with Heb. *šālôm*, "peace." Peace in Hebrew means more than the absence of war. True peace means health, prosperity, and peace with God, i.e., salvation. This understanding of the peace offering, accepted by a number of ancient and modern writers,[10] seems to do most justice to the OT evidence.

Leviticus 7 mentions three different types of peace offering:

---

5. R. Schmid, *Das Bundesopfer in Israel* (Munich: Kösel, 1964).
6. See Introduction V.3, "The Role of Sacrifice" (p. 25 above); D. J. Davies, *ZAW* 89 (1977), pp. 390ff.
7. B. A. Levine, *Presence of the Lord,* pp. 29ff.
8. Among the recent discussions see J. C. de Moor, "The Peace Offering in Israel and Ugarit," *Schrift en Uitleg: FS W. H. Gispen* (Kampen: Kok, 1970), pp. 112–17; L. R. Fisher, "A New Ritual Calendar from Ugarit," *HTR* 63 (1970), pp. 485-501.
9. So de Moor, p. 117.
10. E.g., Calvin II, p. 333; Keil, pp. 298f.; Elliger, pp. 47, 51; and Milgrom, pp. 69f.

confession offerings, vow offerings, and free-will offerings. Salvation (peace) is the common factor in the different situations in which these offerings were presented.

The confession[11] type of peace offering was appropriate in two quite different situations: when someone was seeking God's deliverance, either from his enemies or from sickness. In such cases he might well feel the need to confess his sins, if he thought this was the reason for his present predicament (Judg. 20:26; 21:4; 2 Sam. 24:25). Or he could offer the confession sacrifice after he had been delivered. In this case the confession would center on God's mercy rather than on his own sinfulness. For example:

> My vows to thee I must perform, O God;
> I will render (shillēm) thank offerings (i.e., confession offerings) to thee.
> For thou hast delivered my soul from death, yea, my feet from falling,
> that I may walk before God in the light of life.
>
> (Ps. 56:13–14 [Eng. 12–13])

Here there is a play on the general word for peace offerings (sh^elāmîm) in the word "render" (shillēm).

As the above quotation from Ps. 56 illustrates, there is a close association between the confession peace offering and the vow peace offering. In difficult circumstances men of old often made a vow to the Lord that if he helped them they would do something for God. When they fulfilled their vow, they were expected to bring a peace offering. Jacob made a vow at Bethel, when he was fleeing from home, that if God brought him safe home again "the Lord shall be my God" (Gen. 28:20–21). As a pledge of his vow he poured oil (v. 18) on top of the stone pillar. When at last he did return to Bethel, we find him purifying himself (a prerequisite for a peace offering, Lev. 7:19–20) and building an altar so that he could offer the sacrifice (Gen. 35). Perhaps the best-known vow and peace offering in the OT is found in the story of the birth of Samuel (1 Sam. 1). Every year Elkanah's family went up to Shiloh to offer sacrifice. Though again the sacrifice is not explicitly named, this was a peace offering in which Elkanah distributed portions of meat to different members of his family. We are told that this sacrifice was

---

11. Heb. *tôḏāh* is usually translated "thanksgiving"; but the idea is broader than this. It can cover the confession of sin (Josh. 7:19; Ezra 10:11) as well as confession of faith arising out of a man's experience of God's mercy. C. Westermann, *THWAT* I, pp. 674–682.

an annual one (v. 3). Presumably on most occasions it took the form of a free-will peace offering, but on this occasion Hannah made a vow that she would dedicate any child born to her to be a Nazirite (v. 11). When the child was born and weaned, Hannah brought three bulls (or possibly a three-year-old bull)[12] as a peace offering plus an ephah of flour and a skin of wine. This was a lavish peace offering by any standards, and it probably reflects Hannah's great thankfulness for Samuel's birth as well as Elkanah's relative affluence; he was able, after all, to support two wives (1 Sam. 1:2).

The third kind of peace offering is usually referred to as the free-will offering (Exod. 35:29; Ezra 1:4; 8:28; Ps. 54:8 [Eng. 6], etc.). It was a spontaneous act of generosity by the worshipper, prompted by God's goodness, e.g., at harvest time (Deut. 16:10). Whereas the other kinds of peace offering were closely linked with petitionary prayer, prayers for deliverance or forgiveness or for safety or for children, the free-will offering came as a response to God's unexpected and unasked for generosity. This is perhaps the explanation for men being allowed to bring less than perfect animals for free-will offerings (Lev. 22:23). Where confession of sin or vows were concerned, perfect animals were necessary.

Very often the peace offering is associated with occasions when the covenant was emphasized (e.g., Exod. 24:5; Deut. 27:7; 1 K. 8:63). Here it is difficult to be sure which aspect of the sacrifice was uppermost in the worshippers' minds. It could have been pure gratitude for God's grace in choosing the nation to be God's people. It could have been linked with their vows to keep the covenant (cf. Exod. 24:7; Deut. 27). Or it could be a confession of God's mercy and their own sinfulness of which the laws had reminded them, and a prayer for divine strength to keep them in the future. These different aspects of the peace offering are not mutually exclusive and could be presupposed in all these covenant ceremonies.

Though confession of sin and pleas for deliverance are associated with these sacrifices, more typically they are seen as joyous occasions. These sacred meals were opportunities for rejoicing before the Lord (Deut. 12:12, 18; 27:7; 1 K. 8:66). When God has

12. "Three bulls" in the MT. This seems preferable to "three-year-old bull" of LXX and Peshitta and most modern translations and commentaries. One bull was for the burnt offering, one for the purification offering that was expected after childbirth (Lev. 12), and the third for the peace offering, in payment of her vow. An ephah of flour (1 Sam. 1:24) is approximately three times the normal quantity of flour to be offered with a bull (Num. 15:9), which supports the idea that three bulls were in fact offered on this occasion.

saved and blessed his people, they can and should enjoy worshipping him.

In the ceremony these ideas were expressed in the words as well as in the action. Again we lack a record of what was said, apart from Ps. 100 which was appointed for the confession offering, though several other psalms mention the service (Pss. 26, 50, 54, 107, 116). It is possible that one or more of these psalms was recited as the worshipper placed his hand on the animal's head. No doubt at this point he explained in prayer or praise why he was offering this animal. Then he killed it, and the priest made atonement with the blood (cf. Lev. 17:11). Atonement is not a prominent feature of the peace offering. Where that was the major concern, a burnt offering would have been presented before the peace offering. But even this essentially joyful sacrifice includes a blood rite, a reminder that sinful man is always in need of the forgiveness of his sin.

From this point on, the rite diverged from the burnt offering. Only the fat and the liver and the kidneys were burned, not the whole animal as in the burnt offering. Why should part of an animal be burned in one sacrifice but the whole animal in another? The answer must lie in the different functions of the sacrifices. But to define the reason for the difference more closely eludes us. In the purification offering (Lev. 4:8–10) the same parts of the animal are burned as in the peace offering. In the OT neither blood nor fat may be eaten (Lev. 7:22ff.). We are told why blood is taboo, because atonement is made through it (Lev. 17:11). The reason for the prohibition of eating fat remains obscure. Calvin[13] may well be right in thinking that fat was thought of as specially belonging to God. Certainly fat in the OT can be synonymous with "the best" (Gen. 45:18; Ps. 81:17 [Eng. 16]). By giving the fat the worshipper was giving the best of the animal; and insofar as the animal was thought to represent the man, the worshipper showed he was giving God the best part of his life.

The *kidneys* were also picked out to be burned on the altar as well as the fat surrounding them and the *intestines*. It is likely that some symbolism was attached to this gesture. The kidneys and entrails are referred to in the OT as the seat of the emotions (Job 19:27; Ps. 16:7; Jer. 4:14; 12:2), just as in English we talk of the heart. (The heart in the OT refers primarily to the mind and the will.)

13. Calvin II, pp. 334f. The evidence cited by J. Heller ("Die Symbolik des Fettes im AT," *VT* 20 [1970], pp. 106–108) for supposing that fat symbolizes strength is inconclusive.

It is possible that offering the kidneys and internal fat symbolizes the dedication of the worshipper's best and deepest emotions to God. For the peace offering was often tendered in intrinsically emotional situations, when a man made vows or found himself seeking God's deliverance or praising him for his mercy.

The peace offering closed with a meal. The priests were assigned certain parts of the animal (the breast and the right thigh according to Lev. 7:31–33), and the worshipper and his friends consumed the rest. Though this ritual is passed over in this chapter,[14] it was for the majority of people the most popular part of the service. Much has been made of this meal by scholars, though the Bible tones down its significance. It certainly was not a meal in which God ate some of the food, even if sometimes this idea was mistakenly held by some ancient Israelites. Such a crass view of God is attacked in Ps. 50, a psalm which may well have been used at the peace offering (see v. 14).

> *If I were hungry, I would not tell you,*
> *for the world and all that is in it is mine.*
> *Do I eat the flesh of bulls or drink the blood of goats?*
> (50:12–13)

Rather it was a meal in which God's presence was recognized as specially near, and this made it a particularly joyful occasion (cf. Deut. 12:7). Eating meat was a luxury in ancient Israel. All meat came from animals given by the worshipper to God, and now partly given back to the worshipper by God. This symbolized the way God gave back to the worshipper his life to go on enjoying. The worshipper had made his vows to keep the covenant law, or to do something more specific (e.g., to give Samuel back to the Lord), if the prayer was answered. Now in the sacrificial meal God granted a tangible pledge of his promised blessings. The enjoyment of eating the meat was a physical reminder of all the other blessings that attended the faithful observance of the covenant (Lev. 26:3ff.; Deut. 28:1ff.). A people that kept the law would enjoy peace at home and abroad, abundant crops, large families, and general economic prosperity. It was right and proper for men to look forward to the peace offering. It was a pledge and physical illustration of all the benefits that may be enjoyed by those at peace with God.

---

14. It is mentioned in 7:15–18, where it is specified how quickly the animal is to be eaten up.

The NT and the Peace Offering

The specific term peace offering is never used in the NT. Paul did undertake to pay for the offerings of four men with a vow, and one of these offerings would have been a peace offering (Acts 21:23–26). A more general term for sacrifice is used in the NT which sometimes appears to refer to peace offerings. Hosea's insistence (6:6) that God desires mercy (loving-kindness) rather than sacrifice is twice quoted by our Lord (Matt. 9:13; 12:7). This is a distillation of the essence of the peace offering, which involved the worshipper declaring God's mercies and his own willingness to obey the law. It is taken further in the Epistles. Paul urges the Romans to offer their bodies as a living sacrifice, "which is your spiritual worship" (Rom. 12:1). Hebrews invites us "continually (to) offer up a sacrifice of praise to God, that is, the fruit of lips that acknowledge his name. Do not neglect to do good and to share what you have, for such sacrifices are pleasing to God" (Heb. 13:15–16).

More directly related to the OT peace offering is the Lord's supper. At the last supper[15] Jesus referred to the cup of wine as "the new covenant in my blood" (1 Cor. 11:25). In so doing he alluded to the blood of the old covenant (Exod. 24:8). When the Sinai Covenant had been agreed to by the people, Moses took the blood of the burnt offerings and peace offerings and threw it over the people and said, "Here is the blood of the covenant which the Lord has made with you." The last supper was more like the peace offering than a burnt offering in that the peace offering and the last supper were both meals, while the burnt offering never was. Christ's death on the cross is a closer parallel to the burnt offering. His sharing of his body and blood with his disciples forms the closer parallel to the peace offering.

Other similarities between the Christian communion service and the OT peace offering can be drawn. Both demand that the worshipper should be clean, i.e., in a fit state to participate. "Whoever eats the bread or drinks the cup of the Lord in an unworthy manner will be guilty of profaning the body and blood of the Lord" (1 Cor. 11:27; cf. Lev. 7:20). Divine punishment is promised on those who eat without discerning the body. "That is why many of

15. The last supper may indeed have been a Passover meal (Matt. 26:17–19; cf. John 18:28). This would not invalidate the theological connections we are drawing between the peace offering and the Lord's supper, for the Passover could be described as a specialized type of peace offering that was celebrated once a year by the whole nation.

82

you are weak and ill, and some have died" (1 Cor. 11:30). Here Paul is putting the provisions of Leviticus into more modern terms. The first recorded peace offering was at Sinai, when the ten commandments were given. It is therefore highly appropriate for the Decalog, or our Lord's summary of the law, to be read at the Lord's supper.

As in OT times the worshipper praised God, made vows, and brought his petitions to God at the peace offering, so the Christian should make the communion service an occasion at which he rededicates himself to God's service and brings his prayers and praises to his Lord. God in Christ is now present at his service. Instead of eating meat we now consume bread and wine as physical pledges of God's goodness toward us. They remind us of our salvation achieved through Christ; they assure us of his favor in the present; and they promise that he will continue to bless until he comes again.

The most striking contrast with the old peace offerings is in the use of the blood. Under the old covenant the drinking of sacrificial blood was sternly prohibited. Under the new it is expressly commanded, albeit under the guise of wine. It is blood that makes atonement for sin, and by drinking it the Christian is constantly reminded that he is saved by God and not his own efforts. According to the OT, the life enshrined in the blood was sacred because it was God-given. Man had no right to take God-implanted life. It must be returned directly to its creator. Now, in the NT era, this atoning and life-giving power may be drunk by the creature to purge him of his sins and assure him of God's salvation. The Lord's supper should therefore be, like the peace offering, at once a solemn and joyful occasion: solemn because no human being can lightheartedly enter God's presence and pledge to keep his laws, joyful because God's grace and his promise exceed all that we can ask or think in this life and the next.

The NT does not compare peace offerings and Christian festivities such as Christmas dinners, wedding receptions, baptism parties, and so on, because such occasions had not developed in the way we know them. Yet we could compare the joyful family gatherings of Christian people after matrimonial or baptismal vows have been taken to the meal that followed the peace offering. In a context where vows have been made to God in all sincerity, we can surely celebrate the event and be assured of God's presence at the party. Christmas meals are very often divorced from Christian worship, yet if we have remembered God's greatest gift to man at church, praised him for Christ's coming, and pledged ourselves anew to his service, there is a real place for a festive meal in which we rejoice in his continuing presence which first began at Bethlehem.

4. THE PURIFICATION OFFERING (4:1–5:13)

1 *The Lord spoke to Moses as follows:*

2 *"Tell the Israelites, If anyone sins inadvertently by breaking one of the Lord's commands,*

3 *if it is the anointed priest who sins bringing guilt on the people, he must offer to the Lord for the sin which he has committed a perfect bull as a purification offering.*

4 *He must bring the bull before the Lord to the entrance of the tent of meeting; then he must lay his hand on the head of the bull, and then kill it before the Lord.*

5 *Then the anointed priest must take some of the bull's blood and bring it into the tent of meeting.*

6 *The priest must dip his finger in the blood, and then sprinkle some of the blood seven times before the Lord on the curtain of the holy place.*

7 *Then the priest must put some of the blood on the horns of the spicy incense altar that is before the Lord in the tent of meeting. But he must pour all the rest of the blood at the foot of the altar of burnt offering, which stands in the entrance of the tent of meeting.*

8 *He must also remove all the fat of the bull, all the fat covering the intestines,*

9 *the two kidneys and the fat which is on them at the loins, and he must also take away the long lobe of the liver,*

10 *just as it was removed from the ox of the peace offering; and then the priest must burn them on the altar of burnt offering.*

11 *But he must bring all the rest of the bull, its skin and all its flesh, including its head and legs, its intestines and its dung,*

12 *outside the camp to a clean place to the ash heap. Then he must burn it over a wood fire; beside the ash heap it must be burned.*

13 *If the whole congregation inadvertently breaks one of the Lord's commands and the thing is hidden from the assembly, and then they feel guilty,*

14 *when the sin which has been committed becomes known, the assembly must offer a bull as a purification offering and bring it before the tent of meeting.*

15 *Then the elders of the congregation must lay their hands on the head of the bull before the Lord, and then the bull must be killed before the Lord.*

16 *Then the anointed priest must bring some of the bull's blood into the tent of meeting.*

17 *Then the priest must dip his finger into some of the blood and sprinkle it seven times before the Lord on the curtain.*

18 *But he must put some of the blood on the horns of the altar which is before the Lord in the tent of meeting. But he must pour all the rest*

of the blood at the foot of the altar of burnt offering which stands in the entrance of the tent of meeting.

19 *He must remove all its fat and burn it on the altar.*

20 *He must treat the bull exactly like the bull of the purification offering. The priest shall make atonement for them and they will be forgiven.*

21 *Then he must take the rest of the bull outside the camp and burn it exactly as the previously mentioned bull was burned. It is a purification offering of the assembly.*

22 *If a tribal leader sins by inadvertently breaking one of the commands of the Lord his God, and then feels guilty,*

23 *or the sin that he has committed is brought to his notice, he must bring as his offering a perfect male goat.*

24 *He must lay his hand on the head of the goat, then kill it in the place where the burnt offering is killed before the Lord: it is a purification offering.*

25 *Then the priest must take some of the blood of the purification offering on his finger and put it on the horns of the altar of burnt offering. But he must pour the rest of its blood at the foot of the altar of burnt offering.*

26 *He must burn all its fat on the altar like the fat of the peace offering. The priest shall make atonement for his sin and he will be forgiven.*

27 *If one of the ordinary people sins by inadvertently breaking one of the Lord's commands, and then feels guilty,*

28 *or the sin that he has committed is brought to his attention, then he must bring as his offering a perfect female goat for the sin which he has committed.*

29 *He must lay his hand on the head of the purification offering; and then kill the purification offering in the place of the burnt offering.*

30 *Then the priest must take some of its blood on his finger and put it on the horns of the altar of burnt offering. But he must pour all the rest of the blood at the foot of the altar.*

31 *He must remove all its fat in the same way as the fat of the peace offering, and the priest must burn it on the altar to produce a soothing aroma for the Lord. The priest shall make atonement for him and he will be forgiven.*

32 *If he brings a lamb as his purification offering, he must bring a perfect female.*

33 *He must lay his hand on the head of the purification offering, kill it as a purification offering in the place where the burnt offering is killed.*

34 *The priest must then take some of the blood of the purification offering on his finger and put it on the horns of the altar of burnt offering. But all the rest of the blood he must pour out at the foot of the altar.*

35 *He must remove all its fat, just as the fat of the peace offering is removed, and then the priest must burn it on the altar on top of the Lord's food offerings. The priest shall make atonement for his sin and he will be forgiven.*

5:1 *If anyone sins, in that he heard a public injunction to give evidence, and he was a witness or has seen or knows something—if he does not declare it, he will bear his iniquity.*

2 *If anyone touches anything unclean, for example any dead animal or any dead swarming creature, and it slips his memory, though he is unclean, and then he feels guilty;*

3 *or if he touches any person suffering from any contagious uncleanness and it slips his memory, but then later he discovers it and feels guilty,*

4 *or if anyone makes a rash promise to do something, and it slips his memory, and then later he discovers it and feels guilty about any of these things,*

5 *when he feels guilty in any of these matters, he must confess how he has sinned,*

6 *and then, because of the sin he has committed, he must bring as his reparation to the Lord a female sheep or goat to be used as a purification offering. Then the priest shall make atonement for him because of his sin.*

7 *If he cannot afford as much as a sheep, because he has sinned he must bring as his reparation to the Lord two doves or two pigeons, one for a purification offering and one for a burnt offering.*

8 *He must bring them to the priest and offer the one for the purification offering first, and he must wring its neck without completely severing the head.*

9 *Then he must sprinkle some of the blood from the purification offering over the wall of the altar, but the rest of the blood must be drained out at the foot of the altar. It is a purification offering.*

10 *He must use the second bird as a burnt offering according to the regulation, and the priest shall make atonement for him because of his sin and he will be forgiven.*

11 *If he cannot afford two doves or two pigeons, he must bring as his offering for his sin one tenth of an ephah of flour for a purification offering. But he must not add any oil or incense to it, because it is a purification offering.*

12 *He must bring it to the priest, and the priest shall take a handful of it as a memorial portion and burn it on the altar on top of the Lord's food offerings: it is a purification offering.*

13 *And the priest shall make atonement for him because of his sin in one of these cases, and he will be forgiven. The rest of this purification offering belongs to the priest like the cereal offering."*

The Structure of Leviticus 4–5 (Eng. 6:7)

These chapters deal with the purification offering (4:1–5:13) and the reparation offering (5:14–26 [Eng. 6:7]). Their structure is considered together because the laws about these two sacrifices are arranged in a similar way, which is distinctly different from the arrangement underlying chs. 1–3. Whereas the earlier chapters are organized around the sacrificial victim, so that the more valuable animals are dealt with before the less expensive, in these chapters the value of the animal occupies a secondary place. Here the most important distinction is between inadvertent sins and sins of omission or deliberate sins. The status of the sinners who bring the offerings is also important. Thus:

4:1–35   purification offerings for inadvertent offenses
5:1–13   purification offerings for sins of omission
5:14–19   reparation offerings for inadvertent sin
5:20–26   reparation offerings for deliberate sin
(Eng. 6:1–7)

Each main section begins, "If anyone (*nepesh kî*) sins" (4:2; 5:1, 15, 21 [6:2]), and closes with, "the priest will make atonement for him . . . and he shall be forgiven" (4:35; 5:13, 18, 26 [6:7]). Similar phrases generally mark the close of the paragraphs within each main section, but a different word for "if," *'im*, usually[1] opens each subordinate paragraph (e.g., 4:13, 27, 32; 5:7, 11, 17).

Using these criteria the structure of these chapters can be set out as follows.

Purification Offerings
  4:1–35 for inadvertent sin
    2   general introduction (introductory words *nepesh kî*)
    3–21 blood sprinkled in the holy place
      3–12 for the high priest (*'im*)
      13–21 for the whole congregation (*'im*)
    22–35 blood smeared on the main altar
      22–26 for the tribal leader (*'asher*)
      27–31 for an ordinary person offering a goat (*'im*)
      32–35 for an ordinary person offering a lamb (*'im*)
  5:1–13 for sins of omission
    1–6   offering—lamb or goat (*nepesh kî*)
    7–10   offering—birds (*'im*)
    11–13 offering—flour (*'im*)
Reparation Offerings
  5:14–19 for inadvertent sin
    14–16 offense known (*nepesh kî*)
    17–19 offense known (*'im*)
  20–26 (Eng. 6:1–7) for deliberate sin (*'im*)

---

1. In 4:22 a subordinate case is introduced by "if, whoever" (*'asher*). This is a "rare and peculiar" (*BDB* 83b) use of *'asher*. It may be used here to indicate that a different type of purification offering is about to be discussed, in which the blood is smeared on the main altar outside the tent of meeting.

The triadic arrangement of the material emerges quite clearly in this analysis. This is also a feature of chs. 1–3 (see above). As in Lev. 1–3, there are numerous similarities in phraseology within each paragraph, but it is unnecessary to list them here. It may be noted that the very first paragraph lacks the normal closing phrase, "the priest shall make atonement . . . and he shall be forgiven." This is because the priest is the worshipper and he therefore cannot pronounce his own forgiveness. The laws about the reparation offering are peculiar in not specifying what ritual should be followed. Insofar as the directions for the reparation offering are patterned on those for the purification offering, it seems probable that the animals in both sacrifices were treated alike. This is confirmed by 7:1–7.

The Purification (Sin) Offering

The purification offering is the fourth type of sacrifice discussed in Leviticus. Some of the characteristic features of this offering have already been pointed out above under "The Structure of Leviticus 4–5." Here it may be noted that like the burnt offering and the cereal offering, this was a compulsory offering, though according to Num. 28–29 it was offered less frequently than the burnt and cereal offerings. Unlike these sacrifices the material burned on the altar is relatively unimportant: only once is it said to produce "a soothing aroma for the Lord" (4:31). The most important feature of this rite is the sprinkling of the blood on the altar or the veil. Where the blood was sprinkled depended on the social status of the offerer.

The Name of the Sacrifice

Most translations and commentators render the Hebrew term for this sacrifice (*ḥaṭṭā't*) as "sin offering." This is a natural and obvious translation,[2] because *ḥaṭṭā't* commonly means "sin," even within this very chapter (4:3, 14, 23, 28, etc.), and *ḥāṭā'* is the usual verb for "to sin" (4:2, 3, 22, 27). We have already seen, however, that other sacrifices also atoned for sin, notably the burnt offering (ch. 1), the peace offering (ch. 3), as well as the reparation offering (5:14–26 [Eng. 6:7]). Simply to adopt the rendering "sin offering" for *ḥaṭṭā't* obscures the precise function of this sacrifice. It most certainly has to do with sin, and deals with its consequences. But it was not the one and only atoning sacrifice, as commentators tend to suggest.

2. E.g., RSV, NEB.

Sin disrupts the relationship between God and man, and between man and man. It poses a threat to the covenant relationship by provoking divine anger. But it has other side effects as well. If someone steals something, the owner will not only feel aggrieved but hope for restitution of his property if the thief is caught. Propitiation of divine anger, it has been suggested, is an important element in the burnt offering. Restitution, it will be suggested, is the key idea in the reparation offering. Purification is the main element in the purification sacrifice. Sin not only angers God and deprives him of his due, it also makes his sanctuary unclean. A holy God cannot dwell amid uncleanness. The purification offering purifies the place of worship, so that God may be present among his people. This interpretation of the term seems to be compatible with its root meaning,[3] and to explain the rituals of blood sprinkling peculiar to it.[4]

The Sacrificial Animals

A wider variety of offerings was allowed for the purification offering than for other sacrifices. Bulls, goats (male or female), lambs (female), doves, and pigeons are mentioned. If the worshipper was very poor, he could offer one tenth of an ephah of flour instead.[5] It is notable that the male lamb or ram, the most common animal in burnt offerings, is never used for the purification offering (though female lambs were), while goats, the standard animal for the purification offering, were not used for the regular burnt offerings. Pigeons did not occur in peace offerings because they were too small for a meal, but were permissible in both burnt offerings and purification offerings. A cereal offering always accompanied the sacrificial animal of the burnt offering; it could be offered instead of an animal in the purification offering (5:11–13).

Male and female animals could be used in the purification offering, but only male animals in the burnt offering. This points to the fact that while both types of offering were regarded as essential

---

3. *Ḥaṭṭā't* is a noun formed from the Piel of *ḥāṭā'* (to sin), i.e., *ḥiṭṭē'*, to "de-sin" or "purify." Hence *ḥaṭṭā't* means "purification" or "sacrifice securing purification." So B. A. Levine, *Presence of the Lord,* pp. 101f.; cf. Lev. 8:15; Num. 19:19; Ps. 51:9 (Eng. 7); Ezek. 43:20ff.

4. The interpretation followed here is that of J. Milgrom, which he has developed in a number of works, esp. "The Function of the *Ḥaṭṭā't* Sacrifice" (Hebrew), *Tarbiz* 40 (1970), pp. 1–8; "Two Kinds of *Ḥaṭṭā't,*" *VT* 26 (1976), pp. 333–37; *Cult and Conscience, Encyclopedia Miqrait* 7, cc. 237–240.

5. The *ephah* is a unit of capacity, whose exact size is uncertain. According to de Vaux, *Ancient Israel,* p. 202, 1/10th ephah of flour = 1½ liters or 2 lbs. of flour.

in worship, the burnt offering played the major role. This is confirmed by the list of animals prescribed for festal sacrifices in
Num. 28–29. The burnt offerings required more animals of greater
value than the purification offerings.

The Rite

The purification offering began in the same way as the other sacrifices. The worshipper brought his animal to the entrance of the tent
of meeting, laid his hand on its head, stated why he had brought the
sacrifice,[6] and then killed it.

The rest of the ritual was unique to the purification offering.
In the burnt and peace offerings the blood of the animal was thrown
against the altar. But in the purification offering some of the blood
was caught in a basin and the rest was poured away at the foot of the
altar. The blood which was set aside was used in a variety of ways
depending on who the worshipper was.

If the anointed priest was offering the purification offering,
the blood was sprinkled seven times on the veil[7] of the sanctuary,
that is, the curtain acting as the door into the holy of holies, the
innermost part of the tabernacle. A little blood was also smeared on
the *horns*[8] of the incense altar that stood in front of the veil. These
rites took place in the second most holy part of the tabernacle, *the
holy place*, which only priests were allowed to enter.

If rulers or one of the common people offered a purification
offering, the blood was not taken inside the tent of meeting but was
smeared on the horns of the large altar of burnt offering that stood in
the open court (vv. 22ff.).

Leviticus 16 ordains that on the day of atonement the high
priest should take the blood into the holy of holies itself and smear it
on and in front of the mercy seat, which surmounted the ark.

It is these blood-sprinkling rituals that are the principal focus
of attention in the purification sacrifice. However, the disposal of the
remainder of the animal is also mentioned. The rest of the blood was
poured out at the foot of the altar of burnt offering (as in the burnt
and peace offerings). The fat portions were burned on the altar as in
the peace offering as *a soothing aroma for the Lord* (4:31). When a

6. On analogy with other sacrifices (see above).
7. Understanding *'eṭ pᵉnê pārōḵeṭ (on the curtain, vv. 6, 17)* as the direct object of
sprinkle. Lit. "sprinkle . . . the face (surface) of the curtain." Otherwise *'eṭ-pᵉnê*
may be taken as an alternative to *lipnê*, "before," as in 1 Sam. 2:11.
8. Projections at each corner of the altar that looked like horns.   altar

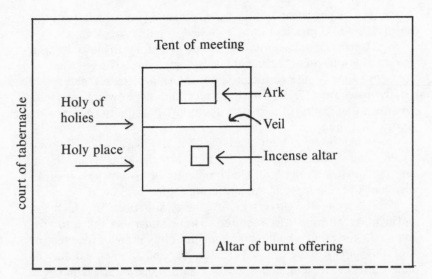

priest offered a purification offering, the rest of the animal, including its skin, flesh, head, legs, entrails, and dung, was taken outside the camp and burned *beside the ash heap*.[9]

If, however, one of the ordinary people brought a purification offering, only the fatty parts were burned and the priest could eat the rest (6:19ff. [Eng. 26ff.]). If the man was too poor to bring even a bird as a sacrifice, he might offer a tenth of an ephah of flour. In this case just a memorial portion was burned (*hiqṭîr*) on the altar, and *the rest*[10] was eaten by the priests (5:11–13).

The Occasions for the Purification Offering

Leviticus specifies various occasions, mainly private, on which the purification offering must be brought. The liturgical calendars in

9. *Burn* (4:12)—here a different word (*śārap*) is used than in v. 10 (*hiqṭîr*). *Śārap* is the ordinary burning leading to destruction. *Hiqṭîr* literally means "to turn into incense" and is the word used of burning things on the altar. Burned there, they ascended to God as a sort of incense, a sweet-smelling savor, or "soothing aroma." *Beside the ash heap* (lit. "on or by the pouring of ash"). *The ash heap* outside the camp is to be distinguished from the ash pit (1:16) (lit. "place of ashes") near the altar of burnt offering. *ʿAl (beside)* may mean "on top of" or "by." The latter would be a neater arrangement. *ʿAl* clearly means "on top of" when reference is made to sacrifices burning on top of each other on the altar (e.g., 1:12; 3:5; 4:35; 8:28).
10. The last clause of v. 13 reads in Hebrew, "it belongs to the priest like the cereal offering." The LXX, followed by most modern translators, correctly interprets "the rest belongs to the priest. . . ."

Num. 28–29 supplement this by prescribing at which festivals purification offerings had to be included in public worship.

A woman unclean as the result of childbirth must bring a purification offering (12:6); so must anyone who has been unclean for some time as the result of a serious skin disease (14:19) or a bodily discharge (15:15). These are all situations in which someone has been unclean for a period, without any possibility of cleansing during that time.

Other less frequent occasions for the purification offering include the dedication of the priests (8:14), the altar (Num. 7:16), and the Levites (Num. 8:8). On completion of his vow the Nazirite also had to bring a purification offering (Num. 6:14).

Leviticus 4–5 covers more general situations in which the purification offering was required. These situations fall into two main categories, of which the first includes unwitting or inadvertent sins, *bishgāgāh* (4:2; cf. vv. 13, 22, 27), and the second sins of omission (5:1–4). Other passages explain more clearly what was meant by inadvertence. Num. 15:27ff. contrasts unwitting sin with sinning "with a high hand" (v. 30), i.e., blatantly or deliberately. The sinner who sins "with a high hand" will not be forgiven, but cut off, whereas one who sins inadvertently can offer sacrifice and enjoy forgiveness. Verses 32–35 apparently give an example of a high-handed sin, gathering sticks on the sabbath, for the convicted man is put to death for it. To remind them to observe the commandments the Israelites must attach tassels to their clothes so that they are not led astray by sinful whims (Num. 15:37–41).

More exactly still, Num. 35 states what cases of homicide merit the death penalty. Whenever a man's death is premeditated, the death penalty must be exacted (35:16–21). But in all other cases where there was no premeditation, where the person was killed inadvertently (*bishgāgāh*), the killer may flee to one of the cities of refuge (Num. 35:11). In vv. 22ff. some examples of inadvertent homicide are given, covering both accidents and other assaults resulting in death that were not planned beforehand.[11]

The second category of sins requiring atonement by means of a purification offering, sins of omission (5:1–4), are regarded by many commentators as examples of inadvertent sins; but the specific phrase *bishgāgāh,* "inadvertently," is not used to characterize these offenses, and it therefore seems better to suppose that a different

11. Cf. B. S. Jackson, *Essays in Jewish and Comparative Legal History* (Leiden: Brill, 1975), pp. 91f.

type of offense is being considered. The common factor in these sins is that someone knows he ought to do something, but then forgets about it, *it slips his memory*[12] (vv. 2, 3, 4). The first case deals with an obligation to give evidence in court (v. 1), the second and third deal with the duty to undergo ritual cleansing after becoming unclean (vv. 2–3; cf. 11:24–28, 39–40; 22:4–7), and the fourth with self-imposed obligations which are then forgotten (v. 4). In each case, when conscience smites the forgetful person, he must confess his sin and bring a purification offering. The appropriateness of this sacrifice is evident where it concerns untreated uncleanness. By failing to purify himself promptly the unclean man may have transmitted uncleanness to the sanctuary (cf. 15:31).

The Meaning of the Purification Sacrifice

Most commentators regard this sacrifice as the principal expiatory offering in ancient Israel. It is *the* sin offering. Hertz writes: "it made the offender against the holiness of God fit to receive the Divine forgiveness."[13] C. F. Keil says, "Sin-offerings were instituted for the purpose of putting an end to the separation between man and God that had been created by sin . . . and of restoring them again to the unimpaired enjoyment of the benefits of God's covenant of mercy and salvation."[14]

Keil interpreted the ritual of the sacrifice as follows: "the offerer transferred the consciousness of sin and the desire for forgiveness to the head of the animal that had been brought in his stead, by the laying on of his hand; and after this the animal was slaughtered, and suffered death for him as the wages of sin."[15] The sprinkling of the animal's blood within the sanctuary protected the sinner from the holiness of God expressing itself in righteous anger. The fat was burned on the altar to symbolize the purification of the human soul from sin. The flesh was burned outside the camp to portray the destruction of sin.[16]

Common though this and similar interpretations of the sin offering are, they seem inadequate for the following reasons. First, laying hands on and killing the animal are features common to all the

12. Lit. "is hidden from him." The context shows that forgetfulness is the cause of the sin.
13. Hertz, p. 22.
14. *Biblical Archaeology* I, p. 299.
15. Keil, p. 305.
16. Keil, pp. 306f.

blood sacrifices in Leviticus. If these acts symbolized the transfer of sin and substitution of the animal's life for the worshipper's in this sacrifice, it is reasonable to suppose that they had a similar significance in the other sacrifices. But then where is the special significance of the purification offering? It may well be that all the animal sacrifices included an element of substitutionary atonement when the sin was transferred to the animal and the animals died in the worshipper's place. But if there was this common core to all the sacrifices, which seems probable, there still remains the question as to what differentiated them.

Keil's discussion of the peculiar features of the sin offering seems a little arbitrary. Why should blood sprinkled in the sanctuary be supposed to protect the worshipper? Why does the flesh burned outside the camp symbolize the destruction of sin, while the flesh burned on the altar symbolized the purification of the worshipper? These are obviously attempts to find a rationale for these rites on the assumption that their overall purpose is expiation. It fails to explain why the blood should be sprinkled on the altar of burnt offering in the case of an ordinary person's sin, why it should be sprinkled on the altar of incense in the case of a national sin or high priest's sin, and why once a year the blood had to be taken into the holy of holies and sprinkled on the mercy seat itself.

Instead of relying on surmise about the symbolism used in these rites, it is better to rely on explicit statements about what they were thought to achieve. In various places the offering of this sacrifice is connected with purification, especially of bodily pollutions (Lev. 12:8; 14:19). These rites are said to cleanse people, "so that they do not die in their uncleanness by polluting my tabernacle which is among them" (15:31). On the day of atonement the blood was sprinkled in the various parts of the tabernacle "to cleanse it and sanctify it from the uncleannesses of the Israelites" (16:19).

These verses clearly express the notion that sin defiles men and particularly God's sanctuary, and that the proper means of purification is animal blood. If there is no purification, death will follow. This is in fact illustrated by the fate of Nadab and Abihu, who presumed to draw near to God, offering incense he had not commanded. For this breach of rules "fire came from before the Lord and consumed them" (Lev. 10:2).

That sin pollutes is not a conception that is readily understood by the Western mind, and so various attempts have been made to explain it. B. A. Levine notes that on the day of atonement blood was sprinkled on various objects that the high priest passed on his way into the holy of holies. He views the entrance of the high priest as a potentially dangerous infection coming right into the presence of God, and rendering God liable to attack by demons. Sin was viewed as a demonic contagion which could be introduced into the sanctuary by human agents.[17]

Such an interpretation might be entertained in some non-Israelite religions, but it hardly seems likely in an OT context. It is not God who is endangered by the pollution of sin, but man. God's holiness may be expressed in wrath, where sin is not atoned for and its guilt is not removed. The great calling of Israel was to be God's holy people among whom he would dwell. His presence was realized in the cloud that came down on Mount Sinai at the law-giving and in the cloud that overshadowed the tabernacle from time to time. The tabernacle was indeed God's dwelling place among his people (Exod. 29:43–46). It had to be kept pure from sin, if God was to remain there and if the people were not to experience God's wrath instead of his mercy. To have God dwelling in your midst is both a great blessing and a great danger. The danger, of course, springs from man's sinfulness, which always arouses God's wrath.

In discussing Lev. 1 we concluded that the burnt offering was the principal atoning sacrifice in ancient Israel. It was the sacrifice that reconciled the sinner with his creator. It was the most frequent sacrifice and also the most costly. Only unblemished animals could be offered and they had to be burned whole; there was no meat left for the priests to eat.

In contrast the purification offering was a less important rite. It was offered less frequently, and less valuable animals were used. It was designed to cope with a subsidiary problem created by human sin—pollution and defilement. This is a notion that is almost a stranger to the modern world. We do treasure the memory of famous people and events, and enjoy visiting the places where they lived or something significant happened. We feel that by going there we may recapture something of the atmosphere and spirit of the great men or of the historic happening. The Bible attaches greater significance to actions than we do. For us they are just memories. For the biblical writers an action has enduring aftereffects. In particular, sins pollute the place where they are committed. Guilt rests on the area where a murder takes place (Deut. 21:1–9). The sins of the Canaanites pol-

17. Levine, *Presence of the Lord*, pp. 68ff.

95

luted the land to such an extent that it vomited them out (Lev. 18:24–30).

Shakespeare was familiar with the idea that sin leaves a stain which no human effort can remove. For example, Lady Macbeth suffered as a sleepwalker as a result of collaborating in murder. Each night she used to rise from her bed and wash her hands repeatedly, because she thought they still had blood on them.

> *"Here's the smell of the blood still:*
> *all the perfumes of Arabia will not sweeten this little hand.*
> *Oh! oh! oh!"*
>
> Macbeth 5.1.55–57

The purification offering dealt with the pollution caused by sin. If sin polluted the land, it defiled particularly the house where God dwelt. The seriousness of pollution depended on the seriousness of the sin, which in turn related to the status of the sinner. If a private citizen sinned, his action polluted the sanctuary only to a limited extent. Therefore the blood of the purification offering was only smeared on the horns of the altar of burnt sacrifice. If, however, the whole nation sinned or the holiest member of the nation, the high priest, sinned, this was more serious. The blood had to be taken inside the tabernacle and sprinkled on the veil and the altar of incense. Finally over the period of a year the sins of the nation could accumulate to such an extent that they polluted even the holy of holies, where God dwelt. If he was to continue to dwell among his people, this too had to be cleansed in the annual day of atonement ceremony (see Lev. 16).

Detailed Exegesis

Leviticus 4 treats the purification offering differently from the previous sacrifices. It is more explicit about the type of animal required from different people in different situations. It is specified that an anointed priest should offer a bull, a ruler a male goat, and a common man a female goat or lamb or birds. The reason for these distinctions is worth further investigation.

The purification offering of the anointed priest (4:3–12)

The anointed priest is an unusual term occurring only in ch. 4 (vv. 3, 5, 16) and in 6:15 (Eng. 22). Aaron and his sons were anointed (Exod. 28:41; 30:30; 40:15; Num. 3:3), and it could therefore refer to any one of them. Most commentators, however, believe that only the high priest is meant, i.e., Aaron. In favor of this Num. 35:25 does seem to regard the unction of the high priest as something special. So "the anointed priest" would most naturally refer to the high priest, though the more common technical term is "the great priest" (Lev. 21:10, etc.).

Bringing guilt on the people (v. 3). When the priest sinned he involved not only himself but the whole nation. Here we have the idea that one man's action can affect the whole nation. Though some commentators[18] say that only a sin of the high priest committed in the course of his official duties is referred to, it seems more probable[19] that any sin by the high priest in his private or public capacity may bring guilt on the whole nation (cf. Lev. 10:6; 22:16). This reflects the very special role of the high priest in ancient Israel.

> The priests were to be the teachers of the people (Deut. 33:10) and therefore had to be an example especially in their private lives; and the high priest, who stood at the head of the priests, had to exhibit in his life the ideal of a holy life to which all could look up.
>
> The high priest is the representative of the nation and its ideal. So long as he is pure and spotless, all Israel fulfilled its obligations through its representative. When however the high priest is tainted through sin and becomes unworthy of representing the nation, all Israel stands guilty before God.[20]

The gravity of high-priestly sin is further underlined in vv. 4–7, by the valuable animal he has to bring and by the provision that he must sprinkle its blood on the veil and incense altar. A bull[21] is the largest animal ever prescribed for the purification offering. The only other occasion it was required was when the whole nation sinned (see vv. 13ff.). Sprinkling the blood within the holy place indicates that the pollution caused by the priest's sin was more serious than a layman's sin, which only required the altar of burnt offering to be cleansed (cf. above and vv. 22ff.).

The purification required for congregational sin (4:13–21)
Sin by the whole congregation required the same rites of purification as a sin by the high priest, though this time the bull was brought by

---

18. E.g., Keil, p. 303.
19. Cf. Hoffmann I, pp. 176f.; Gispen, pp. 71f.
20. Hoffmann I, pp. 176f.
21. Occasionally instead of the normal term for "bull" (*par*) the pleonastic phrase (*par ben-bāqār*), literally "a bovine bull," is found (4:3, 14; 16:3; 23:18). R. Péter, *VT* 25 (1975), p. 492, suggests that this phrase is an archaism dating from a period when *par* simply meant "an adult male animal."

the elders (vv. 14–15) instead of the high priest. But the exact nature of the offense is problematic. Is there any difference between the *congregation* ('*ēḏāh*) (vv. 13, 15) and *assembly* (*qāhāl*) (vv. 13, 14, 21)? What are the circumstances in which the offense is committed and discovered (vv. 13–14)?

Traditional Jewish commentators asserted that the congregation refers to the supreme court of justice in ancient Israel, the Sanhedrin. In the OT, however, "congregation" usually has a much broader meaning than this; sometimes indeed it seems to be co-extensive with the whole nation (Exod. 12:3, 6; 17:1; Num. 20:1, 2). This has led most Christian commentators to regard "congregation" and "assembly" as interchangeable terms, meaning a large group, or gathering of people.

The truth appears to lie somewhere between these extremes. "The congregation is not the whole people, but the people represented by its heads."[22] The congregation was a clearly defined group of people in ancient Israel with representative and legal functions.[23] From time to time we find the congregation acting in a legal capacity, especially in capital cases (Num. 15:33ff.; 27:2; 35:12, 24f.). It is a group alongside Moses and Aaron which comes into prominence in times of leadership crisis (Exod. 16:1, 2, 9; Num. 8:20; chs. 13–14, 16). Probably it was a large body, a sort of parliament with representative and judicial functions. It is tempting to see in Num. 1:2; 14:29 a definition of the "congregation," i.e., "all able-bodied men over the age of twenty." Since the "congregation" contained representatives of every family in Israel, it is easy to see why it could be used occasionally to designate the whole nation.

Assembly (*qāhāl*) has a less precise meaning. It means a gathering of people, whether assembled for a religious or a secular purpose. Most often it refers to religious gatherings at Sinai (Deut. 5:22; 9:10; 18:16), or in the temple (1 K. 8:22, 65). People with bodily injuries or of foreign descent may not enter the assembly, that is, they are forbidden to participate in worship (Deut. 23:2ff. [Eng. 1ff.]). The word can refer more generally to gatherings for war (Gen. 49:6; Ezek. 23:24; 26:7) or simply to a large number of people (Gen. 28:3; 48:4).

The situation here envisaged seems to be as follows: the "congregation" representing all Israel goes astray, but the fault *is*

22. Keil, *Biblical Archaeology* II, p. 316; cf. Saalschütz, pp. 38ff.
23. A. Hurvitz (*Tarbiz* 40 [1971], pp. 261–67) shows that '*ēḏāh*, a term particularly common in priestly literature, fell out of use after the exile.

hidden from the assembly, that is, it is not brought to light in the course of worship in the assembly in the daily services. How this could have come about is obscure. Perhaps a vision or prophecy or operation of the Urim and Thummim is intended. At any rate the fault does not appear to affect the conduct of worship. But the congregation starts to *feel guilty* (v. 13),[24] and then the sin by which they have incurred guilt becomes known. Then the assembly brings the bull as an offering and the sanctuary is cleansed.

Alternatively we may interpret the offense as by one member of the congregation, and it is hidden from the rest of the congregation when it assembles together. Since, however, this seems to be the case envisaged in vv. 22ff., it is preferable to see the fault in 13ff. as a corporate sin of the leaders of Israel. If this is the correct way to interpret the law, Josh. 9 could be an instance of it, when the leaders made a covenant with Gibeon without asking direction from the Lord (v. 14).

The purification offering of a tribal leader (4:22–26)

The sin of a tribal leader was not as serious as the sin of a high priest or of the whole congregation. The leader was required to offer only a male goat, and its blood was sprinkled on the altar of burnt offering. This symbolized the idea that his sin did not bring defilement into the inner sanctuary; it affected merely the outer sanctuary where the altar of burnt offering stood. It further differed from the preceding purification offerings in that the priest was allowed to eat the flesh of the goat (6:17ff. [Eng. 24ff.]; cf. 4:12, 21) after the other parts had been burned.

Tribal leader (*nāśî'*) covers a variety of officers in ancient Israel.[25] Its root meaning is "lifted up"; literally it means someone raised over the people. Most often it refers to the heads of tribes (e.g., Num. 2:3ff.), but it may also refer to the head of small groups within a tribe (e.g., Num. 3:24, 30) and even to the head of the nation (1 K. 11:34; Ezek. 12:10). It is a term particularly associated with the tribal organization of early Israel. With the establishment of the monarchy it seems to have fallen out of use, until Ezekiel

24. "Are guilty" is a possible translation of *'āshēm*, but as Milgrom (*Cult and Conscience*, pp. 7ff.) has pointed out, to translate it "be guilty" makes the remark superfluous. It has just been said that a commandment has been broken. It is clear that the congregation is objectively guilty but does not realize it. *'Āshēm* has the same sense in 4:22, 27; 5:2–5, 17, 23–24 (Eng. 6:4–5).
25. Cf. E. A. Speiser, "Background and Function of the Biblical *Nāśî'*," *Oriental and Biblical Studies*, pp. 113–122.

revived it. He commonly designates the king of the restored Israel as "tribal leader" (e.g., Ezek. 44:3; 45:7, 22, etc.).

Exodus 22:27 (Eng. 28) says, "You shall not revile God, nor curse a ruler (tribal leader) of your people." The leaders of ancient Israel occupied a privileged position which the law attempted to protect. But their position of leadership meant that their sins were correspondingly more serious than those of ordinary people and they had to offer more valuable animals in worship. The purification of the sins of the common man are dealt with last.

Purification offering of the common people (4:27–5:13)

The sin of an *ordinary* person,[26] someone who is not a priest or tribal leader, is the subject of the next section. A layman is not expected to provide such a valuable offering to atone for his sin as one of the rulers or priests. He may bring a she-goat (4:27ff.) or ewe-lamb (vv. 32ff.). If he is poor, he may bring instead a turtledove or pigeon (5:7ff.) or even some fine flour (5:11ff.). Here we have a sliding scale of offerings similar to that for burnt offerings in Lev. 1. Since both the burnt offering and the purification offering were obligatory in certain situations, not optional like the peace offering, the law provided for the poor by allowing them to present a cheaper offering if they could not afford a lamb or goat. The ritual when a layman brought a lamb or goat was very similar to that for the ruler. The offerer laid his hand on the animal and killed it. The priest took some of the blood and sprinkled it on the horns of the altar to purify it. The rest was either burned or consumed by the priests.

5:1–6 specifies some of the sins for which an ordinary layman must bring a purification offering. They can be characterized as sins of omission; see above, "The Occasions for the Purification Offering." *Bear his iniquity* (v. 1)—this phrase commonly refers to sin and its punishment. Here it probably refers to the fulfilment of the curse, pronounced against witnesses who fail to come forward (Judg. 17:2; Prov. 29:24). When the man starts to see the curse coming true, he feels guilty and then brings his offering.

Verses 7–10 specify that a poor man must bring two birds for sacrifice: *one for a purification offering and one for a burnt offering.* If this was the position of a poor man, wealthier people presumably

---

26. Lit. "one of the people of the land," a relatively rare phrase in the Pentateuch (cf. Gen. 23:7, 12–13; Exod. 5:5; Lev. 20:2, 4; Num. 14:9). Gispen (p. 84) points out that since these laws look forward to Israel's settlement in Canaan, this phrase does not necessarily disprove Mosaic authorship.

had to offer a burnt offering too. We have already observed that there is a similar sliding scale for burnt offerings in Lev. 1. This demonstrates that the purification offering deals with only one aspect of the process of atonement. It purifies the tabernacle or temple, so that God may be present with the worshipper. The burnt offering may then be offered to bring reconciliation between man and God and give the worshipper an opportunity to rededicate himself to God's service.

The Purification Offering and the NT

Under the Levitical laws the blood of the purification offering was used to cleanse the tabernacle from the pollution of sin. We have seen that the primary purpose of this purification was to make possible the continuing presence of God among his people. Many other things used in worship are daubed with blood to make them fit for the service of God: besides the various altars, the veil (Lev. 4) and the mercy seat (Lev. 16), the priests' vestments and the priests themselves (Exod. 29:19ff.; Lev. 8:22ff.). As Heb. 9:22 puts it, "Indeed, under the law almost everything is purified with blood, and without the shedding of blood there is no forgiveness of sins."

For the NT writers it is the blood of Christ which cleanses from the defilement of sin. Peter defines Christians as those who are "chosen and destined by God the Father and sanctified by the Spirit for obedience to Jesus Christ and for sprinkling with his blood" (1 Pet. 1:2). For John, fellowship with God and with other Christians is through the blood of Jesus his Son cleansing us from all sin (1 John 1:7). The saints in heaven "have washed their robes and made them white in the blood of the Lamb" (Rev. 7:14). Thus the cleansing from sin that was secured under the old covenant through the purification offering is effected under the new covenant by the death of Christ. Whereas in the Levitical laws it was the place of worship that was purified, under the new dispensation it is the worshipper himself.

John and Peter merely mention the purification offerings in passing; it is Hebrews that goes into their significance for the Christian in most detail (see Heb. 9, 10). Jesus Christ is the true high priest, whose actions Aaron and his sons were only imitating as best they could. Christ "entered once for all into the Holy Place, taking not the blood of goats and calves but his own blood, thus securing an eternal redemption. For if the sprinkling of defiled persons with the

101

blood of goats and bulls and with the ashes of a heifer sanctifies for the purification of the flesh, how much more shall the blood of Christ, who through the eternal Spirit offered himself without blemish to God, purify your conscience from dead works to serve the living God" (Heb. 9:12-14).

The writer goes on to stress the uniqueness and all-sufficiency of Christ's sacrifice. His death achieved a cleansing for sin which animal sacrifices never could. Unlike them it had only to be offered once to achieve its effect. "Therefore, brethren, since we have confidence to enter the sanctuary by the blood of Jesus, by the new and living way which he opened for us through the curtain, that is, through his flesh, and since we have a great priest over the house of God, let us draw near with a true heart in full assurance of faith, with our hearts sprinkled clean from an evil conscience and our bodies washed with pure water" (Heb. 10:19-22). He draws a parallel between the burning of the purification sacrifice outside the camp and Jesus' death outside Jerusalem. This is a reminder to Christians of the way that they should worship God. "We have an altar from which those who serve the tent have no right to eat. For the bodies of those animals whose blood is brought into the sanctuary by the high priest as a sacrifice for sin are burned outside the camp. So Jesus also suffered outside the gate in order to sanctify the people through his own blood. Therefore let us go forth to him outside the camp, bearing abuse for him. For here we have no lasting city, but we seek the city which is to come. Through him, then, let us continually offer up a sacrifice of praise to God, that is, the fruit of lips that acknowledge his name. Do not neglect to do good and to share what you have, for such sacrifices are pleasing to God" (Heb. 13:10-16).

The Christian Application of Leviticus 4-5

As with the other sacrifices in Leviticus, the coming of Christ has made the purification offering obsolete. Christ's death has purified us from the pollutions of sin in a complete and absolute way that need never be repeated. Yet this does not mean that we have nothing to learn about sin, its effects and its remedies, from Lev. 4. The NT writers show otherwise.

Their exegesis by no means exhausts the relevance of Lev. 4 for today's Church. Lev. 4 makes explicit that sin defiles the sanctuary: it makes it impossible for God to dwell among his people.

Though Israel was still the chosen people, when it sinned it no longer enjoyed the benefits of God's presence (cf. Exod. 32; Lev. 10; Num. 14, etc.). In a similar way the Christian is warned not to "grieve the Spirit" (Eph. 4:30) by sin. God's presence is now mediated by the Holy Spirit indwelling the believer (Eph. 2:22); that is why Christ's death has to purify our "conscience" or "heart." There is the continued threat in the NT that sin can drive the Spirit from the believer just as under the law God could be driven from the tabernacle. The Christian is told to walk in the Spirit and be filled with the Spirit (Gal. 5:25; Eph. 5:18).

Leviticus 4 also shows that the sin of Israel's leaders was considered more serious than that of ordinary people. The high priest and congregation had to offer more valuable animals than the ordinary man. So too the NT insists that God's judgment on Church members is proportionate to their responsibility. "Everyone to whom much is given, of him will much be required" (Luke 12:48). "We who teach will be judged with greater strictness" (Jas. 3:1).

These OT laws also show that unintentional sin is just as much sin in God's sight as deliberate wrongdoing. Rash promises, unfulfilled duties are just as liable to God separating himself from us now as under the Old Covenant.

They also show what should be done when our conscience convicts us. "When a man feels guilty in any of these matters he must confess how he has sinned and then bring a purification offering" (5:5–6). So too in the NT, confession of sin is a prerequisite of cleansing. "If we confess our sins, he is faithful and just, and will forgive our sins and cleanse us from all unrighteousness" (1 John 1:9). For a Christian the animal offering is no longer necessary, since Christ's death has brought purification, but confession is, if fellowship with God is to be reestablished.

5. THE REPARATION OFFERING (5:14–26 [Eng. 6:7])

14 *The Lord spoke to Moses as follows:*

15 *"If anyone trespasses and sins inadvertently against the Lord's sacred property, he must bring in reparation to the Lord a perfect ram convertible into silver shekels on the sanctuary standard to be a reparation offering.*

16 *He must also repay what he sinned in the sacred property, add one fifth extra and give it to the priest. The priest shall make atonement for him using the ram of the reparation offering, and he will be forgiven.*

103

THE BOOK OF LEVITICUS

17 *If anyone sins by breaking one of the Lord's commands, but did not realize it, and then feels guilty and bears his iniquity,*

18 *he must bring to the priest a perfect ram or its equivalent (in money) to be a reparation offering, and the priest shall make atonement for him because of his inadvertent mistake which he failed to realize, and he will be forgiven.*

19 *It is a reparation offering. He has made reparation to the Lord."*

20 *(6:1) The Lord spoke to Moses as follows:*

21 *(6:2) "If anyone sins and trespasses against the Lord by cheating his neighbor with regard to any deposit or security, by theft, or by oppressing his neighbor,*

22 *(6:3) or if he finds lost property, and cheats by swearing falsely in in any of these cases in which men sin against each other,*

23 *(6:4) if he sins, and feels guilty, he must return what he stole or extorted, the deposit with which he was entrusted, or the lost property he found,*

24 *(6:5) or anything else about which he swore falsely: as soon as he feels guilty, he must repay in full and add a fifth extra to what he should give him.*

25 *(6:6) He must bring to the priest, as his reparation to the Lord, a perfect ram or its equivalent to be a reparation offering.*

26 *(6:7) The priest shall make atonement for him before the Lord, and he will be forgiven for any of these things by which men bring guilt on themselves."*

The Reparation (Guilt) Offering

The reparation offering (RSV, NEB, guilt offering) concludes the list of sacrifices in Lev. 1–5. As with the other sacrifices, there has been much discussion about its function and purpose in Israelite worship. The word here translated *reparation offering* or "guilt offering" (*'āshām*) in other contexts can mean "reparation" or "guilt," and this has led to confusion about the role of this sacrifice. In Lev. 5:7, according to the RSV translation, a poor man "shall bring, as his guilt offering . . . two turtledoves or two young pigeons, one for a sin offering and the other for a burnt offering." It seems preferable, however, to translate the first phrase "as his reparation" (cf. 5:6, 15, 25 [6:6]; 19:21) rather than "as his guilt offering," for birds are never offered as a guilt offering.

The confusion between the reparation offering and the purification offering (Lev. 4) has been compounded by the old understanding of the purification offering as *the* sin offering. Surely the sin offering and the guilt offering must be closely related? Consequently many commentators take the guilt offering as a kind of sin offering, or vice versa.

Closer examination shows that the two sacrifices were quite distinct. The ritual was different. The sacrificial animals were different. The circumstances in which they were offered differed. The function of the reparation offering was not the same as that of the purification offering. In short, different names denote different sacrifices. Insofar as other sacrifices also had to do with the guilt of sin, there is much to be said for calling this "the reparation offering"[1] or the "compensation offering"[2] to bring out its precise function.

The Sacrificial Animals

Only a *ram* or a male lamb could be offered as reparation offerings (Lev. 5:14ff.; 14:12ff.; 19:21–22; Num. 6:12). The reparation offering is unusual in restricting the choice of animal to one species in this way. Rams and male lambs could be offered as burnt offerings and peace offerings, but other animals could be used too. On the other hand male sheep were never allowed for the purification offering. Bulls, goats, female lambs, and birds could be offered, but not rams or male lambs. The choice of animals is the first clear distinction between the purification offering and the reparation offering.

The Rite (see also Lev. 7:1–7)

The ritual side of the reparation offering is described much more briefly than is the case with the other sacrifices, and it is difficult to be sure of the exact procedure. The brevity of description may correspond to the relative unimportance of the ritual as far as this sacrifice is concerned. The value of the animal presented was more important than the procedure at the altar.

The worshipper brought his unblemished ram to the altar of burnt offering. As with the other sacrifices, it was killed there. We are not told that the worshipper laid his hand on the animal, but Num. 5:7 mentions confession as part of the rite. Since laying on of hands was usually accompanied by confession in other animal sacrifices, it seems likely that it formed part of this one too.

As with the burnt and peace offerings, the blood was thrown against the altar. There were no blood-sprinkling rites such as characterized the purification offering. Finally the fat and entrails of the ram were burned on the altar. The priests were allowed to have

---

1. Milgrom, *Cult and Conscience*, pp. 13f.
2. See N. H. Snaith, "The Sin-Offering and the Guilt-Offering," *VT* 15 (1965), pp. 73–80.

the flesh to cook and eat in a holy place. In allocating the meat to the priests the reparation offering resembled the purification offering of the leader or layman.

The Occasions for the Reparation Offering

The situations requiring the reparation offering are set out in Lev. 5:14–24 (Eng. 6:5); 14:10ff.; 19:20–22; Num. 5:6–10; 6:9–12. The first is defined in Lev. 5:15 as follows, "If anyone trespasses and sins inadvertently against the Lord's sacred property. . . ." The word *trespasses (māʿal)* is used of a wide variety of serious sins in the OT. It may refer to adultery (Num. 5:12, 27), worshipping pagan deities (Num. 31:16; Ezek. 20:27), and marrying foreigners (Ezra 10:2, 10). It also refers to Achan's sin of stealing the consecrated booty (Josh. 7:1), and to Uzziah's fault when he insisted on offering incense in the temple, a privilege confined to the priests (2 Chr. 26:16, 18).

The offense is here more closely defined as sinning *inadvertently*[3] *against the Lord's sacred property.* The word translated *sacred property* is literally "holy things." In the singular this word (*qōḏesh*) means "holiness" or "sanctuary" (e.g., 20:3; 22:2, 32; 10:4, 17–18). The plural seems to refer to offerings made to the priests, which in Lev. 22 and 27 are called "holy things." Only priests and members of their household are allowed to eat the holy things (22:2–13). "Anyone who eats holy food inadvertently must add a fifth to it, and give it to the priest" (22:14). Ch. 27 defines "holy things" as anything dedicated by men to God, e.g., animals, houses, land, tithes.

When a man dedicated something it was valued by the priest, and if the dedicator subsequently changed his mind, he had to pay a fifth extra to redeem the item. "Very holy things," literally "holy thing of holy things," is a technical term for the parts of sacrifices eaten by the priests (e.g., Lev. 2:3, 10).

Quite what constituted an inadvertent sin against the Lord's sacred property (holy things) is not specified. Eating holy food is one possibility (see Lev. 22:14). Perhaps failing to fulfil a dedicatory vow or to present the tithe would also have constituted an offense meriting a reparation offering. Notice that the penalty is in two parts: the man has to restore to the priesthood that of which they had been deprived by his mistake, plus 20 percent. He must also bring a ram

3. On this term see above on 4:2, p. 92.

106

to be slain at the altar. The worshipper had to compensate the man he had offended by giving him back what he lost, and had to acknowledge his guilt before God by bringing the sacrificial ram.

The ram must be *perfect*, i.e., unblemished, and *convertible into silver shekels on the sanctuary standard* (v. 15). This phrase is obscure. The traditional Jewish explanation is that the ram must be worth at least two shekels.[4] More recent studies have explained the phrase differently. The translation adopted here presupposes E. A. Speiser's interpretation.[5] If the man could not bring a ram as a reparation offering, he had to bring an equivalent amount of silver instead. A precise figure is not given for the ram, for its price would vary from time to time. A similar provision is found in Nuzi documents of the second millennium B.C. Jackson,[6] however, suggests that the phrase means "at your assessment of the property," i.e., the guilty person must restore the sacred property plus 20 percent plus a sum equivalent in value to the sacred property. To defend his idea Jackson[7] has to suppose the reference to silver shekels is an interpolation in v. 15, since it is missing in 5:18 and 5:25 (Eng. 6:6). Speiser's explanation, that the phrase in 5:18, 25 is an abbreviation of the full phrase in 5:15, seems preferable.

On the sanctuary standard (v. 15) is literally "in holy shekels." Evidently the sanctuary had its own set of weights, slightly different from other systems.[8] For this important sacrifice the holy weights had to be used.

Verses 17–19 discuss another case of inadvertent trespass against sacred property. It differs from the first where the offense was known, in that this time the offender does not know what he has done wrong: *but did not realize it* (v. 17). This does not seem to refer to ignorance of the law. Men are presumed to know that they must not take priestly property. Nor is it a question of subsequently learning that such and such belonged to the priest. If someone discovered he had inadvertently purloined sacred property, he was expected to return it plus 20 percent plus a ram (see vv. 15–16). Instead, the discovery that he has done wrong comes through his

4. Cf. Elliger, p. 77.
5. See E. A. Speiser, *Oriental and Biblical Studies*, pp. 124–28, followed by Levine, *Presence of the Lord*, pp. 95–100. Milgrom, *Cult and Conscience*, pp. 13ff. Speiser takes the pronominal suffix in ʿerkᵉḵā, "your valuation," as a fossilized form which has lost its meaning, so that ʿerkᵉḵā means "valuation," "monetary equivalent." Cf. bōʾᵃḵāh, "your approach > approach" (Gen. 10:19, 30, etc.).
6. B. S. Jackson, *Theft in Early Jewish Law* (Oxford: Clarendon, 1972), p. 175.
7. *Ibid.*, p. 172.
8. See de Vaux, *Ancient Israel*, pp. 203ff.

conscience. He *feels guilty* and starts to suffer[9] for it, i.e., *bears his iniquity*.

This then is an instance of a suspected trespass against sacred property, one of the most dreaded sins in antiquity.[10] Someone suspects he has sinned, but does not know exactly how. In his uncertainty he fears the worst, and therefore a reparation offering must be brought, *a ram or its equivalent (in money)*. The gravity of sin dealt with by the reparation offering is demonstrated by the fact that unlike the burnt and purification offerings less valuable animals than rams could not be brought instead. However, since the sin was only suspected, not known, there was no restitution of sacred property involved. This sacrifice served then to pacify oversensitive Israelite consciences. The last clause, *He has made reparation to the Lord* (v. 19), underlines the assurance of forgiveness already mentioned in the previous verse.[11]

The third situation where a reparation offering was required was quite different. It is again described as trespassing against the Lord (v. 21 [6:2]). The sin dealt with here is not merely stealing a neighbor's goods, either by blatant robbery, extortion, or by failing to return property entrusted for safe-keeping (vv. 21–22 [6:2–3]), but when challenged about this *swearing falsely* (v. 22 [3]) that one is not guilty. Oaths by the gods were a common means of settling legal disputes, where other evidence was lacking. Exod. 22:6ff. (Eng. 7ff.) prescribes an oath by the Lord for a number of such cases.[12] By abusing the oath, a person took God's holy name in vain, and trespassed against his holiness. Therefore a reparation offering was required to make amends. Milgrom[13] points out that Israel's neighbors also regarded a false oath as a sin comparable with trespass against sacred property.

What is striking about this provision is that although the offense was blatant and deliberate, perjury in a public court, yet

9. For this meaning of "to bear iniquity" cf. Gen. 4:13; Lev. 7:18; 20:17, 20; Num. 5:31; 14:34. On *'āshēm*, "to feel guilty," cf. note on 4:13.
10. Milgrom, *Cult and Conscience*, pp. 76ff.
11. *'Ashōm 'āsham (he has made reparation)* is usually translated "he is guilty." However, a reassertion of the man's guilt is unexpected at this point in the text, for sacrificial laws generally conclude with a statement of forgiveness and atonement. That *'āsham* can mean "to bear guilt, suffer punishment" is clear (e.g., Hos. 5:15; 10:2). Since *ḥiṭṭē'* may mean "to de-sin, cleanse, do the purification offering" (6:19), an analogous meaning may be posited for *'āsham*, to make reparation."
12. For extrabiblical examples see LE 22, 37; LH 9, 23, 106, 120, 126, 131, 206f., 227, 249, 266, 281; MAL A25, 47.
13. *Cult and Conscience*, pp. 21f.

sacrificial atonement was permitted. The other reparation offerings were for inadvertent sins. So too were the purification offerings, though these were also acceptable for sins of omission (5:1–6). It seems likely that atonement for deliberate sins was possible where there was evidence of true repentance, demonstrated by remorse (feeling guilty), full restitution (v. 23 [4]), and confession[14] of sin (cf. Num. 5:6–8).

Another notable feature of this law is the low level of restitution made to the man who had lost his property, in comparison with the law in Exod. 22:6ff. There, for similar offenses, double restitution was the norm (200 percent), whereas here it is only one and one fifth (120 percent) restitution plus a ram. Traditionally this discrepancy has been accounted for as follows: Exodus envisages a situation where the offender is convicted on the evidence presented by the plaintiff, but in Leviticus the culprit confesses his guilt. Making the penalty a low one should have encouraged voluntary surrender.[15]

A reparation offering of a lamb was required, along with a burnt offering and sin offering, when a leper was declared clean (Lev. 14). A reparation offering of a ram is prescribed where a man had intercourse with a betrothed slave-girl (Lev. 19:20–22). Had the girl been free, both would have been put to death as adulterers (cf. Deut. 22:23–24). Since she was a slave, she was not held responsible for her action. The man was, however, expected to bring a reparation offering. Finally, a Nazirite who by force of circumstances broke his vow of total dedication to God had to offer a reparation offering (Num. 6:6–12).

The Meaning of the Reparation Offering

The reparation offering is prescribed for two main types of offenses, trespass against holy things and trespass against God's holy name by uttering false oaths in court. As was pointed out in the Introduction (see VI.2: "Holiness"), contact between the holy and the unclean could result in death (Lev. 10:1–2; Num. 16:16ff.). It could be argued that in this sacrifice the ram was put to death instead of the guilty sinner.

---

14. For detailed discussion of the place of confession and repentance in OT law see Milgrom, *Cult and Conscience,* pp. 105ff.
15. Jackson *(Theft in Early Jewish Law,* p. 175) seeks to align Exodus and Leviticus by supposing that the ram had to be equal in value to the stolen property. Restitution would then be 220 percent. As Milgrom *(Cult and Conscience,* p. 116 n. 428) points out, there would be many cases where the value of the ram would be very different from that of the stolen item.

Alternatively the ram may be seen as making reparation to God, just as the return of property plus a fifth makes restitution to the man or priest whose goods had been stolen.

Both explanations seem to cover the case of the Nazirite whose holiness was polluted by someone dying near him (Num. 6:9). Along with a purification and burnt offering, he must bring a reparation offering, when he renews his vow (6:11–12). The basis for this could be the animal suffering in place of the polluted Nazirite, or compensation to the Lord for the time he had been deprived of the Nazirite's services. Why a cleansed "leper" should have had to offer a reparation offering is not clear (Lev. 14:12). Serious skin diseases made a man unclean, and therefore he was driven out of the camp. It may be that the reparation offering was included in this case because God had somehow been deprived of the man's worship. Or it could be that, since skin diseases were often associated with judgment on sin, especially sins of trespass against holiness (2 Chr. 26:16–19), it was thought fitting that the cleansed "leper" should offer this sacrifice just in case his disease had been caused by such a sin (cf. Lev. 5:17–19). Finally, if breaking the commandment about taking God's name in vain required a reparation offering, it is not surprising that adultery did too (Lev. 19:20–22). But this does not help to decide whether the offered ram died in the sinner's place or provided compensation to God for his loss.

The earliest interpretation of the significance of the reparation offering is found in Isa. 53, where the suffering servant's death is described. "He was wounded for our transgressions, he was bruised for our iniquities" (v. 5). "The Lord has laid on him the iniquity of us all" (v. 6). In these words the idea of substitutionary atonement is clearly set out. The servant suffers instead of us. He bears the penalty of our sins.

In v. 7 it becomes clear that the prophet is thinking in sacrificial terms: the servant is "like a lamb that is led to the slaughter." The word used here (śeh) is less precise than that used for lamb in Leviticus, and may in fact refer to sheep or goats. An allusion to any type of animal sacrifice is therefore possible and may be intended. Nevertheless v. 10 is more specific: "Yet it was the will of the Lord to bruise him; he has put him to grief; when thou shalt make his soul an offering for sin . . ." (RSV "when he makes himself an offering for sin"). "An offering for sin" is literally a reparation offering. The death of the suffering servant compensates for the sins of the people and makes many to be accounted righteous.

110

It may not be necessary, however, to choose between the idea of substitutionary atonement, of the ram dying in the sinner's place, and of reparation, of the ram somehow compensating God for the loss he has suffered as the result of sin. In some degree substitution seems to form part of the theology of all the sacrifices: reparation may be the specific component of the reparation offering, just as purification is the distinctive aim of the purification offering.

The reparation offering draws attention to the fact that sin has both a social and a spiritual dimension. It not only affects our relation with our neighbor, it affects our creator. It influences our relationship vertically with God as well as horizontally with our fellow man. Just as we must put ourselves right with men by paying them back for the wrongs we have done them, so we must compensate our heavenly Father for the debts we run up against him.

The reparation offering thus demonstrates that there is another aspect of sin that is not covered by the other sacrifices. It is that of satisfaction or compensation. If the burnt offering brings reconciliation between God and man, the purification or sin offering brings purification, while the reparation offering brings satisfaction through paying for the sin.

The sacrificial system therefore presents different models or analogies to describe the effects of sin and the way of remedying them.[16] The burnt offering uses a personal picture: of man the guilty sinner who deserves to die for his sin and of the animal dying in his place. God accepts the animal as a ransom for man. The sin offering uses a medical model: sin makes the world so dirty that God can no longer dwell there. The blood of the animal disinfects the sanctuary in order that God may continue to be present with his people. The reparation offering presents a commercial picture of sin. Sin is a debt which man incurs against God. The debt is paid through the offered animal.

The NT and the Reparation Offering

The reparation offering is never mentioned in the NT, but Isa. 53 is quoted several times and its ideas underlie many passages describing Christ's sufferings (v. 1//John 12:38; Rom. 10:16; v. 4//Matt. 8:17; vv. 5–6//1 Pet. 2:24–25; v. 9//1 Pet. 2:22; v. 12//Luke 22:37). The Gospels underline how Christ was scourged, let false accusations go unanswered at his trial, was crucified with two robbers, and was

16. On theological models in atonement theology see J. I. Packer, "What Did the Cross Achieve?" *TB* 25 (1974), pp. 3–45.

buried in a rich man's grave. All these points may be allusions to Isa. 53. Even when not explicitly alluding to Isa. 53, the Evangelists obviously saw the fulfilment of that prophecy in Jesus.

It therefore seems legitimate to regard Christ's death not only as the perfect burnt offering, peace offering, and purification offering, but also as the perfect reparation offering, the sacrifice which metaphorically compensates God for our sin. As with the other sacrifices, it is hard to understand how such a transaction can be applied to God and particularly to relations within the Godhead. We must not suppose that any of these sacrificial analogies or models is an exhaustive description. They are human terms designed to give mere man some insight into the mysteries of our redemption.

Christ's death, the perfect reparation offering, has therefore made it obsolete, along with the other sacrifices. It is no longer necessary to attempt to compensate God for our failure by bringing a ram or a lamb to the altar. Our spiritual debts have been written off in the sacrifice of Christ.

There is another aspect of the reparation offering that still has a relevance today. The reparation offering focuses on the debt we incur to God by breaking faith with him or with our fellow man. Where sin includes a wrong against a neighbor, the neighbor had to receive restitution plus a fifth at the same time as the sacrifice was brought. Divine forgiveness was contingent on reparation to the neighbor and sacrifice to God. Similarly the NT expects us to make amends to our neighbors if we wish to enjoy peace with God.

"Forgive us our trespasses as we forgive those who trespass against us" (Matt. 6:12). "If you are offering your gift at the altar, and there remember that your brother has something against you, leave your gift there before the altar and go; first be reconciled to your brother, and then come and offer your gift" (Matt. 5:23–24). When Jesus came to Zacchaeus' house, Zacchaeus announced, " 'Behold, Lord, the half of my goods I give to the poor; and if I have defrauded anyone of anything, I restore it fourfold.' And Jesus said to him, 'Today salvation has come to this house' " (Luke 19:8–9). In both testaments the way of salvation is through sacrifice and through making amends to those we have wronged.

B. INSTRUCTIONS FOR THE PRIESTS (6:1 [Eng. 8]–7:38)

1. THE BURNT OFFERING (6:1–6 [8–13])

1(8) *The Lord spoke to Moses:*
2(9) *"Command Aaron and his sons as follows: This is the law of the*

burnt offering, the burnt offering which is on the hearth all night till the morning. The fire must be kept burning on it.

3(10) *The priest must put on his linen garment and linen shorts over his flesh and he must remove the ashes produced by the fire of the burnt offering and place them near the altar.*

4(11) *Then he must take his clothes off and put on other clothes, and then take the ashes outside the camp to a clean place.*

5(12) *But the fire must be kept burning on the altar: it must not go out. The priest must burn wood each morning, and lay the burnt offering on the wood, and burn the fat of the peace offerings on it.*

6(13) *A perpetual fire must be kept burning on the altar: it must not go out."*

2. THE CEREAL OFFERING (6:7–11 [14–18])

7(14) *"This is the law of the cereal offering. The sons of Aaron must offer it before the Lord by the altar.*

8(15) *Then the priest must remove with his cupped hand some of the flour and oil and all of the incense on the cereal offering and burn its memorial portion on the altar as a soothing aroma for the Lord.*

9(16) *But the rest of it Aaron and his sons must eat. It must be eaten in the form of unleavened cakes in a holy place: i.e., they must eat it in the court of the tent of meeting.*

10(17) *It must not be baked with leaven. I have given it as their portion from my food offerings. It is most holy like the purification offering and the reparation offering.*

11(18) *Every male descendant of Aaron may eat it. It is a permanent due for your descendants from the Lord's food offerings. Anyone who touches them becomes holy."*

3. THE PRIEST'S CEREAL OFFERING (6:12–16 [19–23])

12(19) *The Lord spoke to Moses as follows:*

13(20) *"This is the offering of Aaron and his sons which they must offer to the Lord from the day he is anointed, a regular cereal offering, one tenth of an ephah of flour; they must offer half of it in the morning and half of it in the evening.*

14(21) *It must be made with oil on a griddle. You must bring it well mixed and offer it in small bits like a crumbled cereal offering as a soothing aroma for the Lord.*

15(22) *The priest who is anointed to succeed him among his sons must do it. This is a permanent due for the Lord: it must be completely burned.*

16(23) *Every priestly cereal offering must be completely burned. It must not be eaten."*

4. THE PURIFICATION OFFERING (6:17–23 [24–30])

17(24) *The Lord spoke to Moses as follows:*

18(25) *"Tell Aaron and his sons: This is the law of the purification offering.*

The purification offering must be killed before the Lord in the place where the burnt offering is killed. It is most holy.

19(26) *The priest who performs the sacrifice must eat it in a holy place: it must be eaten in the court of the tent of meeting.*

20(27) *Anything that touches its flesh becomes holy. You must wash in a holy place any garment on which the sprinkled blood is splashed.*

21(28) *Earthenware vessels used for cooking it must be broken. If it is cooked in a copper vessel, it must be scrubbed and rinsed in water.*

22(29) *Any male member of the priestly families may eat it. It is most holy.*

23(30) *But any purification offering in which blood is brought inside the tent of meeting to make atonement within the sanctuary may not be eaten. It must be burned with fire.''*

5. THE REPARATION OFFERING (7:1–10)

1 *"This is the law of the reparation offering. It is most holy.*

2 *The priest must kill the reparation offering in the place where they kill the burnt offering, and he must splash its blood around the altar.*

3 *He must offer all its fat: he must remove the fat tail, the fat covering the intestines,*

4 *the two kidneys and the fat which is on them at the loins, and the long lobe of the liver near the kidneys.*

5 *The priest must burn them on the altar as a food offering to the Lord. It is a reparation offering.*

6 *Any male member of the priestly families may eat it. It must be eaten in a holy place. It is most holy.*

7 *The same rule applies to the purification offering as to the reparation offering. The priest who makes atonement with it shall have it.*

8 *The priest who offers a burnt offering for someone shall have its skin.*

9 *Every cereal offering baked in an oven, or cooked in a pan or on a griddle, must go to the priest who offers it.*

10 *But every uncooked cereal offering, mixed with oil or dry, must be shared equally among all the sons of Aaron.''*

6. THE PEACE OFFERING (7:11–36)

11 *"This is the law of the peace offering, which must be offered to the Lord.*

12 *If he offers it for a confession offering, he must offer with the confession sacrifice thin unleavened cakes mixed with oil, and unleavened wafers coated with oil, and flour mixed into cakes containing oil.*

13 *He must offer cakes of leavened bread as his offering along with the confession peace offering.*

14 *He must also offer part of every offering as a contribution to the Lord. It shall go to the priest who splashes the blood of the peace offering.*

15 *Meat from a confession peace offering must be eaten on the day that it is offered. None of it may be left till the next morning.*

16 *If his offering is a vow or freewill sacrifice, it must be eaten on the day that he offers it, and anything left over may be eaten the following day.*

17 *But whatever meat is left over on the third day must be burned with fire.*

18 *If any meat from a peace offering is eaten on the third day, the man who offered it will not be accepted. It will not be credited to him. It is rotten. The person who eats it will bear his iniquity.*

19 *Meat which comes in contact with anything unclean may not be eaten. It must be burned. Anyone who is clean may eat meat.*

20 *Any person who eats meat from one of the Lord's peace offerings while he is unclean will be cut off from his people.*

21 *If a person touches something unclean, whether it be human uncleanness or an unclean animal or some abominable uncleanness, and then eats some meat from the Lord's peace offering, that person shall be cut off from his people."*

22 *The Lord spoke to Moses as follows:*

23 *"Tell the Israelites, Do not eat any ox, sheep, or goat fat.*

24 *The fat from an animal that dies naturally or accidentally may be used for any purpose, but you must not eat it on any account.*

25 *For anyone who eats the fat of an animal that can be offered to the Lord as a food offering, the person who eats will be cut off from his people.*

26 *Do not eat the blood of any bird or animal in your dwellings.*

27 *Anyone who eats any blood will be cut off from his people."*

28 *The Lord spoke to Moses as follows:*

29 *"Tell the Israelites, Whoever offers a peace offering to the Lord must bring from it a gift for the Lord.*

30 *His own hands must bring the Lord's food offerings; he must bring the fat on the breast as well as the breast, the breast to be dedicated as a dedication to the Lord.*

31 *The priest must burn the fat on the altar and the breast shall belong to Aaron and his sons.*

32 *You must give the right leg from the peace offering as a contribution to the priest.*

33 *That is for the priest who offers the peace offering blood and burns the fat. The right leg shall be his portion,*

34 *because I have taken the breast of the dedication and the right leg of the contribution from the peace offering of the Israelites and I have given them to Aaron and his sons as a permanent due from the Israelites.*

35 *This is the anointed right of Aaron and his sons from the Lord's food offerings, from the day he presented them to act as priests to the Lord,*

36 *because the Lord commanded that it should be given to them by the Israelites when he anointed them. This is a permanent rule for all their descendants."*

7. SUMMARY (7:37–38)

37 *This is the law for burnt offerings, cereal offerings, purification offerings, reparation offerings, ordination offerings, and peace offerings,*

38 *which the Lord commanded Moses on Mount Sinai, on the day he commanded the Israelites to offer their offerings to the Lord in the wilderness of Sinai.*

The Structure of Leviticus 6:1 (Eng. 8)–7:38

The material in these chapters is set out in nine paragraphs.

6:1–6 (8–13)	The perpetual burnt offering
7–11 (14–18)	The cereal offering
12–16 (19–23)	The priest's cereal offering
17–23 (24–30)	The purification offering
7:1–10	The reparation offering
11–21	The peace offering
22–27	No fat or blood to be eaten
28–36	The priest's portions of the peace offering
37–38	Summary

Each paragraph begins with: "The Lord spoke to Moses" (6:12 [19]; 7:22, 28) or "This is the law of" (6:7 [14]; 7:1, 11, 37). On two occasions both opening phrases occur together (6:1–2, 17–18 [8–9, 24–25]), perhaps indicating major subdivisions of the material. Furthermore there is a slight alteration in the opening formula in 7:22–23, 28–29, addressing the Israelites instead of the sons of Aaron (6:2, 17–18 [9, 24–25]). On these criteria the nine paragraphs fall into three groups of three (A: 6:1–6, 7–11, 12–16; B: 6:17–23; 7:1–10, 11–21; C: 7:22–27, 28–36, 37–38), a triadic arrangement akin to that found in the previous chapters.

The principal theme of these chapters is the eating of the sacrificial meat (e.g., 6:9, 11, 16, 19 [16, 18, 23, 26], etc.): who may eat what, and where. In most cases only priests could eat the sacrifices, but laymen could share in the peace offering, and this is the cue for introducing more general rules about eating in 7:22–27 and about the portions of the peace offering reserved for the priests in 7:28–36.

The section closes with a brief summary of its contents listing the main topics discussed (7:37–38). Concluding summaries like this are also found in 11:46–47; 13:59; 14:54–57; 15:32–33.

The Relationship of Leviticus 6–7 to Chs. 1–5

In these chapters there are further rules for the conduct of worship.

In various respects they overlap with, and to some extent duplicate, the material in chs. 1–5. They deal with the same sacrifices—the burnt offering, the cereal offering, the peace offering, the purification offering, and the reparation offering. This time, however, the sacrifices are dealt with in a different order; the peace offering is dealt with last in Lev. 7, but is the third kind of sacrifice in ch. 3.

The modern reader of Leviticus inevitably asks why there should be this repetition and apparent incoherence in the arrangement of material in the book. Very many suggestions have been advanced by biblical critics to explain the present structure of Leviticus in terms of the process by which it was written. The simplest and least speculative of these theories is that of Hoffmann,[1] who argues that Lev. 6–7 were originally written immediately after Exod. 29. Exod. 29 tells how Aaron and his sons were to be ordained as priests, of the sacrifices that had to be offered on that occasion. Lev. 6–7 explains some of the details of the ritual involved in these sacrifices. Then some time later Lev. 1–5 was written to clarify how and when the ordinary layman should bring sacrifice. Hoffmann rests his case on the close connection between Exod. 29 and Lev. 6–7 and on the fact that the contents of both sections are said to have been revealed on Mount Sinai (Lev. 7:37–38), whereas Lev. 1–5 was revealed in the tabernacle (Lev. 1:1).

This kind of answer only partially deals with the question of the relationship of the material in these chapters. At the level of human authorship it does not explain how the editor of Leviticus understood the mutual relationship of these sections. At the level of divine inspiration we must ask: What are we supposed to learn from this second treatment of the same subject matter? Why did God set out his directions for worship in one form as in Lev. 1–5 and in another as in chs. 6–7?

A comparison of Lev. 1–5 with chs. 6–7 discloses differences of emphasis and arrangement, which may provide a clue to their mutual relationship and particular purpose. Lev. 1:2 and 4:2 preface their remarks on worship by: "Tell the Israelites." Subsequently individual laws begin with "If a man," "If anyone," and so on. Chs. 1–5 are addressed to any Israelite who has to offer a sacrifice. They concentrate on what the worshipper has to do.

In contrast chs. 6–7 focus on the priests' role in worship. 6:2(9) says "Command Aaron and his sons," 6:18(25) "Tell Aaron and his sons." Most of the regulations in these two chapters are for

---

1. Hoffmann I, pp. 70ff.

the priests' information. The rules explain what the priests ought to do, what parts of the sacrifice should be given to them, and so on. Only two paragraphs (7:22ff., 28ff.) are addressed to the people as a whole. They are in fact a kind of digression prompted by the rituals associated with the peace offering, which involved a larger degree of lay participation than the other sacrifices.

The diverse intentions of both sections clarify their different emphases. If you were a layman, you would want to know when to offer a peace offering or a purification offering. You would also be interested in what kind of animals you had to bring for the different sacrifices, and what you had to do at the service. These topics are the dominant concern of Lev. 1–5.

If, however, you were a priest, you would have been more interested in the ritual as such. It was the worshipper's duty to bring the animal on the right occasions, it was the priest's to sacrifice it according to the proper form. He had to know which parts of the animal had to be burned, which could be eaten and which could not. He was also interested in which parts of the sacrifice belonged to him, which had to be shared with his colleagues, and which were to be returned to the worshipper.

This difference in purpose explains the different emphases of the two sections. Chs. 1–5 concentrate on those aspects of sacrifice that immediately concern the worshipper himself, while chs. 6–7 focus on those of concern to the officiating priest. There is not a hard and fast division between these sections: chs. 1–5 also contain details of ceremonial which chiefly concern the priest, whereas chs. 6–7 for their part contain some instruction for the ordinary Israelite.

Within the sections the order of sacrifices also differs. In chs. 1–5 the order is burnt, cereal, peace, purification, and reparation offering. In chs. 6–7 the order is burnt, cereal, priest's cereal (not mentioned in Lev. 1–5), purification, reparation, and peace offering.

In chs. 1–5 the motive for the arrangement seems to be theological: the "food offerings" producing "a soothing aroma for the Lord" are grouped together (chs. 1–3), and then come the purification and reparation offerings (chs. 4–5) securing the forgiveness of sins. In chs. 6–7 the sacrifices are arranged in order of their frequency.[2] The regular daily sacrifices come first, i.e., the burnt

2. See Num. 28–29.

offering, cereal, and priest's cereal offering. This is followed by the purification offering, which was compulsory only at certain festivals or after someone had sinned. The reparation offering was never offered on a regular basis, but was mandatory following certain sins. Finally, the peace offering was generally an optional sacrifice.

The Perpetual Burnt Offering (2–6 [9–13])

The main concern of this paragraph is that the fire on the altar of burnt offering should never go out. The point is made five times (vv. 2, 5, 6 [9, 12, 13]). It was the priest's duty to keep the fire lit with the carcass of the burnt offering smoldering away on top of it. The law focuses on the most difficult part of the task, keeping the fire going all night. It was customary to offer a burnt offering every morning and every evening (Num. 28:3–8). On most days other offerings would be offered during the day, but after the evening burnt offering there would be nothing till the next day, and without careful tending the fire would go out. The priest must not allow this to happen: *the fire must be kept burning . . .: it must not go out* (v. 5 [12]).

In the morning the ash had to be cleared away (vv. 3–4 [10–11]). In approaching the altar the priest had always to wear the correct priestly clothes, especially designed to cover *his flesh*, i.e., his private parts (v. 3 [10]; cf. Exod. 20:26; 28:42–43), even when he was not actually engaged in sacrifice but was merely clearing away the ashes. When he left the altar to carry the ash away to a place outside the camp, he had to put on other clothes. The holy garments were reserved for use in the sanctuary (v. 4 [11]). The holy and the common must not be confused (cf. Lev. 10:10).

What was the purpose of the perpetual fire of the burnt offering? What did it symbolize? Since it is never explicitly explained in Scripture, we can only list the suggestions that have been made. Calvin notes that the first burnt offerings in the tabernacle and in the temple were lit by fire from heaven (Lev. 9:24; 2 Chr. 7:1). The priests had to keep this fire going so "that the offerings should be burnt with heavenly fire."[3] Keil[4] thinks the fire had to be kept burning because the burnt offering "was the divinely appointed symbol and visible sign of the uninterrupted worship of Jehovah." Gispen[5] thinks that it represented the continual consecration of the

3. Calvin II, p. 364.
4. Keil, p. 318.
5. Gispen, p. 104.

people to God. If the burnt offering was also seen as a propitiatory sacrifice,[6] the perpetual fire served as a reminder of the constant need for atonement.

Whichever interpretation is adopted, Christians can draw a lesson from it. If the perpetual fire represents God's eternal presence with his people, the Christian is reminded to keep the divine fire ever burning within him. In the words of Paul, "Do not quench the Spirit" (1 Thess. 5:16ff.). If it speaks of our abiding need for atonement, we are reminded that Christ "always lives to make intercession" for us (Heb. 7:25).

Charles Wesley brings several of these interpretations together in his hymn:

> *O thou who camest from above*
>   *The pure celestial fire to impart*
> *Kindle a flame of sacred love*
>   *On the mean altar of my heart.*
>
> *There let it for Thy glory burn*
>   *With inextinguishable blaze*
> *And trembling to its source return*
>   *In humble prayer and fervent praise.*

The Most Holy Sacrifices (6:7 [14]–7:10)

The cereal offering, purification offering and reparation offering are all termed *most holy* (6:10, 18 [17, 25]; 7:6). That is, they are sacrifices which only the priests may eat. Furthermore they must be eaten in a holy place, in the court surrounding the tent of meeting (6:9, 19 [16, 26]). The focus in this section is on the priests' rights: defining what the priests may or may not take for themselves.

The Cereal Offering (6:7–11 [14–18])

As in chs. 1ff., this offering is described immediately after the burnt offering, which it normally accompanied.

The ritual and significance of the cereal offering have already been discussed (see commentary on ch. 2). These verses add very little to the earlier regulations: they simply underline that all priests are entitled to eat this offering, as long as they consume it in a holy place, such as the court of the tabernacle.

---

6. See above, "The Purpose of the Burnt Offering," pp. 55ff.

Anyone (or anything) *who touches them becomes holy* (v. 11c [18c]). This is probably meant as a warning to lay people to avoid touching the most holy sacrifices. But it is rather difficult to say what "becoming holy" means in this context. Similar expressions are found in v. 20 (27); Exod. 29:37; 30:29; Deut. 22:9. Elliger explains the phrase as follows: "He enters a state in which anyone who is not a priest trained to act discreetly will soon provoke God's special wrath against himself. At least he can only free himself from this state by undergoing a special act of purification."[7]

Certainly Leviticus underlines the dangers attendant on holiness.[8] Judgment falls when the unclean meets the holy (cf. 7:20; 10:1–3). But this text does not explain how long the state of holiness contracted through contact with a sacrifice lasted or what could be done to make the layman "common" again. Verses 20ff. (27ff.) suggest that the holiness could only be removed by destruction of the object or by washing it. It does not actually refer to deconsecration of people. Ch. 27 does deal with ransoming things and people that have been dedicated to the Lord. Broadly speaking the donor must pay 20 percent extra to redeem his gift. When a Nazirite had fulfilled the period of his vow, he had to be deconsecrated by offering every type of sacrifice save a reparation offering (Num. 6:13–20). Whether either of these procedures was adopted in this instance, where the consecration was involuntary, is doubtful.

The Priest's Cereal Offering (6:12–16 [19–23])

This sacrifice is not mentioned in chs. 1–5. The main principle[9] enunciated in this law is that the priest is not to eat the sacrifice offered on his own behalf. *Every priestly cereal offering must be completely burned. It must not be eaten* (v. 16 [23]). A similar principle underlies the rules about the purification offering.[10] When the priest brought one, the whole animal was burned (4:1–12; 6:23 [30]); but when a layman brought a purification offering the priest could eat some of the flesh (6:19 [26]). Similarly cereal offerings donated by lay people could be eaten by the priests (6:9–11 [16–18]),

---

7. Elliger, p. 97.
8. See Introduction, VI.2: "Holiness."
9. There are certain difficulties in translating v. 14 (21). *Well mixed (murbeket)* and *small bits (tupînê)* are rare words, whose exact significance is uncertain. *Tupînê*, "small bits," may be a corruption of *t^eputtennāh*, "You shall crumble it." See the commentaries of Elliger, Gispen, and Hoffmann for fuller discussion.
10. See J. Milgrom, "Two Kinds of *Ḥaṭṭā't*," *VT* 26 (1976), pp. 333–37.

but when the priest offered one for himself, it had to be burned in its entirety (v. 16 [23]).

From the day he is anointed (v. 13 [20]) is literally "on the day he is anointed." This phrase[11] indicates the point at which the sacrifice started to be offered on a daily basis, as *a regular cereal offering*. The daily cereal offering of the priests is mentioned by Josephus.[12]

Hebrews 7:27 refers to these daily sacrifices. Christ's priesthood is superior to Aaron's because he does not have to repeat his sacrifice. "He has no need, like those high priests, to offer sacrifices daily, first for his own sins and then for those of the people; he did this once and for all when he offered up himself." This Levitical law stands as a reminder that though complete forgiveness is available to us as Christians, we still need to claim it daily.

The Purification Offering (6:17–23 [24–30])

This covers much the same ground as ch. 4, clarifying which purification offerings the priest may eat and which he may not. Verse 23 (30) forbids the eating of purification offerings brought by the priest or the congregation (cf. 4:7, 18). Verses 20–22 (27–29) mention what should be done if any of the purifying blood goes astray. Since it is the blood that purifies the altar and other sacred objects, it must not be spilled on other objects. If it is, it must be washed off. If that is impossible, the thing must be destroyed (v. 21 [28]). This is another illustration of the principle of not confusing the holy and the common (cf. commentary on 6:11 [18]).

The Reparation Offering (7:1–10)

Here the ritual of the reparation offering is more fully described than in ch. 5. For a discussion of the ritual and its significance see above.

This section also lists what is to be done with various other offerings. In the burnt offering the whole animal except the skin was burned. The *skin* was given to the priest (v. 8). Verses 9 and 10 deal with cooked and uncooked cereal offerings. Verse 9 appears to say that cooked offerings were eaten by the officiating priest on his own whereas v. 10 suggests that *uncooked* offerings were *shared* between all the priests. It is hard to know what reason there could be for this rule. Keil[13] suggests that cooked offerings tended to be rarer

11. Cf. 5:24 (Eng. 6:5), "as soon as he feels guilty" (lit. "on the day of his guilt").
12. *Antiquities* 3:10:7.
13. Keil, p. 323.

and smaller than uncooked offerings and therefore could be eaten by one man, but uncooked ones needed to be shared out. Hoffmann[14] doubts whether there is any evidence for this difference in size and quantity, and suggests that both types of cereal offering could be shared among all the priests. Verse 10, he suggests, is simply designed to prevent the cereal offerings being shared with laymen.

The Peace Offering (7:11–36)

11–21   The peace offering is the only offering which laymen were allowed to eat. Some parts of the sacrificial animal were given to the priests, but the main part was returned to the worshipper for his own consumption. This section is concerned with regulating this sacred meal, specifying who may eat what, and when. For many Israelites the peace offering was the main, some would say the only, opportunity they had to eat meat. For this reason this section leads into other more general regulations governing the consumption of meat (vv. 22ff.).

This section gives many details not found elsewhere in Leviticus about the purpose and conduct of the peace offering. We have already discussed the more general questions raised by this sacrifice above in ch. 3; now we will focus on the detailed points made here. The significance of some of the details is difficult or impossible to recover, and Calvin's wise words on this section bear repetition: "It is certain, indeed, that God had a reason for dealing more strictly or more indulgently; but to enquire now-a-days as to things unknown, and which conduce not at all to piety, is neither right nor expedient."[15] Modern commentaries contain a fair amount of speculation about some of these rules, but assured results seem as far off as ever.

Verses 11–17 distinguish the peace offering for confession[16] from those offered spontaneously or in connection with a vow. The confession offering was the most solemn kind of peace offering, as two features demonstrate. First, the confession offering had to be accompanied by some sort of cereal offering, *cakes mixed with oil, and unleavened wafers coated with oil, and flour mixed into cakes containing oil* (v. 12), and *cakes of leavened bread* (v. 13). It seems as though all these different types of bread had to accompany a confession offering; they were not alternatives from which the worshipper could bring his favorite food. He had to give one of each sort

14. Hoffmann I, p. 247.
15. Calvin II, p. 371.
16. On the translation "confession" (*tôḏāh*) see above, p. 78 n. 11.

to the officiating priest (v. 14). The second difference between the confession offering and the others was that it had to be eaten on the day of the sacrifice; nothing could be left for the morning. If anything was left over, it had to be burned up; it could not be eaten (v. 15). Other types of peace offering could be eaten on the day following the sacrifice but not on the third day (vv. 16–17).

This rule, that the flesh of sacrifices should be eaten promptly, is not mentioned in connection with any of the other sacrifices. But it seems likely that the meat of the purification and reparation offerings was supposed to be consumed on the same day as the sacrifice was presented, for in 10:19 Aaron justified burning the sin offering by pleading that it was impossible for him to have eaten it that day, the day his sons had died.

The reason for eating the flesh promptly is not clear. We are simply told that if anyone eats the flesh on the third day he "will not be accepted. It will not be credited to him. It is rotten. The person who eats it will bear his iniquity" (v. 18). If the word here translated *rotten* (*piggûl*)[17] has been correctly rendered, we may have the clue to the purpose of this rule. It may be derived from a root meaning "to rot" (*pāgal*). If this is correct etymology of the word, worshippers may not keep the food overnight, lest it spoil and become inedible as the manna did (Exod. 16:19ff.). This then would be another example of the Levitical law's inistence that only perfect animals and people may participate in the worship of God. Those that are damaged or in any way fall short of the ideal are excluded from worship (Lev. 1:3, 10; 21:16ff.). Another reason for not eating flesh had to do with the possibility of its contact with something unclean. Then of course it may not be eaten (vv. 19–21).

Other suggested rationales for this rule include the notion that by insisting that the flesh had to be eaten quickly, the law encouraged the worshipper to share the meal with others, especially the poor. Another idea is that by eating the food up in one day rather than storing it, the worshipper exercised faith that God would provide for his needs day by day.[18]

None of these suggestions really explains why a confession sacrifice had to be eaten within a day, while others could be left for two days. The first explanation seems to have most to commend it. For whatever reason, whoever eats of a peace offering after the

---

17. *Piggûl* is used in only three other passages (Lev. 19:7; Isa. 65:4; Ezek. 4:14). B. A. Levine (*Presence of the Lord,* p. 7 n. 7) translates it "delayed offering."
18. Hoffmann I, p. 251.

prescribed deadline loses any benefit from it. Indeed he is regarded as guilty and is liable to *bear his iniquity*, i.e., to suffer appropriate divine punishment (v. 18; cf. 5:1; 17:16; 19:8).

More severe punishment is allotted to those who are unclean themselves yet presume to eat of the sacrificial offering. He *will be cut off from his people* (vv. 20–21). This phrase indicates direct divine judgment, usually death. It is attached to various sins, mainly of a religious and sexual kind (cf. 7:21, 25, 27; 17:4, 9; 18:29; 19:8; 20:17–18; 22:3, etc.), which by their very nature are hard for human judges to punish. If the culprit does not own up, his guilt is unlikely to be proved in a human court. For this reason a divinely executed punishment is threatened.[19]

The types of uncleanness that debar a man from worship are more fully described elsewhere in Leviticus, especially ch. 22. Contact with dead or diseased people, or unclean animals (see ch. 11), or bodily discharges of any sort (chs. 12–15) all bring uncleanness on a person and preclude his participation in a sacrificial meal, until he has purified himself with the appropriate ceremonies.

No Fat or Blood (7:22–27)

The fat of animals that may be sacrificed, oxen, sheep, and goats, belongs to God (v. 23). It must be burned and not eaten. If, however, the animal dies of natural causes, it can no longer be offered in sacrifice, because only unblemished animals are fit for God. In this situation it is not to be wasted. The fat may be used for any purpose apart from being eaten, presumably for lighting, polish, and other household purposes (v. 24). 11:39–40 and 17:15 allow the flesh of such an animal to be eaten, but state that anyone who does so becomes unclean and must wash afterward. Deuteronomy prefers Israel to maintain her holiness unblemished and recommends giving the carcass to the resident alien or selling it to foreigners (Deut. 14:21).

In no circumstances may blood be consumed. Eating *blood* means eating meat from which the blood has not been drained (e.g., 1 Sam. 14:33). Blood is the means of atonement in all the animal sacrifices and may not be eaten (cf. Lev. 17:10ff.). Both prohibitions were difficult to enforce, but divine retribution is threatened against offenders: that person *will be cut off from his people* (vv. 25, 27).

19. On "cutting off" see below on 17:4.

The Priest's Portions of the Peace Offering (7:28–36)

From every sacrifice presented by a layman the officiating priest received something (cf. 6:19 [26]; 7:6ff.). This was the priest's *anointed right* (v. 35): he was entitled to a share in the sacrifices by virtue of his anointing as priest.[20] From the peace offering he was assigned two parts, *the breast* (v. 30) and *the right leg* (v. 33). It is difficult to know precisely which cuts are intended by these terms. The right leg (*shôq*) might indicate the hindquarter, but Deut. 18 speaks of the shoulder (*z^erôa'*), which suggests the forequarter. In a Canaanite temple at Lachish the right forelegs of several different species were found by the altar. In the light of this evidence it seems likely that both Leviticus and Deuteronomy are alluding to a pre-Mosaic custom of donating the right foreleg to the priest. However, Deut. 18:3 specifies the stomach and cheeks instead of the breast, which suggests there was some flexibility later. Modern consumers often prefer cuts from the leg to those from the breast, but whether this was true of the scraggier animals of ancient Israel is unknown.

The breast is said to be a *dedication* (*t^enûpāh*) (v. 30), whereas the leg is described as a *contribution* (*t^erûmāh*) (v. 34). What is the distinction between these terms? According to traditional Jewish exegesis "contribution" (or heaving) was effected by a vertical, up-and-down action, whereas "dedication" (waving) was done with a sideways action. Etymologically this is quite a natural way to interpret these terms, but it fails to explain the difference between them. And in some cases it is hard to envisage any such motion being involved (e.g., Num. 8:13ff.; Ezek. 45:1).

Modern scholars have therefore looked for other explanations of the terms. Vincent[21] suggested that "dedication" was a sacred gift to God and/or his priests, whereas "contribution" was originally a secular tax. Driver[22] denied that there was really any difference between the "contribution" and the "dedication." Milgrom[23] on the other hand believes the "contribution" represented

---

20. Only here does *mishḥāh* (*anointed right*) have the sense of "portion." Elsewhere it always means "anointing, unction" (e.g., 8:2, 10). As the rest of the verse links their entitlement to a share of the sacrifices with their ordination, I have tried to bring out the connection in translation.
21. A. Vincent, in *Mélanges Syriens offerts à R. Dussaud* I (Paris: Geuthner, 1939), pp. 267–272.
22. G. R. Driver, *JSS* 1 (1956), pp. 100–105.
23. J. Milgrom, "The Leg of the Contribution" (Hebrew), *Tarbiz* 42 (1972–73), pp. 1–11; "The Alleged Wave-Offering in Israel and in the Ancient Near East," *IEJ* 22 (1972), pp. 33–38.

the first stage in giving anything to God. Only certain objects underwent a ritual dedicatory ceremony in the sanctuary itself, called "dedication." The many references to these terms in Scripture[24] are compatible with this distinction, but it would be unwise to regard this as proof.

Leviticus 6–7 and the NT

In commenting on 6:2-6, 13-16 (9-13, 20-23), we observed some similarities between the theology of Leviticus and the NT. But compared with some other passages in the book the NT parallels seem sparse. However, do they exhaust the lessons that a Christian may draw from these two chapters?

These chapters were addressed to the priests of ancient Israel, who led and conducted the services and carried out the sacrifices. Though blood sacrifice has been made obsolete under the New Covenant by Christ's death, those who lead the worship of the new Israel of God may still find guidance as to the correct approach and attitude to adopt in divine service, for it is the same God that we address today.

These laws underline that scrupulous attention to detail and punctilious obedience to God's instructions were expected in priest and worshipper, otherwise "the man who offered it will not be accepted" (7:18).

We express respect and reverence in ordinary life by conforming to the conventions of etiquette in our society. These conventions vary from society to society. What may be regarded as politeness in one culture may be thought very rude in another. Our conventions of worship are utterly different from those of ancient Israel, and differ from denomination to denomination. Careful attention to convention may be one way of demonstrating our reverence and love for God. "Let us offer to God acceptable worship with reverence and awe; for our God is a consuming fire" (Heb. 12:28–29). Paul, in rebuking the leaders of the Corinthian church, advises them to lead the worship of the church with order and dignity, "For God is not a God of confusion but of peace" (1 Cor. 14:33).

Calvin commenting says, "Since God prefers obedience to all sacrifices, he was unwilling that anything should remain doubtful as to the external rites, which were not otherwise of great importance;

24. E.g., "contribution"—Exod. 25:2–3; 30:13ff.; Lev. 10:15; 22:12; Num. 31:29, 41, etc.; "dedication"—Exod. 35:22; Lev. 14:12, 21, 24; 23:15, 17, 20; Num. 8:13ff.

that they might learn to observe precisely, and with most exact care, whatever the Law commanded, and that they should not obtrude anything of themselves."[25]

Jesus said that God must be worshipped in spirit and in truth. And it has become commonplace to contrast spirit and form as if they were incompatible in worship. "The letter killeth but the Spirit giveth life" is a text that out of context (2 Cor. 3:6) can be used to justify slapdash leading of services and other Christian activities. Spontaneity and lack of preparation is equated with spirituality. Lev. 6–7 denies this: care and attention to detail are indispensable to the conduct of divine worship. God is more important, more distinguished, worthy of more respect than any man; therefore we should follow his injunctions to the letter, if we respect him.

A glance at the performing arts dispels the illusion that a great and spirited performance can be achieved without practice and attention to detail. Indeed great actors and musicians spend hours studying and rehearsing the works they are to perform, so that they can recapture the spirit of the author and convey it in their performance. Audiences expect performers to aim at perfection in the concert hall. Worship is also a performance, a performance in honor of almighty God. As no orchestra can give of its best without a competent conductor and meticulous rehearsal, so no congregation is likely to worship our holy God in a worthy manner without careful direction by a well-instructed minister.

25. Calvin II, p. 363.

II. INSTITUTION OF THE PRIESTHOOD
(8:1–10:20)

Preliminary Observations

It comes as a surprise to find the laws in Leviticus suddenly interrupted by a long narrative describing the ordination of Aaron and his sons to the priesthood. We tend to think of Leviticus as a law book, not as a history book. But the reverse is really the truth. Leviticus and the other books of the Pentateuch are basically concerned with the history of God's people. They deal with the way God brought them out of Egypt, what happened in the wilderness, how God made a covenant with them, how divine worship was established, and the like. The history provides a setting for the laws, not vice versa.

It is not just that the narrative explains when and why certain laws were given. It does that. But the events are often as important as the laws. God's saving action is just as significant as his word. Biblical revelation is more than the bare communication of truths about God and his will. The Bible affirms that God directed the course of history in order to create a holy people who knew and did his will.

At the heart of this scheme was the establishment of a pure system of worship, in which God could be honored and praised in a fitting manner, and through which human sin could be atoned for. To this end the tabernacle was erected, so that God's presence could become a permanent and living reality in Israel's religious life. The tabernacle was furnished with the ark and altars, and all the other equipment necessary for making atonement. Sacred garments were made for the priests to wear during the sacrifices (Exod. 35–40). Regulations explaining which sacrifices ought to be offered form the subject matter of Lev. 1–7. But there was still no order of priests to

129

carry out the ministry of atonement. Chs. 8–10 tell how the priest-hood was instituted and the first sacrifices offered. The sudden death of two of Aaron's sons underlined the need for holiness among the priests and the necessity of worshipping God only in accordance with the divinely authorized form.

This narrative then deals with a vital stage in the history of redemption. Israel had been constituted as the people of God through the covenant at Sinai. This relationship of grace conferred both privileges and responsibilities. The Israelites were assured of God's blessing so long as they adhered to the terms of the covenant. But if they broke the covenant, they were warned to expect God's judgment. Indeed after the golden calf was made, God threatened to destroy Israel completely (Exod. 32ff.). That episode emphasized the gravity of sin and the need for atonement. Yet one incident was hardly sufficient to change ingrained attitudes that had grown up over many years. A constant reminder of God's presence and holi-ness was needed together with the means of regular atonement for sin. This was provided by the tabernacle and the priesthood. The tabernacle stood in the center of the camp to bring to mind God's glory and holiness, and it served as a center for worship where forgiveness was offered to the people. The inauguration of this priestly ministry in the tabernacle, therefore, constituted a most significant step in the history of the nation.

The purpose of all these sacred institutions is summed up in Exod. 29:43–46. "There (i.e., in the tabernacle) I will meet with the people of Israel, and it shall be sanctified by my glory; I will conse-crate the tent of meeting and the altar; Aaron also and his sons I will consecrate to serve me as priests. And I will dwell among the people of Israel, and I will be their God. And they shall know that I am the Lord their God, who brought them forth out of the land of Egypt that I might dwell among them; I am the Lord their God."

Before we examine the individual paragraphs in detail, some of the broader features of the account deserve attention. The first phrase that ought to be noted is, "as the Lord commanded Moses." Because it is such a commonplace statement in the Pentateuch we are apt to overlook it. But beginning with 7:38, this or a similar phrase recurs with remarkable frequency in these three chapters (8:4, 5, 9, 13, 17, 21, 29, 34, 36; 9:6, 7, 10, 21; 10:7, 13, 15).

In describing the erection of the tabernacle, Exod. 39f. uses the same technique to emphasize the fidelity with which the divine blueprint was carried out. The obedience of Moses and Aaron to

God's word is also underlined by verbal repetition. The command to ordain Aaron and his sons was given in Exod. 28–29. To stress how faithfully these commands were obeyed, they are echoed closely in the account of their fulfilment in these chapters. Practically every verse in ch. 8 is a quotation or adaptation of commands first given in Exod. 29.[1] In ch. 9 we find rather freer summaries of the laws on sacrifice in Lev. 1–7.[2] In this way Moses' strict adherence to God's declared will is emphasized. Following the precise execution of all these commands, and in fulfilment of the divine promise (9:4, 6), "the glory of the Lord appeared to all the people" (9:23). When God's people obey his word, they can expect to enjoy the fulfilment of his promises.

Chapter 10 makes plain that the converse is also true. The precise nature of Nadab and Abihu's offense is obscure, save that their action was such as the Lord "had not commanded them." But this transgression was enough to turn the fire of blessing (9:24) into the fire of judgment (10:2).

Subsequently in chapter 10 we find the surviving priests paying strict attention to God's commands as mediated by Moses (10:3, 5, 6, 7, 8, 11, 12, 13, 16, 18). Again the previous directions about worship are freely quoted and adapted (10:12–15//6:9 (16) and 7:30, 32; 10:17–18//6:19 (26), 23 (30).

The second remarkable thing about this episode emerges if it is recalled what happened between the giving of the instructions about the appointment of priests (Exod. 29) and their fulfilment in Lev. 8–10. The plans for erecting the tabernacle and installing Aaron as high priest were interrupted by the production of the golden calf. According to Exod. 32 Aaron was not the instigator of this idea, but a very willing accessory. Only through Moses' intercession were the whole people of Israel including Aaron saved from destruction by God's wrath. Exod. 35ff. told how the tabernacle was built in accordance with the original plan. Though the garments for Aaron had been made, Aaron played no part in dedicating the tabernacle in Exod. 40. We are left in suspense. Will Aaron be allowed to become high priest, or is he permanently debarred from that office as a result of the golden calf?

1. Exod. 29:1ff.//Lev. 8:2; 29:4ff.//8:6ff.; 29:7//8:12; 40:9–11//8:10–11; 29:8–9//8:13; 29:10–14//8:14–17; 29:15–18//8:18–21; 29:19–20//8:22–24; 29:22–25//8:25–28; 29:26//8:29; 29:21//8:30; 29:31–32//8:31; 29:34//8:32; 29:35–37//8:33–35.
2. Lev. 9:8ff., cf. 4:3ff.; 9:12–14//1:3–9 (9:15–17); 9:18–21//3:2–5 and 7:30, 33. For discussion of the technical sacrificial terms used in chs. 8–9 see the earlier parallel passages.

The account of his ordination resolves our doubts. God's grace and forgiveness are such that even a sinner like Aaron may be appointed to the highest religious office in the nation. Perhaps the closest biblical parallel to Aaron's experience was that of Peter. In spite of his threefold denial of his Lord at Christ's trial, he was reinstated as leader of the apostles after the resurrection.

The third recurrent feature of this narrative is the centrality of Moses. He is the principal actor in the story. He is the mediator between God and the newly ordained priesthood. He is a priest before the high priest was ordained. The special and unique role of Moses in this story is not peculiar to it; it emerges in many other parts of the Pentateuch. But because his role is so obvious, that does not mean it is therefore unimportant. On the contrary the frequent references to Moses show the prominent place he occupied in the divine economy of salvation. He is the one whom God addressed to make his will known to the people and to Aaron (8:1, 5, 9, 13, 21, 29, 31, 34ff.; 9:6, 7, 10; 10:3). Rarely does God address Aaron alone. Usually it is through, or with, Moses. Here we see Moses as a prophet directly in touch with God and passing on God's will to the people. Such is Moses' authority that a command from him is treated as though it were from God, even when its divine origin is not explicitly referred to (10:4, 6–7; cf. vv. 3, 12). When Moses is satisfied with Aaron's behavior, it is assumed that God is (10:19–20).

Another aspect of the mediatorial prophetic role of Moses is the part he plays in the ordination of Aaron. Since Aaron has no predecessor as high priest, he must be ordained on the explicit instruction of God as mediated by Moses. Moses has to lead the ceremony, there being no other priest who could do so. In the ordination service a ram was offered as a peace offering (8:22ff.). In normal circumstances when a ram was offered, the officiating priest received the breast and the right thigh and various cakes as his portion (7:11ff.), but in this case the perquisites are shared between Moses and God. Moses receives the breast as his share (8:29) and the rest is burned (8:28). In this symbolic fashion it is made clear that God and Moses are involved in instituting the priesthood.

The Structure of Leviticus 8–10

In the legal material in Leviticus a tendency to arrange the laws in groups of three has been noted. This narrative section likewise falls into three scenes.

    (1) Ordination of Aaron and his sons—day 1 (ch. 8)

    (2) Ordination of Aaron—day 8: Aaron's first sacrifices ac-

cepted (ch. 9)

(3) Aaron's sons' offerings rejected (ch. 10)

Each scene to some extent parallels the preceding one in form and content and to some extent contrasts with it. We have here a literary triptych, i.e, three pictures designed to hang together so as to illuminate and enrich the meaning of each other. Musically one could describe it as a theme and two variations. This technique of panel-writing has been noted in other passages in the Pentateuch.[3]

An outline analysis of the chapter may exhibit some aspects of this method of story-telling. Other points will be noted in the detailed analysis of each chapter and in the commentary on them.

Chapter 8	Chapter 9	Chapter 10
1 The Lord tells M	2 M tells A	
2 "Take"	2 "Take"	
4 M did as commanded	5 took as commanded	1 took not commanded
		2 fire from the Lord (cf. 9:24)
5 M says: "This is the thing"	6 M says: "This is the thing"	3 M says: "That is what"
6 M brings near A and his sons	7 M says to A: "Draw near and do"	4 M says to A's cousins: "Carry out A's sons"
7 M clothes A		6 M says to A: "Do not tear clothes"
12 M anoints A		7 Stay in sanctuary (cf. 8:33) anointing oil
14 M offers purification offering	8 A offers his purification offering	8 The Lord tells A
18 M offers burnt offering	12 A offers his burnt offering	10 Distinguish holy, etc.
	15 A offers people's purification offering	
	16 A offers people's burnt offering	
22 M offers peace offering	18 A offers people's peace offering	
31 M tells A and sons: "Eat in sanctuary"		12 M tells A and sons: "Eat in sanctuary"
33 Stay in sanctuary	22 Blessing, fire from the Lord	20 M satisfied

Chapter 8 is a well-structured unit in its own right, and is discussed below. What should be noticed at this point is its relationship with

---

3. See S. E. McEvenue, *The Narrative Style of the Priestly Writer*, pp. 158ff.

the two following chapters. In ch. 8 Moses acts as priest: in the
sacrifices he undertakes all the priestly duties specified in chs. 1–7.
He manipulates the blood (8:15, 19, 23), burns the fat pieces (vv. 16,
20, 28), and receives the priestly portion of the breast (v. 29). Aaron
and his sons, on the other hand, undertake some of the jobs usually
assigned to the laity, such as laying their hands on the animals and
killing them (vv. 14–15, 18–19). Until the ordination ceremony was
complete, Moses had to act as priest.

Chapter 9 describes a very similar sequence of events, but
this time Aaron occupies the center of the stage. He offers the
sacrifices, first for himself (vv. 8ff.) and then for the people
(vv. 15ff.). As the properly constituted high priest he is now entitled
to undertake these duties. Moses can step down from acting as high
priest, and merely mediates God's instructions to Aaron as to what
to do and when (vv. 2, 7). The scene concludes with a public display
of approval on Aaron's first sacrifices. Moses and Aaron go together
into the tent of meeting, bless the people, and then God's glory
appears in the form of fire burning up the sacrifices (vv. 22–24), as
had been promised (vv. 4, 6).

Throughout chs. 8 and 9 the obedience of Moses and Aaron is
constantly stressed (8:4, 9, 13, 17, 21, 29, 36; 9:5, 7, 10, 21). Every
step they take is in obedience to a divine command directly given or
mediated by Moses. Both chapters open with such a word (v. 2). But
the action in ch. 10 commences without any divine directives. In
language very reminiscent of ch. 8 we learn of Nadab and Abihu
taking the initiative themselves. The alert listener or reader at once
senses that there is something wrong. This scene does not begin like
the previous two. It is structured differently. Almost immediately
the narrative explains what is wrong: the fire they offered was "not
commanded." Our unease turns rapidly into shock. "Fire came
from before the Lord" (v. 2). In the previous scene (9:24) this was
the ultimate proof that God had graciously accepted Aaron's sacrifice, a sign that came only at the end of his first day's duties. Here
in contrast God's presence is manifest almost immediately, not in
grace burning up the sacrifice, but in judgment slaying the overcon-
fident young men.

The drastic rearrangement of the formal pattern of chs. 8–9
found in the opening of ch. 10 complements and reinforces the
message of the content of this chapter. By doing what had not been
commanded Nadab and Abihu turned their theological world upside
down. The narrator draws attention to this confusion by upsetting
the narrative structure established in chs. 8 and 9.

Various features in the rest of ch. 10 recall ideas from the previous two (see table), but only slowly does the structure of the narrative revert to the patterns found in chs. 8–9. Like ch. 8, ch. 10 (vv. 12–19) ends with instructions about eating the sacrificial meat in a holy place. The old pattern has reappeared, giving the reader a feeling of security and normality, reinforced by the closing remark: "Moses was satisfied" (v. 20).

A. ORDINATION OF AARON AND HIS SONS (CH. 8)

1 *The Lord spoke to Moses as follows:*

2 *"Take Aaron and his sons, the garments, the anointing oil, the bull for the purification offering, the two rams and the basket of unleavened bread,*

3 *and assemble the whole congregation in the enclosure of the tent of meeting."*

4 *So Moses did as the Lord commanded him, and the congregation assembled in the enclosure of the tent of meeting.*

5 *Then Moses said to the congregation: "This is the thing that the Lord has commanded to be done."*

6 *Then Moses presented Aaron and his sons and bathed them in water.*

7 *He put the shirt and sash on him, dressed him in the cape and put on the ephod and fastened it with the elaborately worked belt of the ephod.*

8 *Then he placed the breast plate on him and put the Urim and Thummim into it.*

9 *Then he placed the turban on his head, and on the turban above his face he placed the gold rosette, as a symbol of holiness, as the Lord had commanded Moses.*

10 *Then Moses took the anointing oil and anointed the tabernacle and all that was in it and sanctified them.*

11 *He sprinkled some of it seven times over the altar, and anointed the altar, all its vessels, the laver and its stand to sanctify them.*

12 *He then poured some of the anointing oil over the head of Aaron and anointed him to sanctify him.*

13 *Then Moses presented the sons of Aaron, and dressed them in their shirts and tied on their sashes and fixed their caps on, as the Lord had commanded Moses.*

14 *Then he brought forward the bull for the purification offering, and Aaron and his sons laid their hands on the head of the purification offering bull.*

15 *Then he killed it, and Moses took (some of) the blood and put it with his finger on and around the horns of the altar and cleansed the altar from sin, and (the rest of) the blood he poured out at the foot of the altar, and he sanctified it by making atonement for it.*

16 *Then he took all the fat over the intestines, the long lobe of the liver, the two kidneys and their fat, and Moses burned them on the altar.*

17 *But the rest of the bull, namely its skin, meat, and dung, was burned*

135

in a fire outside the camp, as the Lord had commanded Moses.

18 Then the ram for the burnt offering was presented and Aaron and his sons laid their hands on the ram's head.

19 Then he killed it and Moses splashed the blood over the altar.

20 He chopped up the ram into pieces, and Moses burned them, the head, the pieces, and the fat.

21 But he washed the intestines and hind legs with water, and Moses burned the whole ram on the altar. It was a burnt offering producing a soothing aroma, a food offering to the Lord, as the Lord had commanded Moses.

22 Then the second ram, the ordination ram, was presented and Aaron and his sons laid their hands on the head of the ram.

23 Then he killed the ram, and Moses took some of the blood and put it on the lobe of Aaron's right ear, on his right thumb, and on his right big toe.

24 Then the sons of Aaron were presented, and Moses put some of the blood on the lobes of their right ears, on their thumbs, and on their big toes, and Moses splashed the rest of the blood over the altar.

25 Then he took the fat, the fat tail, all the fat over the intestines, the long lobe of the liver, the two kidneys and their fat, and the right thigh;

26 and from the basket of unleavened bread which was before the Lord he took one unleavened cake, one cake made of bread and oil, and one wafer, and he placed them on top of the fat pieces and the right thigh.

27 Then he put the whole lot into the hands of Aaron and his sons, and he dedicated them as a dedication before the Lord.

28 Then Moses took them out of their hands and burned them on the altar on top of the burnt offering: they made up the ordination offering producing a soothing aroma, a food offering to the Lord.

29 Then Moses took the breast and dedicated it as a dedication before the Lord: it became Moses' portion from the ordination ram, as the Lord had commanded Moses.

30 Then Moses took some of the anointing oil and some of the blood which was on the altar and sprinkled it over Aaron on his clothes and over his sons and their clothes and he sanctified Aaron, his clothes, his sons, and their clothes.

31 Then Moses said to Aaron, "Cook the meat in the enclosure of the tent of meeting and eat it there, as well as the bread which is in the basket of ordination offerings, as I commanded, 'Let Aaron and his sons eat it.'

32 But the rest of the meat and bread must be burned with fire.

33 For seven days you must not leave the enclosure of the tent of meeting, until the period of your ordination is fulfilled, because your ordination takes seven days.

34 As has been done today, the Lord has commanded to be done to make atonement for you.

35 You must stay in the enclosure of the tent of meeting day and night for seven days and keep the Lord's watch, so that you do not die; for

thus I have been commanded."
36 *Aaron and his sons did all these things which the Lord commanded them through Moses.*

The Structure of Leviticus 8

The narrative presupposes a knowledge of the more detailed instructions found in Exod. 29. The frequent refrain, "as the Lord commanded," and the introductory remarks "The Lord spoke" provide clues to the organization of the material.

1–3	God's double command to Moses	
	2 Take Aaron, clothes, oil, etc.	A
	3 Assemble congregation	B
4–30	Moses' obedience	
	4–5 Congregation assembled	B
	6–9 Aaron's clothes put on	
	10–13 Aaron anointed	
	14–17 Purification offering	A
	18–21 Burnt offering	
	22–30 Peace offering	
31–35	Moses' command to Aaron	
36	Aaron's obedience	

The chiastic arrangement (AB–BA) of the material in vv. 2–30 should be noted. In God's command the instructions about Aaron and his clothes and so on (v. 2) precede the injunction to assemble the congregation (v. 3). In the description of Moses' obedience this order is reversed. Chiasmus brings out the unity of these events. The closing verses (31–36) bridge the gap between the first day of Aaron's ordination (8:33) and its completion a week later (9:1), and also link this chapter with the dominant concern of chs. 6–7, how priestly food should be eaten.

The Congregation Assembled (1–5)

The high-priesthood was the most holy office in Israel, and a man could be appointed to this job only if he had been called of God and had then submitted to the rites of ordination. These involved both the offering of sacrifice and anointing with oil, and had been specified in detail in Exod. 29. Now all that was necessary was a brief reminder of what had to be done (vv. 2–3).

Moses may have been told privately to ordain Aaron, but the ceremony was of such significance that it had to be carried out in public. *The whole congregation*[4] (v. 3, cf. 4–5), that is to say, the body of elders representing all Israel, were summoned to witness the ordination in *the enclosure of the tent of meeting*. This phrase has elsewhere been translated "entrance of the tent of meeting" (cf. 1:3; 3:2; 4:4, etc.). But here and in vv. 33, 35 it seems to designate more than the curtained doorway into the holy place, or even the the area immediately in front of the doorway, and possibly refers to the whole tabernacle precinct, which was separated off from the camp by curtains. We may picture all the "congregation" gathered around the great bronze altar to watch the service.

Other momentous occasions in the history of the nation witnessed by the congregation included the invitation to bring gifts to build the tabernacle (Exod. 35:1), the national census (Num. 1:18), the dedication of the Levites (Num. 8:9), and the water from the rock (Num. 20:8). These milestones had to be observed by all the national leaders.

Aaron's Uniform (6–9)

Modern society uses uniforms rarely and finds difficulty in seeing any point in them at all unless it be sentimental attachment to old-fashioned custom. Even those homes of archaic practices, the church and the universities, are discarding or minimizing their use of traditional robes. It is the more important therefore to think carefully why uniforms were used in the past, if we are to understand this passage.

Essentially a uniform draws attention to the office or function of a person, as opposed to his individual personality. It emphasizes his job rather than his name. In Britain the mayor wears a chain, the judge wears a wig, the policeman wears a blue helmet, and the clergyman a clerical collar. A uniform enables the rest of society to identify immediately figures of authority, and to pay them appropriate respect. Furthermore we can see that, in general, the more prestigious the office, the more splendid the uniform. The crack guards regiments in the British army have a more striking ceremonial uniform than other army units. In general Ph.D. hoods and gowns are much more colorful and expensive than B.A. robes. Cardinals dress more splendidly than parish priests.

Aaron's priestly robes are fully described in Exod. 28 and 39. Here we are simply told that in obedience to God's command these

4. On "congregation" see above on 4:13.

dazzling garments were now put on Aaron. In putting on these clothes he took to himself all the honor and glory of the high-priesthood. In a religion the principal doctrine of which was the holiness of God, the high priest, who mediated atonement between God and man, was an extremely important person. His glorious clothing symbolized the significance of his office. Probably symbolic significance was also attached to individual items in the priestly attire, but that now escapes us.[5]

Moses *bathed Aaron and his sons in water* (v. 6) as was prescribed in Exod. 29:4. But according to Exod. 30:17ff. the priests had to wash themselves every time they went on duty in the taber-nacle (cf. Lev. 16:4). Washing also ensured cleansing after a cure from "leprosy" (Lev. 14:8–9) and after bodily discharges (Lev. 15). Washing in the Bible is an outward physical action representing the desire for an inner spiritual cleansing, as the coupling "clean hands and a pure heart" (Ps. 24:4; 73:13; Isa. 1:16) makes clear.

The shirt was a long undergarment worn next to the skin. It was also worn by laymen (Gen. 37:32) and ordinary priests (Exod. 39:27). The priests' shirts were made of fine linen (Exod. 28:39). The *sash* was long and embroidered, and tied around the waist (Exod. 28:39). *The cape* was a specifically high-priestly vestment (Exod. 28:31–34; 39:22–26). It was made of blue material and was worn over the "shirt" like a poncho. *The ephod,* described in some detail in Exod. 28:5ff.,[6] seems to have been a sort of vest (waistcoat) worn over the cape. It supported the *breast plate,* the most striking piece of the high priest's outfit. The breast plate (described in Exod. 28:15ff.) was about 10″ (25 cm.) square, made of similar material to the ephod, and was studded with jewels symboliz-ing the tribes of Israel. In it there was a pouch for the Urim and Thummim (v. 8). These are Hebrew words which literally mean "lights and perfections." Since we are ignorant of their precise nature, the Hebrew words are usually left untranslated. They seem to be some sort of dice by which God's will was made known. They were capable of giving a positive, negative, or neutral reply to a question. The king or leader of the nation would ask the priest

---

5. Keil, *Biblical Archaeology* I, pp. 216ff., offers a possible interpretation of the symbolism associated with the high priest.
6. Other ephods are mentioned in Judg. 8:27; 17:5; 18:17ff.; 1 Sam. 2:28; 14:3; 21:10 (Eng. 9); 22:18; 23:9; 30:7. Many scholars suggest that these ephods were different in design from the priestly vestment, yet they had important features in common with the high priest's. They were made of valuable materials, they housed the Urim and Thummim, and were used for divination.

whether a proposed course of action was approved by God and would meet with success. We read of the Urim and Thummim being consulted on various occasions in early Israel, but by postexilic times they had dropped out of use (Num. 27:21; Deut. 33:8; 1 Sam. 14:41 (LXX); cf. 23:9–10; 28:6; Ezra 2:63; Neh. 7:65).

The *turban* was made out of blue material and attached to it was a golden plate on which were inscribed the words "Holy to the Lord" (Exod. 28:36ff.), described here as the *gold rosette . . . a symbol of holiness.*[7]

These beautiful vestments drew attention to the supreme dignity and holiness of the high-priestly office. He was the mediator between God and man. He secured atonement for the nation's sin, and his costly garments symbolized the value of his ministry to the nation.

The NT insists that the high-priesthood of Christ is far superior to that of Aaron (Heb. 4:14ff.). As Aaron in OT times entered the tabernacle with the gold rosette on his head so that Israel could be accepted, so Christ entered heaven and ever lives to make intercession for us. The book of Revelation takes up the symbolism of clothes to stress the worth of Christ's ministry for his people. He is clothed with a long robe ("cape") and with a girdle ("sash") round his breast (Rev. 1:13).

The nation of Israel as a whole was called to be a kingdom of priests (Exod. 19:6), and the church is also (1 Pet. 2:5; Rev. 1:6). Israel could see in the glorious figure of the high priest the personal embodiment of all that the nation ought to be both individually and corporately. In a similar way the Christian is called to look at Christ and imitate his deeds and attitudes. Clothing metaphors are frequently used therefore to describe these Christian virtues. "Put on the breastplate of faith and love, and for a helmet the hope of salvation" (1 Thess. 5:8). "Put on then . . . compassion, kindness, lowliness, meekness and patience" (Col. 3:12).

The Anointing (10–13)

In further obedience to God's commands (Exod. 40:9–11), Moses

---

7. *Rosette.* Heb. *tsîts* (lit. "flower"), traditionally supposed to have been in the form of a narrow band, hence the older translation "plate." *Symbol of holiness* (*nēzer haqqōḏeš*) could be translated "crown of holiness," "holy crown" (RSV). *Symbol of holiness* (cf. NEB "symbol of holy dedication," TEV "sacred sign of dedication") reverts to the interpretation of the LXX and Vulgate, a crown being a symbol of dedication to high office.

now carries out various ceremonies with the special oil, anointing various items in the tabernacle and Aaron himself. The recipe for this oil is given in Exod. 30:23ff. By pouring oil on these things he dedicated them to God's service. When Saul and David were anointed king, the Spirit came upon them (1 Sam. 10:1ff.; 16:13). Similarly Isa. 61:1 says, "the Spirit of the Lord God is upon me, because the Lord has anointed me." Since the Spirit brings unity and blessing, this may explain the reference to this ceremony in Ps. 133.

The *laver* (v. 11) was a large basin in which the priests had to wash before they began divine worship (Exod. 30:17ff.; 38:8). Both people and things are dedicated to God through ceremonial anointing with oil.

13 The sons of Aaron are appointed to the priesthood. They wear a simpler version of the high-priestly garments. No mention is made of their wearing an ephod, breastplate, or rosette.

The Purification Offering (14–17)

If God was to be present at the sacrifices offered by the priests, his sanctuary had to be purged from sin's pollution, specifically of those pollutions introduced by the priests themselves. To this end, the first sacrifice was a purification offering on behalf of Aaron and his sons: they lay their hands on the bull (v. 14). The sacrifice follows exactly the instructions in Exod. 29:10–14, and is very similar to the ritual laid down for a priest's purification offering in Lev. 4. Here, however, Moses officiates in place of the priests, who are yet to be ordained, and the blood is smeared on the altar of burnt offering rather than on the veil and altar of incense (Lev. 4:6–7).

We have argued that the blood purifies the object on which it is smeared, and this is confirmed in v. 15, *and cleansed*[8] *the altar from sin*. Why was it thought necessary to purify the outer altar of burnt offering at this stage rather than the inner altar of incense? The narrative does not make it clear. Perhaps it was because the priests had yet to enter the inner sanctuary, and as a result they had not polluted it; or perhaps it was because they were about to offer a burnt offering on this altar, and it was necessary to purify it beforehand.

---

8. *Ḥiṭṭēʾ*, "to de-sin, cleanse." So Levine, *Presence of the Lord*, p. 101. Cf. 6:19 (Eng. 26); 9:15; 14:49, 52.

The Burnt Offering (18–21)

This sacrifice follows the instructions given in Exod. 29:15–18 and the ritual of Lev. 1. Once again the unusual feature is that it is Moses who performs the priestly side of the ritual and the priests-to-be take the part of the ordinary worshipper[9] (cf. vv. 15ff.). Here Aaron and his sons seek reconciliation with God by offering up a ram in their place as a ransom for their sins. In identifying themselves with the immolated animal they dedicate themselves to God. In Paul's phrase, they died unto sin that they might live unto righteousness (Rom. 6:5ff.).

The Ordination Peace Offering (22–30)

This follows the prescriptions of Exod. 29:19ff. and broadly corresponds to the ritual for the peace offering outlined in Lev. 3. As in the earlier sacrifices, Moses fulfils the priest's role and takes the *breast . . . as a dedication,*[10] that is, the part of the animal that was normally assigned to the priest (v. 29). In the standard peace offering the priests also received the right thigh. On this occasion the *right thigh* was included in God's portion burned on the altar (v. 25). Perhaps this distribution of the priestly perquisites represents the idea that the ordination of Aaron is carried out jointly by God and Moses.

The most striking divergence from the usual procedure with peace offerings is to be found in the treatment of the *blood.* Normally the blood was thrown against the altar (Lev. 3:2, 8, 13), but in this case some of it is smeared on the right ear, right thumb, and right toe and on the clothes of Aaron and his sons (vv. 23–24, 30). The rest of the blood was thrown on the altar as usual.

There are several levels of meaning in this ritual. That Aaron and the altar are both anointed first with oil and then with blood symbolizes the intimate connection of the priesthood with sacrifice. Through the blood from the altar Aaron is ordained to offer sacrifice at the altar.

9. N.b. RSV "Moses killed" (vv. 15, 19, 23) is incorrect. The subject is unnamed, and by analogy with chs. 1 and 4 it should be presumed that the offerer, i.e., Aaron, killed, chopped up, and washed the animal. V. W. Turner (*The Ritual Process;* London: Routledge and Kegan Paul, 1969, pp. 94ff.) has observed that installation rituals often contain an element in which the man being elevated to high office has to do something humiliating that he will never have to do again once he is installed.

However, *was burned with fire* (v. 17) appears to be an impersonal use of the third singular active "he burned" (cf. vv. 18, 22, 24), since Aaron was confined to the tabernacle court (vv. 31–35).
10. On this term cf. 7:30.

Other parallels to this ceremony point to another level of meaning. The cleansed "leper" offers a reparation offering, and blood from it is smeared on his right ear, thumb, and toe (Lev. 14:14). Here the altar represents the divine and the blood-smearing rite indicates the "leper" is now back in communion with God. A similar interpretation fits the ceremonies ratifying the Sinai Covenant described in Exod. 24. The blood indicates that in the covenant Israel has become the people of God. So here the blood links God and Aaron, showing in a visible way that he is now God's man, his special representative among Israel.

Finally, peace offerings were offered for confession or sealing a vow (cf. 7:12ff.), and this allows a third interpretation of the rite. In the first case the blood could have served to purify Aaron and his sons from the pollution of sin, sanctifying them so that they were fit to enter God's presence. In the second it may have served to seal their ordination vows.

All the evidence points toward the former interpretation. Verse 30 states that the oil and blood "sanctified Aaron and his clothes." Exod. 29:34 insists that any meat left over from the offering till the second day must be burned. This is compatible with its being a confession peace offering but not with a vow. Further, there is no mention in the text of vows forming part of the ordination rites. If, then, this peace offering was essentially confessional, what was the content of Aaron's confession? We cannot be certain, but it may have consisted of a confession of God's mercy in choosing Aaron to be high priest and a prayer that he would be blessed in his ministry.

Only the tip of the *right ear,* the *thumb* of the right hand, and *big toe* of the right foot are smeared with blood. Why should these points of his body be singled out for purification? It is an example of a part standing for the whole: the righthand side was considered the more important and favored side (Gen. 48:17ff.; Matt. 25:34, 41). "The priest must have consecrated ears ever to listen to God's holy voice; consecrated hands at all times to do holy deeds; and consecrated feet to walk evermore in holy ways."[11]

Further Instruction to Aaron (31–36)

Verses 31–36 summarize the instructions already given in Exod. 29:31ff. Though Aaron and his sons in this sacrifice are in the role of worshippers rather than priests, they are told that they must

11. Dillmann, p. 465.

eat the flesh of the peace offering within the precincts of the tabernacle. For lay worshippers it was not specified where they should eat the peace offerings. Aaron and his sons are being ordained to the priesthood, therefore they must eat the flesh of the sacrifice in the holy place.

For seven days (vv. 33, 35)—A man may defile himself in a moment, but sanctification and the removal of uncleanness is generally a slower process. After healing from serious skin diseases or bodily discharges a seven-day transition period is prescribed (14:8ff.; 15:13–14, 28–29). Other events of great significance were also marked by a seven-day break from the normal social contacts (e.g., birth, Lev. 12, cf. Gen. 17; marriage, Gen. 29:27; and mourning, Gen. 50:10).

According to Exod. 29:35 a bull was to be offered on each of the following six days as a purification offering.[12] This may also have been accompanied by the daily burnt offerings as specified in Exod. 29:38ff. Rather uncharacteristically Lev. 8 does not make it clear whether these instructions were fulfilled to the letter, but that may be the implication of vv. 35–36. A warning is given about the necessity of exact obedience to divine prescriptions for worship: *Keep the Lord's watch, so that you do not die.*[13] It was not the first time such a warning had been given (see Exod. 19:21). That warning is repeated here. It anticipates and explains the disaster that overtook Nadab and Abihu, who presumed to offer fire "which he had not commanded."

Leviticus 8 and the NT

In this section one doctrine emerges very clearly: the universality and pervasiveness of sin. The men chosen to minister to God in the tabernacle pollute the tabernacle and therefore purification offerings have to be offered. Their clothes and bodies are stained with sin and they must be smeared with blood to purify them. These sacrifices are not offered just once; they have to be repeated, because sin is deep-rooted in human nature and often recurs. There is no once-for-

12. Keil (*Biblical Archaeology* I, 226 n. 3) argues that the peace offering and the anointing of the priests and altar were repeated each day for a week. This is a possible reading of the text, but, in my opinion, not the most likely.
13. Milgrom, *Studies*, p. 10, regards this as a reference to the priests' duty to guard the sanctuary, but it may be a more general injunction to obey strictly God's commands; cf. RSV, "performing what the Lord has charged."

all cleansing known to the OT. It is the incorrigibility of the human
heart that these ordination ceremonies bring into focus. In the words
of the psalmist,

> They have all gone astray,
> they are all alike corrupt;
> there is none that does good,
> no, not one.
> Ps. 14:3; cf. Rom. 2–3

The sinfulness of the priests and the ineffectiveness of their
sacrifices to remove sin is one of the main themes of Hebrews (see
Heb. 5–10). Christ's coming achieved all that the old priests
attempted.

"He has no need, like those high priests, to offer sacrifices
daily, first for his own sins and then for those of the people; he did
this once for all when he offered up himself" (Heb. 7:27). Like
Aaron, Christian people still need a daily forgiveness of their sin
(1 John 1:8–9), but unlike him they do not need to offer animal
sacrifice, for "the blood of Jesus cleanses us from all sin"
(1 John 1:7).

Another point clearly made in this chapter is the unique
mediatorial role of Moses. He is the priest who ordains Aaron. He is
the prophet who declares God's will to Aaron. In Deut. 18:15 Moses
says, "The Lord your God will raise up for you a prophet like me."
For the NT writers this prophet is Christ (Acts 3:22). Like Moses
Jesus declared God's will to men (John 1:17–18; 5:30ff.). Like
Moses, who appointed Aaron "to instruct the Israelites" (10:11), the
Lord chose his apostles to "go to the lost sheep of the house of
Israel" and to "preach" (Matt. 10:6–7). These men in their turn
continued the practice of calling and ordaining successors, often
picked out by prophecy, to continue the work of teaching and
preaching the gospel (Acts 13:1–3; 1 Tim. 1:18; 3:1ff.; 4:11ff., etc.).

B. AARON'S FIRST SACRIFICES (CH. 9)

1 *On the eighth day Moses called Aaron and his sons and the elders of
   Israel,*
2 *and he said to Aaron, "Take for yourself a perfect bull calf for a
   purification offering and a perfect ram for a burnt offering and offer
   them before the Lord.*
3 *Speak to the Israelites as follows: "Take a male goat for a purifica-*

145

tion offering and a perfect one-year-old calf and lamb for a burnt
offering,

4 and an ox and a ram to sacrifice them before the Lord as a peace
offering, and a cereal offering mixed with oil, for today the Lord is to
appear to you.' "

5 Then they took what Moses had commanded before the tent of
meeting, and all the congregation approached and stood before the
Lord.

6 Then Moses said: "This is the thing that the Lord has commanded
that you should do in order that the glory of the Lord may appear to
you."

7 Then Moses said to Aaron, "Approach the altar and make your
purification offering and burnt offering, and make atonement for
yourself and for the people, and make the people's offering and
make atonement for them, as the Lord has commanded."

8 Then Aaron approached the altar and killed the calf of the purification offering that was for himself.

9 Then the sons of Aaron presented the blood to him, and he dipped
his finger in the blood and put it on the horns of the altar, but the rest
of the blood he poured out at the foot of the altar.

10 He burned on the altar the fat, the kidneys, and the long lobe of the
liver which came from the purification offering, as the Lord had
commanded Moses.

11 But the meat and the skin he burned with fire outside the camp.

12 Then he killed the burnt offering, and the sons of Aaron presented
the blood to him and he splashed it over the altar.

13 Then they handed the burnt offering to him, piece by piece, and also
the head, and he burned them on the altar.

14 Then he washed the intestines and the hind legs and burned them on
the altar on top of the burnt offering.

15 Then he presented the people's offering. He took the goat of the
purification offering which was for the people, and killed it and
made cleansing for sin as with the previous one.

16 Then he presented the burnt offering and did it according to the
regulations.

17 Then he presented the cereal offering, took a handful from it, and
burned it on the altar beside the morning burnt offering.

18 Then he killed the ox and the ram of the peace offerings for the
people. The sons of Aaron presented the blood to him, and he
splashed it over the altar.

19 But as for the fat from the ox and the ram, the fat tail, the fat
covering the intestines, the kidneys, the long lobe of the liver,

20 they placed the(se) fat pieces on top of the breasts and burned the
fat pieces on the altar.

21 But he dedicated as a dedication before the Lord the breasts and the
right thigh, as Moses had commanded.

22 Then Aaron lifted up his hands toward the people and blessed them.
Then he came down from doing the purification offering, burnt
offering, and peace offering.

23 *Then Moses and Aaron entered the tent of meeting, came out again,*
and blessed the people. Then the glory of the Lord appeared to all
the people.

24 *Fire came from before the Lord and consumed upon the altar the*
burnt offering and the fat pieces. When all the people saw it, they
shouted aloud and fell on their faces.

Aaron's First Sacrifices (Lev. 9)

After a week of ordination services Aaron is now fully approved as
high priest. No longer does he have to rely on Moses to offer
sacrifices on his behalf. He is now qualified to offer them himself.
This chapter tells of the first services which Aaron conducted.

The service described here bears some resemblance to that of
the day of atonement mentioned in Lev. 16. On both occasions two
sets of sacrifice were brought, first some on behalf of the priests,
then others on behalf of all the people. On this occasion, though, there
was no scapegoat, but instead peace offerings. This made it a more
festive occasion than the day of atonement.

The Structure of Leviticus 9

As has already been pointed out (see above, "The Structure of
Leviticus 8–10"), the structure of this chapter closely resembles
that of the preceding one and gains much of its significance through
contrast with it. On the same criteria as used in ch. 8, this chapter
divides as follows:

1–4	Moses' command to Aaron and the congregation
5–6	The congregation obeys
7	Moses' command to Aaron
8–21	Aaron obeys
	8–11 by offering his purification offering
	12–21 by offering other sacrifices
22–24	Fire from the Lord

Moses' Commands to Aaron and the Congregation (1–4)

On the eighth day (v. 1), exactly a week after the sacrifices described in ch. 8, Aaron was ready to begin his priestly ministry. But
even the high priest was subject to Moses, the prophetic mediator
between God and man. Moses is said to have told or commanded
what should be done some five times in seven verses (9:1, 2, 5, 6, 7).
The elders of Israel are summoned to join in the worship (v. 1). They

seem to be roughly identical with the *congregation*[1] in v. 5 (cf. 8:3–5).

Take for yourself a perfect bull calf (v. 2). Jewish commentators have long noted the irony of this command to Aaron. The first sacrifice he has to offer is a calf, as if to atone for his sin in making the golden calf (Exod. 32), while the ram for a burnt offering recalls the same animal offered by Abraham instead of Isaac (Gen. 22). The sinfulness of man is certainly underlined by this command. For seven days sacrifices have been offered to purge Aaron's sins in the ordination service. Yet in the first services that he conducts Aaron offers sacrifice both on his own and the people's behalf.

The purpose of these sacrifices is twice stated: *for today the Lord is to appear to you* (v. 4);[2] *in order that the glory of the Lord may appear to you* (v. 6).[3] *The glory of the Lord* is God's visible presence among his people. It is described in Exod. 24:16–17: "The glory of the Lord settled on Mount Sinai and the cloud covered it six days. . . . Now the appearance of the glory of the Lord was like a devouring fire on the top of the mountain." "The glory of the Lord" seems to be an alternative way of describing the pillar of cloud and fire that regularly accompanied Israel through her pilgrimage in the wilderness (Num. 14:10ff.). It appeared on Mount Sinai, at the completion of the tabernacle, and at other great historic occasions. But God's glory was not always present in the tabernacle, absenting itself from time to time (Exod. 40:34ff.). The return of God in his glory was always something to be looked for. There was a recognition that if God was not present in the tabernacle then all worship there was meaningless. These sacrifices are designed to make fellowship between God and man possible again.

The Congregation Obeys (5–6)

They took (v. 5) exactly echoes the command in v. 3.

This is the thing that the Lord has commanded (v. 6). Cf. 8:5. The similarity in phraseology draws attention to the similarity between the first and last days of Aaron's ordination. But this time *the glory* will appear (v. 6).

---

1. On the meaning of "congregation" see on 4:13–14.
2. The Hebrew verb form here is unusual, in that perfect forms rarely have a future meaning. *Nir'āh* would normally be translated "has appeared" but the context here demands "is to appear." Alternatively the participle *nir'eh* may be intended.
3. "In order that"; weak *waw* with imperfect has final force (GK 165a).

Moses' Command to Aaron (7)

This supplementary command serves to specify more precisely the order in which the various sacrifices mentioned in vv. 2–3 were to be offered. The sacrifices on behalf of the priests were to be presented before the sacrifices for the people.

Aaron Obeys (8–21)

Although purification and burnt offerings had been offered for Aaron on the preceding seven days, he now had to offer one of each on his own behalf (vv. 8–14). His action in carrying out these sacrifices served as a public admission of his own sinfulness and need for forgiveness. The ritual for both sacrifices follows the normal procedure[4] for burnt and purification offerings set out in chs. 1 and 4, except that the blood of the purification offering is smeared on the outer altar of burnt offering. Normally in the high priest's purification offering the blood was smeared on the altar of incense (4:3ff.). The reason for this deviation may be that the incense altar did not yet need cleansing, since Aaron had not yet entered the tent of meeting where it stood.

Four sacrifices were brought on behalf of the people (vv. 15–21): a goat as a purification offering to cleanse the altar,[5] a calf and a lamb as a burnt offering, a cereal offering, and an ox and a ram as peace offerings. These are fairly modest offerings in comparison with those offered at the principal feasts (see Num. 28–29), and negligible compared with those brought by Solomon at the consecration of the temple (1 K. 8:62ff.). But it is not the quantity but the variety that is the point here. On Aaron's first day in office he offers every kind of sacrifice, except reparation offerings, which were reserved for specific offenses (see ch. 5), and most kinds of sacrificial animal.[6] This indicates that the purpose of these sacrifices was not to atone for specific sins, but for the general sinfulness of the nation, to dedicate the whole people to the worship of God according to his appointed means, and to pray for God's blessing on them.

Fire from the Lord (22–24)

Using the altar of burnt offering as a platform Aaron turned to

---

4. See v. 16: *according to the regulation.*
5. On *ḥiṭṭē'*, "cleanse" (v. 15), cf. note on 8:15.
6. Birds, which were optional alternatives for the poor, were not included in this national sacrifice.

address the people and pronounce God's blessing (v. 22), perhaps using the words of Num. 6:23ff.

> The Lord bless you and keep you:
> The Lord make his face to shine upon you,
>   and be gracious to you:
> The Lord lift up his countenance upon you,
>   and give you peace.

Then Moses and Aaron entered into the tent of meeting. This was the place where God usually spoke to Moses (Exod. 40; Lev. 1; Num. 12). So it seems probable that they went in at this time to commune with God, and to pray that he would fulfil his promise to appear in glory (cf. vv. 4 and 6). Their conviction that God intended to bless his people was strengthened by their time of communion, and emerging they jointly blessed the people. Their words were then miraculously underwritten by the appearance of the glory of God. This takes the form of fire coming down on the altar and burning up in a flash all the sacrificial portions smoldering there. The narrative makes it clear that they were already being burned when the divine fire appeared (vv. 10, 14, 17, 20). But it would take some time to burn all the animals mentioned in this chapter, and the process was incomplete when God dramatically demonstrated his acceptance of them by burning them up completely.

On three other occasions God showed his approval of a burnt offering by sending heavenly fire to burn it up: when the birth of Samson was announced to Manoah and his wife (Judg. 13:15ff.), when Solomon dedicated the temple (2 Chr. 7:1ff.), and when Elijah challenged the prophets of Baal on Mount Carmel (1 K. 18:38ff.). Each time, confronted by the awe-inspiring reality of God, the worshippers fell to the ground and praised God. Lev. 9:24 says *they shouted*. The word translated "shout" means a loud cry, usually one of joy. It is often found coupled with other words expressing praise and joy at God's ways and works (e.g., Isa. 49:13; Jer. 31:7; Ps. 20:6 [Eng. 5]; 33:1; 35:27; 59:17 [16]; 95:1). These episodes show that the worship of God involves a total response of man to God. The presence of God was greeted with a shout, not silence. More than that, they *fell on their faces* (v. 24). God's greatness and holiness cannot be ignored; he must be acknowledged by our whole being. Nothing less is adequate.

Leviticus 9 and the NT

This chapter brings out very clearly the purpose and character of OT worship. All the pomp and ceremony served one end: the appearance of the glory of God. Aaron's gorgeous garments, the multiplicity of animal sacrifices, were not ends in themselves but only means to the end, namely, the proper worship of God. These elaborate vestments and sacrifices helped simple human minds appreciate the majestic holiness of God. But all the ritual in the OT would have been pointless if God had not deigned to reveal himself to the people. The clothing and the sacrifices merely helped to put the worshippers in a state of mind that was prepared for God's coming, and removed the obstacles of human sin that prevented fellowship, but they did not necessarily ensure God's presence.

The NT is equally aware of the emptiness of a ritual where God is not present. It is Christ or the Spirit that reveals the glory of God in the NT era. On various occasions in the life of Christ, we read of the glory of God appearing: at Christ's birth (Luke 2:9) and transfiguration (Luke 9:31), in his miracles (John 2:11), and at his second coming (Matt. 16:27; 25:31). Christ himself is described as the glory of God (1 Cor. 2:8; John 1:14). Christ is present where two or three meet in his name (Matt. 18:20). Worship must be in Spirit and Truth (John 4:24). When the Spirit came at Pentecost he was in the form of fire; under his inspiration the believers spoke of "the mighty works of God" (Acts 2:11). Repeatedly in Acts we read of the Spirit falling on disciples and prompting them to praise God, sometimes in strange tongues.

Spontaneous and heartfelt praise is thus a feature of true worship common to both testaments. So is the aspect of fear. In ancient Israel "they fell on their faces." Similarly on the day of Pentecost we read, "fear came upon every soul" (Acts 2:43). Hebrews reminds us to "offer to God acceptable worship, with reverence and awe; for our God is a consuming fire" (Heb. 12:28f.).

Much of the time the worship of Israel and the modern Church falls short of these ideals, despite Christ's prayer that all his disciples might see his glory (John 17:24). In the heavenly city that prayer will be fulfilled: "the city has no need of sun or moon to shine upon it, for the glory of God is its light, and its lamp is the Lamb" (Rev. 21:23).

C. JUDGMENT ON
NADAB AND ABIHU (CH. 10)

1 *Then Nadab and Abihu, sons of Aaron, each took his censer, put fire in it, and placed incense on top of it and offered before the Lord a strange fire which he had not commanded them.*

2 *Then fire came from before the Lord, and consumed them, and they died before the Lord.*

3 *Moses said to Aaron "That is what the Lord meant when he said,*
   '*I must be sanctified among those who are near me, and*
   I must be honored in the presence of the whole people!'
   Aaron was silent.

4 *Moses called Mishael and Elzaphan, the sons of Uzziel, Aaron's uncle, and said to them, "Come near, carry your brothers away from the sanctuary out of the camp."*

5 *So they came near, and carried them in their shirts out of the camp, as Moses had commanded.*

6 *Moses said to Aaron and his sons, Eleazar and Ithamar, "Do not untidy your hair or tear your clothes, lest you die and He become angry with the whole congregation. But let your brothers, the whole house of Israel, bewail the fire which the Lord has sent.*

7 *You must not leave the enclosure of the tent of meeting lest you die, because the Lord's anointing oil is on you."*
   They did as Moses said.

8 *The Lord spoke to Aaron as follows:*

9 *"Do not drink wine or strong drink, whenever you or your sons enter the tent of meeting, so that you do not die. This is a permanent rule for your descendants.*

10 *It is your duty to distinguish between the holy and the common, and between the unclean and the clean.*

11 *and to instruct the Israelites in all the rules which the Lord has spoken to them through Moses."*

12 *Then Moses said to Aaron, and Eleazar and Ithamar, his surviving sons, "Take the cereal offering which is left over from the Lord's food offerings, and eat it in the form of unleavened bread near the altar, for it is most holy.*

13 *You must eat it in a holy place because it is your due and your sons' due from the Lord's food offerings, for so I have been commanded.*

14 *You and your sons and your daughters must eat the dedicated breast and the contributed thigh in a clean place. For they have been given as your due and your sons' due from the Israelites' peace offerings.*

15 *They must bring the contributed thigh and the dedicated breast with the food offerings of the fat pieces to offer as a dedication before the Lord, and you and your sons shall have it as a permanent due, as the Lord commanded."*

16 *But Moses carefully inquired about the goat of the purification offering, and discovered it had already been burned. He was angry with Eleazar and Ithamar, the surviving sons of Aaron, and said:*

17 *"Why did not you eat the purification offering in the holy place,*

because it was most holy and it was given to you to bear the iniquity of the congregation to make atonement for them before the Lord.

18 *Since the blood was not brought into the holy place you ought to have eaten it in the sanctuary as I commanded."*

19 *Aaron said to Moses, "Even though they offered before the Lord their purification offering and burnt offering today, things like these have happened to me. If I had eaten a purification offering today, would the Lord have been satisfied?"*

20 *When Moses heard this, he was satisfied.*

The Death of Nadab and Abihu (Lev. 10)

Tragedy and triumph go hand in hand in the Bible and in life. On the very first day of Aaron's high-priestly ministry his two eldest sons died for infringing God's law. In the life of our Lord his baptism by the Spirit was followed by temptation in the wilderness, his triumphal entry into Jerusalem by his crucifixion six days later. In the early Church the healing of the lame man was succeeded by the death of Ananias and Sapphira (Acts 3–5).

These glaring contrasts are upsetting to the cosy bourgeois attitudes that often pass for Christian. In many parts of the Church the biblical view of divine judgment is conveniently forgotten or supposed to be something that passed away with the OT. Heine's famous last words, "God will forgive me. That's his job," have become the unexpressed axiom of much modern theology. This short story is therefore an affront to liberal thinkers. It should also challenge Bible-believing Christians whose theological attitudes are influenced by prevailing trends of thought more often than they realize.

The Structure of Leviticus 10

The main features of this chapter are discussed above (see "The Structure of Leviticus 8–10"). It falls into the following sections.

1–3	Fire from the Lord
4	Moses' command to Mishael, etc.
5	Mishael's obedience
6–7a	Moses' command to Aaron
7b	Aaron's obedience
8–11	The Lord's commands to Aaron
12–18	Moses' commands to Aaron
19	Aaron's reply
20	Moses satisfied

The regular pattern of the narrative of the preceding chapters, of a command followed by its fulfilment, is disrupted in this chapter, most obviously by Nadab and Abihu's presumption in offering fire that was "not commanded" (vv. 1–2). The pattern is reestablished in vv. 4–5, where Mishael and Elzaphan promptly obey Moses, and reaffirmed in vv. 6 and 7 when Aaron does the same. But then in vv. 8–11 the Lord speaks directly to Aaron, and gives him certain instructions, the fulfilment of which is not mentioned in this chapter.

Despite appearances, this second deviation from the command-fulfilment pattern does not signal Aaron's disobedience, rather the reverse; it is a confirmation of his high-priesthood and a reminder of his continuing duties. This is proved by the fact that this is the only place in Leviticus where God addresses Aaron alone without Moses' intervention. The presumptuous behavior of his two sons Nadab and Abihu cast a cloud over the whole priesthood. This word of God to Aaron is in effect a reassurance that he still has a part to play in teaching Israel the way of holiness. His fulfilment of the command is the subject of the succeeding narrative and provides an important link with chs. 11–15, which discuss the rules about uncleanness. Finally Moses' commands to Aaron in vv. 12–18 are not carried through immediately. Instead Aaron explains his action (v. 19). Yet Moses is satisfied (v. 20). In other words Aaron is reinstated not only in the eyes of God (vv. 8ff.), but in the eyes of Moses the covenant mediator (v. 20).

Fire from the Lord (1–3)

Nadab and Abihu (v. 1) were the two eldest of Aaron's four sons (Exod. 6:23). They had accompanied their father and Moses up Mount Sinai (Exod. 24:1). Along with Aaron and their brothers, Eleazar and Ithamar, they had just been ordained as priests (Lev. 8:30). It may be assumed, therefore, that they had the right to offer incense. Certainly v. 1 is full of words that in chs. 8–9 describe priestly work, e.g., *took (lāqaḥ)* (8:15, 16, 23, 25; 9:2, 15); *put (nātan)* (8:15, 24; 9:9); *placed (śîm)* (9:20; cf. 8:8–9, 26); *offered (hiqrîb)* (8:18, 22; 9:2, 9, 15, 16, 17). Even the word for *incense*[1] *(qᵉṭōreṭ)* resembles the word "to burn" sacrifices on the altar *(hiqṭîr)* (8:16, 20, 21, 28; 9:10, 13, 14, 17, 20).

These verbal echoes of the preceding chapters evoke memories of great and moving occasions when God's plan for creat-

1. On this term see M. Haran, *VT* 10 (1960), pp. 113–129.

ing a holy people made a significant advance. Then suddenly our euphoria is shattered by the last five (Hebrew) words of the sentence: "strange fire which he had not commanded them."

Strange fire. The reader would dearly love to know the precise nature of their sin.[2] What made the fire "strange"? Incense was produced by mixing aromatic spices together, which were then vaporized by putting them in a censer containing glowing lumps of charcoal, i.e., "fire." According to Lev. 16:12 these coals had to be taken from the altar. Did they this time perhaps come from somewhere else? Daily incense offerings were prescribed in Exod. 30:7–8. Did Nadab and Abihu offer it at the wrong time of day? This could be deduced from Exod. 30:9, which prohibits "strange incense."[3] Elsewhere in the law "strange" *(zār)* refers to people who are not priests (Exod. 30:33; Lev. 22:12; Num. 17:5 [Eng. 16:40]), or to outsiders (Deut. 25:5). Perhaps "unauthorized" might be an alternative translation. At any rate the Hebrew term seems fairly imprecise.

What really mattered is stated next: it was fire *which he had not commanded them.* The whole narrative from 8:1 has led us to expect God's ministers to obey the law promptly and exactly. Suddenly we meet Aaron's sons doing something that had not been commanded.

Fire came from before the Lord (v. 2). Exactly the same phrase occurs in 9:24. On the first occasion divine fire came only after all the sacrifices had been offered. This time it came instantly, and *consumed them;* cf. 9:24, "consumed" the sacrifices. This was a fire of judgment: *they died before the Lord.* The first time it was proof of God's blessing. Then they shouted. Now *Aaron was silent* (v. 3).

Moses, God's spokesman, does have a word for the occasion. He explains God's action in a poetic couplet.

> *"I must be sanctified among those who are near me,*
> *and I must be honored in the presence of the whole*
> *people"* (v. 3).

I must be sanctified[4] *(' eqqāḏēsh).* Holiness *(qdsh)* is one of the great themes of Leviticus.[5] The whole nation was called to be holy, but

---

2. For recent discussion see J. C. H. Laughlin, "The 'Strange Fire' of Nadab and Abihu," *JBL* 95 (1976), pp. 559–565.
3. Keil, p. 351.
4. As frequently in the laws the imperfect has imperative force: "I shall" = "I must"; cf. comment on 1:2.
5. See Introduction, VI.2: "Holiness."

how much more responsibility rested on the priests whose duty was to perform the sanctifying rituals and to teach the people the way of holiness. They preeminently were *near (qārōḇ)* to God, for they drew near to him themselves (*qārēḇ*) (e.g., 9:7–8) and brought near the sacrifices (*hiqrîḇ*) (e.g., 7:9, 33; 9:9, etc.). *Honored* or "glorified" is the verbal form (*kāḇēḏ,* Niphal) of the word for "glory" (*kāḇôḏ*) (cf. 9:23). God's holiness and glory are also mentioned together in Isa. 6:3:

> Holy, holy, holy is the Lord of hosts;
> the whole earth is full of his glory.

It has been well said that God's "holiness is his hidden, concealed glory. . . . But his glory is his holiness revealed."[6]

Moses' words may be loosely paraphrased, "the closer a man is to God, the more attention he must pay to holiness and the glory of God." The unspoken implication is that the sons of the high priest ought to have known better than to act so presumptuously. The same theological point is made in many different ways in the OT. It is because Israel is God's covenant people that she faces the covenant curses listed in Lev. 26 and Deut. 28. Amos says that while other nations deserve God's punishment for their grave sins against humanity, Judah and Israel will be punished just because they have not kept the law (Amos 2–3). Holy men within Israel are judged by an even higher standard: they are expected to follow out God's injunctions to the last jot and tittle. In their case, the slightest transgression tends to attract the most startling punishment. The greatest of all Israel's leaders, Moses, was denied the fulfilment of his lifelong ambition for slightly deviating from God's commands (Num. 20), "because you did not believe in me, to sanctify me in the eyes of the Israelites" (Num. 20:12). Some of the men of Bethshemesh, a priestly city (Josh. 21:16), died for not treating the ark reverently (1 Sam. 6:19). 1 K. 13 tells of a prophet, who having faithfully fulfilled his mission to preach against the altar of Bethel, failed to hurry home as he had been directed, and then was killed by a lion. Gehazi, Elisha's servant, and King Uzziah were both struck down with "leprosy" for their sins (2 K. 5:20ff.; 2 Chr. 26:16ff.).

Commenting on this passage Calvin wrote: "if we reflect how holy a thing God's worship is, the enormity of the punishment will by no means offend us. Besides, it was necessary that their religion should be sanctioned at its very commencement; for if God had

6. Herntrich quoted by O. Kaiser, *Isaiah 1–12* (London: S.C.M., 1972), p. 79.

suffered the sons of Aaron to transgress with impunity, they would have afterwards carelessly neglected the whole law. This, therefore, was the reason for such great severity, that the priests should anxiously watch against all profanation."[7]

Moses' Command to Mishael and Elzaphan (4)
Their Obedience (5)
Moses' Command to Aaron and his Surviving Sons (6–7a)
Their Obedience (7b)

After the death of Nadab and Abihu the narrative reverts to the usual command-fulfilment pattern, as if to underline the effect of their death on the spectators: God's commands are not to be tampered with.

Priests were forbidden to go near the dead, because corpses brought defilement which would preclude their officiating in the sanctuary (Lev. 21). This ban was absolute in the case of the high priest (21:10ff.), but other priests were allowed to bury their nearest relatives. We should have expected the brothers of Nadab and Abihu to have buried them; instead the task is delegated to Aaron's cousins[8] Mishael and Elzaphan (v. 4).

Aaron and his sons are also forbidden to join in the customary rites of mourning. *Do not untidy your hair or tear your clothes* (v. 6; cf. 13:45; Gen. 37:29, etc.). This rule normally applied just to the high priest (Lev. 21:10); here it is extended to his sons as well. It is not explained why Eleazar and Ithamar could not join in mourning their brothers' deaths. It is simply stated that if they did, they would *die* and God's wrath would fall on *the whole congregation* (v. 6). Perhaps it was because Nadab and Abihu had not suffered a natural death, but a direct judgment from God. The surviving priests, even though they were brothers, had to identify themselves entirely with God's viewpoint and not arouse any suspicion that they condoned their brothers' sins. Had they joined in the traditional customs of tearing their clothes, they might have been tempted in their grief to blame God for their brothers' deaths. Rare are men like Job, who can mourn the loss of relatives and praise God at one and the same time (Job 1:20–21).

7. Calvin III, p. 431. For a fuller discussion of the biblical doctrine of judgment see J. W. Wenham, *The Goodness of God* (London: IVP, 1974).
8. For family tree see Exod. 6:16ff.

Total dedication to God's service is required of the priests: they must not leave *the enclosure of the tent of meeting* (v. 7)[9] even for the funeral (cf. Matt. 8:21–22; Luke 9:59–60; 14:26–27).

Away from the sanctuary out of the camp (v. 4, cf. 5). Their dead bodies are unclean and must be removed from the holy area into the realm of the unclean outside the camp (cf. 4:12, 21, etc.). They are treated like the useless parts of the sacrificial animals.

In their shirts (v. 5). The garments that symbolized their high calling (8:13) were now used as shrouds for their ignominious burial.

Let the whole house of Israel bewail the fire which the Lord sent (v. 6). Though the priests were not to mourn, "God allowed the dead men to be bewailed by the people, lest the recollection of their punishment should too soon be lost."[10]

The Lord's Commands to Aaron (8–11)

The Lord spoke to Aaron. Only here in Leviticus does God speak to Aaron directly and by himself; elsewhere it is always with or through Moses. This shows the importance of what follows, and that Aaron, despite his sons' misdeeds, was still high priest, able to mediate between God and man.

The commands given to Aaron, however, are strange. Why should a ban on drinking alcohol be introduced here, and then be coupled with instructions about teaching the Israelites? Hoffmann[11] suggests that it was customary to ply mourners and others in distress with drink to cheer them up (cf. Prov. 31:6–7). The remarks about drink would then be consonant with earlier injunctions forbidding the priests to indulge in the usual mourning customs (v. 6). Gispen,[12] following earlier Jewish commentators, believes the ban was provoked by Nadab and Abihu's drunkenness, which had led them into such error. But there is nothing explicit in the text to prove that they had been drinking too much.

The OT writers were well aware that too much alcohol could lead to lightheadedness and lack of understanding (Prov. 20:1; Hos. 4:11; 7:5). *It is your duty.*[13] The essence of the priest's job was

9. On this phrase cf. comment on 8:3.
10. Calvin III, p. 434.
11. Hoffmann I, p. 296.
12. Gispen, p. 166.
13. *It is your duty to distinguish* (*ûlᵃhabdîl*) is an unusual construction. Hoffmann I, p. 296, compares Exod. 32:29, where again an imperative is followed by *waw* and infinitive, apparently continuing the imperative sense of the first verb.

to make decisions, as to what constituted the difference between *the holy and the common, and between the unclean and the clean* (v. 10).[14] To make a mistake in these matters provoked God's judgment and could lead to death. So to reduce the risk of such errors, the priests were forbidden to drink before going on duty. The Nazirites, another group of holy men in ancient Israel, had to abstain for as long as they were under their vow (Num. 6:3–4; Judg. 13:4–5; Luke 1:15). Ordinary laymen could enjoy wine as a gift of God (Ps. 104:15), but excessive drinking was castigated (Prov. 23:29ff.). Leaders in the NT Church had also to be temperate in their use of drink (1 Tim. 3:3, 8; Tit. 2:2–3).

To instruct the Israelites (v. 11). The priests were not just men who offered sacrifices, but were also teachers. To "instruct" (*lᵉhôrôt*) the people involved teaching the law (*tôrāh*), which included both teaching the revealed *rules* and making decisions about difficult cases not explicitly covered in the Sinai revelation (Deut. 17:9ff.).

Moses' Commands to Aaron (12–18)

Moses checks that the priests have completed the sacrifices mentioned in ch. 9. The final act in most sacrifices was the consumption of the edible portions by the priests.

The cereal offering (v. 12) refers to the one that accompanied the people's burnt offerings (9:4). Apart from the memorial portion, this was all eaten by the priests[15] (9:17; cf. 2:2–3, 9–10, etc.) in a "holy place," i.e., the court of the tabernacle (6:9ff. [Eng. 16ff.]). Similar regulations applied to the priestly perquisites from the peace offerings: *the dedicated breast and the contributed thigh* (v. 14; cf. 7:29ff.). Moses reminds Aaron and his sons that despite the disaster of Nadab and Abihu's death, the priestly privileges are not forfeited. By God's command these parts of the sacrifice are their *permanent due* (vv. 13, 15; cf. 7:34, 36).

In the case of purification offerings priests did not have an automatic right to the meat. It depended on what was done with the blood of the sacrifice. If the blood was smeared inside the tent of meeting, the animal's carcass was burned outside the camp (4:1–21). If, however, the blood was smeared on the altar of burnt offering

---

14. On these distinctions see Introduction, VI.2: "Holiness."
15. *Eat it in the form of unleavened bread* (v. 12). *Unleavened bread* is in explanatory apposition to *it*, hence this translation or TEV "make unleavened bread with it and eat it."

outside the tent of meeting, the priests were entitled to eat the meat
(6:18ff. [Eng. 25ff.]). Ch. 9 mentions two purification offerings, one
for Aaron[16] (9:8ff.) and one for the people,[17] namely, a goat (9:15).
Moses' anger is roused because they have not followed the rules
with the second offering. They have burned the meat instead of
eating it themselves as they were entitled to (vv. 16–18). Since[18] the
blood was not brought into the *holy place,* i.e., the outer part of the
tent of meeting, *you ought to have eaten it.*

Aaron's Reply (19)
Moses Satisfied (20)

By presenting a purification and burnt offering for themselves
(9:8ff.), Aaron and his sons had striven to avert God's wrath. Yet
they had failed: *Things like these have happened to me,* says Aaron
referring to the divine fire of judgment (10:2). Given the circumstances, Aaron's fear of eating "most holy" things such as the
meat of the purification offering was understandable.

    When Moses heard this, he was satisfied (v. 20). This sug-
gests, perhaps, that God is more gracious to those who make mistakes because they fear him than to those who carelessly and impu-
dently enter his presence, as Nadab and Abihu did (cf. vv. 1–3).

Leviticus 10 and the NT

Nowhere in the NT is this particular episode referred to, though
there are a number of lines of theological continuity linking this
passage with NT teaching. The disciple must put allegiance to Christ
before family obligations (vv. 6–7; Matt. 8:21–22). Ministers, like
Aaronic priests, should be temperate (v. 9; 1 Tim. 3:3, 8). But the
most striking principle endorsed by the NT is that the closer a man is
to God the stricter the standard he will be judged by (v. 3). Our Lord
said: "Everyone to whom much is given, of him will much be
required" (Luke 12:48). Peter: "Judgment begins with the household of God" (1 Pet. 4:17). James (3:1): "We who teach shall be
judged with greater strictness." The story of Nadab and Abihu
vividly illustrates these NT sayings.

---

16. On the anomaly in the ritual here see commentary on 9:8ff.
17. *Bear the iniquity* (v. 17); cf. 5:1; 7:18.
18. *Hēn (since,* v. 18; *though,* v. 19) calls attention to some fact upon which action
is to be taken, or a conclusion based (BDB 243b).

III. UNCLEANNESS AND
ITS TREATMENT (11:1–16:34)

Leviticus 11–15: Preliminary Observations

Chapter 11 opens a new section of the book of Leviticus. Chs. 11–15 deal with various kinds of uncleanness and how men may be cleansed from them. Ch. 11 differentiates between clean and unclean foods, i.e., which animals may be eaten and which may not. Ch. 12 deals with the pollution associated with childbirth, and chs. 13 and 14 deal with skin and fungus diseases. Ch. 15 deals with bodily discharges. These five chapters look back to 10:10: you are "to distinguish between the holy and the common . . . the unclean and the clean," and serve to prepare the way for ch. 16, which describes the great day of atonement. The ceremonies on that day were ordained "because of the uncleannesses of the Israelites" (16:16). These chapters then help to explain what is meant by uncleanness. The relationship between chs. 11–15 and 16 may be compared to that between chs. 1–7 and 8–10. Chs. 1–7 explain the sacrifices offered on the occasion of the institution of the priesthood (8–10): chs. 11–15 provide essential background for understanding the significance of the day of atonement (16).

These chapters of law are sandwiched between two sections of historical narrative (chs. 8–10 and 16). Because the quantity of law so outweighs the history here and throughout Leviticus, we tend to forget that the narrative frames the law and not the reverse. The preponderance of law tends to give it the appearance of timelessness, whereas the context makes it plain that these laws were given in a specific situation to a specific people. They are part of the blueprint for making the people of Israel holy. "I am the Lord who brought you up out of the land of Egypt to be your God; you must therefore be holy, for I am holy" (11:45). They are not necessarily to be taken as universal and eternal prescriptions. They express God's will for his people at a particular time, but as the NT makes clear they were not intended to apply forever or to Gentiles (Mark 7:14ff.; Acts 10; 15; 1 Cor. 10:23ff.). But this does not relieve the Christian commentator of the need to search for the significance of these laws in the life of ancient Israel. Why were they given and what were they supposed to achieve? If we can see why such regulations were first imposed on Israel, we may discover both why they were abrogated under the new covenant and what they can still teach us today.

A. UNCLEAN ANIMALS (CH. 11)

1 *The Lord spoke to Moses and Aaron:*

2 *"Speak to the Israelites as follows: These are the creatures which you may eat from all the land animals:*

3 *all among the land animals which have divided and cloven hoofs and chew the cud, you may eat them.*

4 *But the following divided-hoofed or cud-chewing animals you must not eat: the camel, for although it chews the cud, it does not have divided hoofs: you must regard it as unclean.*

5 *The coney, for although it chews the cud, it does not have divided hoofs: you must regard it as unclean.*

6 *The hare, for although it chews the cud, it does not have divided hoofs: you must regard it as unclean.*

7 *The pig, for although it has divided and cloven hoofs, it does not chew the cud: you must regard it as unclean.*

8 *Do not eat their flesh, and do not touch their carcasses. You must regard them as unclean.*

9 *You may eat these among the water animals. Anything that has fins and scales and dwells in the waters, i.e., the seas or the rivers, you may eat.*

10 *But anything which dwells in the seas or rivers and does not have fins or scales, or anything that swarms in the waters or other living creatures in the waters, you must regard them as detestable.*

11 *You must regard them as detestable. Do not eat their flesh but treat their carcasses as detestable.*

12 *Anything in the waters which does not have fins or scales, you must regard as detestable.*

13 *You must detest these among the birds. They may not be eaten. They are detestable: the griffon vulture, the bearded vulture, the black vulture,*

14 *the kite, every kind of buzzard,*

15 *every kind of raven,*

16 *the ostrich, the night hawk, the seagull, every kind of falcon,*

17 *the little owl, the fisher-owl, the long-eared owl,*

18 *the barn owl, the tawny owl, the Egyptian vulture,*

19 *the stork, every kind of heron, the hoopoe, and the bat.*

20 *All winged insects that go on all fours you must regard as detestable.*

21 *But you may eat any winged insect that goes on all fours if it has jumping legs to hop with.*

22 *You may eat these: every kind of desert locust, every kind of cricket, every kind of long- or short-horned grasshopper.*

23 *But all winged insects which have only four legs you must regard as detestable.*

24 *By these you will make yourselves unclean. Anyone who touches their carcass becomes unclean until the evening.*

25 *Anyone who carries part of their carcass must wash his clothes and he becomes unclean until the evening.*

26 *Every animal which has divided but not cloven hoofs and does not chew the cud, you must regard as unclean. Anyone who touches them becomes unclean.*

27 *Any four-legged animal which walks on paws you must regard as unclean. Anyone who touches their carcass becomes unclean until the evening.*

28 *Anyone carrying their carcass must wash his clothes and becomes unclean until the evening. You must regard them as unclean.*

29 *These are the animals that swarm on the ground that you must regard as unclean: the mole-rat, the mouse, every kind of dabb lizard;*

30 *the gecko, the monitor lizard, the lizard, the skink, and the chameleon.*

31 *You shall regard these as unclean among all the swarming animals. Anyone who touches them when they are dead becomes unclean until the evening.*

32 *Anything on to which any of them falls becomes unclean when they are dead, until the evening: that applies to any wooden article, piece of clothing, skin or sacking, or any article which is in use. It must be placed in water, and it remains unclean until the evening, and then it will be clean.*

33 *But the contents of any earthenware vessel into which one of them falls becomes unclean and you must break it.*

34 *Any food which could otherwise be eaten, on which water (from such a vessel) comes, becomes unclean, and any drink in such a vessel which could otherwise be drunk becomes unclean.*

35 *Everything on which the carcass falls becomes unclean: an oven or stove must be broken up. They are unclean. You must regard them as unclean.*

36 *But springs, wells, and water cisterns will be clean, but the man who touches the carcass becomes unclean.*

37 *If one of the carcasses falls on seed for sowing, it is clean.*

38 *But if water is placed on the seed, and then a carcass falls on it, you must regard it as unclean.*

39 *If an animal that may be eaten dies, anyone who touches its carcass becomes unclean until the evening.*

40 *Anyone who eats any of its carcass or carries it must wash his clothes and remain unclean until the evening.*

41 *Everything that swarms on the ground is detestable: it must not be eaten.*

42 *'Everything that swarms on the ground' covers crawling creatures, swarming things that have four or more legs. Do not eat them. They are detestable.*

43 *Do not make yourselves detestable by any swarming things. Do not pollute yourselves through them or become unclean by them.*

44 *For I am the Lord your God, and you must sanctify yourselves and be holy because I am holy. Do not pollute yourselves with any swarming thing that crawls on the ground.*

45 *For I am the Lord who brought you up out of the land of Egypt to be your God; you must therefore be holy, for I am holy.''*

46 *This is the law about animals, birds, all living creatures that swim in the water, and all creatures that swarm on the ground,*

47 *in order to make a distinction between the unclean and the clean, between the animal which may be eaten and that which may not be eaten.*

Note on Translation Problems

The meaning of many of the Hebrew terms for birds and reptiles is uncertain. One expert[1] in this field suggested that only 40% of the Hebrew terms could be identified with accuracy. I have simply followed the consensus of recent studies.[2] Where the experts disagree, I have usually adopted the renderings of Bare and the *Encyclopedia Miqrait*.

The Structure of Leviticus 11

The structure of this chapter is quite clear. Both subject matter and also key words and phrases mark the principal divisions. The chapter falls into six main sections, each introduced by "this" or "these" (vv. 2, 9, 13, 24, 29, 46). The main sections are further subdivided into paragraphs, usually signalled by inclusions, that is, the repetition of an opening clause or phrase at the end of the paragraph; e.g., "you may eat all the land animals . . ." (vv. 2–3, cf. 4, 8, 9 [2x]); "anything which does not have fins or scales . . . you must regard them as detestable" (vv. 10, 12, cf. 20, 23). "Anyone who touches their carcass . . . unclean until the evening" (vv. 24–25, 27–28; "You must regard as unclean" (vv. 29, 38).

---

1. F. S. Bodenheimer quoted by G. Bare, *Plants and Animals of the Bible* (United Bible Societies: 1969), p. iii.
2. See G. Bare, *Plants and Animals of the Bible;* G. S. Cansdale, *Animals of Bible Lands* (Exeter: Paternoster, 1970); G. R. Driver, "Birds in the OT," *PEQ* 87 (1955), pp. 5–20; *Encyclopedia Miqrait* (Jerusalem: Bialik, 1965–76), and the lexicons of W. Baumgartner and W. L. Holladay.

Clean and Unclean Animals: Definitions (1–23)

    1–8   Land creatures
          2–3   edible
          4–8   inedible—unclean
    9–12 Water creatures
          9   edible
          10–12   inedible—detestable
    13–23 Flying creatures
          13–19   inedible—detestable birds
          20–23   insects—detestable (20)
                          edible (21–22)
                          detestable (23)

Pollution by Animals and its Treatment (24–47)

    24–28 Land creatures
    29–45 Swarming creatures
                  general principles (29–38)
                  clean animals (39–40)
                  concluding exhortation (41–45)
    46–47 Summary

The threefold categorization of creatures into those that inhabit the land, sea, and air has affinities with Gen. 1:20ff. The
author's fondness for organizing his material into groups of three has
already been noted in earlier chapters.

Leviticus 11: Clean and Unclean Animals

These laws have fascinated and perplexed generations of biblical
scholars. Why did God decree that certain foods could be eaten and
others must be rejected? There has been a great variety of suggestions but to this day no consensus has emerged. Before outlining
the various possibilities, the regulations themselves should be
summarized.

    (1) Cloven-hoofed, cud-chewing land animals (e.g., sheep and
        cattle) may be eaten. Other mammals are unclean (e.g.,
        pigs and camels) and may not be eaten (vv. 2–8).
    (2) Only fishes which have fins and scales may be eaten (vv.
        9–12).
    (3) Certain named birds, probably birds of prey, may not be
        eaten (vv. 13–19).

(4) Flying insects may not be eaten, but hopping insects are edible (vv. 20–23).
(5) Touching the dead carcass of an unclean animal makes a person unclean. He must wash himself (vv. 24–28).
(6) Other swarming animals, such as mice and lizards, are also unclean. If they are found dead inside a vessel, the vessel becomes unclean and must be destroyed or purified (vv. 29–38).
(7) Clean animals that die of natural causes become unclean, unfit to eat and a source of pollution (vv. 39–40).

The uncleanness associated with certain animals is less serious than other kinds of uncleanness dealt with in subsequent chapters of Leviticus. This comes out in two ways: only contact with a dead carcass makes a man unclean, and to purify oneself from such uncleanness requires only a wash and a wait till evening. Other pollutions require a much longer time to clear, as well as the offering of sacrifice (see chs. 12–15).

These rules about unclean animals are relatively straightforward, but their rationale is quite obscure and has been a subject of discussion from pre-Christian times. Why can sheep and grasshoppers be eaten, but pigs and mice must be shunned? What is the point of dividing land animals into cloven-hoofed cud-chewers which are clean and others which are not? Before embarking on the detailed exegesis of these laws it is appropriate to consider the general principles and the different approaches to them.

Four different types of explanation have been offered for these laws: the distinctions between clean and unclean animals are arbitrary, cultic, hygienic, or symbolic.

(1) The distinctions are arbitrary. Their rationale is known only to God, who revealed them to man as a test of obedience. Though this was the view of some rabbis[3] and may be the conclusion to which one is driven if no other explanation seems to work, it is basically a negative approach and should be adopted only as a last resort.

(2) The cultic explanation holds that the unclean animals are either those used in pagan worship or those associated with particular non-Israelite deities. As a mark of their fidelity to the covenant Israel must shun these animals entirely.[4]

3. See Hertz, p. 93.
4. See M. Noth, *The Laws in the Pentateuch and Other Studies* (Edinburgh: Oliver and Boyd, 1966), pp. 56ff.

In favor of this explanation is its antiquity.[5] The law's own statement of its purpose also lends it plausibility. The covenant was designed to separate Israel from all the peoples and to create a holy nation (Exod. 19:5–6; cf. Lev. 11:44–45). Isa. 65:4 speaks of the ungodly "who eat swine's flesh" probably as part of some Canaanite ritual. Archeologists have also discovered quantities of pig bones in pre-Israelite levels at Tell el-Farah (North), which suggest the pig may have been a sacred animal.[6]

Unfortunately this hypothesis explains too little of the evidence to be of real use. In general the Canaanites sacrificed the same general range of animals as Israel. Why were they not declared unclean? In particular why was the bull not prohibited in the OT, since it was an important cultic animal in both Egyptian and Canaanite ritual? It seems unlikely that uncleanness derives solely from the use made of some animals in pagan religion. It may be that when the Canaanites used a beast which for other reasons the Israelites considered unclean, that animal became even more abhorrent in covenant eyes, but pagan usage hardly explains the initial categorization of clean and unclean.

(3) The hygienic interpretation holds that the unclean creatures are unfit to eat because they are carriers of disease. The clean animals are those that are relatively safe to eat. This explanation is adopted by many modern writers. Pork can be a source of trichinosis. The coney and hare are carriers of tularemia. Fish without fins and scales tend to burrow into the mud and become sources of dangerous bacteria, as do the birds of prey which feed on carrion.[7]

This interpretation is particularly attractive to twentieth-century Western readers, obsessed as we are by health care and medical science. And it may well be that God in his providence did give rules that contributed to the health of the nation. But just because we can see hygienic considerations underlying some of the laws does not mean that the human authors of Scripture did too. There are good reasons for believing that they did not see these provisions as hygienic.

First, hygiene can only account for some of the prohibitions. Some of the clean animals are more questionable on hygienic

5. Origen, *Contra Celsum* 4:93.
6. R. de Vaux, "Les sacrifices de porcs en Palestine et dans l'Ancient Orient," *BZAW* 77 (1958), pp. 250–265.
7. See for example Clements, p. 34.

grounds than some of the unclean animals.[8] If ancient Israel had discovered the dangers of eating pork, they might also have discovered that thorough cooking averts it. In any event, trichinosis is rare in free-range pigs. Among the Arabs camel flesh is regarded as a luxury, though Leviticus brands it as unclean.

Secondly, the OT gives no hint that it regarded these foods as a danger to health. Motive clauses justifying a particular rule are a very characteristic feature of OT law, yet there is never a hint that these animal foods must be avoided because they will damage health. Yet this would surely have constituted an excellent reason for avoiding unclean food.

Third, why, if hygiene is the motive, are not poisonous plants classed as unclean?

Finally, if health were the reason for declaring certain foods unclean in the first place, why did our Lord pronounce them clean in his day? Evidence is lacking that the Middle Eastern understanding of hygiene had advanced so far by the first century A.D. that the Levitical laws were unnecessary. Indeed, if the primary purpose of the food laws was hygienic, it is surprising that Jesus abolished them.

(4) The symbolic interpretation of the food laws views the behavior and habits of the clean animals as living illustrations of how the righteous Israelite ought to behave, while the unclean represent sinful men. This type of explanation goes back to pre-Christian Jewish writers, and has been advocated by more recent commentators. Aristeas[9] suggested that chewing the cud made an animal clean, because it reminded men to meditate on the law. Bonar[10] argued that the sheep was clean because it reminded the ancient Israelite that the Lord was his shepherd, whereas the dirty habits of the pig spoke of the "filth of iniquity." Others[11] have supposed that some animals were considered unclean because of their associations with death or sin.

Interesting and imaginative as these older attempts at symbolic interpretation are, they are at best partial, covering only part of the data, and at worst whimsical and capricious. There seems to be no criterion for preferring one interpretation to any other. Biblical

---

8. J. Simoons, *Eat Not This Flesh: Food Avoidances in the Old World* (Madison: University of Wisconsin, 1961), pp. 37ff.
9. Letter of Aristeas, 154f.; this was probably composed in the 2nd century B.C.
10. Bonar, pp. 214f.
11. Keil, pp. 357ff.; Hoffmann I, pp. 315ff.

exegesis without controls is apt to run away into total subjectivity.

The works of social anthropologist Mary Douglas appear to avoid these dangers. She argues that the uncleanness laws do have symbolic significance, but her interpretation is based on a comprehensive reading of all the laws and a reliance on the distinctions emphasized in Leviticus itself, not on points that fascinate the modern reader.

In our Introduction[12] it was suggested that the notion underlying holiness and cleanness was wholeness and normality. The priests, for example, had to be free from physical deformity (21:5–6, 17ff.). Mixed crops, mixed clothing, and mixed marriages are incompatible with holiness (18:23; 19:19).

The same insistence on wholeness underlies the uncleanness laws in this chapter. The animal world is divided into three spheres: those that fly in the air, those that walk on the land, and those that swim in the seas (cf. Gen. 1:20–30). Each sphere has a particular mode of motion associated with it. Birds have two wings with which to fly, and two feet for walking; fish have fins and scales with which to swim; land animals have hoofs to run with. The clean animals are those that conform to these standard pure types. Those creatures which in some way transgress the boundaries are unclean. Thus fish without fins and scales are unclean (Lev. 11:10; Deut. 14:10). Insects which fly but which have many legs are unclean, whereas locusts which have wings and only two hopping legs are clean (Lev. 11:20–23). Animals with an indeterminate form of motion, i.e., which "swarm," are unclean (Lev. 11:41–44). "Holiness requires that individuals shall conform to the class to which they belong."[13] Insofar as some animals do not conform, they are unclean.

This analysis explains the main divisions between clean and unclean, but it does not explain why pigs are unclean, but sheep and goats are reckoned to be clean. Douglas thinks a rationale for this differentiation may be discerned if the social background to the laws is borne in mind. Sheep and goats would have been the standard meat of pastoralists, so it was natural for them to be regarded as clean. But pigs and camels did not conform exactly to the norms of behavior defined by sheep and goats and were therefore unclean. They transgress the boundaries of clean animals in not chewing the cud or in lacking cloven feet. In other words, there is a parallel

12. See Introduction, VI.2: "Holiness."
13. M. Douglas, *Purity and Danger*, p. 53.

between the holiness looked for in man and the cleanness of animals: man must conform to the norms of moral and physical perfection, and animals must conform to the standards of the animal group to which they belong.[14]

Further analysis[15] demonstrates that each sphere of the animal realm is similarly structured. Water creatures divide into the clean and the unclean, but land and air creatures further subdivide into clean animals that may be eaten and clean animals that may be sacrificed as well as eaten. This threefold division of animals—unclean, clean, and sacrificial—parallels the divisions of mankind, the unclean, i.e., those excluded from the camp of Israel, the clean, i.e., the majority of ordinary Israelites, and those who offer sacrifice, i.e., the priests. This tripartite division of both the animal world and the human realm is no coincidence, as is demonstrated by various laws in the Pentateuch, which apply similar principles to man and beast (Gen. 1:29–30; Exod. 13:2, 13; 20:10; 21:28ff.; 22:28–29 [Eng. 29–30]; Lev. 26:22). Once it is admitted that the animals symbolize the human world, the uncleanness of the birds of prey becomes intelligible: they are detestable because they eat carrion and flesh from which the blood has not been drained properly, acts that make men unclean (Lev. 11:13–19; cf. 11:40 and 17:10ff.).

Douglas therefore contends that there was a system underlying the uncleanness regulations and their symbolism was consciously felt in ancient Israel. They expressed an understanding of holiness, and of Israel's special status as the holy people of God. The division into clean (edible) foods and unclean (inedible) foods corresponded to the division between holy Israel and the Gentile world. Among those animals that were clean there were a few types that could be offered in sacrifice. Similarly there was a group of men within Israel who could offer sacrifice, namely the priests. Through this system of symbolic laws the Israelites were reminded at every meal of their redemption to be God's people. Their diet was limited to certain meats in imitation of their God, who had restricted his choice among the nations to Israel. It served, too, to bring to mind Israel's responsibilities to be a holy nation. As they distinguished between clean and unclean foods, they were reminded that holiness was more than a matter of meat and drink but a way of life characterized by purity and integrity.

14. *Ibid.*, pp. 54f.
15. M. Douglas, "Deciphering a Meal," *Daedalus* 101 (1972), pp. 61–81, reprinted in *Implicit Meanings* (London: Routledge, 1975), pp. 249–275.

The strongest argument in favor of Douglas' interpretation of the food laws is its comprehensiveness and coherence. Additional support may be found in the earliest explanation of these laws for a Greek audience in the second century B.C., the Letter of Aristeas. He says that men must behave like the clean birds which eat grain, not like the wild and carnivorous unclean birds.[16] These regulations teach Israel to act "with discrimination according to the standard of righteousness—more especially because we have been distinctly separated from the rest of mankind."[17]

Finally it may be noted that the NT appears to regard the food laws as symbolic of the division between Jew and Gentile, and their abolition under the New Covenant is of a piece with breaking down the wall of partition. This is discussed more fully below.[18]

Edible Land Creatures (1–3)

The Lord spoke to Moses and Aaron (v. 1). It is rare for laws to be addressed to Aaron and Moses together; much more commonly Moses is spoken to alone (e.g., 1:1; 4:1). Hoffmann[19] plausibly suggests that Aaron is specifically included here and in 13:1; 14:33; and 15:1 because these are sections dealing with uncleanness, and in 10:10 the priests were commissioned "to distinguish . . . between the unclean and clean" and "to instruct the Israelites."

These are the creatures . . . from all the land animals (v. 2). "Creature" (Heb. *ḥayyāh*), literally "living thing," frequently denotes wild beasts (e.g., Gen. 7:14; Lev. 17:13), whereas "land animal" (*bᵉhēmāh*) often refers to domesticated ones (e.g., Exod. 20:10; Lev. 1:2). But as the parallel in Deut. 14:4 makes clear, both terms have a broader meaning here.

Which have divided and cloven hoofs and chew the cud (v. 3). This definition covers oxen, sheep, and goats, the principal domesticated animals, and the wild game listed in Deut. 14:5. In animals with cloven hoofs "the five basic digits of the foot have been reduced and only two functional ones are left; these end in hoofs and the animals are, in effect, walking on two toes of each foot."[20]

Cows, sheep, and goats also "chew the cud." This English phrase means they swallow their food without chewing it very much,

16. Letter of Aristeas, lines 145–49.
17. Aristeas, line 151.
18. See also my article "The Theology of Unclean Food," *EQ* [forthcoming].
19. Hoffmann I, p. 302.
20. G. S. Cansdale, *Animals of Bible Lands*, p. 43.

store it temporarily in one of their stomach compartments, then later at their leisure regurgitate it and rechew it thoroughly, and then swallow and digest it. It seems clear that this technical definition of chewing the cud is not quite what Hebrew means by the phrase, since various animals which do not technically "chew the cud," e.g., the camel, coney, and hare, are said to "chew the cud" in vv. 4–6. These animals do appear to chew their food very thoroughly like true ruminants, and this is what the law is insisting on. Clean animals are those which have cloven hoofs and chew their food thoroughly. They may be eaten.

Inedible (Unclean) Land Creatures (4–8)

After giving a general definition of what constitutes an edible or clean animal, the law goes on to make it clear that both qualifications for cleanness are required. Clean animals must chew the cud *and* have cloven hoofs. One without the other makes the animal unclean. The *camel* (the one-humped dromedary is meant), the Syrian *coney* or rock hyrax, and *hare* chew their food thoroughly like true ruminants, but do not have *divided hoofs*.[21] Therefore they are unclean. The *pig* is also classed as unclean, because it has only half the necessary qualifications, divided hoofs, but it does not chew the cud (v. 7).

Do not eat their flesh, and do not touch their carcasses (v. 8). These unclean beasts made a person unclean only if he ate them or touched their dead body. One could ride a camel, for example, without contracting uncleanness (Gen. 24:10ff.). Only eating them or touching them after they had died was polluting, and the latter was true of clean animals and human corpses as well (vv. 39–40; 21:2, etc.). It was the prohibition against eating them that was peculiar to unclean animals.

The main attempts to explain this law have already been discussed above. Here it may be noted that neither the cultic nor hygienic explanation really does justice to the qualifications for cleanness reiterated in the text—cloven hoofs and chewing the cud. The symbolic interpretation of Douglas understands this rule as follows. Sheep, goats, and oxen were the standard sacrificial animals of pastoralists. They have in common cloven hoofs and rumination. Interpreting this theologically one might say that as God had limited his "diet" to these animals, so must his people. It is man's duty to

21. For descriptions see Cansdale, *Animals,* pp. 64–70, 129–132.

imitate his creator (vv. 44–45). When the Israelite restricted his food to God's chosen animals, he recalled that he owed all his spiritual privileges to divine election. As God had chosen certain animals for sacrifice, so he had chosen one nation "out of all the peoples that are on the face of the earth" to be "a kingdom of priests and a holy nation" (Deut. 7:6; Exod. 19:6). It is noteworthy that Deuteronomy (14:1–2) introduces the regulation about clean animals with a reference to Israel's election, while Leviticus (11:44–45) concludes its regulations with similar remarks. The law demands total commitment to the Lord: half-castes and the halfhearted do not enjoy the covenant blessings (e.g., Lev. 20:2; Deut. 20:8; 23:3 [Eng. 2]). Animals with only half the required characteristics were on similar grounds unclean: they symbolized those who attempted to blur the edges of the covenant community and detract from its holiness. Only those subscribed fully to the law, "the cloven-hoofed ruminants," could count themselves as true members of the elect nation.

Edible and Inedible Water Creatures (9–12)

The sole criterion for distinguishing between clean and unclean fish and other water creatures is whether they have fins and scales. Fishes, which usually have fins and scales, may be eaten (v. 9). Other aquatic animals without fins and scales may not be eaten (vv. 10–12). The one rule applies both to fresh- and salt-water sources. No examples to illustrate this general rule are given: the principle is simply stated.

What is the thinking underlying this division into scaly, finned fish, which are clean, and other water creatures, which are unclean? Various suggestions have been made. Hygiene is often appealed to. "Fish which do not have scales and fins are shallow water fish. They easily become carriers of various harmful bacteria."[22] Keil justifies their prohibition symbolically. "Of water animals, all serpent-like fishes and slimy shell-fish, and of small creeping things, all except some kinds of locusts, partly because they recall the old serpent, partly because they seek their food in all sorts of impurities, and partly because they crawl in the dust, and represent corruption in the slimy character of their bodies."[23] Gispen[24] points out that Romans and Egyptians did not eat fish without scales.

Douglas suggests that the fins and scales are mentioned be-

22. Clements, p. 34.
23. Keil, *Biblical Archaeology* II, p. 119.
24. Gispen, p. 181.

cause they are the normal means of propulsion among fishes. Elsewhere in the chapter the number and character of an animal's feet is of great importance for determining whether it is clean or not (vv. 3ff., 21ff., 27, 42ff.). Indeed the means of locomotion and the mode of eating are the two types of test used to distinguish between clean and unclean beasts. In Genesis and Leviticus the world is divided into three spheres: air, land, and water. Each sphere has its own kind of animal life. "In the firmament two-legged fowls fly with wings. In the water scaly fish swim with fins. On the earth four-legged animals hop, jump or walk. Any class of creatures which is not equipped for the right kind of locomotion in its element is contrary to holiness. . . . Thus anything in the water which has not fins and scales is unclean. Nothing is said about predatory habits or scavenging. The only sure test for cleanness in a fish is its scales and its propulsion by means of fins."[25] Put more simply, fishes which swim normally are clean. In limiting themselves to eating the normal members of the fish world, Israel was reminded that its life was to conform to the norms of God's world in a moral and spiritual sense as well as physically, and that God had chosen them to be a holy nation.

Inedible Birds (13–19)

The list now goes on to mention various birds which are *detestable* (v. 13). This may be a stronger term than "unclean," but the principles applying to what is detestable seem to be much the same as "unclean." The identification of the species listed presents problems, but most commentators generally agree that the birds in question are birds of prey or eaters of carrion.[26] The *bat* is not strictly speaking a bird, though it is classed as one also by the Arabs.[27]

Again commentators disagree as to the reason for this prohibition. "Birds of prey, which eat carrion, are dangerous disease carriers."[28] "All animals are unclean which bear the image of sin, of death and corruption. . . . Of winged creatures not only birds of prey . . . but also marsh birds and others, which live on worms, carrion and all sorts of impurities."[29] Most modern commentators agree that it is the symbolism of preying on other animals that makes birds of

25. *Purity and Danger*, p. 55.
26. A view as old as the Letter of Aristeas.
27. Keil, p. 365.
28. Clements, p. 34.
29. Keil, *Biblical Archaeology* II, pp. 118f.

prey unclean. They are killers, or blood-drinkers; and thus they break the law. Douglas[30] points out that in Israel animals were expected to obey covenant law. Both man and his beasts are required to keep the sabbath (Exod. 20:10). The first-born of animals were consecrated to sacrifice (Exod. 22:28–29 [Eng. 29–30]), just as the first-born among men were dedicated to the priesthood. Because these birds' eating patterns break the fundamental principle of not eating flesh with blood in it, they are declared unclean just as men who eat flesh without draining off the blood become unclean (Lev. 17).

Insects (20–23)

Verse 20 states that *all winged insects that go on all fours* should be detested. The Heb. *sherets* is a broader term than the English translation *insects* suggests; "swarming things" or "swarmers" expresses its meaning more aptly. They are small creatures that often occur in swarms and move to and fro in haphazard fashion. "Swarmers" are to be found on land, in the sea, and in the air. Here *winged insects* is quite an appropriate translation, but it obscures the distinguishing feature of swarming. *Going on all fours* is the opposite of walking uprightly: the number of legs is irrelevant. Everything that swarms is *detestable* because, according to Douglas, they have no clear-cut motion peculiar to their sphere of life. Birds have two wings with which to fly and two legs for walking. Land animals have four legs. Fishes have fins and scales. But swarmers swarm whether they are on land, in the air, or in the sea They break down the categories of movement. Flying insects fly in the air with wings and then walk on their numerous feet on the ground.

Four kinds of locusts or grasshoppers are pronounced clean (vv. 21–23). They are characterized by having *jumping legs to hop with* (v. 21; lit. "hind legs [cf. 1:9, 13, etc.] above their feet"). These enable them to have a distinctive hopping motion as opposed to swarming. It makes them more like a bird with its wings and two feet. Because they have a motion appropriate to their sphere, they are clean. Douglas says: "The case of the locusts is interesting and consistent. The test of whether it is a clean and therefore edible kind is how it moves on the earth. If it crawls it is unclean. If it hops it is clean."[31] No other commentator has produced an explanation of why locusts are edible and other insects prohibited. Douglas' view

30. *Daedalus* 101 (1972), p. 75.
31. *Purity and Danger*, p. 56.

has the great merit of accepting the explanation given in Leviticus itself, however odd this distinction may seem to us.

The identity of the locusts is difficult to establish.[32] Little seems to hang on the identification. It is probable that just a few specific examples are given to illuminate the general principle. For centuries locusts have been a regular part of the diet of the Middle East, and are said to be very nutritious.[33] John the Baptist lived in the desert on locusts and wild honey (Mark 1:6).

Pollution by Animals and its Treatment (24–45)

Hitherto this chapter of Leviticus has simply defined which animals are clean or detestable and which are not. It is permissible to eat clean animals but not others, and these clean animals only if they have been ritually drained of blood. But having said this, there are a host of questions left unanswered. If an animal is unclean, does this mean that anyone who touches it is polluted? Does it make any difference to its uncleanness whether the animal is alive or dead? What happens if you touch an unclean animal or accidentally eat unclean flesh? These are the problems that the rest of the chapter discusses.

First (vv. 24, 27, 31, 39) it is made clear that only dead animals pollute men. Uncleanness of dead animals is contagious; as long as they are alive they may be unclean in themselves but they do not affect others. Second, all dead animals are unclean unless they have been ritually slaughtered. So even clean animals are unclean if they die naturally (v. 39). They may not be eaten and anyone who touches them is made unclean (vv. 39–40). Third, the uncleanness caused by dead animals is temporary. It only lasts until the evening of the day on which it was contracted (vv. 24, 25, 27, 28, etc.). In this respect it differs from other kinds of pollution which may last a week (15:13), two months (12:5), or indefinitely (13:45–46). Fourth, household articles which come in contact with dead carcasses also become unclean, and have to be purified by washing (vv. 25, 28, 32, 40).

The rules about death point up the strength of the uncleanness it causes. While no living unclean animal pollutes, all corpses

32. See Bare, *Plants and Animals,* pp. 30, 44ff., 48, 102; *Encyclopedia Miqrait* I, pp. 520–26.
33. Cansdale, *Animals of Bible Lands,* p. 244.

do. This accords well with our understanding of the clean as the whole and the normal, and the unclean as the subnormal or abnormal. Death is at the opposite pole from normal healthy life. In between these two extremes are found disease and deformity. Disease may make a man contagiously unclean (Lev. 15), whereas deformity is simply a bar to priestly service (21:17ff.). Death is the greatest disorder that can affect human affairs. It is the ultimate contradiction of the covenant promises of life and health (Lev. 26), and it nullifies God's creative purpose (Gen. 1–2). On this analysis one might expect uncleanness caused by death to be treated more severely than that caused by sickness. It may be suggested that contact with dead animals was too frequent to make such a regulation practical.[34]

Land Creatures (24–28)

Verses 24–25 explain how these rules apply to the flying insects mentioned in the previous section. Verse 26 restates the principle that only animals that are cloven-hoofed and chew the cud are clean. Verse 27 puts the same law the other way round. *Any four-legged animal which walks on paws . . . is unclean.* Animals such as cats and dogs, bears and lions, have paws, not hoofs, and are therefore unclean. The word translated "paw"[35] *(yāḏ)* usually means "hand." Douglas, however, suggests that "hand" may be a better translation here. Animals with handlike paws are behaving "unnaturally" by

---

34. The gradations between life and death, altar and Sheol (realm of the dead), holy men and unclean, perfect sacrificial and dead animals can be represented diagrammatically as follows:

Life Normality		increasingly $\longrightarrow$ abnormal		Death Total Disorder	
Holy of Holies	Altar	Tabernacle Court	Camp	Outside Camp	Sheol
God	Priests	Deformed Priests	Israelites	Unclean	Dead
	Perfect Sacrificial	Blemished Sacrificial	Edible (clean)	Inedible (unclean)	Carcasses

---

35. The only other time it is translated "paw" in the AV is 1 Sam. 17:37, "out of the paw of the lion, and out of the paw of the bear." In 1 Sam. 17 it could be an idiomatic phrase—"from the power of the lion."

using their hands for walking. By using an inappropriate means of locomotion they are shown to be unclean.[36]

Swarming Creatures and the Pollution They Cause (29–38)

The animals listed in vv. 29 and 30 are described as swarming. Modern naturalists are fairly sure that only small animals such as mice and lizards are meant, since they are described as climbing over and falling into various household utensils. These creatures are unclean because they swarm, that is, they dart hither and thither in unpredictable fashion. Swarming is expressly contrary to holiness in biblical thought, according to Douglas. Order not chaos is the goal of creation, and this principle applies as much to motion as to species. "Since the main animal categories are defined by their typical movement, 'swarming,' which is not a mode of propulsion proper to any particular element, cuts across the basic classification. Swarming things are neither fish, flesh nor fowl. Eels and worms inhabit water, though not as fish; reptiles go on dry land, though not as quadrupeds; some insects fly, though not as birds. There is no order in them. . . . The prototype and model of the swarming things is the worm. As fish belong in the sea, so worms belong in the realm of the grave with death and chaos."[37] If this explanation is correct, the underlying theology is the same as before. Only animals that are true examples of each type are clean. Others which transgress the norms of locomotion are unclean in themselves and convey impurity to others when dead.

These "swarming creatures" present their own special problems. Like other animals their corpses pollute. But because they tend to enter houses, they come into contact with all sorts of household objects and pollute them. Some typical situations in which this may occur are therefore outlined and an appropriate remedy for the defilement is specified.

The basic principle governing the following laws is stated in v. 32, *Anything on to which any of them falls becomes unclean when they are dead.* The usual English translation (cf. RSV) may suggest that only the dead corpse of the animal actually falling on something pollutes. The Hebrew allows, however, for the possibility of a live

---

36. *Purity and Danger*, p. 56, followed by Porter, p. 90. Douglas also suggests this could explain why the animals listed in vv. 29–30 are banned: their forefeet are uncannily handlike! More probably they are unclean for swarming.
37. *Purity and Danger*, p. 56.

animal falling onto or into something and dying there. Anything with which the dead body of the animal comes in contact is defiled.

What is to be done with the polluted object? That depends on what it is. If it is made of wood, or is a garment, or leather or sack, *or any article which is in use* (v. 32), it may be cleansed. This is done by placing the thing in water, and probably leaving it to soak till evening (v. 32). But the rule could mean that it was sufficient to dip the polluted object in water, and leave its pollution to clear itself by evening. At any rate by evening the pollution was removed and the vessel or other object was then ritually clean.

However, pottery vessels, ovens, and stoves (v. 35)[38] could not be purified this way. They had to be broken to preclude their re-use. Similarly any food or drink contained within the vessel became impure and therefore could not be consumed. Logically, if a small vessel containing water becomes impure when one of these creatures falls into it, it should follow that large containers such as cisterns should also become polluted if an animal falls into them (v. 36). This would have drastic consequences in a country where drinking water is often in short supply. So immediately an exception to the general principle is stated: if an animal falls into a spring or cistern, neither the container nor the water becomes impure. Only the person who fishes out the dead animal contracts impurity.

It is difficult to be sure why a polluted wooden vessel is treated differently from a polluted earthenware vessel (vv. 32–33). Why does one only require washing but the other must be destroyed? A similar rule is enunciated in 6:21 [Eng. 28] with regard to the purification offering. It is usually explained by saying that impurity soaks into an earthenware vessel and is hard to remove by washing, whereas in the case of a wooden vessel it only remains on the surface. This would be true if the pottery were not glazed, and the wood were highly polished. But since glazed pottery was indeed made in Palestine, this explanation does not seem entirely convincing. If this was the thinking, would not impurity have sunk into garments and sacking and be equally difficult to remove (v. 32)? It seems possible that the distinction is between vessels and implements used for ordinary work and cooking vessels. Impurity in food would be more serious than on clothes.

Both explanations may have a bearing on the final case dealt

---

38. *Oven,* Heb. *tannûr,* means a large pot for boiling or baking. *Stove, kîrayim,* is used only here in the OT. According to the Mishnah, Shabbat 3:1, it was a kind of cooking range with two holes on which to put cooking pots.

with by the law, pollution of grain (vv. 37–38). If dry seed grain comes in contact with an animal's carcass, it is not polluted. If wet grain comes in contact with an animal, it becomes unclean. It is usually said that the water enables the impurity to penetrate the grain and make it unclean. But it may be that wet grain is being prepared not for sowing but for cooking or brewing, and this might be the reason why wet grain becomes unclean, but dry grain does not.

Pollution from Clean Animals (39–40)

Even clean animals that die naturally, instead of being ritually slaughtered and drained of blood, become unclean and may not be eaten. People who become unclean through contact or eating them must wash and remain unclean till the evening.

Concluding Exhortation (41–45)

To conclude this section of complicated legislation, one of the simpler rules is reiterated: "Everything that swarms on the ground is detestable: it must not be eaten" (v. 41, cf. 29). This single example stands for the whole set of food laws. To ignore them makes a man detestable, polluted, and unclean (v. 43). This is incompatible with Israel's calling. Israel was chosen to be God's holy people (Exod. 19:6). More than this, Israel is called to act like God: to *be holy, for I am holy.* Twice in two verses this ideal is stated. Verse 45 recalls the first covenant revelation to the people at Mount Sinai (Exod. 19ff.) and looks back beyond this event to their redemption from Egypt. These laws, which may strike the modern reader as quaint and pedantic, had a very different import to ancient Israel. They were perpetual reminders of God's grace to Israel. As the laws distinguished clean from unclean animals, so the people were reminded that God has distinguished them from all the other nations on earth to be his own possession. If the distinction between clean and unclean was sometimes obscure to Israel, the reason for God's election of Israel was too. It rested in God's inscrutable will, not on national merit (Deut. 7:6–8).

This call to "be holy, for I am holy" is one of the slogans of Leviticus. It is repeated twice here (vv. 44, 45) and comes again another three times (19:2; 20:7, 26). Man's highest duty is to imitate his creator. "You, therefore, must be perfect as your heavenly Father is perfect" (Matt. 5:48).

Summary (46–47)

This lists the laws in the chapter and states their purpose: *to make a distinction between the unclean and the clean*. This phrase harks back to the duties imposed on the priests in 10:10, "to distinguish . . . between the unclean and the clean . . . and to instruct the Israelites." Similar summaries are found at the end of chs. 13, 14, and 15.

The Food Laws in the NT

The Levitical laws relating to food caused one of the great controversies in the NT Church, and we find references to them by most of the NT writers. The controversy was due to two factors. First, the observance of these laws had become the mark of the faithful Jew; his abstinence from certain foods and his adherence to various rituals distinguished him from the Gentiles. As a result of the dispersal of Jews throughout the ancient world and the incorporation of Judaea into foreign empires, the Jews had become acutely aware of their distinctiveness, a distinctiveness that was focused and expressed in their food laws. Those in daily contact with Gentiles were continually reminded of the differences, and not least that Israel was God's chosen people and a holy nation. These laws, therefore, occupied a central place in Jewish life and thought, and for that matter still do today. The second reason for the controversy was our Lord's insistence that the food laws did not really matter, and the apostolic decision that they need not be observed unless it gave offense to the scrupulous.

Before discussing the theological motive underlying this radical reappraisal of the food laws, we should review the NT passages discussing the question. Matt. 15:10–20 (//Mark 7:14–23) is part of a sermon by Jesus attacking the custom of the Pharisees, which allowed men who made a donation to the temple to escape the obligation imposed by the fifth commandment to look after their parents. The custom made Pharisaic tradition more important than the word of God. Then Jesus turns to another traditional practice which he said tended to be regarded as more important than moral principle. He said that it was more important to have a pure heart than to wash hands before meals. "Whatever goes into the mouth passes into the stomach, and so passes on. But what comes out of the mouth proceeds from the heart, and this defiles a man. For out of the heart come evil thoughts, murder, adultery, fornication, theft, false witness, slander. These are what defile a man; but to eat with unwashed hands does not defile a man" (Matt. 15:17–20; cf. 23:25–28). Mark, commenting on Jesus' remarks, says, "Thus he declared all foods clean" (7:19). In other words Jesus was abrogating the distinction between clean and unclean animals. In John's Gospel we see Jesus putting his teaching into practice by asking for a drink from a Samaritan woman. In 4:9 the woman expresses surprise that Jesus as a Jew should be prepared to accept a drink from a Samaritan, "For Jews do not drink from the same vessels as Samaritans" (cf. NEB translation). The food laws were an assertion of Israel's distinctiveness; to remove them was to put into question her special status.

This comes out more clearly in the story of Cornelius. Like the conversion of Paul, this is a story which Luke recounts three times, a clear sign of its importance in the development of the early Church. We are told that Peter had a vision in which "he saw the heaven opened, and something descending, like a great sheet, let down by four corners upon the earth. In it were all kinds of animals and reptiles and birds of the air. And there came a voice to him, 'Rise, Peter; kill and eat.' But Peter said, 'No, Lord; for I have never eaten anything that is common or unclean.' And the voice came to him again a second time, 'What God has cleansed, you must not call common.' This happened three times, and the thing was taken up at once to heaven" (Acts 10:11–16). Soon afterward men come and invite Peter to go to Cornelius' house. When Peter arrives there, he explains why he has gone. "You yourselves know how unlawful it is for a Jew to associate with or to visit anyone of another nation; but God has shown me that I should not call any man common or unclean" (Acts 10:28). Then he preaches to them, and the Spirit comes upon Cornelius and his household and they are baptized. Reporting his actions to the other apostles, Peter points to the gift of the Spirit as proof that God has removed the barriers between Jew and Gentile. What is striking about the narrative from our point of view is the way Peter links the vision abolishing the distinction between clean and unclean animals with the distinction between clean and unclean men, i.e., between Jew and Gentile.

The issue of clean and unclean foods was discussed again at

the Council of Jerusalem (Acts 15), when it was debated whether it was necessary to circumcise the Gentiles and charge them to keep the law of Moses (v. 5). It was decided to require from Gentile believers only that they should abstain from the pollutions of idols, from unchastity, from what is strangled, and from blood. In other words, the requirement of circumcision and the distinction between clean and unclean animals were abolished. This is sometimes seen as a compromise between the Jewish and Gentile wings of the Church. There may well have been an element of this in their decision, but it is possible to see a theological basis for their conclusion. The rite of circumcision and the distinction between clean and unclean animals were particularly associated with the special status of Israel as the covenant people, whereas the prohibition on blood (and strangled meat) went back earlier to the time of Noah (Gen. 9:4). It was the laws distinguishing Israel from the other nations that were set aside, not the older moral principles that applied to all men.

In Paul's Epistles the question of food is discussed in various passages. Paul does indeed advise that the Christian should abstain from certain foods if the circumstances warrant. This is not because any foods are unclean in themselves; "the earth is the Lord's, and everything in it" (1 Cor. 10:26). The reason for abstaining is now different: it is the law of love. The Christian according to Paul may eat anything as long as he gives no offense in so doing. But should this freedom lead to a fellow Christain stumbling, he should avoid those foods which lead to suspicion. "If your brother is being injured by what you eat, you are no longer walking in love. Do not let what you eat cause the ruin of one for whom Christ died" (Rom. 14:15).

The Christian Value of Leviticus 11

The NT teaches that the OT food laws are no longer binding on the Christian. These laws symbolized God's choice of Israel. They served as constant reminders of God's electing grace. As he had limited his choice among the nations to Israel, so they for their part had to restrict their diet to certain animals. At every turn these laws reminded them of God's grace toward Israel. In the new era when salvation was open to all men, and Israel was no longer the only object of divine grace, the laws lost their particular significance. They could only serve to divide mankind into Jew and Gentile, whereas in the age which has now begun God's further purpose is revealed "in Christ . . . to unite all things in him" (Eph. 1:10). The distinction between clean and unclean foods is as obsolete as the distinction between Jew and Gentile.

This is not to say that these laws have nothing to teach the Christian. As we have seen, they were constant reminders to Israel that they were chosen to be a holy people, that they were called to imitate God, and that the laws were a reminder to give thanks for this calling. The NT believer is in a very similar position. The Church is now "a chosen race, a royal priesthood, a holy nation, God's own people" (1 Pet. 2:9). They are bidden to set their "minds on things that are above, not on things that are on the earth" (Col. 3:2), to "give thanks in all circumstances" (1 Thess. 5:18). Though the Christian is so much more privileged than ancient Israel, it is easy to take for granted the grace that has been given him and fail to acknowledge it. The ancient food laws were designed to curb such forgetfulness.

These laws were not only reminders of Israel's redemption, they were "like signs which at every turn inspired meditation on the oneness, purity and completeness of God. By rules of avoidance, holiness was given a physical expression in every encounter with the animal kingdom and at every meal. Observance of the dietary rules would then have been a meaningful part of the great liturgical act of recognition and worship which culminated in the sacrifice of the temple."[39] Douglas has showed that there is a connection in biblical thinking between wholeness, holiness, and integrity. God demands integrity of character and wholeness of physical form in his worshippers. These rules were symbols of a moral order. Only the normal members of each sphere of creation, e.g., fishes with fins, counted as clean. This definition, which identified "perfect" members of the animal kingdom with purity, was a reminder that God looked for moral perfection in his people. Carrion-eating birds and carnivorous animals were unclean because they also typified a man's sinful, destructive, and murderous instincts. In a real sense, then, Jesus was drawing out the meaning of the symbolism of the Levitical laws in insisting that it was what comes out of man that defiles him, "evil thoughts, murder, adultery, etc." These rules in Leviticus served not only as reminders of redemption but of moral values. With the law of God written on his heart by the Spirit, the Christian ought not to need such tangible reminders of God's will and charac-

39. Douglas, *Purity and Danger,* p. 57.

ter. He also has ready access to the Bible, which holds up a mirror to his conduct. Let us follow James' advice to look into that perfect law, the law of liberty, and act (Jas. 1:25).

B. UNCLEANNESS OF CHILDBIRTH (CH. 12)

1 *The Lord spoke to Moses:*
2 *"Speak to the Israelites as follows: If a woman conceives and gives birth to a boy, she becomes unclean for seven days, as unclean as she is during her menstrual period.*
3 *On the eighth day the flesh of his foreskin must be circumcised.*
4 *For another thirty-three days she must stay at home until her blood is cleansed. She must not touch anything holy, and she must not go to the sanctuary till her time of purification is complete.*
5 *But if she gives birth to a girl, for two weeks she becomes as unclean as during her menstruation, and then she must stay at home for sixty-six days, because her blood is being cleansed.*
6 *When the time of her purification is complete, for a boy or a girl, she must bring to the priest at the entrance of the tent of meeting a one-year-old lamb for a burnt offering, and a pigeon or a dove for a purification offering.*
7 *Then he must offer them before the Lord to make atonement for her and she will be purified from her discharge of blood. This is the law for the woman who gives birth to a boy or a girl.*
8 *If she cannot afford a sheep, she may take two doves or pigeons, one for the burnt offering and one for the purification offering. The priest will make atonement for her and she will be clean."*

The Structure of Leviticus 12

1	Introduction
2–5	Uncleanness following birth
	2–4 of a boy
	5 of a girl
6–7a	Sacrifice after birth
7b	Summary
8	Additional provision for the poor

The structure of this short law is clear. First there is a definition of how long a woman is unclean after childbirth, and what she must do during this time (vv. 2–5). The main case—uncleanness following the birth of a boy—is introduced by *kî* (v. 2), whereas the subsidiary case is introduced by *'im* (v. 5). For this pattern elsewhere in Leviticus see especially chs. 1 and 4–5. When the period of uncleanness expires, appropriate sacrifices are specified

(vv. 6–7). There is a summary of the contents of the law (v. 7), and finally a provision for the poor (v. 8).

This basic structure reappears in the following chapters:

Period of uncleanness	12:2ff.	13:1ff.	15:1ff.	25ff.
Sacrifice	6–7	14:1ff.	15:14–15	29-30
Summary	7	13:59; 14:32, 54		32-33
Provision for the poor	8	14:21ff.		

Uncleanness after Childbirth

After dealing with the uncleanness associated with animals, the law moves on to consider various bodily defilements. Ch. 12 deals with the ritual defilement that follows childbirth, chs. 13 and 14 with the uncleanness caused by skin diseases, and ch. 15 with the uncleanness associated with reproduction, including the woman's monthly cycle. This is referred to in vv. 2, 5 of this chapter, anticipating the law discussed in more detail in 15:19ff. Whereas the previous chapter dealt with causes of pollution that are external to man, these chapters deal with internal sources of pollution; they arise from the constitution of man, not from his environment. Insofar as man can pollute himself through his own bodily functions as well as through his contact with animals, these uncleanness laws reflect the fact that Israel's status as a holy nation faces challenges inside and outside. Sin is not merely a matter of environment but of individual failure.

The law is short and simple. When a baby is born, the mother is contagiously unclean for one or two weeks, *as unclean as she is during her menstrual period* (v. 2, cf. 5). This is more fully explained in 15:19–24. In the week following menstruation a woman was not only unclean in herself and unable to visit the sanctuary, but anyone or anything she touched became unclean as well. On the eighth day a boy had to be circumcised (v. 3; cf. Gen. 17:10ff.), but the woman remained unclean in herself, though she would no longer pollute other people. She had, therefore, to refrain from touching anything holy, e.g., from eating meat from a peace offering (7:20–21), and if she was a priest's wife from eating the priestly portions to which she was entitled (22:3ff.). She was also debarred from going to church (vv. 4, 5). This is another illustration of the principle that the unclean must be kept separate from the holy.[1]

After the period of purification is over (40 days for a boy, 80

---

1. See Introduction, VI.2: "Holiness."

for a girl), the mother must bring a purification offering and a burnt offering (vv. 6, 8). Sacrifice was generally required when a person's uncleanness lasted more than seven days (cf. ch. 15). The purification offering was presented first to cleanse the sanctuary.[2] Although she had not entered the sanctuary after the child had been born, her presence in the camp had still contaminated the altar (cf. 15:31), and the blood of the purification offering cleansed it. Then the burnt offering was brought to secure the forgiveness of sins and to express the mother's gratitude for the birth of her child and her renewed dedication to God. As elsewhere it was provided that the poor could bring a bird instead of a lamb as a burnt offering (v. 8; cf. 1:14ff.; 14:21ff.).

Though the ritual is straightforward, it is not easy to understand the thinking behind this law. Why should a woman become unclean by bearing children? This is what the creator had told her to do (Gen. 1:28). The same question arises with the other bodily sources of defilement mentioned in Lev. 15. Reproduction is essential to the survival of the human race, yet intercourse makes both man and wife unclean (15:18). If birth caused such serious and prolonged uncleanness, by far the most serious kind of uncleanness apart from uncured skin diseases dealt with in chs. 13–14, one would have supposed that ancient Israel would have frowned on childbearing. But as many stories make clear, childlessness was looked on as the height of misfortune (Gen. 15ff.; 1 Sam. 1) and sometimes as the judgment of God (Lev. 20:20; Deut. 28:18), whereas a large family was looked on as a great blessing from God (Lev. 26:9; Deut. 28:11; Ps. 127:3–5). The second main problem posed by these laws is why a girl should require twice as long a period of uncleanness as a boy.

Various answers are given by commentators. Some[3] suggest that in this law we have a relic of older pre-Israelite practice, which regarded the new mother as unclean. In view of the fact that other people do make the new mother taboo, this is a possible view; but we still must explain why God saw fit to incorporate this law into Leviticus, but did not endorse other age-old customs. Another explanation[4] is that women who had recently given birth to children were particularly prone to attack by demons. Reference is made to the beliefs of other nations and to Gen. 3:1 and Exod. 22:17

2. See commentary on ch. 4.
3. Heinisch, p. 59; cf. C. J. Vos, *Woman in OT Worship*, pp. 62ff.
4. Elliger, pp. 157f., and Bertholet, p. 41.

(Eng. 18). But there is no mention of demons here, and it is a risky procedure reading beliefs into a text when there is no clear evidence for them.

The law itself does provide a clear answer to the first question. It is not the birth itself that makes the woman unclean. There is no mention of the baby being unclean, but it is the discharge (lochia) that follows childbirth that make the woman unclean. Three times *her blood* or *discharge of blood* is mentioned in this law (vv. 4, 5, 7). For the first few days after delivery this discharge is bright red, then it turns brown and later becomes paler. It may last from two to six weeks. Because the first phase of lochia resembles the menstrual discharge, it is consistent for the woman to be treated as contagiously unclean as she is when she menstruates. Since the postnatal discharge lasts longer than a week, the woman continues to be unclean for an additional 33 or 66 days, making a total of 40 or 80 days.

On the more fundamental question of why any discharge should make a person unclean, the Bible gives no explicit answer. Keil[5] suggests that because decaying corpses discharge and cause pollution, so every bodily discharge is a reminder of sin and death. For Douglas,[6] a bleeding or discharging body lacks wholeness and is therefore unclean. Loss of blood can lead to death, the antithesis of normal healthy life. Anyone losing blood is at least in danger of becoming less than perfect and therefore unclean. Thus blood is at once the most effective ritual cleanser ("the blood makes atonement," 17:11) and the most polluting substance when it is in the wrong place. This is profound. Our greatest woes result from the corruption of our highest good, e.g., speech, sex, technology, atomic power.

No convincing explanation has been offered why the birth of a girl makes the mother unclean for twice as long as the birth of a boy. There does seem to have been a belief in antiquity that the postnatal discharge lasted longer in the case of a girl.[7] More recently a physician[8] has argued that there is scientific justification for such a belief. The figures he produces, however, hardly justify a doubling of the time.[9] Possibly there may be some reflection on the relative status of the sexes in ancient Israel. For instance, the redemption price of women is about half that of men (Lev. 27:2-7).

5. Keil, pp. 374f.
6. Douglas, *Purity and Danger,* p. 51, followed by Porter, p. 94.
7. Dillmann, p. 506.
8. D. I. Macht, "A Scientific Appreciation of Leviticus 12:1-5," *JBL* 52 (1933), pp. 253-260.
9. Cf. C. J. Vos, *Woman in OT Worship,* pp. 68f.

Leviticus 12 and the NT

These rituals are mentioned in Luke 2:22–24. "When the time came for their purification according to the law of Moses, they (Mary and Joseph) brought him up to Jerusalem . . . to offer a sacrifice . . . 'a pair of turtledoves, or two young pigeons.' "

The Anglican Book of Common Prayer provides a short service entitled "The Thanksgiving of Women after Childbirth commonly called the Churching of Women," in which the woman expresses gratitude for deliverance from "the great pain and peril of childbirth."

C. UNCLEAN DISEASES (CH. 13)

1 *The Lord spoke to Moses and Aaron as follows:*

2 *"If anyone has a swelling on his skin or an eruption or a shiny patch and it turns into the affliction of a serious skin disease on the skin of his body, he must be brought to Aaron the priest or one of his sons who are also priests.*

3 *The priest must look at the affected area in his skin. If the hair in the affected area has turned white and the affliction appears deeper than the skin, it is the affliction of a serious skin disease. When the priest sees it, he must declare him unclean.*

4 *If the shiny patch is white and does not appear to be deeper than the skin and the hair has not turned white, the priest must shut up the afflicted person for seven days.*

5 *On the seventh day the priest must look at him and if as far as he can see the affliction has not become any worse, that is, it has not spread in the skin, the priest must shut him up again for another seven days.*

6 *On the seventh day the priest must look at him again, and if the affliction is pale, and it has not spread in the skin, the priest shall declare him clean: 'it is just an eruption.' He must wash his clothes and be clean.*

7 *But if the eruption spreads in the skin after he has appeared before the priest for his cleansing, he must appear again before the priest.*

8 *Then the priest must look, and if the eruption has spread in the skin, he must declare him unclean: 'it is a serious skin disease.'*

9 *If anyone is afflicted with a serious skin disease, he must be brought to the priest.*

10 *The priest must look, and if there is a white swelling in the skin which has turned the hair white and if there is a speck of raw flesh in the swelling,*

11 *it is an old serious skin disease in his body and the priest must declare him unclean. He need not shut him up, for he is unclean.*

12 *If the serious skin disease breaks out in the skin and covers the whole skin of the afflicted man from head to foot, as far as the priest can see,*

13 *the priest must look, and if the serious skin disease does cover his whole body, he must declare the afflicted man clean. He has turned completely white: he is clean.*

14 *But when raw flesh is seen in him, he becomes unclean.*

15 *The priest must look at the raw flesh and declare him unclean. The raw flesh is unclean: it is a serious skin disease.*

16 *But then if the raw flesh retreats and becomes white, he may go to the priest.*

17 *And the priest must look at him, and if the affliction has turned white, the priest must declare the afflicted man clean. He is clean.*

18 *If anybody has a boil in his skin, which heals up,*

19 *and then a white swelling or reddish-white shiny patch comes up where the boil was, he must appear before the priest.*

20 *The priest must look, and if it seems deeper than the skin and its hair has turned white, the priest shall declare him unclean. It is. an affliction of a serious skin disease. It has broken out in the boil.*

21 *If when the priest looks at it, the hair in it has not turned white and it is not deeper than the skin but is pale, the priest must shut him up for seven days.*

22 *If it then spreads in the skin, the priest must declare it unclean. It is an affliction.*

23 *But if the shiny patch stays in one place and does not spread, it is just the scar of a boil, and the priest must declare him clean.*

24 *Or if anyone has a burn in his skin, and the living tissue becomes a reddish-white or white shiny patch,*

25 *the priest must look at it. If the hair in the shiny patch has turned white and it appears deeper than the skin, it is a serious skin disease. It has broken out in the burn and the priest must declare him unclean. It is an affliction of a serious skin disease.*

26 *But if when the priest looks at it, there is no white hair in the shiny patch and it is no deeper than the skin and it is pale, the priest must shut him up for seven days.*

27 *On the seventh day the priest must look at him, and if it has spread in the skin the priest must declare him unclean. It is an affliction of a serious skin disease.*

28 *But if the shiny patch has stayed in one place, and it has not spread in the skin and is pale, it is the swelling from a burn; the priest must declare him clean, for it is just a burn scar.*

29 *If a man or woman has an affliction in his scalp or beard,*

30 *the priest must look at it. If it seems deeper than the skin and the hairs in it are yellowish and thin, the priest must declare him unclean: it is a severe infection, a serious skin disease of the scalp or the beard.*

31 *If the priest looks at an affliction from a severe infection, and it seems no deeper than the skin but there are no black hairs in it, the priest must shut up the man afflicted with the severe infection for seven days.*

32 *On the seventh day the priest must look at the affliction, and if the*

severe infection has not spread, and there is no yellowish hair in it, and the severe infection seems no deeper than the skin,

33 *he must shave himself except for the severely infected area and the priest must shut up the severely infected man for another seven days.*

34 *Then on the seventh day the priest must look at the severe infection, and if it has not spread and seems no deeper than the skin, the priest must declare him clean. He must wash his clothes and he becomes clean.*

35 *If after his cleansing the severe infection spreads in the skin,*

36 *the priest must look at him. If the severe infection has spread in the skin, the priest must not look for the 'yellowish' hair: he is unclean.*

37 *But if the severe infection has not become any worse as far as he can see, and black hair has grown in it, the severe infection is cured. He is clean, the priest shall declare him clean.*

38 *If a man or woman has shiny patches on his body, that is, white shiny patches,*

39 *the priest must look, and if there are pale white patches on his body, it is vitiligo which has broken out in the skin; but he is clean.*

40 *If a man loses his hair, he is bald, but clean.*

41 *If he loses his hair from the edge of his face, he is 'bald in front,' but clean.*

42 *But if there is a reddish-white affliction in the baldness or front baldness, it is a serious skin disease breaking out in the baldness.*

43 *The priest must look, and if there is a reddish-white swelling of an affliction in the baldness similar in appearance to the serious skin disease on the body,*

44 *he is a man with a serious skin disease and he is unclean. The priest must declare him unclean; his affliction is on his head.*

45 *The man with a serious skin disease must have his clothes torn and his hair hanging loose and cover his moustache and call out 'unclean, unclean.'*

46 *All the days that he has the affliction he shall be unclean: he is unclean. He must live alone; his home must be outside the camp.*

47 *If a garment is affected with a serious skin disease, whether it is a woollen or linen garment,*

48 *in the warp or woof of linen or wool, or in leather or anything made of leather,*

49 *if the affliction is greenish or reddish in the garment or leather or the warp or woof or in any leather object, it is the affliction of a serious skin disease, and it must be shown to the priest.*

50 *The priest must look at the affliction and shut it up for seven days.*

51 *On the seventh day he must look at it. If the affliction has spread in the garment, the warp or the woof, the leather or anything made of leather, the affliction is a persistent serious skin disease. It is unclean.*

52 *He must burn the garment or the warp or the woof, whether it is wool or linen, or the leather article which has the affliction in it, because it is a persistent serious skin disease. It must be burned.*

53 *If the priest sees that the affliction has not spread in the garment, the warp or the woof, or in any leather article,*

54 *the priest must order them to wash the afflicted object and he must shut it up for another seven days.*

55 *After it has been washed the priest must look at the affliction, and if its appearance has not changed, even though it has not spread, it is unclean and you must burn it. It is corrosive whether in the front or the back.*

56 *If the priest looks and the affliction is pale after it has been washed, he must tear it out of the garment or the skin, or the warp or the woof.*

57 *And if it appears again in the garment or the warp or the woof or in any leather article, it is breaking out. You must burn the thing that is afflicted.*

58 *But any garment, warp or woof, or leather article, which you wash and the affliction leaves it, must be washed a second time and is then clean."*

59 *This is the law about serious skin disease in woollen or linen garments, warp or woof, or leather objects for declaring them clean or unclean.*

The Structure of Leviticus 13–14

These chapters deal with "serious skin disease" *(tsāra'at)*, in people (13:2–46; 14:1–32), clothes (13:47–58), and houses (14:33–53). It is difficult to find one English word to cover these diverse conditions. Inspired by the Greek translation *(lepra)*, traditional English translations have rendered *tsāra'at* by "leprosy." This is obviously inappropriate in the case of mold and mildew in clothes and houses. As for the various skin complaints covered by the Hebrew term, it is doubtful if any of them corresponds to true leprosy (Hansen's disease).

It may seem strange to modern ears to give the same name to such diverse conditions as mildew and psoriasis. Yet the Hebrew mind saw enough similarities between them to do so. All these afflictions, categorized as *tsāra'at*, are unclean, and may be recognized by discoloring of the surface (13:3, 49; 14:37) affecting part of an object, not its totality (13:9–13; 14:37, 42, 55), being more than superficial (13:3; 14:37), and actively spreading (13:7, 51; 14:44). These symptoms are clearly abnormal, and by disfiguring the appearance of man and his works, destroy the wholeness that ought to characterize the creation. For this reason these conditions are pronounced unclean.

The fondness for threefold division that characterizes other parts of the Levitical law is again very marked in these chapters. They fall into three large sections, each introduced by "The Lord spoke to Moses (and Aaron)" (13:1; 14:1, 33) and closing with "This is the law for . . ." (13:59; 14:32, 54). These sections are in turn subdivided into shorter paragraphs, where again triadic patterns are prominent.

The overall structure of these chapters is therefore as follows:

13:1–59 Serious skin disease in men and clothing: diagnosis and treatment.

14:1–32 Ritual cleansing after cure of serious skin disease.

14:33–57 Serious skin disease in houses; diagnosis, treatment, and cleansing.

The Structure of Leviticus 13

This chapter divides into two main sections, the diagnosis and treatment of human skin disease (vv. 2–46) and the diagnosis and treatment of "skin" diseases in clothing and similar articles (vv. 47–58). Twenty-one different cases of skin disease are distinguished in the first section, and three different cases of diseased garments in the second.

The formal description of each case is quite stereotyped. Each diagnosis usually contains the following items. First, a preliminary statement of the symptoms, e.g., "if anyone has a burn" (v. 24). Second, a priestly inspection, "the priest must look" (vv. 3, 10, etc.). Third, a statement of the specific symptoms on which the priest must base his diagnosis, e.g., "If the hair in the affected area has turned white" (v. 3). Fourth, the priestly diagnosis and prescribed treatment, e.g., "it is the affliction of a serious skin disease . . . he must declare him unclean" (v. 3). The declaration of uncleanness leads to the treatment prescribed in vv. 45–46. Sometimes where the initial priestly inspection proves inconclusive, the suspect may be shut up for a week and then inspected again (v. 26). Another week and another priestly inspection is required in some cases (vv. 5, 33). Occasionally the priestly inspection could be dispensed with (vv. 40–41).

Using these formal criteria as a guide, the law can be divided into sections as follows. It should be noted how often the main case (introduced by noun + *kî*, "if") is followed by two subsidiary cases (introduced by *'im*, "if"). This triplet pattern emerges elsewhere in the Levitical law.[1]

---

1. The same forms and triplet pattern recur in the laws about the skin diseases in clothing (vv. 47–58), but of course in these cases the infected article is treated differently from an afflicted man (cf. vv. 52 and 45–46).

The Identity of "Serious Skin Disease"

Until recently, Heb. *tsāra'at* has generally been translated "leprosy" following the Greek translation *lepra,* despite the fact that the term is also applied to infections of clothes (13:47–58) and houses (14:34–53). True leprosy (Hansen's disease) is a gruesome complaint

194

that affects the skin, and makes other parts of the body become numb and insensitive to pain, while the bones are deformed, and eventually the sufferer dies. It is still widespread in parts of the East and Africa. It is also contagious, and until recently was incurable. If leprosy was the disease in question here, there would be no problem in understanding why the sufferer was declared unclean.

Modern medical opinion is agreed, however, that leprosy is not one of the diseases being described.[2] There are various reasons for this. First, archeological evidence from Egypt reveals no evidence of people suffering from leprosy before the fifth century A.D. It is true that written records show that people had recognized leprosy before then, but it was certainly rare in Palestine in pre-Christian times.[3] Second, the symptoms of leprosy do not correspond to the description of the complaints in Leviticus. According to Browne, none of the biblical references to *tsāra'at* "includes any of the indubitable signs and symptoms of leprosy, and those that are mentioned tell against rather than for leprosy. Furthermore, none of the pathognomonic features of leprosy are so much as hinted at; these are, anaesthetic areas of the skin, painless and progressive ulceration of the extremities, and facial nodules. These are obvious departures from the normal that would be noticed by observant laymen, and were in fact noted in other lands when true leprosy began to occur."[4] Finally, the Greek *lepra* did not designate true leprosy, for which a different term was used, *elephantiasis*.[5]

But if *tsāra'at* is not leprosy, can it be identified with any specific complaints? In several passages *tsāra'at* is compared to snow (Exod. 4:6; Num. 12:10; 2 K. 5:27). English translations attempt to make the comparison more precise by rendering the phrase "leprous, as *white* as snow." There is no justification for adding "white" to the simile. The point of comparison may well be the flakiness of snow (cf. Ps. 68:15 [Eng. 14]; 147:16).[6] Hulse[7] argues that the comparison between "leprous" Miriam and a stillborn baby may well lie in the fact that when a fetus that has died in the womb is

2. S. G. Browne, *Leprosy in the Bible* (London: Christian Medical Fellowship, 1970); E. V. Hulse, "The Nature of Biblical 'Leprosy' and the Use of Alternative Medical Terms in Modern Translations of the Bible," *PEQ* 107 (1975), pp. 87–105.
3. Browne, pp. 9ff.
4. Browne, p. 8.
5. Browne, pp. 14f.
6. Browne, p. 7.
7. Hulse, p. 93.

delivered, its skin flakes off. Etymologically the Greek term *lepra* seems to refer to scaliness,[8] and Heb. *tsāra'at* may also.[9] It seems likely that the Hebrew term denotes a scaly skin disease of some sort.

Browne[10] holds that it is impossible to make an accurate diagnosis on the basis of the description in Lev. 13. Hulse is more sanguine, however. He believes the "serious skin disease" referred to in 13:2ff. is probably psoriasis, the disease of the head or the beard (vv. 29ff.) is favus, and the harmless spots of vv. 38–39 are vitiligo (leucoderma). He suggests that severe forms of other skin diseases, such as eczema, could sometimes have led to the patient being classified as unclean. The periods of confinement prescribed by Leviticus enabled the priest to distinguish these long-term skin diseases from skin troubles caused by other diseases, such as scarlet fever. After a week or two the skin would return to normal after a fever, but not if it were one of the complaints listed by Hulse.

Before examining the text of Lev. 13 in detail, it is well to have some modern medical definitions of the diseases in question.

"*Psoriasis* is a chronic, non-infectious skin disease characterized by the presence of well-demarcated, slightly raised reddish patches of various sizes covered by dry greyish-white or silvery scales. The disease is usually localized, particularly to the scalp, elbows, knees, shins, outer aspects of the arms and the lower part of the back, but can sometimes become more widespread. The lesions are itchy and when scratched the scales come off in flakes and leave a moist shiny red surface."[11] The severity of the disease varies. In some cases the symptoms may disappear for months or years. It generally does not affect the general health of the sufferer. In temperate regions 1–2 percent of the population tend to suffer from psoriasis, but it is much rarer in warmer climates.[12]

"*Favus* is a much more severe and damaging infection in which the fungus invades both the hair and the full thickness of the skin. The disease appears chiefly on the scalp and only rarely elsewhere. Yellow cup-shaped crusts are formed round loose wiry hairs which are the colour of hay and a mouse-like odour is present. Scar tissue develops in the deeper parts of the skin which results in

---

8. Hulse, p. 93.
9. Browne, p. 5; cf. BDB 863b.
10. Browne, pp. 5f.
11. Hulse, p. 96.
12. Hulse, pp. 99f.

permanent loss of hair leaving a smooth, glossy, thin, white patch."[13] It is infectious.[14]

"*Leucoderma* is a slightly disfiguring condition in which patches of otherwise normal skin lose their natural colouring and become completely white."[15] It differs from psoriasis and favus in affecting only the color of the skin and not penetrating below the surface.

Introduction (1)

The Lord spoke to Moses and Aaron. This is one of several laws in this section addressed to Aaron as well as Moses (11:1; 14:33; 15:1). The priests had a duty to distinguish between clean and unclean, and to teach the people the difference (10:10–11). These laws on the uncleanness resulting from skin disease particularly concerned the priests, and so Aaron, the high priest, is specifically addressed as well as Moses.

First Set of Tests for Skin Diseases (2–8)

This section gives general principles for distinguishing a *serious skin disease,* which involves uncleanness, from less important complaints, which do not. A "serious skin disease" may begin with some sort of *swelling* or *shiny patch*[16] on the skin (v. 2). If the layman suspects it is "serious" he must go to the priest, who then determines whether it is unclean or not.

The first test applied by the priest is whether the hair has turned white and how deep the trouble seems to lie. If the hair has turned white and the trouble is deeper than the skin, it is "serious" and the man is pronounced unclean (v. 3). He is then excluded from the camp and has to live alone, with his hair hanging loose and clothes torn, and must warn any who approach of his uncleanness (vv. 45–46). Since skin diseases do not affect the pigmentation of the hair, Hulse suggests the hair turns white as a result of the white scales clinging to the hairs.[17]

If, however, the scaliness only appears superficial and the

13. Hulse, pp. 96f.
14. Hulse, p. 100.
15. Hulse, p. 95.
16. *Baheret* (*shiny patch*); cf. AV "bright-spot," RSV "spot," NEB, TEV "inflammation." The variety of translations illustrates the uncertain meaning of the more general terms in this chapter. Etymology (*bhr*, "shine") and the early versions seem to connect it with brightness and shining, but clinical precision is impossible.
17. Hulse, p. 98.

hair has not become white, the priest has to suspend judgment. The suspect is shut up for a week, and the affected area reexamined by the priest a week later. If the scaliness has not spread, he is again confined for a week and reexamined. If the disease has still remained static and the affected area is *pale* [18] or "dim" (psoriasis is characterized by shiny scales), the man is pronounced clean (vv. 6–7). This quarantine period would help distinguish acute from chronic diseases. The disease had to become visibly worse for at least two weeks, when the hair and flesh were otherwise unaffected.

The Second Set of Tests for Skin Disease (9–17)

The second set of tests hangs on the presence of *raw* (living) *flesh* [19] in the affected area. If the hair has become white and there is raw flesh, this is a sure sign of a "serious skin disease." It is an *old* (v. 11) disease and no quarantine period is necessary. The exact meaning of *raw* is hard to determine here. It may refer to the inflammation of the skin making it red. Hulse suggests it refers to the tiny areas of bleeding that occur when the scales of psoriasis are rubbed off. [20] If the skin all over his body was affected by the disease and he turned white, this did not matter; but if "living" flesh was seen, the man was unclean (v. 13). The "serious skin disease" was therefore a patchy condition, such as psoriasis. "Thus, any very extensive skin disease which entailed peeling of the skin, such as exfoliative dermatitis or, again, the exfoliative stage of scarlet fever, was not biblical leprosy." [21]

Tests for Skin Disease Associated with Scars (18–28)

Similar tests are applied to more localized inflammations (vv. 18–28) on the site of a boil or burn. The presence of white hair and deep infection is a sure symptom that the disease is serious. In cases of doubt a period of two weeks quarantine is prescribed. This could be a description of favus or patchy eczema, but Hulse suggests that psoriasis is more likely. "It is well recognized that psoriasis can occur on scars and at sites of burns and other injuries." [22]

---

18. *Kēhāh* (lit. "has become pale"); cf. vv. 21, 26, 28, 39, 56. The root is also used of poor sight (Gen. 27:1) and weak spirits (Ezek. 21:12 [Eng. 7]).
19. *Speck of raw flesh (miḥyaṭ bāśār ḥay)* (lit. "living tissue [cf. v. 24] of living flesh").
20. Hulse, p. 98.
21. Hulse, p. 95.
22. Hulse, p. 98.

Tests for Skin Disease in the Scalp or Beard (29–37)

These verses deal with infections of the scalp and beard. A different word is used in v. 30 to describe these complaints. *Severe infection* renders Heb. *neṭeq.* As v. 30 makes plain it is nevertheless regarded as a kind of "serious skin disease," though its more usual description "severe infection" is one hint that a different complaint is here being referred to. Another is the juxtaposition of "serious skin disease" and "severe infection" in the summary of these chapters in 14:54. Finally, though the treatment of this disease is similar to that for the disease dealt with earlier, the priest is told to look out for yellow thin hair (v. 30) rather than white hair (cf. vv. 3, 4, 21, etc.). Yellowing of the hair is characteristic of favus rather than psoriasis. So Hulse[23] argues that favus is the disease referred to here.

The method of diagnosis of favus is similar to that of psoriasis. The priest has to look for yellowing hair and signs that the infection is deeper than the skin. If he fails to find them, the suspect is quarantined for up to two weeks. After the first week, he must shave his hair off apart from the area affected by the "severe infection."

Verse 31, *there are no black hairs in it,* seems to contradict the principles of diagnosis enunciated in vv. 30, 32, 36, 37. One would expect to read "and it seems no deeper than the skin and there are no yellow hairs in it," whereas it actually says "no black hairs in it." Keil[24] would like to read *tsāhōḇ* (yellow) instead of *shāḥōr* (black), but most commentators do not think the emendation is necessary. Any black hair in the infected area was sufficient to warrant a man being declared clean (cf. v. 37).

A Clean Skin Disease (38–39)

Most commentators recognize that the complaint referred to here is vitiligo or leucoderma, in which patches of the skin go completely white. In Arabic it is termed *bahaq,* in Hebrew *bōhaq.* It is not counted as defiling. Unlike the other complaints it does not go deeper than the skin and the hairs are not discolored by scales flaking off.

Baldness and Skin Disease (40–44)

These verses deal with other afflictions of the scalp. Baldness as

23. Hulse, p. 99.
24. Keil, p. 381.

such does not constitute uncleanness (v. 40), but serious skin diseases may attack the scalp of a bald man as well as someone who has not lost his hair. The same diagnostic tests apply to the scalp as to other parts of the body. Hulse[25] thinks that again psoriasis is the disease most likely to manifest the symptoms described here.

Treatment of Those with Serious Skin Disease (45–46)

When the priest has confirmed that the skin disease is serious and defiling, the sufferer must tear his clothes, untidy his hair, and cover his lip and cry "Unclean" to prevent people from defiling themselves by touching him. Furthermore, he must go and live by himself outside the camp. As someone who is permanently unclean, he must separate himself from the holy camp of Israel where God is present (Num. 5:1–4; cf. Deut. 23:11ff. [Eng. 10ff.]).

These two verses give some insight into the religious ideas associated with unclean skin diseases. Tearing the clothes, untidying the hair, and covering the moustache are signs of mourning. The word for "tear" *(pāram)* is a rare one, used in Leviticus only, in this passage and in 10:6; 21:10. In the other two passages it is connected with letting the hair loose as an act of mourning for the dead. It is something high priests should not do. Rending *(qāra')* one's clothes can be a sign of sorrow for death (Gen. 37:34; 2 Sam. 1:11) or for sin and its consequences (Num. 14:6; 2 K. 22:11, 19; Ezra 9:5) or other calamity (2 K. 11:14; 19:1). Covering the moustache[26] is specifically associated with mourning for the dead in Ezek. 24:17, 22, while in Mic. 3:7 it is a sign of shame for the seers who fail to receive an answer from God.

The diseased person has to live alone outside the camp. A solitary existence was viewed as a calamity in itself in ancient times (cf. Lam. 1:1). It is a modern idea to want to "get away from it all." Biblical man knew he was meant to live in society, to be a member of God's people. Living outside the camp would, therefore, have occasioned great distress. It was not that everywhere outside the camp was unclean; there were clean places outside the camp (e.g., 4:12). But it was the place farthest removed from God, the place to which the sinner and the impure were banished (10:4–5; Num. 5:1–4;

25. Hulse, p. 98.
26. *Śāpām (moustache,* "upper lip"—AV, RSV, NEB) is used too rarely to be sure of its exact meaning. The phrase "do the *śāpām*" (2 Sam. 19:25 [Eng. 24]) suggests facial hair is involved.

12:14–15; 31:19–24). It was the place where wrongdoers were executed (Num. 15:35–36).

The holiest area, where one was closest to God, was the tabernacle. It was here that the holy men, the priests, worked. The tabernacle was surrounded by the camp where Israel the holy people of God lived. This in turn was encircled by the area outside the camp, which was populated by non-Jews, sinners, and the unclean. To live outside the camp was to be cut off from the blessings of the covenant. It was little wonder that when a man was diagnosed as unclean he had to go into mourning. He experienced a living death; his life as a member of God's people experiencing God's blessing came to an end. Gen. 3 presents a similar picture. Man was warned that disobedience to God's command meant death (Gen. 2:17). In fact, physical destruction was not the immediate consequence of the fall, but exclusion from Eden (3:24), with the loss of all the benefits associated with it (3:16ff.), followed at once. As Adam and Eve experienced a living death when they were expelled from Eden, so every man who was diagnosed as unclean suffered a similar fate.

Elsewhere in Scripture we are told that this penalty was indeed enforced. When Miriam, Moses' sister, suffered from a skin disease she was shut out of the camp for seven days (Num. 12:9ff.). 2 K. 7:3ff. tells of four lepers who lived outside the city gate.

Death often follows sickness, and the OT writers sometimes bring out this connection. One goes down to Sheol when one dies, and when one is seriously ill (Ps. 18:6 [Eng. 5]; 30:4 [3]; 116:3; Isa. 38:10). In Sheol a miserable existence awaited the wicked (Isa. 14:10). Outside the camp the man afflicted with uncleanness was similarly deprived of the usual covenant mercies.

Serious "Skin Disease" in Clothing (47–58)

The modern mind sees little in common between human skin diseases and mold affecting garments or other household articles. The ancient Israelites saw things differently. They used the same word for both, *tsāraʻat*, which we have translated "serious skin disease." From the standpoint of appearance, there are areas of resemblance between the two complaints. Both are abnormal surface conditions that disfigure the outside of the skin or garment. Both cause the surface to flake or peel. These verses draw out other points of similarity in the diagnostic tests that are applied to distinguish clean from unclean fungal infections.

201

If the owner notices a greenish or reddish mold growing in a garment made of wool or linen, he has to bring it to the priest to be inspected. The same rule applies to things made of leather, to leather itself, and to parts of a garment, the "warp" and the "woof." This phrase *warp or woof* occurs several times, only in this chapter (vv. 48, 49, 51, 52, 53, 56, 57, 58). This, the traditional translation of the terms, refers to the lengthwise and cross threads in a woven garment. But such an interpretation is fraught with problems. How could mold grow in the warp and the woof and not in the garment itself? How could it grow in the warp without the woof being affected as well? Commentators offer two different solutions to this problem. The first is that the phrase refers to two types of yarn, one used for the warp, the other for the woof. It is suggested that the yarn for different parts of the process was prepared differently and stored separately.[27] Alternatively the expression refers to different stages in the manufacture, perhaps the spun yarn and the woven material.[28] The former explanation is probably preferable.

The test applied by the priest is quite simple. After examining the affected article he shuts it up for a week. If the mold or mildew spreads in the article during that week, it is *a persistent*[29] *serious skin disease,* and the article is therefore unclean and must be burned (v. 52). If, however, the mold does not seem to spread during the week that it is shut up, the article has to be washed and shut up for another week. If the appearance of the affected area does not change during that week, it is *corrosive*[30] and unclean and the whole article must be burned (v. 55). If the affected patch seems to fade during the week, only the affected area has to be torn out (v. 56), though if the infection breaks out again, the whole garment must be destroyed (v. 57).

Summary (59)

In this chapter certain maladies are described, and the priests are told how to distinguish between clean and unclean. Modern writers have attempted to identify these complaints and give them their modern names. Though this is a proper and worthwhile exercise it

27. E.g., Keil, p. 383; Hoffmann I, p. 390.
28. Snaith, p. 98.
29. *Mam'eret (persistent).* A rare term found only in 13:51–52; 14:44; and Ezek. 28:24. Of uncertain etymology. The context is the best guide to its meaning.
30. *Peḥeṭet.* Used only here and meaning dubious. BDB 809a associate it with *pḥṭ,* "perforate."

should not be supposed this is what the priests were trying to do. They were not doctors trying to decide whether a man was suffering from psoriasis or eczema. The symptoms as such were what caused a man to be pronounced unclean, not the underlying cause of these symptoms. If a man looked bad, he was declared unclean. It was not that the disease as such was thought to be infectious or would result in his death, but the symptoms were incompatible with full membership of the covenant people.

The symptoms that led to a verdict of uncleanness were as follows. The "skin disease" had to be long and lasting. It had to be old (v. 11) or last at least a week or two (vv. 4ff., 26ff., 33ff., 50ff.). It had to be deeper than the skin (vv. 3, 20, 25, 30) or irremovable by washing (v. 55). It was something that affected only part of a person. It was patchy. If it covered the whole body, it did not defile (vv. 12–13). With garments and articles it is clear that only part of the object was affected, since v. 56 speaks of tearing out the affected spot.

This last observation perhaps gives the clue as to why certain diseases were regarded as unclean and others were not. Holiness in Leviticus is symbolized by wholeness. Animals must be perfect to be used in sacrifice. Priests must be without physical deformity. Mixtures are an abomination. Men must behave in a way that expresses wholeness and integrity in their actions. When a man shows visible signs of lack of wholeness in a persistent patchy skin condition, he has to be excluded from the covenant community. Temporary deviations from the norm do not attract such treatment, but if the symptoms last for more than two weeks, he must go to live outside the true Israel. These laws on skin diseases are again eloquent testimony to the importance of purity and holiness in ancient Israel. Anyone might fall victim to these complaints and face the prospect of being cut off from his family and friends for the rest of his days. Yet it was considered so important to preserve the purity of the tabernacle and the holiness of the nation that individuals and families might be forced to suffer a good deal. Individual discomfort was not allowed to jeopardize the spiritual welfare of the nation, for God's abiding presence with his people depended on uncleanness being excluded from their midst (cf. Isa. 6:3–5).

D. CLEANSING OF DISEASE (CH. 14)

1 *The Lord spoke to Moses as follows:*

2 *"This is the law about the man with a serious skin disease on the occasion of his cleansing. He must be brought to the priest.*

3 *and the priest must go outside the camp and look, and if the affliction of a serious skin disease has healed in the affected man,*

4 *the priest must command that they take for the one who is being cleansed two clean live birds, some cedar wood, scarlet cord, and hyssop.*

5 *Then the priest must order them to kill one of the birds over an earthenware vessel containing fresh water.*

6 *But he must take the living bird, the cedar wood, the scarlet cord, and hyssop and dip them into the blood of the bird which was killed over the fresh water.*

7 *Then he must sprinkle it seven times over the one who is being cleansed from the serious skin disease, and he must declare him clean and let the living bird fly away in the open.*

8 *The cleansed man must wash his clothes, shave off all his hair, and wash his body in water, and he is then clean. Afterward he may enter the camp but must live outside his tent for a week.*

9 *On the seventh day he must shave off all his hair, that is, his head, his beard, and his eyebrows. He must shave off all his hair; then he must wash his clothes and himself in water, and then he is clean.*

10 *On the eighth day he must take two perfect male lambs and one perfect ewe-lamb a year old, three tenths of an ephah of fine flour for a cereal offering mixed with oil, and one log of oil.*

11 *The officiating priest must stand them and the man who is being cleansed before the Lord in the entrance of the tent of meeting.*

12 *Then the priest must take one male lamb and offer it as a reparation offering, and the log of oil, and dedicate them as a dedication before the Lord.*

13 *He must kill it in the place where he kills the purification and burnt offerings in the sanctuary, because the reparation offering is like the purification offering; it is most holy and belongs to the priest.*

14 *Then the priest must take some of the blood of the reparation offering and put it on the lobe of the right ear of the man being cleansed, on his right thumb, and on the big toe of his right foot.*

15 *The priest must take some of the oil and pour it into the palm of his left hand.*

16 *Then the priest must dip his right finger into the oil in his left-hand palm, and sprinkle some of it with his finger seven times before the Lord.*

17 *And some of the remaining oil in his hand the priest must put on the man's right ear lobe, the right thumb, and right big toe, on top of the blood of the reparation offering.*

18 *Then the priest must put the rest of the oil in his palm on the head of the man who is being cleansed, and the priest must make atonement for him.*

19 *The priest must do the purification offering and make atonement for the cleansed man because of his impurity, and afterward he must kill the burnt offering.*

20 *The priest must offer the burnt offering and the cereal offering on the altar and make atonement for him, and then he is clean.*

21 *If he is poor and cannot afford it, he must take one male lamb as a reparation offering for a dedication, to make atonement for himself, and a tenth of an ephah of fine flour mixed with oil for a cereal offering, a log of oil,*

22 *and two doves or pigeons, whichever he can afford. One is for a purification offering and one for a burnt offering.*

23 *On the eighth day of his cleansing he must bring them to the priest to the entrance of the tent of meeting before the Lord.*

24 *Then the priest must take the lamb of the reparation offering and the log of oil and dedicate them as a dedication before the Lord.*

25 *Then he must kill the lamb of the reparation offering, and then the priest must take some of the blood of the reparation offering and put it on the lobe of the right ear of the man being cleansed and on his right thumb and right big toe.*

26 *Then the priest must pour some of the oil into the palm of his left hand,*

27 *and sprinkle some of it with his right finger seven times before the Lord.*

28 *Then the priest must put some of the oil in his palm on the lobe of the man's right ear, on his right thumb, and on his right big toe, where the blood of the reparation offering had been placed.*

29 *But the priest must put the rest of the oil in his palm on the man's head to make atonement for him before the Lord.*

30 *Of the birds he can afford, whether doves or pigeons, he must use*

31 *whatever he can afford, one as a purification offering and one as a burnt offering along with the cereal offering, and the priest must make atonement for the man being cleansed before the Lord."*

32 *This is the law for the man with a serious skin disease who cannot afford his cleansing.*

33 *And the Lord spoke to Moses and Aaron as follows:*

34 *"If, when you come to the land of Canaan which I am giving you to possess, I put upon a house in the land you possess the affliction of a serious skin disease,*

35 *the owner of the house must come and tell the priest: 'Something that looks to me like an affliction is in the house.'*

36 *Then the priest must give orders that they clear out the house before the priest comes to look at the affliction, so that nothing in the house becomes unclean. Afterward the priest must come to look at the house.*

37 *He must look at the affliction, and if the affliction in the walls of the house consists of greenish or reddish spots, and it seems deeper than the wall surface,*

38 *the priest must come out of the house to the doorway and shut it up for seven days.*

39 *On the seventh day the priest must go back and look. If the affliction has spread in the walls of the house,*

40 *the priest must give orders that the stones which are affected by the*

205

affliction must be pulled out and dumped outside the city in an unclean place.

41 *He must have the interior of the house scraped, and they must pour the plaster which they have scraped away outside the city in an unclean place.*

42 *Then they must take other stones and put them in place of the old stones and take fresh plaster and plaster the house.*

43 *If then the affliction recurs and breaks out in the house after he has pulled out the stones, has scraped the house and replastered it,*

44 *the priest must come and see that the affliction has spread in the house. It is a persistent serious skin disease in the house. It is unclean.*

45 *He must pull down the house, the stones, the woodwork and all the plaster of the house, and bring it outside the city to an unclean place.*

46 *Whoever enters the house during the period it is officially shut up becomes unclean until the evening.*

47 *Whoever sleeps or eats in the house must wash his clothes.*

48 *But if the priest enters the house and sees that the affliction has not spread in the house after it has been replastered, the priest can declare the house clean because it has recovered from its affliction.*

49 *He must take to purify the house two birds, cedar wood, scarlet cord, and hyssop.*

50 *He must kill one bird over an earthenware pot containing fresh water,*

51 *and he must take the cedar, the hyssop, the scarlet cord, and the living bird, and dip them in the blood of the one that has been killed and in the fresh water, and sprinkle the house seven times.*

52 *Then he must purify the house with the bird's blood, the fresh water, the living bird and cedar wood, hyssop, and scarlet cord.*

53 *He must let the living bird go out of the city into the open countryside and make atonement for the house, and it is then clean."*

54 *This is the law for every affliction of a serious skin disease, for a severe infection,*

55 *for serious skin diseases in garments or houses,*

56 *and for swellings, eruptions, and shiny patches,*

57 *to show when they are unclean and when they are clean. This is the law for serious skin disease.*

The Structure of Leviticus 14

This chapter is intimately connected with the preceding one and some preliminary observations about its arrangement have already been made; see above, "The Structure of Leviticus 13–14" and "The Structure of Leviticus 13."

It divides into two halves; the first deals with the ritual cleansing of a man whose skin disease has cleared up (14:1–32), and the second with the treatment of the "skin disease" of houses (vv. 33–53). Each part subdivides into three paragraphs.

Ritual Cleansing after Cure of Serious Skin Disease (2–32)

The procedures described in this chapter are not curative but ritual. The priests did not do anything to cure the sick person. Their duty was to diagnose when a man was unclean and when he was clean again, and to make sure that the correct rituals were carried out when the disease cleared up and the man was readmitted to the community. To use a modern analogy, the priest in ancient Israel was more like a public health inspector than a physician. He determined whether a person was infected; he did not attempt to cure him. In this respect Israel differed from her neighbors, who went in for exorcism and magical rites in attempts to cure disease. In Israel a man had to seek help directly from God in prayer, not rely on the dubious remedies of folk medicine.

The rites prescribed here are long and complicated, as befits the great change in status involved in becoming clean. When someone was pronounced ritually unclean with a skin disease he was excluded from the covenant community. When his complaint cleared up he was readmitted to a life of fellowship within the holy nation. This transition from death to life is marked first by ceremonies outside the camp. Then readmission to full membership of Israel is secured by offering the four main types of mandatory sacrifice—the purification offering, the burnt offering, the reparation offering, and the cereal offering.

Rituals outside the camp (2–9)
If a man thinks he has recovered from a skin disease, the priest is

207

summoned to examine him outside the camp. If the priest is satisfied that the man is cured, two clean birds are brought. One has to be killed and its blood caught and mixed with fresh water contained in an earthenware vessel. Some of it is sprinkled over the man, using cedar wood, scarlet cord, and hyssop. The living bird is also dipped into the blood and then allowed to fly free. Then the man himself must shave all over and wash himself and his clothes. He is then clean enough to enter the camp, but not to live at home.

On the seventh day the man shaved again and underwent another ritual bath to cleanse himself and make himself fit to enter the court of the tabernacle the following day (v. 9).

These rituals are termed by anthropologists "rites of aggregation," i.e., ceremonies in which a person who is in an abnormal social condition is reintegrated into ordinary society. Shaving, washing, and offering sacrifice are regular ingredients of such rites.[1] The shaving and washing obviously portray cleansing from the pollution caused by the skin disease and the life of uncleanness implicit in dwelling outside the camp.

The bird rites are more difficult to interpret. There are some resemblances between them and the day of atonement rituals where goats were used (Lev. 16). On that occasion one goat was offered as a purification offering, while the other, the scapegoat, was driven out into the wilderness symbolically bearing the nation's sins (16:6ff.).

The first clue to the meaning of this ritual is to be found in the selection of two clean birds. Clean animals in OT thought symbolize Israel.[2] The birds must represent the healed Israelite who is about to reenter the covenant community. This symbolic equation is confirmed by dipping the one bird in the blood of the other and sprinkling that blood on the worshipper. This action at least establishes a visible relationship between the worshipper and the birds. This has been seen by older commentators. For example, Keil asserts that the bird let loose in the open country is "a symbolical representation of the fact that the former leper was now imbued with new vital energy, and released from the fetters of his disease, and could now return . . . into the fellowship of his countrymen."[3] The other bird also symbolized the cured man. Its death, according to Keil, portrays the

---

1. E. R. Leach, *Culture and Communication,* pp. 78f.
2. See above on ch. 11. Specifically sacrificial birds such as doves or pigeons are not prescribed; this may be deliberate as they could be equated with the priest.
3. Keil, p. 385.

fate that would have overtaken a man but for God's mercy in healing him.

Davies prefers to identify the role of the released bird more closely with that of the scapegoat: "it carried away into the outside world the problem afflicting the man and society."[4] The scapegoat carried away the nation's sins whereas the bird carried away the polluting skin disease.

Comparison with the day of atonement ceremony may also clarify why the other bird was sacrificed. In Lev. 16 the second goat serves as a purification offering to cleanse the tabernacle "from the uncleannesses of the Israelites" (16:19). The blood was sprinkled seven times over the mercy seat (16:14–15). In this case too the blood of the bird is sprinkled seven times over the worshipper, and the priest then declares him clean (14:7). Indeed, this rite is very similar to the poor man's purification offering (5:7–10) except that that was held in the court of the tabernacle whereas this one took place outside the camp. The use of cedar wood, scarlet, and hyssop is also in place in a rite of purification (cf. Num. 19:6; Ps. 51:9 [Eng. 7]; Isa. 1:18), though we cannot be sure of the precise symbolic significance of these items.

For seven days the man had to live outside his tent (v. 8). In other words, his reintegration into the covenant community was not complete, until on the eighth day he was permitted to bring sacrifice in the tabernacle. Calvin draws a parallel with circumcision being delayed till the eighth day after birth. "As infants on the eighth day . . . were grafted into the church; so now the eighth day is prescribed for the restoration of those who, in the cure they have received, are as it were born again; for they are accounted dead whom the leprosy had banished from the holy congregation."[5]

Rituals inside the court of the tabernacle (10–32)
On the eighth day the process of reincorporating the cured man into the covenant was completed by sacrifice and certain ritual anointings. These ceremonies find their closest parallels in the concluding covenant rituals described in Exod. 24 and in the ordination service described in Lev. 8–9.

The importance of this occasion emerges in the type of sacrifices prescribed: all the mandatory sacrifices, burnt (cf. Lev. 1),

---

4. D. J. Davies, "An Interpretation of Sacrifice in Leviticus," *ZAW* 89 (1977), p. 397; cf. Porter, p. 108.
5. Calvin II, p. 26.

cereal[6] (cf. Lev. 2), purification (Lev. 4), and reparation (Lev. 5), had to be presented. Only peace offerings (Lev. 3), which were almost always voluntary, are missing. For the animal sacrifices lambs were prescribed, but doves could be substituted for lambs in the case of the burnt and purification offering, if the cost of providing three lambs was too heavy. The reparation offering could not be less than a lamb, though.

The function of these sacrifices has already been discussed. Only the presence of the reparation offering is unexpected in this list. Usually after a man had been declared clean after long-term uncleanness, he simply had to offer a purification offering to cleanse the sanctuary, and a burnt offering, which brought reconciliation with God and represented a rededication of his life to God's service. The cereal offering was a pledge of allegiance. All these motives are clearly intelligible in the context of a man being readmitted to full membership of the covenant. But why was the reparation offering required?

Three different situations in which a reparation offering was required are described in 5:14–26 (Eng. 6:7): trespass against sacred property, suspected trespass, or false oaths. It is possible, as Milgrom[7] argues, that the reparation offering had to be presented by the cured man, because he might suspect that his serious skin disease had been caused by a trespass, though he was not certain how he had sinned. On a number of occasions in the OT people do develop "serious skin disease" following sacrilegious behavior (e.g., Num. 12:9ff.; 2 K. 5:27; 2 Chr. 26:17ff.). Aware that sacrilege could be punished in this way, a devout Israelite who broke out with skin disease might consider it appropriate to offer a reparation offering just in case some lapse of his was the cause of his suffering. Alternatively, it could be that the reparation offering, the basic function of which is to compensate God for loss, was thought appropriate in this case to repay all the sacrifices, tithes, and firstfruits which the afflicted man had been unable to present during his uncleanness.

The most unusual feature of these rituals is the use to which the blood of the reparation offering is put. It is smeared on the right ear, thumb, and big toe of the cured man (vv. 14, 17; cf. 8:23ff.). Presumably, as in other cases where sacrificial blood is smeared on

6. The volume of an ephah (vv. 10, 21) is uncertain, probably about 15 liters or 20 lbs. of flour. The log is also uncertain, possibly about a pint or half a liter. Cf. de Vaux, *Ancient Israel*, pp. 200–203.
7. Milgrom, *Cult and Conscience*, pp. 80ff.

objects, this action purifies the recipient. Seven days earlier a similar rite had been enacted outside the camp using the blood of a bird, and this served as an initial cleansing. Now the blood of a sacrificial lamb was used to complete the purifying process. The blood sprinkled on the altar was also smeared on the cured man, thus indicating that he was again in contact with the grace of God. This message is underlined by the next step. Oil, first dedicated to God, and placed in the priest's left hand, was sprinkled seven times before the Lord, and some of it was put on the cured man's right ear, thumb, and big toe and over his head (vv. 15–17, 26–29). If the blood served to unite him with the altar, the oil spoke of union between God, the priest, and the worshipper. Once readmitted to full membership of the covenant, the healed man could offer the standard sacrifices expected of all Israel, the burnt, cereal, and purification offerings (vv. 19–20, 30–31).[8]

The Infections of Houses (33–53)

The laws relating to serious skin diseases close with a section on infected houses. Like garments they too can be affected with mildew or possibly dry rot. Tests similar to those applied to garments and human skin diseases are used to determine whether the infection is serious. The color and depth of the infection—if it is *greenish or reddish* (14:37; cf. 13:49) and is *deeper than the wall surface* (14:37; cf. 13:3, 20–21, 26, etc.)—is significant. A similar quarantine period of seven days is also imposed. If the disease spreads during this time, action is taken to eradicate it (14:38–39; cf. 13:4–5, 26). If the disease is not cured by rebuilding the infected part of the house, the whole house must be pulled down (14:39–45). If it is cured, the ritual with the two birds is performed on behalf of the house (14:48–53; cf. 3–7). When this has been done, the house is regarded as clean and may be inhabited again (cf. vv. 46–47). No real sacrifices (cf. 14:10–31) are required, since buildings simply have to be clean, not in communion with God.

This law looks forward to the time when Israel would reside in houses in the promised land of Canaan (vv. 33–34). It therefore not only talks about stone-built houses but about the city (vv. 41, 45,

---

8. Verses 30–31 contain a possible case of textual corruption. In the Hebrew "he can afford" appears at the end of v. 30 and again in a slightly different form at the beginning of v. 31. Most commentators believe the repetition is an example of dittography. This may well be so, though tentatively in the translation I have retained it in both verses (cf. Hoffmann I, p. 406; Gispen, pp. 225f.; and probably the NEB).

53). The earlier laws on the other hand speak of tents (14:8) and the camp (13:46; 14:3, 8). These laws about houses can be seen as an extension of the laws dealing with garments and materials. When a tent started to grow mildew, it was presumably treated in accordance with the rules set out in 13:47ff. The same word *persistent (mam'eret)* is used to describe the disease in 13:51–52 and 14:44. This law is thus an extension, an application of the old law about garments in the new situation created by the settlement in Canaan. The old principles for distinguishing "serious skin diseases" from less significant ones still apply, but the treatment differs. One can destroy an infected garment by burning it (13:52), but a stone house needs to be pulled down (14:45). This process of reinterpretation, or more correctly reapplication of old laws to new circumstances, is something that has to be faced with every new situation. Christian interpreters are most often confronted with the problem when they try to find the relevance of OT law in NT situations. But even within the OT itself it was necessary to be ready to look for new applications of old laws (cf. Num. 27, 36; Lev. 24:10ff.; 2 Chr. 30:16ff.).

Summary (54–57)

This summary covers all the laws in chs. 13–14. For similar formulas see 11:46–47; 12:7; 13:59; 14:32; 15:32–33.

These laws form part of the teaching that the priests had to be familiar with, so that they could instruct the people in the difference between clean and unclean (v. 57; cf. 10:10–11). Holiness, as we have already seen, is defined in Leviticus in terms of wholeness. Skin diseases disfigured the surface of things and thereby destroyed their wholeness. Only the perfect and holy could enjoy the presence of the holy God, therefore the unclean were expelled from the camp. In the case of material objects this meant destruction either by fire or by dumping outside the city in an unclean place. In the case of persons they were compelled to live outside the camp and *ipso facto* out of contact with the tabernacle through which God's grace was made present with men. As outcasts they were dead to the community and cut off from divine grace.

Such persons could be readmitted only if their complaint cleared up. As was usual in ancient Israel, their ritual cleansing and sanctification was secured by the offering of sacrifice.[9]

It is not stated anywhere in these laws that these skin diseases

9. Cf. Introduction, VI.2: "Holiness," VI.3: "The Role of Sacrifice."

were caused by particular sins. Indeed, the fact that inanimate objects like garments and houses could be afflicted evidently rules out such a strict connection between sin and "skin diseases." Nevertheless, in several cases skin disease is definitely viewed as the consequence of specific sins: Num. 12:9ff.; 2 K. 5:26–27; 2 K. 15:5; 2 Chr. 26:19ff.

It seems likely that even in OT times "skin diseases" and their treatment were regarded as symbolic of sin and its consequences. When a man was afflicted with a disfiguring skin disease he did visibly "fall short of the glory of God" (Rom. 3:23), the glory that he had been given in his creation (Ps. 8:6 [Eng. 5]). His banishment from human society and God's sanctuary was a reenactment of the fall, when Adam and Eve were expelled from Eden (Gen. 3). The infection of garments and houses with "skin disease" served as a reminder of the interaction of man and his environment. Throughout Scripture, human sin has implications not just for mankind but for the rest of creation (Gen. 3:17–18; 6:13–14; Deut. 28:15ff.; Amos 4:7ff.; Rom. 8:20ff.). If a connection between sin and skin disease was recognized in OT times, it is natural that healing from such disease should be coupled with offerings prescribed for sinners.

The NT and Skin Disease

The NT refers to skin disease in a number of places. Though the word used in Greek is *lepra,* modern medical opinion is uncertain whether this would have included leprosy or only the "skin diseases" mentioned by Leviticus.[10] "Lepers" *(leproi)* were among those healed by Jesus in the course of his ministry (Matt. 8:2–4; 11:5; Mark 14:3; Luke 17:11–19). The Levitical law provided no means of curing "skin diseases." The sufferer had to wait in hope of a cure from God, without human aid. Only then could he present himself to the priest. But with the coming of Christ, God himself sought out the "lepers" and healed them. Jesus came to seek and save that which was lost. His outreach to the lepers was on a par with his ministry to other sick people and social outcasts, such as tax-collectors and prostitutes. In Jesus a new age had come. The kingdom of God was present, and salvation was available to all who had faith. In this new age the old barriers were obsolete because God was calling all men into his new community. In the day of grace,

10. Browne, pp. 13ff.; Hulse, p. 91.

outward ailments no longer mattered. Jesus had come to heal them. The laws of Leviticus were not abrogated by Jesus; in fact he tells the healed "lepers" to observe them (Matt. 8:4; Luke 17:14). But the new era of salvation made obsolete the idea that the diseased should be banished from human and divine society. Jesus' ministry and that of his disciples (Matt. 10:8) was one which brought reconciliation between God and man. Therefore the old laws isolating men because of their unsightly appearance had become inappropriate and out of date. Like the rules about unclean animals, they did not fit in with the new program, which was to climax in the creation of a new heaven and a new earth, in which men of every class and nation would be redeemed (Rev. 7:9).

E. UNCLEAN DISCHARGES (CH. 15)

1 *The Lord spoke to Moses and Aaron as follows:*

2 *"Speak to the Israelites and tell them: If a man is discharging from his 'flesh,' he is unclean because of his discharge.*

3 *This is his uncleanness when he discharges, whether his 'flesh' runs with his discharge or whether it is blocked by the discharge (he is unclean so long as his 'flesh' is discharging or his 'flesh' is blocked by his discharge): this is his uncleanness.*

4 *Any bed on which the man with a discharge lies becomes unclean, as well as any piece of furniture he sits on.*

5 *If anyone touches his bed, he must wash his clothes and bathe in water and be unclean until the evening.*

6 *Whoever sits on a piece of furniture which the man with a discharge used to sit on must wash his clothes, bathe in water, and be unclean until the evening.*

7 *Whoever touches the flesh of a man with a discharge must wash his clothes, bathe in water, and be unclean until the evening.*

8 *If the man with a discharge spits on a clean man, he must wash his clothes, bathe, and be unclean until the evening.*

9 *Any saddle on which the man with a discharge rides becomes unclean.*

10 *Whoever touches anything that has been under him becomes unclean until the evening, and whoever carries them must wash his clothes, bathe in water, and be unclean until the evening.*

11 *Anyone whom the man with a discharge touches without washing his hands in water must wash his clothes, bathe in water, and be unclean until the evening.*

12 *An earthenware vessel which the man with a discharge touches must be broken, and a wooden vessel must be scoured with water.*

13 *When a man with a discharge is cleansed from his discharge, he must count seven days for his purification, wash his clothes, bathe his flesh in fresh water, and he is then clean.*

14 *On the eighth day he must take two doves or pigeons, and come before the Lord to the entrance of the tent of meeting and give them to the priest.*

15 *Then the priest must use one for a purification offering and the other for a burnt offering, and the priest must make atonement for him before the Lord because of his discharge.*

16 *If a man suffers an emission of semen, he must bathe his whole flesh in water and be unclean until the evening.*

17 *Any garment or skin with which the semen comes in contact must be washed in water, and is unclean until the evening.*

18 *If a woman has sexual intercourse with a man, they must bathe in water and be unclean until the evening.*

19 *If a woman has a discharge, that is, a discharge of blood in her 'flesh,' her menstrual uncleanness lasts seven days. Anyone who touches her becomes unclean until the evening.*

20 *Anything she lies or sits on during her menstrual period becomes unclean.*

21 *Anyone who touches her bed must wash his clothes, bathe in water, and be unclean until the evening.*

22 *Whoever touches any piece of furniture she sits on must wash his clothes, bathe in water, and be unclean until the evening.*

23 *If he touches the bed or the piece of furniture which she sits on, he becomes unclean until the evening.*

24 *If a man lies with her and her menstrual uncleanness comes on him, he becomes unclean for seven days and any bed he lies on becomes unclean.*

25 *If a woman has a discharge of blood for a number of days outside her menstrual period or beyond her menstrual period, for as long as her discharge persists her uncleanness is like that of her menstrual period; she is unclean.*

26 *Any bed she lies on during her discharge becomes unclean like a bed during her menstrual period, and any piece of furniture she sits on becomes unclean like the impurity of her menstrual period.*

27 *Anyone who touches them becomes unclean and must wash his clothes, bathe in water, and be unclean until the evening.*

28 *If her discharge clears up, she must count seven days and afterward she will be clean.*

29 *On the eighth day she must take two doves or pigeons and bring them to the priest at the entrance of the tent of meeting.*

30 *Then the priest must use one for a purification offering and the other as a burnt offering, and the priest must make atonement for her before the Lord because of the discharge that made her impure.*

31 *You must separate the children of Israel from their uncleanness so that they do not die in their uncleanness by polluting my tabernacle which is among them."*

32 *This is the law of a man with a discharge and of the emission of semen which makes for uncleanness,*

33 *and for the woman unwell with her period, for discharges among men and women, and for a man who lies with a woman who is unclean.*

215

This chapter, concluding the regulations on uncleanness, discusses the defilement associated with the reproductive processes. To the modern mind it would seem more natural to group the laws in this chapter with those of ch. 12 dealing with childbirth. But evidently some other principle underlies the present arrangement of Leviticus. Could it be the duration of uncleanness? The uncleanness laws start with uncleanness that is permanent: that associated with various animals and food (ch. 11). Then they deal with the uncleanness of childbirth, which may last up to eighty days (ch. 12). Chs. 13 and 14 deal with uncleanness of indefinite duration; it all depends how long the serious skin disease persists. Finally, ch. 15 deals with discharges associated with reproduction, pollutions which usually only affect a person for up to a week. Whatever the explanation of the order of the material within chs. 11–15, these laws illuminate the day of atonement rituals, which are designed to cleanse the tabernacle "of the uncleannesses of the Israelites" (16:16). Without these chapters we should be at a loss to know what was the purpose of the ceremonies described in ch. 16.

The Structure of Leviticus 15

This chapter deals with four main cases, each introduced by "If a man/woman" (*'îsh/'ishshāh kî*) (cf. chs. 12–14). Each type of pollution is defined, its consequences are described, and an appropriate rite of purification, usually a wash and a wait till evening, is prescribed.

The chapter thus divides as follows:

1	Introduction	
2–18	Male Discharges	
	2–12 Long-term	*(kî)*
	13–15 cleansed by sacrifice	
	16–17 Transient	*(kî)*
	18 and intercourse	
19–30	Female Discharges	
	19–23 Transient (menstruation)	*(kî)*
	24 and intercourse	
	25–27 Long-term	*(kî)*
	28–30 cleansed by sacrifice	
31	Purpose of Law	
32–33	Summary	

The balance and symmetry of the arrangement is striking. Two types of discharge, long-term and transient, are distinguished. Since they can affect both sexes, that gives four main cases. It should also be noted that the discharges of women are discussed in the reverse order to those of men. This gives an overall chiastic pattern (AB-BA). Chiasmus is regularly used in Hebrew to bring out the unity of a doublesided event.[1] It is a most appropriate device to employ in these particular laws, focusing as they do on the unity of mankind in two sexes. Form and content here complement each other to express the idea that "God created man in his own image . . . male and female created he them" (Gen. 1:27). The unity and interdependence of the sexes finds its most profound expression in the act of sexual intercourse, and very fittingly this is discussed in v. 18, the midpoint of the literary structure.

The Uncleanness of Human Discharges

1 For this introductory formula cf. 11:1; 13:1; 14:33 and the comments there.

Long-term Male Discharges (2–15)

This chapter deals with various discharges from the sexual organs. Verses 16–24 deal with the normal short-term discharges of men and women, and vv. 25ff. with a long-term discharge from a woman. With the exception of the first paragraph it is clear that the discharges come from the sexual organs. This first section merely states that the discharge comes from the man's *flesh* (vv. 2–3). This word *(bāśār)* is quite common in Hebrew and has a wide range of meanings. Its basic meaning is "flesh" or "meat" (Lev. 4:11); it can also denote the "body" as a whole (Lev. 14:9); or even "man" as weak and mortal as opposed to God (Gen. 6:3; cf. Isa. 31:3). A few commentators have suggested, therefore, that a discharge from the penis may not necessarily be implied here; it could be a case of hemorrhoids. This is unlikely, though, for two reasons. First, there is no mention of any loss of blood, which Leviticus would hardly fail to mention if hemorrhoids were involved. Second, v. 19 uses the same word "flesh" for the woman's vagina, so it is most natural to suppose that in vv. 2–3 the corresponding male organ is intended.

As early as the Septuagint the complaint in question has been

1. See F. I. Andersen, *The Sentence in Biblical Hebrew* (The Hague: Mouton, 1974), pp. 120ff.

identified as gonorrhea, and most commentators accept this diagnosis. But apart from the fact that an abnormal discharge from the male organ is being described, few specific details are given here. The *discharge* is called a "flow" *(zôḇ)*—the noun is used only in this chapter; the related verb "to flow" is rare,[2] apart from the standard description of Canaan as a land "flowing with milk and honey" (Exod. 3:8; Num. 13:27, etc.). In v. 3 further details are given.[3] The discharge may be quite runny; the word *runs (rār)* is used only here but it is connected with the word for saliva *(rîr)* (Job 6:6; 1 Sam. 21:14 [Eng. 13]). Or it may block (lit. "cause to seal") the male organ, presumably because it is thick and coagulates. But whether the discharge is runny or coagulates, it makes the affected man unclean.

It is the uncleanness of the man and its consequences that are the main concern of this section. The striking thing about the uncleanness associated with these discharges is that not only the affected person becomes unclean, but also people and objects that come in contact with him, and these in their turn can become secondary sources of uncleanness. In this regard the uncleanness described here is much more "infectious" than the uncleanness of skin diseases dealt with in chs. 13–14, or unclean animals in ch. 11. In these cases only the person that comes in direct contact with the source of uncleanness is defiled. He does not become a source of uncleanness himself. In this respect, then, gonorrhea in men and menstrual and other female discharges are viewed as much more potent sources of defilement than others.

For example, any *bed* (vv. 4–5),[4] chair (v. 6), or *saddle* (v. 9)[5] which the affected man sits or lies on becomes unclean, and also a source of secondary pollution to others. If someone touches the polluted bed, he becomes unclean and must wash himself and his clothes and be unclean till the evening. The factor linking the bed, chair, and saddle seems to be alluded to in v. 10. They are things that have been under him, i.e., have been in close contact with his infected organ.

---

2. Only Ps. 78:20; 105:41 of flowing water, and Jer. 49:4.
3. The clause in brackets in our translation of v. 3 is not found in the Hebrew MT, but only in the Samaritan version and the Septuagint. It seems easier to suppose that it was omitted from the MT by homoeoteleuton, than that it was a deliberate insertion in the Hebrew text from which the LXX and Samaritan Pentateuch are derived. However, it makes little difference to the passage's interpretation.
4. A bed: probably more like a piece of carpet or simple mattress than our elaborate pieces of furniture.
5. *Merkāḇ,* literally something for riding; it could also refer to a cart or part of it.

Direct contact with an unclean man also transmits uncleanness (v. 7). Though the same word "flesh" is used in this verse as in vv. 2 and 3, most commentators seem to think that any part of the body is meant here, not just his penis. This seems to be confirmed by v. 11. If the man does not wash his hands before touching someone, he transmits pollution. If he does wash his hands, he does not convey impurity. Spittle from an infected man also pollutes (v. 8). Cooking vessels touched by an infected man must also be destroyed (v. 12; cf. 11:32–33).

Though these rules would occasion great inconvenience, they seem to imply that a man with a discharge may continue to live at home. He is neither driven out into the wilderness like those afflicted with serious skin disease[6] (13:45–46), nor does he have to undergo the elaborate cleansing rituals described in ch. 14. When he recovers, he simply has to wait seven days, wash, and offer the two cheapest sacrifices (v. 14; contrast 14:10–20). This suggests that the uncleanness caused by discharges was viewed as less serious than that associated with skin disease.

Transient Male Discharges (16–18)

Emission of semen,[7] in intercourse (v. 18) or at other times (vv. 16–17), also causes pollution. This idea is attested in many different cultures including the Babylonian, Egyptian, Greek, Roman, and Arab.[8] It is referred to in several other places in the OT (Exod. 19:15; Lev. 22:4ff.; Deut. 23:10ff. [Eng. 9ff.]; 1 Sam. 21:5ff. [4ff.]; 2 Sam. 11:11). No sacrifice was required to purify a person from this kind of pollution: the man (and his wife when she was involved) had simply to wash and wait until evening (vv. 16, 18). The practical effect of this legislation was that when a man had religious duties to perform, whether this involved worship or participation in God's holy wars, sexual intercourse was not permitted.

Menstrual Discharge (19–24)

Whereas long-term discharges in men are discussed before transient discharges, women's discharges are discussed in the reverse order: menstruation is dealt with first. A possible reason for this change of

---

6. Num. 5:2–4 seems to contradict this. But Saalschütz, pp. 242f., plausibly suggests that this was an enactment which applied only during the desert wanderings, when the camp was viewed as particularly holy.
7. Lit. "outpouring of seed," according to H. M. Orlinsky, *JBL* 63 (1944), pp. 37–39.
8. Gispen, p. 230.

order has been suggested above (see "The Structure of Leviticus 15").

The uncleanness *(niddāh)* associated with the monthly period has already been mentioned in 12:2, 5. Though a different term is used, the idea is alluded to in 2 Sam. 11:4. It was a common belief of ancient peoples, including Egyptians, Persians, and Arabs, that menstruation entailed cultic uncleanness.[9] Here the biblical concept is explained more fully. During the seven days following menstruation a woman is unclean in the same way as a man suffering from a long-term discharge. Anybody who touches her becomes unclean for the day and must wash himself and his clothes (v. 19, cf. vv. 7, 11). Similarly, anything the menstrual woman lies or sits on becomes a secondary source of pollution, which will in its turn pollute anyone who touches it (vv. 20–23, cf. vv. 4–10).

Finally, should a woman's period commence while she is having intercourse with her husband, he becomes unclean like her. His uncleanness lasts seven days, and anything he lies on becomes a secondary source of pollution (v. 24, cf. vv. 19–23). This interpretation[10] of v. 24 is more probable than the alternative, that intercourse at any time in the seven days following menstruation leads to the man contracting this severe type of uncleanness.[11] Sexual intercourse during a woman's period is expressly forbidden elsewhere in Leviticus (18:19; cf. Ezek. 18:6; 22:10), and those involved are liable to be "cut off" (Lev. 20:18), i.e., to suffer divine punishment. There is no conflict between these regulations; rather they approach the same topic from different angles. In this chapter we are dealing with rules of impurity, in ch. 18 with categorical prohibitions, and in ch. 20 with punishments consequent on various sins.[12]

It should be noted that though menstrual impurity is viewed as just as contagious as gonorrheal discharges (vv. 2–15), no sacrifices are required to atone for it. In this respect it resembles normal seminal emissions from men (vv. 16–17). A period of waiting and a wash is all that is required for the person to be free from impurity. Only if they fail to observe the appropriate period of waiting, or do not wash, can they be said to sin and become liable to judgment. The sexual processes thus make men unclean, but that is not the same as saying they are sinful. Uncleanness establishes boundaries of action, but as long as these are not transgressed no guilt is incurred.

9. Gispen, p. 230.
10. See Saalschütz, p. 243; Keil, p. 394; Gispen, p. 235.
11. Hoffmann I, p. 428; Snaith, p. 108; Maarsingh, p. 128.
12. Cf. Maarsingh, pp. 128–29.

Long-term Discharges from Women (25–30)

The complaint in question is a discharge of blood outside the normal period of menstruation (v. 25), such as the woman mentioned in the Gospels suffered from (Mark 5:25; Luke 8:43). A number of different complaints could cause such bleeding. What is important for Leviticus is that it is an irregular discharge, like gonorrhea, and therefore it is treated similarly. As long as it lasts, the woman herself is unclean, and makes anyone she touches unclean, as well as the things she sits or lies on (vv. 26–27). If her complaint clears up, she must wait seven days and then offer the minimum sacrifices, one bird for a burnt offering and one bird for a purification offering. Sacrifices are required here, because like childbirth (ch. 12), skin disease (chs. 13–14), and gonorrhea (15:2–12), the uncleanness lasts more than a week.

The Purpose of These Regulations (31)

You must separate (v. 31).[13] The verb used here (*hizzîr*) occurs in this form only five other times, in Num. 6 (vv. 2, 3, 5, 6, 12) referring to the vows of the Nazirite. A related form is used in Lev. 22:2. In Num. 6 separation is positively "to the Lord" and negatively from wine and strong drink (Num. 6:3). Here it is a separation *from their uncleanness, so that they do not die in their uncleanness by polluting my tabernacle.* Those who were unclean could not participate in divine worship in the tabernacle. If they did, they not only polluted the tabernacle but were liable to death at the hands of God. This had been emphasized at the law-giving on Sinai. On that occasion the people were told to wash (Exod. 19:10) and refrain from sexual intercourse (19:15) on pain of death (vv. 12, 21, etc.). The danger of entering into the tabernacle in an unfit condition has been illustrated by the fate of Nadab and Abihu (Lev. 10). Though some types of uncleanness only require a period of waiting and washing to be purged, repeated warnings are given about the consequences of ignoring these rituals. "He will bear his iniquity" (17:16; 19:8; 22:9), "he will be cut off" (20:18, etc.). Clearly the layman had to know when he was unclean, lest by infringing these regulations he became liable to these severe penalties. It was the purpose of these laws to explain the conditions that made a man unclean, so that he might avoid actions that might bring down God's wrath upon him.

13. The Samaritan Pentateuch and the ancient versions read *hizhîr,* "warn," instead of *hizzîr,* "separate." The MT is probably to be preferred as the more difficult reading.

The Function of These Laws

Verse 31 explains why these laws are included in Leviticus. They were given to the people, so that they might avoid falling into more serious sin through ignorance of how they ought to act when unclean. But why were these particular conditions regarded as unclean in the first place? The text itself does not explicitly answer this question, so it is no surprise that commentators give a variety of answers.

Clements[14] supposes that hygienic motives underlie these laws. But here, as elsewhere in Leviticus, this covers only a few of the cases discussed and is therefore dismissed by most commentators. Elliger[15] and Kornfeld[16] suggest that sex was associated with demonic powers and therefore brought uncleanness. Since there is nothing in these laws about demons, this suggestion is just speculation. Bertholet[17] and Heinisch[18] do not attempt to explain the function of these laws, but simply note that other ancient religions have similar concepts. Older commentators including Calvin,[19] Bonar, and Keil view these discharges as symbolizing sin and death. Even the natural processes of reproduction make a man unclean. These laws serve as a constant reminder that every man is a sinner, and sin affects his most intimate thoughts and actions. Gispen[20] partially endorses this view, but adds that it also helped to underline Israel's need to be holy and to differentiate the nation from the Canaanites and their customs.

Douglas has not discussed these laws as fully as those found in ch. 11, but she has made some instructive observations about them. Holiness is symbolized by physical perfection. Blemishes preclude animals from being used in sacrifices or priests from officiating in the sanctuary. Men with skin diseases are driven out of the camp. Similarly all bodily discharges are defiling and disqualify a person from approaching the temple.[21] Discharges are not just incompatible with holiness, understood as physical normality, they symbolize breaches in the nation's body politic. "When rituals express anxiety about the body's orifices the sociological counterpart

14. Clements, p. 43.
15. Elliger, p. 197.
16. Kornfeld, pp. 99f.
17. Bertholet, p. 49.
18. Heinisch, p. 69.
19. Calvin II, p. 32; Bonar, pp. 287ff.; Keil, *Biblical Archaeology* I, pp. 378ff.
20. Gispen, p. 230.
21. Douglas, *Purity and Danger*, p. 51.

of this anxiety is a care to protect the political and cultural unity of a minority group." Throughout their history the Israelites were a hard-pressed minority. They believed that all the bodily issues—blood, pus, excreta, semen—were polluting. "The threatened boundaries of their body politic would be well mirrored in their care for the integrity, unity and purity of the physical body."[22] In other words, the rules about bodily discharges give symbolic expression to the laws barring intermarriage with the Canaanites and the prohibitions against foreign customs and religion, which conflicted with Israel's special status as the one elect and holy nation.

Finally, Douglas also points out that uncleanness rules can serve to undergird morality, or at least reflect the moral principles accepted in society. By affirming that certain actions entail uncleanness, the act is itself discouraged. This is especially useful in the area of private morality where legal sanctions are not likely to be effective.[23]

Douglas does not explore this aspect of Israelite pollution rules. But where the rules about discharges were respected, they certainly had implications for morality and religion (e.g., 1 Sam. 21:5ff.; 2 Sam. 11:11). They would tend to encourage restraint in sexual behavior. This is most obvious in the rules concerning intercourse (v. 18) and the monthly period (vv. 19–24). Because sexual intercourse made both partners unclean, and therefore unable to participate in worship for a whole day, this regulation excluded the fertility rites and cult prostitution that were such a feature of much Near Eastern religion. It also served to make ordinary prostitutes social outcasts. Evidently ancient Israel, like many other societies, was unable to ban prostitution altogether (cf. Prov. 7), but this rule deprived the prostitute of social respectability and therefore helped to undergird the stability of family life. Similarly the prohibition on intercourse in war should have protected conquered women from abuse (cf. Num. 25).

The laws concerning the menstrual period on first inspection seem very harsh to the modern mind. At face value they seem to consign every adult woman in Israel to a state of untouchability for one week a month. But as has been pointed out, it is probably a fairly recent phenomenon for women to suffer a menstrual period once a month between adolescence and the menopause. This is not

22. *Ibid.*, p. 124. More general discussions of the symbolic significance of these rituals may be found in *Implicit Meanings*, especially pp. 60ff., 249ff., 276ff.
23. See *Purity and Danger*, pp. 129ff.

because female physiology has changed, but because of the different social habits of modern Western society. In ancient Israel three factors would combine to make menstruation very much rarer, at least among married women. These were early marriage, probably soon after puberty, and late weaning (perhaps at the age of two or three years), and the desire for large families (Ps. 127:4–5). The only women likely to be much affected by the law of Lev. 15:19–24 would be unmarried teenage girls. The relative frequency of their periods and the contagiousness of the uncleanness associated with menstruation should have made any God-fearing young man wary of physical contact with a girl he did not know well, for if he went to worship in an unclean condition, he was liable to God's judgment. In this way these regulations may have promoted restraint in relations between the sexes and have acted as a brake on the passions of the young.

Leviticus 15 and the NT

The laws in this chapter are not formally discussed in the NT. They are, however, alluded to, and form the background to several episodes in the Gospels. The clearest case is that of the woman who had suffered from bleeding for twelve years, who came up to Jesus in the crowd, touched him, and was healed of her complaint. Under the Levitical law such a woman should have been cut off from society and isolated, lest by touching others they became unclean. This law explains why the woman was so fearful when Jesus revealed what she had done. Her flouting of the uncleanness regulations would have made many other people unclean, and they might well have turned on her in anger. Jesus reassured her, "your faith has made you well; go in peace" (Mark 5:34).

Jesus' action on this occasion was typical of his attitude to the uncleanness regulations in general. We find him touching other classes of people whose physical condition made them unclean and therefore social outcasts, notably "lepers," the dead (Mark 5:41), and "sinners" (Luke 7:36ff.). His actions demonstrated that with his coming a new age had dawned in God's dealings with men. In Christ, God had drawn near to men and was calling sinners to repentance. The Levitical laws tended to separate man from God. Jesus showed by his deeds that anyone who repented could be accepted by God. His attitude to the laws about bodily uncleanness was of a piece with his attitude to the food laws. Both types of law symbolized the sole election of Israel: Jesus proclaimed that the kingdom of God was open to all believers.

Jesus' teaching inevitably brought him into conflict with the Pharisees, and they challenged him about hand-washing (Matt. 15//Mark 7). Evidently on the basis of Lev. 15:11 they insisted that before every meal a man should wash lest he pass on uncleanness to anyone else. By washing on every occasion they avoided offending against the law inadvertently. Jesus declared that "not what goes into the mouth defiles a man, but what comes out of the mouth, this defiles a man" (Matt. 15:11). According to Jesus, uncleanness was more a matter of the mind than the body. He thus pointed beyond the letter of the OT cleanness regulations to the moral principles that informed them.

I have suggested that one of the functions of these uncleanness rules may have been to stigmatize irregular sexual behavior and to encourage restraint among the unmarried. In this respect NT ethics are at one with the OT (cf. Matt. 5:27ff.; 1 Cor. 6:9ff.; 1 Tim. 5:2; Heb. 13:4; 1 Pet. 3:2ff.). But uncleanness rules are unlikely to be effective except in a homogeneous society where they are universally accepted. The NT Church was not in this position, but was a small minority in an alien world. It therefore relied almost entirely on exhortation to uphold biblical principles of morality (e.g., 1 Cor. 6:15ff.; 2 Pet. 1:4ff.). Only in extreme cases did it use excommunication as a means of enforcing these principles (1 Cor. 5:1–5).

F. PURIFICATION OF THE TABERNACLE FROM UNCLEANNESS (CH. 16)

1 *The Lord spoke to Moses after the death of the two sons of Aaron, when they approached the Lord and died.*

2 *The Lord said to Moses, "Tell Aaron your brother that he should not go at any time into the sanctuary behind the curtain in front of the mercy seat which is on the ark, so that he does not die, because I appear in a cloud over the mercy seat.*

3 *Aaron must enter the sanctuary with the following: with a young bull as a purification offering and a ram as a burnt offering.*

4 *He must wear a holy linen shirt, have linen shorts over his loins, bind on a linen sash, and fasten on a linen turban: these are the holy garments. He must wash his body in water and then put them on.*

5 *From the congregation of the Israelites he must take two male goats for a purification offering and one ram for a burnt offering.*

6 *Aaron must present the bull of his purification offering and must make atonement for himself and for his household.*

7 *Then he must take the two goats and stand them before the Lord at the entrance of the tent of meeting.*

8 *Aaron must cast lots for the two goats, one lot for the Lord and one lot for Azazel.*

9 *Aaron must present the goat on which the Lord's lot comes up and use it as a purification offering.*

10 *But the goat on which Azazel's lot comes up must be stood, while it is still alive, before the Lord to make atonement for it and to send it to Azazel into the wilderness.*

11 *Aaron must present the bull of his purification offering and make atonement for himself and for his household and then he must slay the bull of his purification offering.*

12 *He must next take a censer full of burning coals from off the altar before the Lord and two handfuls of fine spicy incense and then carry them inside the curtain.*

13 *He must place the incense on the fire before the Lord in order that the cloud of incense may cover the mercy seat which is above the ark of the testimony, so that he does not die.*

14 *Then he must take some of the blood of the bull and sprinkle it with his finger on the front of the mercy seat, and in front of the mercy seat he must sprinkle some of the blood with his finger seven times.*

15 *Then he must kill the goat for the people's purification offering and bring its blood inside the curtain, and do with its blood as he did with the bull's blood and sprinkle it on and in front of the mercy seat.*

16 *He must make atonement for the sanctuary because of the uncleannesses of the Israelites and because of their offenses, for all their sins: so he must do for the tent of meeting which is pitched with them in the middle of their uncleanness.*

17 *But no one may be in the tent of meeting from the time he enters to make atonement in the sanctuary till the time he comes out. He must make atonement for himself, for his household, and for the whole assembly of Israel.*

18 *Then he must come out to the altar which is before the Lord and make atonement for it by taking some of the blood of the bull and the goat and putting it round about, on the horns of the altar.*

19 *Seven times he must sprinkle some of the blood over it with his finger, cleanse it, and sanctify it from the uncleannesses of the Israelites.*

20 *He must finish cleansing the sanctuary, the tent of meeting and the altar, and then he must present the living goat.*

21 *Aaron must lay his two hands on the head of the living goat and confess over it all the iniquities of the Israelites, all their transgressions, all their sins, and he must place them on the head of the goat and drive it, with the help of a man appointed for the job, into the wilderness.*

22 *The goat must carry away all their iniquities into a region that is cut off and he shall drive it into the wilderness.*

23 *Aaron must enter the tent of meeting, take off the linen garments which he had put on when he entered the sanctuary and leave them there.*

24 *Then he must bathe his body with water in a holy place and put on*

his clothes. Then he must come out and make his burnt offering and the burnt offering of the people and make atonement for himself and for the people.

25 *The fat of the purification offering he must burn on the altar.*

26 *The man who sent the goat to Azazel must wash his clothes, and bathe his body in water, and afterward he may reenter the camp.*

27 *As for the bull and goat for the purification offering, the blood of which was brought in to make atonement in the sanctuary, they must be brought out of the camp and their skins, flesh, and dung be burned with fire.*

28 *The man who burns them shall wash his clothes, bathe his body in water, and afterward may reenter the camp.*

29 *It shall be a permanent rule for you that on the tenth day of the seventh month you must afflict yourselves and not do any work, that includes both the native inhabitant and the resident alien who lives among you.*

30 *Because on this day atonement will be made for you to cleanse you: you shall cleanse yourselves before the Lord from all your sins.*

31 *It is a sabbath of solemn rest for you and you must afflict yourselves: it is a permanent rule.*

32 *The priest who is anointed and ordained to officiate as priest in his father's place must put on the holy linen garments,*

33 *and purify the holy sanctuary and the tent of meeting and the altar; he must make atonement on behalf of the priests and all the people of the assembly.*

34 *This shall be a permanent rule for you to make atonement for the Israelites from all their sins once a year." And he did as the Lord commanded Moses.*

Leviticus 16: The Day of Atonement

This chapter begins with a reference back to ch. 10 (16:1–2; cf. 10:1ff.). The intervening chapters (11–15) have been concerned with explaining the difference between clean and unclean, for the duty of teaching the people about these differences had been imposed on the priests in 10:10–11. Thus the theological point of departure for this new section, dealing with the day of atonement, is, like that of chs. 11–15, also to be found in ch. 10. That chapter showed how priests who dared to approach God without due care and self-preparation might die suddenly in the fire of divine judgment. Thus ch. 16 sets out the proper rituals that the high priest must carry out if he is to preserve himself from a similar fate (16:2).

But this is not the only point of contact between ch. 16 and the preceding material. Chs. 11–15 have disclosed that all men are liable to contract uncleanness, through food, through death, through sex, or through disease. As we have seen, uncleanness is not necessarily morally culpable; it does not always require a sacrifice to eliminate its effects. But it does make a person unfit to enter the sanctuary. Yet the uncleanness rules are so wide-ranging that inevitably someone is going to infringe them unwittingly and thereby pollute the sanctuary and make it unfit for the presence of God. The main purpose of the day of atonement ceremonies is to cleanse the sanctuary from the pollutions introduced into it by the unclean worshippers (cf. 16:16, 19). Without a purpose such as this there would have been little point in the high priest putting his life at risk by entering into the holy of holies. The aim of these rituals is to make possible God's continued presence among his people.

The Structure of Leviticus 16

The day of atonement ceremonies were complex, and their description in this chapter is correspondingly involved. A certain amount of repetition of key phrases (e.g., "make atonement for himself," etc., vv. 6, 11, 17, 24, 33, 34; "a permanent rule," vv. 29, 31, 34) is found, but on the whole the style is more discursive than elsewhere in the book. It may be analyzed as follows:

The prescriptions for the day of atonement
- 1–2   Introduction
- 3–5   Animals and priestly dress needed for the ceremonies
- 6–10   Outline of the ceremonies
- 11–28 Detailed description of the ceremonies
    - 11–19 the blood-sprinkling rites
    - 20–22 the scapegoat
    - 23–28 cleansing of the participants
- 29–34 The people's duty

The introduction (vv. 1–2) is typical of Leviticus. The final section (vv. 29–34) also contains a summary of the main rituals (vv. 32–33) analogous to those found at the end of chapters 11, 13, 14, and 15. An outline of the ceremonies is given (vv. 6–10) and then they are described in detail (vv. 11–28). The same pattern is found elsewhere in Scripture (e.g., in Deut. 27 cf. vv. 2–3 with 4–8).

Introduction (1–2)

After the death of the two sons of Aaron (v. 1). This flashback to ch. 10 places the laws about the day of atonement firmly in a specific historical context: they were revealed to Moses to prevent any other priests meeting an untimely death when they served in the tabernacle. This shows once again that Leviticus is basically concerned to relate the history of Israel, in the course of which the Law was given.[1]

The Lord said to Moses (v. 2). As in chs. 8–10 the laws that concern the priests are not revealed directly to the priests or even to the high priest Aaron, but to Moses. This underlines Moses' special place in the Israelite hierarchy: he is superior even to Aaron the high priest. He is the great mediator between God and man. The peculiarly exalted role of Moses runs through Exodus to Deuteronomy, and it is evident here as well.

The basic precaution that Aaron must take to protect himself is *not to go at any time into the sanctuary behind the curtain* (v. 2). He cannot enter into the innermost part of the tabernacle, the holy of holies where the ark was kept, "at any time." The Hebrew phrase translated here "not . . . at any time" could imply a total prohibition against entry. However, the context makes it clear that with proper precautions the high priest may enter the holy place once a year. The reason why Aaron may not enter the innermost sanctuary whenever he likes is that it houses the ark on which the *mercy seat*[2] is found. It is there that God comes to his people. In the heart of the tabernacle, hidden in a cloud (cf. Exod. 24:15ff.), God used to appear. Before the tabernacle had been built God had come to his people on Mount Sinai. Now he dwells among them in the innermost part of the sanctuary. Familiarity can breed contempt. These laws drive home the truth that God is just as holy and demands just as much reverence when he dwells permanently with Israel as on the first occasion when he appeared on Sinai (Exod. 19).

1. Cf. comments on 1:1 and ch. 8: "Preliminary Observations."
2. Heb. *kappōreṯ*. The most appropriate way to translate this term is disputed. Probably it is connected with *kipper*, "to make atonement," as is suggested by the Greek translation *hilastērion* (propitiation) and the other ancient versions. The English rendering *mercy* seat reflects the idea that this part of the ark was used for atonement. The notion of it being a "seat" comes from remarks such as Ps. 99:1, "the Lord reigns. . . . He sits enthroned upon the cherubim." These cherubim flanked the mercy seat (Exod. 25:17–22), making it look like a throne.
   Many scholars, however, have associated *kappōreṯ* with Arab. *kafara*, "to cover," and translate it "lid, cover." The plausibility of this etymology depends on *kipper* meaning "to cover sin." If this is rejected (see our discussion above on pp. 59ff.), it seems unlikely that *kappōreṯ* means merely "lid." It was a sort of lid for the ark, but it was much more. It was the place where God's glory appeared and where atonement was made once a year. The etymology of *kappōreṯ* does not concern the biblical writers: what is stressed here and in Exod. 25:22 is that it is the place where "I will meet with you . . . and speak with you." M. Görg, *ZAW* 89 (1977), pp. 115–18, suggests an Egyptian derivation, and that *kappōreṯ* means *Fussfläche* (footplate).

Basic Requirements for the Ceremonies (3–5)

Certain things had to be prepared in advance for the ceremonies of the day of atonement. These included a bull for a purification offering and a ram for a burnt offering, both sacrificed on behalf of the high priest (v. 3), and two goats and another ram for the congregation (v. 5). Regulations governing the selection of sacrificial animals are found in Lev. 1 and 4.

The high priest also had to wear a special set of vestments for most of the ceremony, listed in v. 4: a shirt, shorts, sash, and turban all made of linen. In other words a simpler, less flamboyant dress than usual must be worn by the high priest. His proper high-priestly uniform is described in Exod. 28. Beautiful colored materials, intricate embroidery, gold and jewelry made him look like a king.[3] On the day of atonement he looked more like a slave. His outfit consisted of four simple garments in white linen, even plainer than the vestments of the ordinary priest (Exod. 39:27–29). The symbolic significance of these special vestments is nowhere clearly explained. Undoubtedly they draw attention to the unique character of the occasion. On this one day the high priest enters the "other world,"[4] into the very presence of God. He must therefore dress as befits the occasion. Among his fellow men his dignity as the great mediator between man and God is unsurpassed, and his splendid clothes draw attention to the glory of his office. But in the presence of God even the high priest is stripped of all honor: he becomes simply the servant of the King of kings, whose true status is portrayed in the simplicity of his dress. Ezekiel (9:2–3, 11; 10:2, 6–7) and Daniel (10:5; 12:6–7) describe angels as dressed in linen, while Rev. 19:8 portrays the saints in heaven as wearing similar clothes.

Outline of the Ceremony (6–10)

Verses 6–10 summarize the order of the day's events.

(1) Aaron offers the bull as a purification offering for himself and the priests (v. 6).

(2) Aaron casts lots to decide which goat is to be sacrificed as a purification offering for the people, and which is to be sent into the wilderness (vv. 7–8).

(3) The goat for the purification offering is sacrificed (v. 9).

3. On the symbolic significance of the high priest's garments see above on 8:6–9.
4. Cf. E. R. Leach, *Culture and Communication,* p. 86, for the symbolic significance of the different parts of the tabernacle.

(4) The other goat is brought before the Lord and then despatched to the wilderness (v. 10).

Verses 8 and 10 both describe the goat sent into the wilderness as the goat *for Azazel*. The meaning of this phrase is discussed further in the comments on v. 22.

The Main Ceremony Described in Detail (11–28)

The blood-sprinkling rites (11–19)

The first part of the ceremony is a purification offering on behalf of Aaron and the priests (vv. 11–14). This bears certain resemblances to the purification offering for the anointed priest described in 4:3–12: in both cases a bull is the sacrificial animal (16:11; cf. 4:3), there is a seven-fold sprinkling of its blood (16:14; cf. 4:6), and the unused parts are burned outside the camp (16:27; cf. 4:11–12). Where this purification sacrifice differs from those described in ch. 4 is in the place where the blood is sprinkled. In the ordinary priestly purification sacrifice the blood was sprinkled on the outside of the curtain leading into the holy of holies, and on the incense altar which was also outside the curtain.[5] This time, however, the blood is taken into the innermost sanctuary and sprinkled on the mercy seat on top of the ark (v. 14).

Entry into the holy of holies is fraught with danger. To protect himself from the wrath of God, the high priest has to prepare a censer full of hot charcoal taken from the altar of burnt offering in the outer court and put in it fine incense. The smoke of the incense was to *cover the mercy seat,* so that the high priest would not be killed (vv. 12–13). The most obvious explanation is given by Hertz: "the purpose of the incense-smoke was to create a screen which would prevent the High Priest from gazing upon the Holy Presence."[6] Keil[7] suggests that the incense was to prevent God seeing the sinner. Insofar as the incense is said to cover the mercy seat rather than the high priest (v. 13), the former interpretation seems the more plausible. Nevertheless, sometimes incense can avert God's wrath (Ps. 141:2; Num. 17:11ff. [Eng. 16:46ff.]), and this idea may underlie the use of incense[8] here.

In the detailed account of the ceremony (vv. 11–28) the second stage, the casting of lots over the goats, is passed over. All that

---

5. For the location of these items the reader is referred to the diagram on p. 91.
6. Hertz, p. 156; cf. Hoffmann I, p. 447.
7. Keil, p. 399.
8. See further M. Haran, *VT* 10 (1960), p. 128.

needs explanation has been said in the summary in vv. 7–8. The Mishnaic tractate Yoma fills out the details of this part of the ceremony. While its law probably reflects the practice in Jerusalem before the destruction of the temple in A.D. 70, and it is uncertain whether the same procedure was followed in OT times, its description has some interest in the absence of other information.

The two goats were stood before the high priest, one on the right and one on the left. Two lots were put into an urn, one inscribed "to the Lord," the other "to Azazel." The high priest put his hand into the urn and took out one lot in each hand and placed them on the head of the goats. Then everyone could see which would be used as a purification offering and which would be sent into the wilderness.[9]

The third phase of the ceremony (vv. 15–19) involves the sacrifice of the goat "for the Lord" as a purification offering on behalf of the people. The bull was offered on behalf of the priests; the goat is offered on behalf of the people and its blood is used in the same way as the bull's. It is sprinkled seven times on and before the mercy seat (v. 15). Presumably on this occasion too Aaron could enter only under the protection of a cloud of incense (v. 15, cf. 12–13).

The obscure phrase in the second half of v. 16, *so he must do for the tent of meeting,* seems to refer to a similar sprinkling of blood in the outer half of the tent where the altar of incense stood.[10] Exod. 30:10 says that the incense altar must be sprinkled with the blood of a purification offering once a year. The rituals in this part of the tent are again alluded to in the summary in v. 20: *the sanctuary,* i.e., innermost holy of holies; *tent of meeting,* i.e., outer part of the tent; *altar,* i.e., the altar of burnt offering in the main courtyard.

After the holy of holies and the holy place had been cleansed, the outer shrine had to be purified by a seven-fold sprinkling of the main altar[11] of burnt offering with the blood of the bull and the goat (v. 18). Using the blood of both animals symbolized the fact that the altar had to be cleansed from the defilements of priests and people.

9. See Yoma 4:1f.
10. Keil, p. 400.
11. Verse 18, "the altar which is before the Lord," is taken by Jewish commentators (e.g., Hertz, p. 158, and Hoffmann I, p. 450) to refer to the golden incense altar in the holy place. This is described as being "before the Lord" in 4:7 and 18, and they identify the action commanded here with that in Exod. 30:10. However, most commentators believe that the altar of burnt sacrifice is intended here. Sacrifices on this altar are said to take place before the Lord (e.g., 1:3, 5, etc.). Where the incense altar is referred to, it is defined as being "within the tent of meeting" as well as "before the Lord" (see 4:7, 18). Some commentators (e.g., Snaith, p. 115; Elliger, p. 213) suppose that no sprinkling of the golden altar took place on this occasion, this being a late

Verses 16, 19–20 explain the purpose of all these blood rituals to *cleanse and sanctify* the sanctuary and altars *from the uncleannesses of the Israelites*.[12] The uncleanness that affects every man and woman to a greater or lesser degree (see Lev. 11–15) pollutes the sanctuary. These atonement-day rituals make the impossible possible. By cleansing the sanctuary they permit the holy God to dwell among an unholy people (vv. 16–17; cf. Isa. 6:3ff.; Ps. 15; 24:3ff.). Verse 17 underlines the fact that only one man, the high priest, may enter into the holy of holies. Under both testaments there is but one mediator between God and man (cf. 1 Tim. 2:5).

The scapegoat (20–22)

Verses 20–22 (cf. v. 10) describe the fourth and most striking phase of the day of atonement ceremony, the despatch of the scapegoat into the wilderness.[13] After being chosen by lot (vv. 7–8), the animal is brought before the high priest, who places both his hands on the goat's head and confesses all the nation's sins. This action symbolically transfers the sins to the goat (v. 21). It is then led off into the wilderness by *a man appointed for the job*.[14]

The symbolism of this ceremony is transparent. As vv. 21 and 22 explain, this ceremony removes the sins from the people and leaves them in an unclean place, the desert. The basic idea is clear enough, but certain details are quite obscure. What is meant by the "region that is cut off" (v. 22) and "Azazel" (vv. 8, 10, 26)?

A region that is cut off is literally "a land of cutting off." "Cutting off" could refer to the fact that the place to which the goat was led was "cut off" from the camp, perhaps by a deep valley, so that the animal had no chance of returning to Israel and bringing back the guilt of their sins. Alternatively, it could refer to the fact that it was taken to a place where its life was "cut off." In later

---

concept found in Exod. 30 but not in Lev. 16. The implausibility of this interpretation is well argued by Hoffmann I (pp. 450ff.). I prefer the interpretation of Keil (p. 401) and Gispen (p. 248) that the incense altar was sprinkled with blood and that this is referred to summarily in vv. 16 and 20. See the exegesis of these verses.

12. (*For*) *all their sins* (vv. 16, 21) (*lᵉkol-ḥaṭṭōʼtām*) specifies more precisely the preceding words *uncleannesses* and *transgressions*. For other examples of *lᵉkol* of nearer specification cf. 5:3–4; Exod. 28:38; 36:1.

Alternatively if *ḥaṭṭāʼṭ* here means "purification" (cf. ch. 3 n. 3), the phrase could be translated "for their complete purification," "to purify them all."

13. For some possible Hittite parallels to the scapegoat ritual see O. R. Gurney, *Some Aspects of Hittite Religion* (1977), pp. 47ff.

14. *ʼittî*, "ready," from *ʼēṭ*, "time." Hence "made ready," *appointed for the job*; cf. TEV and Gispen, p. 249.

times, the Mishnah records that the goat was led to a steep cliff and pushed over backward to kill it.[15]

This goat is said to be *for Azazel* (vv. 8, 10, 26). What is meant by the term is uncertain. Different etymologies are suggested to fit in with different interpretations.[16] The most popular explanation among commentators is that Azazel is the name of a demon that lived in the wilderness. Three arguments are adduced in favor of this view. First, Azazel is in direct contrast with the Lord (v. 8). Would "the Lord" (Heb. *YHWH*), God's personal name, be contrasted with something impersonal? Second, in later Jewish literature Azazel (Enoch 8:1; 9:6) is the name of a demon. Third, the OT looks on the wilderness as the haunt of demons and similar creatures (Lev. 17:7; Isa. 13:21; 34:14; cf. Matt. 12:43, etc.).

Those who adopt this interpretation insist that the goat was not viewed as a sacrifice or gift to Azazel. The sins of Israel were simply being sent back to their author, Azazel, who lived in the desert. Despite this disclaimer, it is not difficult to see the rite being misinterpreted as a gift to the demon, if Azazel is a demon's name. There is, therefore, force in Hertz's objection to this view. "The offering of sacrifices to 'satyrs' is spoken of as a heinous crime in the very next chapter (17:7); homage to a demon of the wilderness cannot, therefore, be associated with the holiest of the Temple-rites in the chapter immediately preceding."[17]

Hoffmann[18] and Hertz[19] prefer another interpretation, namely, that Azazel is a rare Hebrew noun meaning "complete destruction."

A third possibility is that Azazel means "rocky precipice"; this was Rashi's explanation. "It was a precipitous and flinty

---

15. Yoma 6:6.
16. The etymology of *ᵃzā'zēl* is uncertain and various suggestions have been made. 1. Keil, p. 398; Hertz, p. 154; *BDB*, p. 736b derive it from *'āzal*, "to drive away, remove;" *'zlzl 'z'zl*, "something driven away," e.g., "demon," or "dismissal, entire removal."

    2. LXX, Vulgate seem to derive it from *'ēz*, "goat"; *'āzal*, "go away." So Snaith, p. 113: "the goat has gone away"; de Vaux, *Ancient Israel*, pp. 508f.; cf. English versions: "(e)scape-goat."

    3. Driver, *JSS* 1 (1956), p. 98, suggests it is related to Arab. *'azāzu*, "rough ground," hence "precipice." For further discussion see C. L. Feinberg, "The Scapegoat of Leviticus 16," *Bibliotheca Sacra* 115 (1958), pp. 320–333, and J. Milgrom, *EJ* 5, cc. 1384–87.
17. Hertz, p. 156.
18. Hoffmann I, p. 444.
19. Hertz, p. 154.

rock."[20] More recently this interpretation has been endorsed by
G. R. Driver,[21] who gives a fresh derivation of the term.

If v. 22 is an expansion of what is said earlier in v. 10, as I
have argued, Rashi would be justified in taking "land of cutting off"
as interpretative of Azazel. If this phrase is understood to mean a
land that is cut off, it would support Azazel as meaning "rocky" or
"craggy." If it means a place that cuts off, Azazel may be better
interpreted "total destruction" as suggested by Hertz and
Hoffmann.

Whatever we understand by Azazel, there is little doubt
about the total meaning of the ceremony. "Whether Azazel means,
the mountain where the goat is destroyed, the sin which is given to
destruction, or the evil angel who is given a bribe so that he does not
become an accuser, it all comes back to the same basic idea: that sin
is exterminated from Israel."[22]

The cleansing of the participants (23–28)

After the goat had carried all the nation's sins away into the wilderness, it was important that the camp and sanctuary should not be
immediately recontaminated. These verses, therefore, remind all the
participants to wash before resuming their normal activities (vv. 24,
26, 28). Aaron also had to remove his special linen garments, wash,
and put on his normal high-priestly clothes (vv. 23–24; cf. 4). Wearing these vestments, he offered the rams as burnt offerings on behalf
of himself and the nation (v. 24; cf. 3, 5), and burnt the fat of the
purification offerings on the altar (v. 25; cf. 4:10, 26, etc.).

The People's Duty (29–34)

Up to this point the law has concentrated almost entirely on what the
high priest and his helpers had to do on this holy day. Yet his
ministrations were on behalf not only of himself and the priests but
of the whole nation (e.g., v. 17). We learn here what the nation had to
do on the day of atonement.

"It is a permanent rule . . . that you must afflict yourselves
and not do any work" (v. 29). *Permanent rule* is quite commonly
used to underline the importance of carrying out a particular religious duty (e.g., passover, Exod. 12:14; keeping the candlestick lit,

20. Rashi, p. 73b.
21. G. R. Driver, *JSS* 1 (1956), pp. 97f.
22. Hoffmann I, p. 444.

Exod. 27:21; giving the priests their dues, Lev. 7:36). The threefold repetition of this phrase (vv. 29, 31, 34) must, therefore, underline how important it was for the people to do their part.

On the tenth day of the seventh month (approximately October) they had to afflict themselves and refrain from work. It was a *sabbath of solemn rest* (v. 31; cf. 23:3, 24, 32, 39). No resident aliens were allowed to work either. They were also bound by the fourth commandment to observe the weekly sabbath (Exod. 20:10).

The phrase *afflict yourselves* is rare (Lev. 23:27, 32; Num. 29:7, of the day of atonement; Isa. 58:3, 5; Ps. 35:13). In Isaiah it is associated with fasting. Ps. 35 suggests a wide range of penitential practices were involved, including self-examination and prayer.

> *"I wore sackcloth,*
> *I afflicted myself with fasting,*
> *I prayed with my head bowed on my bosom."*
>
> Ps. 35:13

However impressive the ceremonies enacted by the high priest to atone for sin may be, they were insufficient. The law insists that if they are to be effective, the whole nation, Israelites and foreigners alike, must demonstrate true penitence.

Verses 32–34 summarize the law. See above on "The Structure of Leviticus 16."

The Significance of the Day of Atonement Ceremonies

The purpose of these laws is to prevent Aaron, in theory the holiest man in Israel, suffering sudden death when he enters the tabernacle (vv. 2, 13). The rites teach that no man, however holy, can approach the presence of God without appropriate atonement being made.

The blood-sprinkling rites are described as purification offerings. The meaning of this sacrifice has been more fully discussed in ch. 4 (see above). Here it is simply stated that these rites cleanse the different parts of the tabernacle from the uncleanness of the people of Israel (vv. 16, 19). Blood is the appointed means of cleansing and sanctification. Israel's sin and uncleanness are conveyed to the building in which the people worship. Unless they are cleansed, God will condemn his people to judgment.

The most memorable feature of the day was the despatch of one goat into the wilderness. This is explained as sending the nation's sins away from the people (vv. 21–22). The need for the nation as a whole to be purged of sin is portrayed vividly here. The rites in the holy of holies were unseen by the general public. The scapegoat ceremony was seen by all and could be understood by all. It was a powerful visual aid that demonstrated the reality of sin and the need to eliminate it.

This point was further underlined by the total embargo on work and the exercise of penitential practices such as fasting. By itself the scapegoat might have led some to suppose that it was an easy task to purify the nation from its sinful ways. The commandment to "afflict yourselves" (vv. 29, 31) underlined the need for every individual to examine himself and repent of his sins.

The Day of Atonement in the NT

Many of the ceremonies of the day of atonement are discussed in the book of Hebrews, especially in ch. 9. The author draws out many theological lessons from the rituals. But even more important in his thinking is the crucifixion of Christ. For Hebrews, the day of atonement prefigures the crucifixion. Christ on the cross achieved what the high priests of the Old Covenant had attempted to do on the day of atonement. The effectiveness of his atonement was demonstrated by the veil of the temple being rent in two (Matt. 27:51; Mark 15:38; Luke 23:45). For Hebrews, the tearing of the veil corresponds to the tearing of Christ's flesh. Now all believers have the right to enter into the presence of God (Heb. 10:19ff.).

Under the New Covenant the theological situation has completely changed.[23] There is no longer any need for a day of atonement each year. The first Good Friday was the definitive day of atonement when man's sins were purged once and for all. Now every man who is in Christ has the right, once reserved only for the high priest, to enter into the presence of God. He could go in but once a year; we can draw near at any time.

Though strictly speaking the day of atonement is no longer relevant to the Christian, from studying it he can learn a great deal about the nature of sin, the necessity of atonement, and the superiority of Christ's sacrifice. In a series of contrasts Hebrews brings out how the Christian enjoys far greater privileges than Aaron, for our high priest Christ is far superior to Aaron.

(a) Aaron was a sinner who needed to offer sacrifice for

---

23. See Introduction, VII: "Leviticus and the Christian."

himself before making atonement for the people. Christ is pure and sinless and needs to offer no sacrifices for himself (Heb. 7:26ff.).

(b) Aaron had to repeat the sacrifices regularly. Christ secured an eternal redemption by his own death (9:6–14, 25ff.).

(c) Aaron's rituals secured him entry into the earthly sanctuary; Christ's death led him into the heavenly (9:24).

(d) The repetition of Aaron's sacrifices was a constant reminder of the persistence of sin. Christ's once-for-all sacrifice secured permanent forgiveness of sin (10:1–18).

All this should give us the "confidence to enter the sanctuary by the blood of Jesus" (10:19).

The NT makes nothing of the scapegoat led away into the wilderness; but ever since the epistle of Barnabas, written c. A.D. 200, Christians have seen in the scapegoat a type of Christ. As it was led out to die in the wilderness bearing the sins of the people, so Christ was crucified outside Jerusalem for the sins of his people.[24]

Nor does the NT make anything of the requirement that the day of atonement should be a solemn sabbath and day of affliction. It may be noted, though, that after discussing the rituals of that day, Hebrews does make an appeal for an appropriate Christian response: "Let us draw near with a true heart in full assurance of faith, with our hearts sprinkled clean from an evil conscience and our bodies washed with pure water. . . . Let us consider how to stir up one another to love and good works, not neglecting to meet together . . ." (Heb. 10:22–25).

If, finally, one looks on Good Friday as the Christian equivalent of the day of atonement, one may approve the custom in many countries of making that day a public holiday, "a sabbath of solemn rest," on which Christians can attend church, recall their Savior's death, and lament their sins that were its cause.

24. Micklem, pp. 79f.

IV. PRESCRIPTIONS FOR PRACTICAL HOLINESS (17:1–27:34)

A. BASIC PRINCIPLES ABOUT SACRIFICE AND FOOD (CH. 17)

1 *The Lord spoke to Moses as follows:*

2 *"Speak to Aaron and his sons and to all the Israelites and say to them: This is the thing which the Lord has commanded.*

3 *If any Israelite kills an ox, sheep, or goat inside or outside the camp,*

4 *and does not bring it to the entrance of the tent of meeting to present it as an offering to the Lord before the tabernacle of the Lord, that man is reckoned to be guilty of bloodshed: he has shed blood and that man will be cut off from among his people.*

5 *This is in order that the Israelites may bring their sacrifices, which they are sacrificing in the open country, that they bring them to the Lord to the priest at the entrance of the tent of meeting. They must sacrifice them as peace offerings to the Lord.*

6 *The priest must splash the blood against the Lord's altar in the entrance of the tent of meeting and burn the fat to make a soothing aroma for the Lord.*

7 *They must not continue offering their sacrifices to the goat-demons, to which they are prostituting themselves. This must be a permanent rule for them and their descendants.*

8 *You must also say to them, If any Israelite, or resident alien who dwells among them, offers a burnt offering or sacrifice,*

9 *but does not bring it to the entrance of the tent of meeting to offer it to the Lord, that man will be cut off from his people.*

10 *If any Israelite, or resident alien who dwells among them, eats any blood, I shall set my face against the person who eats blood and cut him off from his people,*

11 *because the life of the body is in the blood, and I have given it to you on the altar to make atonement for your lives: for the blood makes atonement by the life.*

12 *Therefore I said to the Israelites that no person among you may eat blood, nor may the resident alien who dwells among you eat blood.*

13 *If any Israelite, or resident alien who dwells among them, hunts game, that is, birds or animals that may be eaten, he must pour out its blood and cover it with earth.*

14 *For the life of every animal, its blood is its life, and I said to the Israelites, 'You must not eat the blood of any animal, because the life of every animal is its blood.' All who eat it will be cut off.*

15 *Any person, whether native or resident alien, who eats meat from an animal that died naturally or was killed by other animals must wash his clothes, bathe in water, and be unclean until the evening. Then he becomes clean.*

16 *If he does not wash his clothes or bathe his body, he will bear his iniquity."*

The Structure of Leviticus 17

Chapter 17 is systematically arranged. It begins with an introductory formula typical of Leviticus (vv. 1–2; cf. 1:1; 4:1; 6:1; 7:28; 11:1; 15:1; 16:1–2; 18:1–2; 19:1–2). Four paragraphs follow, dealing with sacrifice and the consumption of meat. Each paragraph begins in similar fashion: "If any Israelite or resident alien who dwells among them" (vv. 3, 8, 10, 13), continues with a definition of the sin (vv. 3–4, 8–9, 10, 13–14), prescribes the punishment of "cutting off" for disobedience (vv. 4, 9, 10, 14), and generally closes by giving an additional reason for obeying the law (vv. 5–7, 11–12, 14).

The material thus divides itself as follows:

1–2   Introduction
3–7   No domestic animals to be killed outside the tabernacle
8–9   No sacrifices to be offered outside the tabernacle
10–12 No blood to be eaten
13–16 Rules about hunting game

The laws in this chapter deal with various problems connected with sacrifice and eating meat. These matters have already been discussed in chs. 1–7 and 11 (cf. 7:26–27 with 17:10ff. and 11:39–40 with 17:15–16). This chapter draws together themes that run through the previous sixteen: in particular it explains the special significance of blood in the sacrifices (vv. 11ff.).

Unlike the regulations in the preceding chapters, this section says very little about the role of the priests. It concentrates on the mistakes a layman is apt to make: he may be tempted to kill animals outside the tabernacle (vv. 3–7) or forget to drain out the blood before eating the meat (vv. 10ff.). In this respect these laws have more in common with those that follow in chs. 18–26, which are designed to promote the holiness of all Israel. For this reason modern critics usually affirm that ch. 17 belongs with the succeeding chapters and forms part of the Holiness Code, which is believed to antedate the opening chapters of Leviticus.

This view, however, is not without its problems. For example, ch. 17 lacks most of the phraseology characteristic of chs. 18ff., and has certain features in common with the preceding material.[1] I prefer to view ch. 17 as a hinge linking the two halves of the book: chs. 1–16 containing the ritual regulations for public life and worship, and chs. 18–25 regulating the personal and private affairs of individuals. For a fuller discussion of the critical problems the reader is referred to the Introduction.[2]

Introduction (1–2)

1 Cf. 1:1; 4:1; 6:1; 7:28, etc. See comments on 1:1 and 16:1.

2 *This is the thing which the Lord has commanded.* Identical phraseology is used in 8:5; 9:6.

No Domestic Animals to Be Killed outside the Tabernacle (3–7)

This law bans the killing of the main sacrificial animals, ox, sheep, or goat, anywhere except in the tabernacle. The word *kills* may cover slaughter for nonsacrificial purposes (e.g., Gen. 37:31; 1 Sam. 14:32), though it is most commonly used for the ritual slaughter in sacrifice (cf. Lev. 1:5, 11, etc.). The point made by this law is that in the wilderness no secular slaughter is permitted. If an Israelite wished to eat meat, he must bring his chosen animal to the tabernacle as a peace offering. There the priest would kill it in the approved way, sprinkle the blood and burn the fat (vv. 5–6). The one offering it would then receive back the flesh of the animal to eat (see 3:1ff.; 7:22ff.).

The penalty for disregarding this rule is set out in v. 4. *That man is reckoned to be guilty of bloodshed . . . and will be cut off from among his people.* In other words, this offense is as serious as murder.[3] *He has shed blood,* consequently he will be punished by God directly. This is the traditional understanding of the phrase "to be cut off," and it does seem to fit the different contexts in which it is found (e.g., Exod. 30:33; Lev. 7:20ff.; 20:17ff.).

1. Cf. R. Kilian, *Literarkritische und formgeschichtliche Untersuchung des Heiligkeitsgesetzes,* pp. 176ff.; Hoffmann I, p. 469.
2. Cf. Introduction, II: "The Structure of Leviticus," and III: "The Sources of Leviticus."
3. Cf. J. Milgrom, *JBL* 90 (1971), pp. 154f.

An eminent Israeli lawyer has described the penalty: "The threat of being 'cut off' by the hand of God, in His own time, hovers over the offender constantly and inescapably; he is not unlike the patient who is told by his doctors that his disease is incurable and that he might die any day. However merciful, because of its vagueness and lack of immediacy, this threat of punishment may seem to modern criminals, in ancient times its psychological effect must have been devastating. The wrath of the omnipotent and omniscient God being directed particularly at yourself of all people, and being certain to strike at you with unforseeable force and intensity any day of the year and any minute of the hour, was a load too heavy for a believer to bear."[4]

Other interpretations have been suggested. One is that it is a demand for the death penalty to be imposed by human agency following conviction in the courts. But though death does seem to be envisaged by the phrase, it is unlikely that judicial execution is intended, because many of the crimes to which this penalty is attached are secret sins which would be difficult to prosecute in the court (e.g., Exod. 30:38; Lev. 7:20–21; Num. 15:30–31). Moreover, God sometimes threatens to cut people off himself. Such a threat would be unnecessary if capital punishment were mandatory (17:10; 20:3ff.).

Another possibility is that "being cut off from his people" means being expelled from the nation. Support for this idea can be found in the Laws of Hammurabi § 154, which provides for banishment in a case akin to Leviticus (20:17). But the same objections apply to this as to the previous interpretation, namely, the difficulty of prosecution in many cases and the fact that God exacts the penalty in others.

Death in the OT is often referred to as sleeping with one's fathers (e.g., 1 K. 1:21) or being buried with the fathers (1 K. 14:31). It appears, therefore, that this phrase may not only refer to premature death at the hand of God, but hint at judgment in the life to come. Offenders will be cut off from their people forever. Indeed under the judicial systems of Israel's neighbors, attempts were made to prevent the souls of heinous criminals enjoying rest in the life to come.[5]

---

4. H. H. Cohn, *Israel Law Review* 5 (1970), p. 72. For an older discussion of the question see Saalschütz, pp. 476ff.
5. E.g., by denying the body of the executed proper burial, MAL A53; prohibited in Deut. 21:22–23; cf. Gilgamesh Epic 12:152ff.

The motive underlying this severe law is spelled out in vv. 5–7. It is to prevent sacrifices to the *goat-demons* who inhabited the wilderness (see above on 16:20ff.). The translation of the Hebrew (*śeʿîrîm*) is problematic. Usually it simply means "goats." It seems likely, therefore, that the demons were thought to take the shape of goats, rather like the satyrs of classical mythology. To offer sacrifices to demons was a flagrant breach of the first commandment to "have no other gods but me." This explains why those involved were to be cut off. Exod. 22:19 (Eng. 20) insists, "Whoever sacrifices to any god, save to the Lord only, shall be utterly destroyed."

Anyone involved in secret demon worship might claim that he merely killed the animal outside the camp. To plug this potential loophole it is enjoined that all animals must be killed in the tabernacle (v. 5).

This law could be effective only when eating meat was a rare luxury, and when everyone lived close to the sanctuary as during the wilderness wanderings. After the settlement it was no longer feasible to insist that all slaughtering be restricted to the tabernacle. It would have compelled those who lived a long way from the sanctuary to become vegetarians. Deut. 12:20ff. therefore allows them to slaughter and eat sheep and oxen without going through the sacrificial procedures laid down in Leviticus, though the passage still insists that the regulations about blood must be observed (Deut. 12:23ff.; cf. Lev. 17:10ff.).

No Sacrifices to Be Offered outside the Tabernacle (8–9)

This law deals with other types of sacrifice which people might be tempted to perform outside the tabernacle, namely, the burnt offering and the peace offering, here simply called a sacrifice. There would be little likelihood of people bringing cereal offerings, which were basically gifts to the priesthood, or purification offerings to purify the tabernacle, anywhere except to the tabernacle. There would have been no point.

Though it is not stated why burnt offerings and sacrifices outside the tabernacle were banned, probably it was for the same reason as given in vv. 5–7, namely, that they could be offerings to demons. Other possible motives include sectarianism, breaking up the unity of Israel's worship, or avoidance of the charges levied by the official priesthood. Whatever reason people may have had for wishing to sacrifice outside the tabernacle, they faced the prospect of being cut off (v. 9). This rule is just as binding on the resident alien, the foreigner who has settled in Israel, as on the native Israelite (v. 8, cf. vv. 10, 12, 15).

The *resident alien* (v. 8), often translated "sojourner" (Heb. *gēr*),[6] figures frequently in the Pentateuchal laws. As a foreigner he was in an awkward situation. Like all foreigners in an alien culture he was liable to exploitation, and many of the laws urge charity and fair play for the alien (e.g., Exod. 22:20 [Eng. 21]; Lev. 19:10; Deut. 26:11, etc.). Often he is grouped with the orphan and the widow as among those classes specially deserving of charity (e.g., Deut. 24:19ff.). More than once the native Israelite is reminded that he should be sensitive to the aliens' problems because they themselves had been sojourners in Egypt (e.g., Exod. 23:9).

On the other hand the resident alien was expected to conform to the main rules of Israelite society. For example, he must observe the sabbath (Exod. 20:10) and the day of atonement (Lev. 16:29). He must refrain from heathen worship (Lev. 20:2) and blasphemy (24:16). If he refuses to accept these laws he faces the same penalties as native Israelites (24:16, 22). That the law finds it necessary to specify that certain rules did apply to sojourners seems to imply that in some matters resident aliens were allowed to preserve their traditional customs.

No Blood to Be Eaten (10–12)

As a direct consequence of limiting the slaughter of animals to the tabernacle, the blood of these animals could not be "eaten," that is, drunk or eaten in meat which had not been drained of blood. The importance of this principle is underscored emphatically here six times in five verses (vv. 10–14). This rule is traced back to the time of Noah, who was allowed to eat meat on condition that he avoided the blood (Gen. 9:4). It is restated in Lev. 7:26–27; Deut. 12:16, 23; 15:23; 1 Sam. 14:32ff. It is a rule that applies as much to resident aliens as to natives (vv. 10, 12). Its contravention involves the guilty in being "cut off" (v. 10) (see above on v. 4). Evidently it was a religious rule of the first importance.

Yet its precise significance is elusive. Two explanations are offered for the prohibition: first, *because the life of the body is in the blood* (v. 11, cf. v. 12).[7] The Heb. *nepeš*, translated here *life*, has a

6. See de Vaux, *Ancient Israel,* pp. 74ff.
7. In v. 14 the translation of *its blood is its life* presents problems. Literally the Hebrew says, "its blood is *in* its life." Most translations and commentators regard the preposition "in" as expressing essence and therefore omit it in translation.

broad range of meaning covering such different English concepts as "throat," "appetite," "soul," "life," "person."[8] But in this context the most appropriate rendering is "life." This verse virtually identifies the life of an animal with its blood. At a basic level this is obvious: when an animal loses its blood, it dies. Its blood, therefore, gives it life. By refraining from eating flesh with blood in it, man is honoring life. To eat blood is to despise life. This idea emerges most clearly in Gen. 9:4ff., where the sanctity of human life is associated with not eating blood. Thus one purpose of this law is the inculcation of respect for all life.[9]

A second reason for the ban is given in v. 11. "I have given it to you on the altar to make atonement for your lives: for the blood makes atonement by the life." This, the most explicit statement about the role of blood in sacrifice, has already been discussed at length above (see on 1:4). Here it suffices to say that *make atonement* literally means "pay a ransom" or "ransom," and 11c could be paraphrased "the blood ransoms at the price of life."[10] In other words the ransom price for man's life is not a monetary payment (as in Exod. 21:30) but the life of an animal represented by its blood splashed over the altar. Because animal blood atones for human sin in this way, it is sacred and ought not to be consumed by man.

Rules about Hunting Game (13–16)

The previous laws have been dealing with domesticated animals, e.g., sheep and goats (v. 3), and particularly with sacrificial animals that had to be killed near the altar (vv. 6, 8–9, 11). But only selected domestic animals could be offered in sacrifice (1:2). Did the same rules apply to wild game? Did they have to be killed in the court of the tabernacle (cf. vv. 3–4)? Could their blood be eaten? What happens if an animal is found that has died naturally or been killed by other animals? May one eat it? This paragraph answers such questions.

Only the blood prohibition applies to wild game. Since there

8. See H. W. Wolff, *The Anthropology of the OT* (London: SCM, 1974), pp. 10–25, and C. Westermann, *THWAT* II, pp. 71–96.
9. Hertz, p. 168; J. Milgrom, *Interpretation* 17 (1963), pp. 288–301 and "A Prolegomenon to Lev. 17:11," *JBL* 90 (1971), pp. 149–156.
10. Many writers, e.g., de Vaux, *Sacrifice*, p. 93, understand this verse to mean the blood atones for sin by setting free the animal's life. I believe the interpretation followed here does more justice to the usage elsewhere in Scripture. See on 1:4 above and also the discussions of Milgrom, *JBL* 90 (1971), pp. 150f., and Levine, *Presence of the Lord*, p. 68.

was no question of wild animals being offered in sacrifice, it did not matter where they were killed. Moreover, it would have been impracticable to suggest that every gazelle be chased into the tabernacle before it was killed. But when someone catches game "he must pour out its blood and cover it with earth. . . . You must not eat the blood of any animal" (vv. 13–14). In other words to drink the blood of wild animals is just as sacrilegious as drinking other animal blood.

If an animal dies naturally, or as the result of an attack by another creature, one cannot be sure whether its blood has drained away properly. Therefore if a man eats meat from it he may become unclean and he must wash himself and change his clothes to rid himself of potential impurity (vv. 15–16). An additional cause of uncleanness would be contact with the carcass of an animal which dies: that is polluting in itself (11:39–40).

Similar regulations about the hunting and eating of game are found in Deut. 12:15–16, 22ff. It is recommended there that animals found dead be disposed of differently; they should not be eaten by native Israelites, but may be consumed by resident aliens or (visiting) foreigners. There is no conflict of principle between the provisions of Deuteronomy and Leviticus. Deuteronomy fails to mention the consequences of eating this sort of meat, but the fact that it instructs the full-born Israelites to avoid eating it suggests it concurred with Leviticus that such meat does cause uncleanness. Whereas Leviticus allows both Israelite and sojourner to become unclean and insists on washing afterward, Deuteronomy simplifies the rule by forbidding such meat entirely to Israelites, but allowing sojourners to eat it at will. This seems to be a case of upholding a principle while varying its detailed application.[12]

Leviticus 17 and the NT

Throughout history God's people have tended to forget that they owe exclusive allegiance to God. Within a few years of the promulgation of this law we read of their joining themselves to the Baal of Peor (Num. 25:1ff.). Deut. 32:17 says, "they sacrificed to demons which were no gods." The later histories tell of a continuing struggle between the worship of the Lord and Baal (e.g., Judg. 2:11ff.; 1 K. 16:29ff., etc.). Christ warned his disciples that they could not serve God and mammon (Matt. 6:24; Luke 16:13). Paul warned the Corin-

11. On "bearing iniquity" cf. 5:1; 7:18.
12. Cf. Introduction, VII: "Leviticus and the Christian."

thians against participating in heathen worship, because this involved the worship of demons. "What pagans sacrifice they offer to demons and not to God. I do not want you to be partners with demons. You cannot drink the cup of the Lord and the cup of demons. You cannot partake of the table of the Lord and the table of demons. Shall we provoke the Lord to jealousy? Are we stronger than he?" (1 Cor. 10:20–22). In new guises both materialism (mammon) and demonology still seek to woo the Christian from total commitment to Christ.

The notion that "the blood makes atonement" is of course the presupposition underlying the NT understanding of the death of Christ. "Without the shedding of blood there is no forgiveness of sins" (Heb. 9:22). According to the NT the sacrificial rituals of Leviticus anticipate and foreshadow the only perfect and effective redeeming sacrifice, the death of Christ. The typology of the different sacrifices has already been discussed (see esp. chs. 1, 3, 4, and 16).

But the prohibition on drinking animal blood deserves special comment. It is one of the few ritual obligations from the OT whose observance was enjoined on the early Church. The Council of Jerusalem, having discussed whether Gentile converts should be circumcised and compelled to keep the law of Moses, decided that all that was necessary was that "you abstain from what has been sacrificed to idols and from what is strangled and from unchastity" (Acts 15:29). If an animal was killed by strangulation its blood would not drain out, therefore it fell into the category of the meat mentioned in Lev. 17:11ff.

For the modern interpreter the Jerusalem decrees raise problems. Were they intended to be permanently binding? Or were they a compromise to avoid offending Jewish sensitivities (cf. Rom. 14)? Clearly unchastity *(porneia)* was never approved (1 Cor. 5; Rev. 2:14). But Paul does allow Christians to eat food offered to idols as long as the meal does not take place in a pagan temple and it is not misinterpreted by pagan friends (1 Cor. 8; 10:25ff.). It seems likely, therefore, that Paul did not view eating blood as something that was intrinsically wrong, but held that it should be avoided whenever it might offend Jewish Christians (cf. Rom. 14:2–3, 14–15). Some groups in the Church continued to abstain from blood as late as Tertullian's day (early 3rd century).

In the teaching of Christ the identification of life with blood is reaffirmed. It may be that the Pauline view of the blood prohibition has its roots in our Lord's teaching, for in it the Levitical identification of blood with life is at once reaffirmed and transfigured. According to Leviticus "the blood is the life," and therefore must not be drunk. Those who ignore this rule will be cut off. According to our Lord it is his blood that gives eternal life, and those who wish to enjoy it must drink his blood. "He who eats my flesh and drinks my blood has eternal life, and I will raise him up at the last day" (John 6:54). Each time the Lord's supper is administered, the worshipper is reminded through Christ's words, "This is my blood," that it is only through his Savior's death upon the cross that he enjoys eternal life.

B. BASIC PRINCIPLES OF SEXUAL BEHAVIOR (CH. 18)

1 *The Lord spoke to Moses as follows:*

2 *"Speak to the Israelites and say to them, I am the Lord your God.*

3 *You must not behave as they do in the land of Egypt, where you have been living; and you must not behave as they do in the land of Canaan, which I am bringing you to; you must not follow their rules.*

4 *You must do my laws and keep my rules to follow them; I am the Lord your God.*

5 *You must keep my rules and my laws; if a man does them, he will enjoy life through them: I am the Lord.*

6 *No man among you may approach any of his close relatives to have sexual intercourse: I am the Lord.*

7 *Do not have intercourse with your parents: she is your mother; do not have intercourse with her.*

8 *Do not have intercourse with your father's wife; she is one with your father.*

9 *Do not have intercourse with your sister, your father's daughter or your mother's daughter, whether she belongs to local kindred or distant kindred.*

10 *Do not have intercourse with your granddaughter, because she is one with you.*

11 *Do not have intercourse with your step-sister, if she belongs to your father's kindred; she is your sister.*

12 *Do not have intercourse with your father's sister; she is your father's relative.*

13 *Do not have intercourse with your mother's sister, because she is your mother's relative.*

14 *Do not uncover the nakedness of your uncle; you shall not approach his wife; she is your aunt.*

15 *Do not have intercourse with your daughter-in-law; she is your son's wife; do not have intercourse with her.*

16 *Do not have intercourse with your brother's wife; she is one with your brother.*

17 *Do not have intercourse with a woman and her daughter; do not take her son's daughter or her daughter's daughter to have intercourse with her; they are relatives, it is wickedness.*

18 *Do not marry a woman as well as her sister to distress her by having intercourse with her while she is alive.*

19 *Do not approach a woman during her menstrual uncleanness to have intercourse with her.*

20 *Do not lie sexually with your neighbor's wife and become unclean as a result.*

21 *Do not allow any of your children to be offered to Molech, and do not profane the name of your God: I am the Lord.*

22 *Do not lie with a male as with a woman: it is an abomination.*

23 *Do not copulate with any beast to become unclean as a result. A woman must not stand in front of a beast to couple with it: it is confusion.*

24 *Do not make yourselves unclean with all these things, because with all these things the nations which I am driving out before you have become unclean.*

25 *The land became unclean and I punished it for its iniquity and the land vomited out its inhabitants.*

26 *You must keep my rules and my laws and you must not do any of these abominations, that covers both the native and the resident alien who lives among you.*

27 *because all these abominations were done by the people in the land before you and the land became unclean.*

28 *Lest the land vomit you out for making it unclean as it vomited out the nation which was before you.*

29 *For every person who does any of these abominations will be cut off from his people.*

30 *But you must keep my charge and not do any of the abominable rules which used to be done before you so that you do not make yourselves unclean in them. I am the Lord your God.*

The Structure of Leviticus 18

This chapter divides into four sections:

    1–5   Exhortation to avoid the customs of the heathen

    6–18   A list of unions regarded as incestuous

    19–23   Other Canaanite customs (mainly sexual deviations) to be avoided

    24–30   Warning of the consequences of neglecting these rules

The order of the material in this chapter loosely resembles the covenant-treaty form, which is present elsewhere in biblical literature (e.g., Exod. 20, Deuteronomy).[1]

    2   Preamble: "I am the Lord your God"

1. See D. J. McCarthy, *Treaty and Covenant* (Rome: Biblical Institute Press, 1963), pp. 109ff., and commentaries on Deuteronomy by J. A. Thompson and P. C. Craigie.

3   Historical retrospect: "Egypt, where you have been living"
4   Basic stipulation: "Do my laws"
5   Blessing: "He will enjoy life"
6–23 Detailed stipulations
24–30 Curses

Chapter 17 opened a new section in Leviticus, dealing with private religion and morality as opposed to official worship which was the principal concern of the first sixteen chapters of the book. This chapter goes further in setting out the fundamentals of Israelite morality and defines which sexual unions are compatible with Yahwistic principles.

There is a strong polemical thrust in these laws. Seven times it is repeated that the Israelites are not to behave like the nations who inhabited Canaan before them (vv. 3 [2x], 24, 26, 27, 29, 30). Six times the phrase "I am the Lord (your God)" is repeated (vv. 2, 4, 5, 6, 21, 30). Israel's sexual morality is here portrayed as something that marks it off from its neighbors as the Lord's special people. Ch. 17 also stressed that Israel was not to compromise her witness by worshipping demons, or eating blood. This chapter insists that certain standards of sexual morality are equally decisive marks of religious allegiance.

Hertz[2] argues that the order of the laws in chs. 18–20 is significant. These chapters set out "the foundation principles of social morality. The first place among these is given to the institution of marriage . . . the cornerstone of all human society. . . . Any violation of the sacred character of marriage is deemed a heinous offence, calling down the punishment of Heaven both upon the offender and the society that condones the offence."

Exhortation to Avoid Heathen Customs (1–5)

1–2a For this introductory formula compare 1:1–2; 4:1–2; 12:1–2; 20:1–2, etc.

I am the Lord your God (vv. 2, 4). This phrase, or the shorter form "I am the Lord," is a characteristic refrain in this and the succeeding chapters of Leviticus, though it is also found in Exodus and Numbers.

An almost identical[3] phrase introduces the ten commandments in Exod. 20:2//Deut. 5:6. For this reason it can be described

2. Hertz, p. 172.
3. The English translations disguise the fact that Hebrew uses different words for "I" and "your" in the Decalog.

as a preamble[4] corresponding to those found in Hittite treaties of the second millennium B.C. It may also be described as the covenant formula. This has merit because this short phrase, only three words in Hebrew, encapsulates the fundamental truths about the Sinai Covenant.

The terseness of the phrase disguises the rich association of ideas that it evoked in ancient Israel. It occurs in three main types of context. First, it looks back to the redemption of Israel from slavery in Egypt.[5] When God revealed the full meaning of his name Yahweh to Moses, he linked this revelation to a promise that he would save his people from slavery in Egypt and bring them into the land of Canaan. "I am the Lord, and I will bring you out from under the burdens of the Egyptians, and I will deliver you from their bondage . . . and I will take you for my people, and I will be your God; and you shall know that I am the Lord your God" (Exod. 6:6-7). This short phrase, "I am the Lord your God," was a reminder of what God had done for Israel and how he had chosen to make them his people.

Second, Israel, as the people of God, was expected to imitate God, to be holy.[6] "For I am the Lord your God, and you must sanctify yourselves and be holy, because I am holy" (Lev. 11:44).

Third, this phrase often provides the motive for observing a particular law. Under the covenant the people of God were expected to keep the law, not merely as a formal duty but as a loving response to God's grace in redemption.[7]

In this very short formula the Israelites were reminded constantly who they were and whom they served.

You must not behave as they do in the land of Egypt . . . in the land of Canaan (v. 3). The prevalence of the customs denounced here as Egyptian and Canaanite perversions is well attested in Scripture and in nonbiblical sources. In the Egyptian royal family brothers married sisters. The laws of Hammurabi and the Hittites ban some of the incestuous relationships listed here,[8] but by implication allowed other unions mentioned here. Even the patriarchs disregarded some of these rules: Abraham married his half-sister[9] (Gen.

4. E.g., *ANET,* pp. 202f.
5. Lev. 11:45; 19:34, 36; 23:43; 25:38, 55; 26:13, 45; Num. 15:41.
6. Cf. Lev. 19:2; 20:7, 24.
7. Lev. 18:4, 30; 19:3-4, 10, 25, 31; 23:22; 24:22; 25:17; 26:1.
8. LH 154-58; HL 189f.; cf. vv. 7-8, 15.
9. It may be noted that by David's time such a union was forbidden; hence Amnon's great frustration in not being allowed to wed Tamar (2 Sam. 13:2). Cf. G. J. Wenham, *VT* 22 (1972), pp. 342f.

20:12; cf. Lev. 18:9) and Jacob was married to two sisters simultaneously (Gen. 29; cf. Lev. 18:18).

Homosexuality (v. 22) is referred to among the Canaanites (Gen. 19:5ff.) and also attested in Mesopotamia.[10] Bestiality (v. 23) is also known from Egyptian, Canaanite, and Hittite sources. There was a cult in the Eastern delta that involved the cohabitation of women and goats. Indeed Ramses II, possibly the Pharaoh of the exodus, claimed to be the offspring of the god Ptah, who took the form of a goat.[11] Ugaritic texts speak of gods copulating with animals.[12] The Hittite laws (c. 1500 B.C.) legislate against certain forms of bestiality while permitting others.[13]

In connection with the offerings to Molech, the charred bones of children found in a temple near Amman, destroyed at about the time of the Conquest (late Bronze Age), show that the pre-Israelite inhabitants of the land practiced child sacrifice[14] (v. 21).

"You must not follow their rules" (v. 3).

Follow (hālak) is more literally "to walk." The idea of life as a journey is common in Scripture,[15] and in later Christian literature, e.g., *Pilgrim's Progress.*

Rule (ḥōq)[16] is one of a number of words for law in the Pentateuch. It is derived from the verb "to inscribe" *(ḥāqaq),* which is used for example in Job 19:23 and Isa. 49:16. The noun denotes something inscribed by God, a boundary line for the sea which it may not cross (e.g., Jer. 5:22). When *ḥōq* is used of a law it draws attention to the givenness of the law, that it is a decree or a rule handed out by the law-giver, whether he be human or divine (e.g., Exod. 5:14; 15:25; Ps. 2:7). It is therefore a particularly appropriate term for the rules that follow: there is a givenness about them; little attempt is made to justify these rules, e.g., by arguing that they represent love for your neighbor. "I am the Lord" is sufficient motive for keeping them. They are also rules that define the bounds

10. See *Reallexikon der Assyriologie* 4, pp. 459–468. See also M. H. Pope, "Homosexuality," *IDBS* pp. 415–17.
11. W. Krebs, *Forschungen und Fortschritte* 37 (1963), pp. 19-21.
12. A. van Selms, *Marriage and Family Life in Ugaritic Literature* (London: Luzac, 1954), pp. 81f.
13. HL 187f., 199f.
14. J. B. Hennessey in a letter to the author. See also Hennessey's preliminary report in *PEQ* 98 (1966), pp. 152–162, and V. Hankey, *Levant* 6 (1974), p. 131. For a broad survey of other evidence see A. R. W. Green, *The Role of Human Sacrifice in the Ancient Near East* (1975).
15. Cf. Lev. 26:3; Deut. 5:33; Ps. 1:1; Prov. 2:20; Matt. 7:13–14; John 8:12; Rom. 13:13.
16. See *THWAT* I, pp. 626–633.

which may not be transgressed in sexual relationships. The other word for *law (mishpāṭ)* in this chapter (vv. 4, 5, 26) also conveys a sense of authoritative givenness. A *mishpāṭ* is a legal decision, the sentence passed by a judge *(shōpēṭ)* (Deut. 17:11; 19:6).

He will enjoy life through them (v. 5). Literally "he will live through them." For the OT writers life means primarily physical life. But it is clear that in this and similar passages more than mere existence is being promised. What is envisaged is a happy life in which a man enjoys God's bounty of health, children, friends, and prosperity. Keeping the law is the path to divine blessing, to a happy and fulfilled life in the present (Lev. 26:3–13; Deut. 28:1–14).

But what about life after death? The OT envisaged life continuing in Sheol, a shadowy, depressing version of life on earth. And in a few passages there are hints that the righteous will enjoy a much better existence in the presence of God himself (e.g., Ps. 73; Dan. 12:1–3). But it is Jesus and Paul who insist that the full meaning of life is eternal life. If anyone can keep the law, he will enjoy eternal life (Matt. 19:17; Rom. 10:5; Gal. 3:12). In John's Gospel man must keep the new law—the word of Christ. "If anyone keeps my word, he will never see death" (John 8:51).

Forbidden Unions (6–18)

No man among you may approach any of his close relatives to have sexual intercourse (v. 6). This states the general principle underlying the detailed rules given in the following verses. "Close relative" is literally "flesh of his flesh" (cf. Gen. 2:23). "To have sexual intercourse"—a more literal translation would be "to uncover the nakedness of" (cf. v. 14). The phrase covers intercourse within marriage and outside it. Effectively then these rules define the limits within which a man may seek a wife for himself.

The unspoken assumption underlying these rules is that a man will seek a partner among his own people. Marriages with non-Israelites are firmly forbidden elsewhere (e.g., Deut. 7:3). Preference was shown for marriages within the tribe (Num. 36; cf. Judg. 21) and even between cousins (Gen. 24). But anyone more closely related than this was excluded by these rules. They regulate only the man's choice, because he generally took the initiative in biblical times (Judg. 14:1ff.). A woman who consented to an illicit union, however, was regarded as equally culpable and suffered the same punishment as her partner (Lev. 20:10ff.).

253

These rules may be summarized in the following table:

A man may not marry his:

Mother (v. 7)	Aunt (vv. 12, 13), i.e., father's or mother's sister	Step-mother[17] (v. 8)	Aunt by marriage (v. 14), i.e., uncle's wife
Sister or half-sister (v. 9)	Step-sister (v. 11) Step-daughter (v. 17)	Sister-in-law (v. 16) Daughter-in-law (v. 15)	
Granddaughter (v. 10)	Step-granddaughter (v. 17)		

There is one striking omission from this table. Marriage with one's daughter is not proscribed. This is probably because it was already accepted that such a union was illicit (Gen. 19:30ff.). It is expressly forbidden both in the laws of Hammurabi (LH 154) and in the Hittite laws (HL 195). In other words these regulations extend the prohibitions on incest already accepted in other parts of the ancient Near East.

"No man among you may approach any of his close relatives to have sexual intercourse" (v. 6). The above table explains what is meant: sexual intercourse is forbidden between people who are consanguineous to the first and second degree.[18] Thus a man may not marry his mother or his sister (first-degree consanguinity, vv. 7, 9) or his aunt or his granddaughter (second-degree consanguinity, vv. 12–13, 10). In addition he may not marry the wife of a close blood relation, e.g., his brother's or his uncle's wife or his step-mother (vv. 16, 14, 8). These rules are not concerned with marriage during the lifetime of the brother or uncle, which is covered by the prohibition of adultery (v. 20; Exod. 20:14). Marriage after the death of the woman's first husband or after she has been divorced is what is prohibited here.

The underlying basis of these rules is explained in the motive clauses.[19] For example, "Do not have intercourse with your granddaughter, because she is one with you" (v. 10). *She is one with you*

---

17. The term step-mother translates Heb. "father's wife," and this covers any second wife whether a man marries again following his first wife's death or following divorce, or polygamously. Polygamy was possible but rare in OT times.

18. Using the definitions of consanguinity current in modern genetics, as opposed to Roman or canon law.

19. See F. L. Horton, Jr., "Form and Structure in Laws Relating to Women," *SBL* 1973 Seminar Papers, pp. 20–33; and G. J. Wenham, "The Biblical View of Marriage and Divorce," *Third Way* 1.21 (3 Nov., 1977), pp. 7–9 and "The Restoration of Marriage Reconsidered," *JJS* 30 (1979), pp. 36–40.

could be translated more literally "because she is your nakedness" (cf. vv. 8, 14, 16), or as we might say, "she is your flesh and blood." The law in fact uses an expression like this in vv. 12, 13, 17. *She is your father's relative* is literally "she is your father's flesh."

With our understanding of biology we readily see that our children are an extension of ourselves; they are in a vertical blood relationship with us. But foreign to our way of thinking is the idea that a wife's nakedness is her husband's nakedness[20] and vice versa (vv. 7, 8, 16). In other words, marriage, or more precisely marital intercourse, makes the man and wife as closely related as parents and children. In the words of Gen. 2:24, "they become one flesh." Marriage thus creates both vertical blood relationships in the form of children and horizontal "blood" relationships between the spouses. The girl who marries into a family becomes an integral and permanent part of that family in the same way that children born into the family do. Even if her husband dies, or divorces her, she still has this horizontal "blood" relationship with the family. In Hebrew thinking marriage made a girl not just a daughter-in-law, but a daughter of her husband's parents (Ruth 1:11; 3:1). She became a sister to her husband's brother. For this reason, if her husband dies, her brother-in-law may not marry her (v. 16). Brothers may not marry sisters (v. 9).

The basic principles underlying the rules in vv. 6–18 are therefore clear: a man may not marry any woman who is a close blood relation, or any woman who has become a close relative through a previous marriage to one of the man's close blood relations. All the relationships prohibited here can be seen to be outworkings of these two basic principles. But certain phrases in this section are difficult to understand and require further discussion.

"Do not have intercourse with your sister, your father's daughter or your mother's daughter, whether she belongs to local kindred or distant kindred" (v. 9). Most commentators understand this to be a prohibition on marriage of a man and his full sister *(father's daughter)* or his half-sister *(mother's daughter)*. The final phrase *local kindred or distant kindred* is more difficult. It is generally understood to be a more detailed explanation of the rule forbidding marriage with a full sister or half-sister. The full sister was born

---

20. A more literal translation of v. 7 brings out clearly the idea that a woman's nakedness is her husband's. Cf. RSV "You shall not uncover the nakedness of your father, which is the nakedness of your mother; she is your mother, you shall not uncover her nakedness."

within the family whereas a half-sister was born outside, hence RSV "whether born at home or born abroad." Such redundancy in a legal text is unlikely and therefore other explanations have been sought. Hoffmann[21] and Hertz[22] believe "local kindred or distant kindred" means "legitimate or illegitimate." But it seems unlikely that a fringe case should be picked out in a table of basic rules. The third explanation, presupposed in our translation, also appears to underlie the NEB's rendering "whether brought up in the family or in another home."[23] This takes the Hebrew terms in their most natural sense and finds legal significance in every phrase. This rule presupposes that marriage with a full sister is unlawful (*your sister*) and then specifies less obvious cases (*half-sisters*).

"Your father's daughter or your mother's daughter." A half-sister through a man's mother presupposes an earlier marriage by his mother. In her first marriage the woman had a daughter. When she remarried her daughter could be brought up in her mother's new home ("local kindred") or left behind with her parents or brothers ("distant kindred"). No matter where her first daughter was brought up, any son by her second marriage could not marry her daughter. In other words "whether she belongs to local kindred or distant kindred" refers only to "your mother's daughter." "Your father's daughter" would automatically be classed as local kindred, since she would grow up in her father's home.

"Do not have intercourse with your step-sister, if she belongs to your father's kindred" (v. 11). *Step-sister* is literally "a daughter of your father's wife." Most commentators equate "daughter of your father's wife" with "daughter of your father" and say that what is meant here is a half-sister through one's father, whereas "your father's daughter" in v. 9 means a full sister. We have already argued that this is an unlikely interpretation of "your father's daughter," which *prima facie* includes half-sisters as well as full sisters.

Saalschütz' view seems much more likely. He takes "daughter of your father's wife" to be a step-sister, not a half-sister. One may envisage the following situation. Man A marries woman B and has daughter C, while man D marries woman E and produces son F. Normally C could marry F without objection. But what happens if

21. Hoffmann II, p. 14.
22. Hertz, p. 178.
23. But Porter, p. 146, commenting on the NEB, puts the usual interpretation on this phrase. The interpretation adopted here is a modification of Saalschütz's view, pp. 770f. He thinks the woman's first marriage produced a son and her second a daughter.

man A and woman E die, and then man D marries woman B? Can the children of the first unions marry, or have their parents' second marriage made them brother and sister? Can C still marry F?

This law says a man (F) may not marry his step-sister (C) *if she belongs to your father's kindred*.[24] It is this last clause that leads most commentators and translators to suppose that a man's half-sister as opposed to his step-sister is meant, for they take *kindred (môledet)* to mean "offspring, family, or birth." But in Genesis *môledet* clearly defines a wider grouping than the nuclear family, including cousins. Perhaps "patrilineage" or "extended family" might be a suitable translation.[25] At any rate a man could certainly seek a wife from within his father's *môledet* as long as she was not too closely related to him (Gen. 24:4). This rule states that a man may not marry his step-sister if she was also counted as one of his "father's kindred."

Do not have intercourse with your brother's wife (v. 16). This rule exemplifies the general principle about the choice of marriage partners. There are to be no unions with close relatives or their wives. This law is not condemning an adulterous situation. The wickedness of adultery is presupposed (cf. v. 20). Rather it envisages the termination of "your brother's" first marriage through death or divorce. After the death of her husband a woman may not marry her brother-in-law. Deut. 25:5ff. states an exception to this principle. Should a woman be widowed before she has borne a son, her brother-in-law has a duty to marry her "to perpetuate his brother's name" (v. 7). This custom of Levirate, attested elsewhere in Scripture and the ancient Orient,[26] illustrates the paramount importance of having children in ancient times. Heirs prevented the alienation of family property and ensured the parents' support in their old age, in times when pensions and other welfare services were unknown.

Do not marry a woman as well as her sister (v. 18). This is another example of the basic principle that through marriage a

---

24. Saalschütz, pp. 769f., actually translates this clause "if she (the father's wife) bears children for your father," understanding *môledet* to be a participle meaning "bearing." In other words, if the second marriage of D and B produces offspring, the children of their first marriages C and F may not marry. This is unlikely, for nowhere else in Scripture does *môledet* appear to mean "bearing," and if it were a participle its subject would be "daughter," not "wife" as Saalschütz' view demands.
25. Gen. 12:1; 24:4; 31:3, 13; 43:7; 48:6; cf. Num. 10:30.
26. Gen. 38; Ruth 4; Matt. 22:23ff.; cf. MAL A30–33; HL 193.

woman's sisters became her husband's sisters. Therefore he may not take any of them as a second wife.[27]

To distress her. This may mean "to be a rival wife." Certainly rivalry and distress were characteristic of bigamous marriages, especially between sisters. The history of Jacob's family is eloquent commentary on the wisdom of this law (Gen. 29ff.; cf. 1 Sam. 1:6–7).

While she is alive limits the application of this rule to the woman's lifetime. Should her husband divorce her he may not marry her sister, but if she has died he may. This custom of sororate marriage is analogous to the Levirate law just discussed (Deut. 25:5ff.), but unlike the Levirate was not compulsory. It was also known among the Assyrians and Hittites.[28] The rabbis regarded this sort of arrangement as most praiseworthy, "as no other woman would show the same affection to the orphaned children of the deceased sister."[29]

Other Canaanite Customs to Be Avoided (19–23)

19 Cf. Lev. 15:19ff.; 20:18; 2 Sam. 11:4.

20 Adultery: cf. Exod. 20:14; Lev. 20:10; Deut. 22:22. The OT definition of adultery, in common with that of other ancient societies, was rather narrower than that in the NT. It was defined as sexual intercourse with a married or betrothed woman by someone who was not her husband. Intercourse by a married man with an unattached woman, though disapproved of, was not adulterous and did not warrant the death penalty.[30]

21 *Do not allow any of your children to be offered*[31] *to Molech.* Offerings to Molech are condemned on a number of occasions in the OT (cf. Lev. 20:2–5; 1 K. 11:7; 2 K. 23:10; Jer. 32:35). Though a number of ideas[32] as to what constitutes a sacrifice to

27. J. Murray, *Principles of Conduct* (London: Tyndale, 1957, pp. 251ff.), argues that bigamy in general is being condemned here. He translates it "Do not marry a woman as well as another." Though the Hebrew could mean this, it is unlikely, because elsewhere in this chapter sister always denotes sister, and nowhere in the OT is bigamy regarded as illegal as opposed to inadvisable.
28. MAL A31; HL 192.
29. According to Hertz, p. 180.
30. Gen. 34; Exod. 22:15–16 [Eng. 16–17]; Deut. 22:28–29; cf. J. J. Finkelstein, *JAOS* 86 (1966), p. 359.
31. *Offered (he'ebîr)* (lit. "to pass through") is different from the term for orthodox sacrifice—*hiqrîb,* "to bring near."
32. E.g., Snaith, "children were given . . . to be trained as temple prostitutes" (p. 125).

Molech have been advanced, it is now fairly certain that it involved child sacrifice[33] (cf. Deut. 12:31; 18:10).

The remnants of Molk-sacrifices have been found in North Africa, and there is evidence to suggest that it derived from Phoenicia. It has often been supposed that these sacrifices involved throwing the children alive into the flames. De Vaux points out that only one contemporary description of Carthaginian practice may imply this; the others state that the babies were killed first.[34] He suggests that this custom was practiced in Israel only from about the seventh century B.C., at about the time this part of Leviticus was being composed on normal critical theory.[35] Since he wrote, evidence of child sacrifice has been discovered in Jordan from the period of the Conquest. Interestingly it comes from a temple at Amman, in the territory of the Ammonites, whose deity was Molech according to 1 K. 11:7.

Profane the name of your God. This phrase or a very similar one recurs several times in Leviticus (19:12; 20:3; 21:6; 22:32). To "profane"[36] means to make something unholy. The object of the verb is always something holy, e.g., God's sanctuary, 21:12, 23; the holy foods (22:15); the sabbath, Isa. 56:2, 6; Ezek. 20:13, 16, etc. Profaning God's name occurs when his name is misused in a false oath (Lev. 19:12), but more usually it is done indirectly, by doing something that God disapproves of (e.g., by idolatry, Ezek. 20:39; by breaking the covenant, Jer. 34:16; by disfiguring oneself, Lev. 21:6). By these actions Israel profanes God's name; that is, they give him a bad reputation among the Gentiles (Ezek. 36:20–21). This is why they must shun Molech worship.

22 Homosexuality is condemned throughout Scripture (Gen. 19; Lev. 20:13; Judg. 19:22ff.; Rom. 1:27; 1 Cor. 6:9). *Abomination,* a term of strong disapproval in Hebrew *(tôʻēḇāh),* is used five times in this chapter (vv. 22, 26, 27, 29, 30) and in 20:13. It is more common in Deuteronomy (17 times), in Proverbs (21 times), and in Ezekiel (43 times). Other writers use it less often. It comes from a root meaning "to hate" or "abhor."[37] An abomination is literally something detestable and hated by God (e.g., Prov. 6:16; 11:1).

---

33. De Vaux, *Sacrifice,* pp. 56–90.
34. *Ibid.,* p. 81.
35. *Ibid.,* p. 75.
36. Heb. *ḥillēl;* see *THWAT* I, pp. 570–75, and Introduction, VI.2: "Holiness."
37. Heb. *tôʻēḇāh,* "abomination," *tāʻaḇ,* "to detest"; *THWAT* 2, pp. 1051–55.

23 Bestiality is condemned in most of the legal collections in the Pentateuch (Exod. 22:18 [Eng. 19]; Lev. 20:15–16; Deut. 27:21), because *it is confusion.*[38] Such a nation is unnatural; it transgresses the God-given boundaries between man and the animal. Holiness in the Pentateuch is a matter of purity,[39] of keeping apart what God has created to be separate. This law is one of a number condemning various kinds of mixtures regarded as unnatural (Lev. 19:19; Deut. 22:5, 9–11).

Final Warnings and Exhortations (24–30)

This concluding epilog warns Israel of the dangers of adopting Canaanite practices. If they do, they will pollute themselves and suffer the same punishment as their predecessors: *Lest the land vomit you out . . . as it vomited out the nation which was before you* (v. 28). This most unusual and striking expression (cf. v. 25 and 20:22) personifies the land of Canaan, which finds the customs of its inhabitants so revolting that it vomits them out just as the whale spat out Jonah (2:11 [Eng. 10]), or like a man who has too much to drink (Isa. 19:14).

It was customary for ancient treaties and collections of law to conclude with a series of curses on those who break them. This pattern is found in Scripture too (cf. Exod. 23:20–21; Lev. 26:14ff.; Deut. 28:15ff.). This passage has this function, though in style it more closely resembles the persuasive rhetoric of Deuteronomy.

Leviticus 18 and the NT

For most Christians it is self-evident that the moral rules enunciated in this chapter still apply today. The NT writers assume that the laws on incest (vv. 6–18; cf. 1 Cor. 5:1ff.), adultery (v. 20, e.g., Rom. 13:9), idolatry (v. 21; cf. 1 Cor. 10:7ff.; Rev. 2:14), and homosexuality (v. 22; Rom. 1:27; 1 Cor. 6:9) still bind the Christian conscience.

Indeed as far as adultery is concerned the NT is stricter than the OT. According to Jesus, "Everyone who divorces his wife and marries another commits adultery, and he who marries a woman divorced from her husband commits adultery" (Luke 16:18; cf. Matt. 19:3–12; Mark 10:2–12). Whereas under OT law a married man could take a second wife, with or without divorcing the first, or have an affair with an unattached woman, and not be accused of

38. *Teḇel,* used only here and 20:12 (from the verb *bālal,* "to mix").
39. See Introduction, VI.2: "Holiness."

adultery, this saying brands all three acts as adulterous. In so teaching Jesus introduced full reciprocity between the sexes: unfaithful husbands are just as adulterous as unfaithful wives. Yet this new definition of adultery is not such a break with the OT as may at first appear. It takes the principle underlying the incest laws in Lev. 18 to their logical conclusion: if marriage makes a man one flesh with his wife, he may not later desert her and take another.[40]

This is not to say that the Christian accepts the interpretation placed on v. 5, "if a man does them, he will enjoy life through them," by some of Paul's Pharisaic opponents. They argued that this showed that keeping the law brought man into a right relationship with God (Gal. 3:12; Rom. 10:5). Paul argued that keeping the law is the fruit of justification rather than the means of justification. His exegesis is more faithful to the original setting of Lev. 18:5. The law was given to the covenant people after their redemption from Egypt (v. 3), not as a moral hurdle they had to clear if they wished to be saved.

Just because these laws appear morally right from a Christian standpoint, we may fail to note the incongruity in accepting these as still valid while dismissing those in the previous chapter as obsolete and no longer binding on the Christian conscience. Systematic theologians have traditionally justified this differentiation by arguing that the laws in this chapter are moral whereas the others are ceremonial. In the introduction I have argued that this division is foreign to biblical thinking. The reason why these laws apply to us and others do not, lies in our situation. Man's moral predicaments change very little with time. We still need guidelines to regulate man's treatment of his fellow men. But the believer's situation with regard to salvation has altered drastically; there is no need to continue with animal sacrifice now that the true Lamb of God has appeared.

C. PRINCIPLES OF NEIGHBORLINESS (CH. 19)

1 *The Lord spoke to Moses as follows:*

2 *"Speak to the whole congregation of the Israelites and say to them: You must be holy, for I the Lord your God am holy.*

3 *Each one of you must reverence his mother and his father and observe my sabbaths: I am the Lord your God.*

---

40. For further discussion see G. J. Wenham, "The Biblical View of Marriage and Divorce: NT Teaching," *Third Way* 1.22 (17 Nov., 1977), pp. 7–9.

4 *Do not turn to idols or make yourselves molten gods: I am the Lord your God.*

5 *If you sacrifice a peace offering to the Lord, you must sacrifice it so that you may be accepted,*

6 *but it must be eaten on the day of the sacrifice or the day after, and what is left over to the third day must be burned with fire.*

7 *If anything is actually eaten on the third day, it is rotten; it will not be accepted.*

8 *Whoever eats it must bear his iniquity because he has profaned the Lord's holy thing, and that person will be cut off from his people.*

9 *When you reap the harvest of your land, do not go right up to the corner of your field to reap and do not gather up the gleanings of your harvest.*

10 *Do not glean your vineyard or pick up the windfalls. Leave them for the poor and the resident alien. I am the Lord your God.*

11 *Do not steal and do not cheat and do not defraud your fellow citizen.*

12 *Do not swear falsely in my name and profane the name of your God: I am the Lord.*

13 *Do not oppress your neighbor and do not rob. Do not keep a hired man's wages by you until the morning.*

14 *Do not curse a deaf man or put a stumbling block before the blind but fear your God: I am the Lord.*

15 *Do not practice injustice in court; do not show favoritism to the poor or deference to the great. In justice you must judge your fellow citizen.*

16 *Do not go around spreading slander among your people; do not stand up against your neighbor on a capital charge: I am the Lord.*

17 *Do not hate your brother in your heart: rebuke your fellow citizen so that you do not incur sin because of him.*

18 *Do not take revenge or harbor a grudge against your own people, but love your neighbor as yourself: I am the Lord.*

19 *Keep my rules. Do not cross-breed your cattle; do not sow two kinds of seed in your field; do not wear a garment containing a mixture of fibers.*

20 *If a man sleeps with a slave-girl who has been assigned to another man, but not fully redeemed or given her freedom, damages must be paid. They must not be put to death, because she was not free.*

21 *He must bring his reparation to the Lord to the entrance of the tent of meeting, a ram as a reparation offering.*

22 *The priest must make atonement for him before the Lord with the ram of the reparation offering because of the sin he committed, and he shall receive forgiveness for the sin he committed.*

23 *When you come into the land and plant any fruit tree you must treat its fruit as uncircumcised; for three years it shall be uncircumcised for you and must not be eaten.*

24 *In the fourth year all its fruit shall be a holy praise offering to the Lord.*

25 *But in the fifth year you may eat its fruit and so increase its produce for yourselves: I am the Lord your God.*

26 *Do not eat flesh with blood in it. Do not practice divination or soothsaying.*

27 *Do not round off the edges of your hair or spoil the tip of your beard.*

28 *Do not make incisions in your body for the dead or give yourselves tattoos. I am the Lord.*

29 *Do not profane your daughter by making her a prostitute, so that the land does not prostitute itself and be filled with wickedness.*

30 *Observe my sabbaths and reverence my sanctuary: I am the Lord.*

31 *Do not turn to spirits and do not seek out mediums and become unclean through them: I am the Lord your God.*

32 *Stand up before the elderly and honor the old, and fear your God: I am the Lord.*

33 *If an alien resides with you in your land, do not oppress him.*

34 *Let the resident alien among you be treated like one of yourselves as a native. Love him as yourself, because you were resident aliens in the land of Egypt. I am the Lord your God.*

35 *Do not practice injustice in any legal decision, in measures of length, weight, or volume.*

36 *You must have fair scales, fair weights, a fair ephah and a fair hin: I am the Lord your God who brought you out of the land of Egypt.*

37 *You must keep all my rules and carry out all my decisions: I am the Lord."*

The Structure of Leviticus 19

This chapter covers such a variety of topics that the modern reader finds difficulty in seeing any rhyme or reason in its organization. But once it is recognized that "I am the Lord (your God)" marks the end of a paragraph, its structure becomes much clearer. The chapter falls into sixteen paragraphs, arranged in three sections (4, 4, 8).

1–2a	Introduction	
2b–10	Religious Duties	
	2b	Be holy
	3	Honor parents and sabbath
	4	No idolatry
	5–10	Sacrifices and food
11–18	Good Neighborliness	
	11–12	Honesty
	13–14	No exploitation
	15–16	Justice in court
	17–18	Love your neighbor
19–37	Miscellaneous Duties	
	19–25	No mixed breeding
	26–28	No pagan practices
	29–30	No sacred prostitution

31   No necromancy
32   Respect the old
33–34 Love the alien
35–36 Fair trading
37   Closing exhortation

The first section (vv. 2b–10) consists of four paragraphs, each concluding with the motive clause "I am the Lord your God." The second section (vv. 11–18), also of four paragraphs each concluding with "I am the Lord," is more tightly structured and builds up to a climax in "Love your neighbor as yourself" (v. 18). The third section is longer and uses both "I am the Lord" and "I am the Lord your God" as a refrain. Its opening and close are marked by an inclusion, "Keep my rules" (vv. 19, 37).

Other rhetorical devices in this chapter help to give it a unity. The command to "love your neighbor as yourself" (v. 18) is echoed in the command "love the resident alien as yourself" (v. 34). Children must reverence their parents and "observe my sabbaths" (v. 3); in their turn parents must not prostitute their daughters and must "observe my sabbaths and reverence my sanctuary" (vv. 29–30). The fear of God is motive for treating the weak fairly (v. 14) and for honoring the old (v. 32). Another unifying theme in this chapter is the Decalog. All ten commandments are quoted or alluded to, and sometimes expounded or developed in a new way.[1] The diversity of material in this chapter reflects the differentiation of life. All aspects of human affairs are subject to God's law.

Rules for Practical Holiness
Introduction (1–2a)

Compare 4:1; 8:1; 18:1, etc. *Congregation:* cf. 4:13.

Religious Duties (2b–10)

Be holy (2b)

"You must be holy, for I the Lord your God am holy" (cf. 11:44–45; 20:26) could be described as the motto of Leviticus. For a full exposition of its meaning see the Introduction, VI.2: "Holiness." This motto reminds Israel of its fundamental calling to be a "holy nation" (Exod. 19:6). The people of Israel are to imitate God, whose

---

1. Verse 4, cf. Exod. 20:3–6; v. 12, cf. Exod. 20:7; vv. 3, 30, cf. Exod. 20:8–12; v. 16, cf. Exod. 20:13; vv. 20–22, 29, cf. Exod. 20:14; vv. 11, 13, cf. Exod. 20:15; vv. 15–16, cf. Exod. 20:16; vv. 17–18, cf. Exod. 20:17.

essential nature is holiness (Isa. 6:3; Ps. 99:9, etc.). The meaning of holiness in everyday life is spelled out in the precepts that follow.

> Developing the idea of holiness as order, not confusion, this list upholds rectitude and straight-dealing as holy, and contradiction and double-dealing as against holiness. Theft, lying, false witness, cheating in weights and measures, all kinds of dissembling such as speaking ill of the deaf (and presumably smiling to their face), hating your brother in your heart (while presumably speaking kindly to him), these are clearly contradictions between what seems and what is.[2]

Holiness is expressed in moral integrity, which is in turn symbolized by physical wholeness. The quest for holiness means that priests and sacrificial animals must have no physical deformities (Lev. 21:17ff.) while ordinary people must undergo ritual washings to purify themselves from their discharges (Lev. 15). So in this chapter mixtures (vv. 19ff.) and bodily disfigurements (vv. 27–28) are incompatible with holiness.

> Holiness is thus not so much an abstract or a mystic idea, as a regulative principle in the everyday lives of men and women. . . . Holiness is thus attained not by flight from the world, nor by monk-like renunciation of human relationships of family or station, but by the spirit in which we fulfill the obligations of life in its simplest and commonest details: in this way—by doing justly, loving mercy, and walking humbly with our God—is everyday life transfigured.[3]

Honor parents and the sabbath (3)
Reverence his mother and his father. Holiness begins in the home. Exod. 20:12//Deut. 5:16 says "honor." The word translated *reverence* here is that used in vv. 14, 32 of "fearing God" (cf. Prov. 1:7). As far as a child is concerned, his parents are in the place of God: through them he can learn what God is like and what he requires. It is therefore fitting that in his younger years a child should honor and fear his parents, as in later years he will fear God.

Observe my sabbaths (cf. Exod. 20:8ff.//Deut. 5:12ff.). "The connection of these two precepts is significant. Even as honoring of parents stands foremost among human duties, the sanctification of the Sabbath is the first step towards holiness in his spiritual life."[4]

---

2. M. Douglas, *Purity and Danger*, pp. 53f.
3. Hertz, pp. 190f.
4. Hertz, p. 192.

No idolatry (4)

Do not turn to idols or make yourselves molten gods. Cf. Exod.
20:3–6 // Deut. 5:7–10; Exod. 20:23; 32:23; cf. Deut. 4:16. The word
here translated *idol* is used only twice in the law (here and Lev. 26:1)
but is more frequent in Isaiah (e.g., Isa. 2:8, 18, 20; 10:10–11, etc.).
Two different etymologies have been suggested for it: either it is a
diminutive of god (*'ēl*)—"godling," or it is derived from a Semitic
root meaning "to be weak." If this is the root, we could bring out the
hidden nuances by translating it as "weakling." At any rate this
term is always used to disparage heathen gods and show up their
powerlessness.[5]

Or make yourselves molten gods—echoing Exod. 34:17; cf.
Deut. 27:15. The archetypal molten god was the golden calf made by
Aaron while Moses was up on Mount Sinai (Exod. 32; cf. Deut. 9:12,
16; Neh. 9:18; Hos. 13:2). Though it is described as a molten calf,
quite likely only parts of the image were actually cast in metal. Other
parts probably consisted of gold-plated wood (cf. Jer. 10:3–4; Isa.
44:9ff.). This explains how it could be burned (Exod. 32:20).

Sacrifices and food (5–10)

Chapter 17 insists that only meat properly sacrificed as a peace
offering may be eaten. Both laws in this paragraph regulate which
food may be eaten and under what conditions. The rules for peace
offerings (vv. 5–8; cf. 7:15–20) given here cover the points that
affect the layman when he brings a peace offering. They are less
complicated than those found in ch. 7, perhaps because this version
is meant for laymen whereas ch. 7 was intended for the priests, who
had to know the finer points of the law.

9–10 Gleanings by the poor: cf. Lev. 23:22; Deut. 24:19–22.
This is one of a number of laws in the Pentateuch[6] specifically aimed
at relieving the plight of the poor, such as widows, orphans, and
resident aliens. These people rarely had land of their own, and had
to rely on selling their labor to buy food. This law entitled them to a
small amount of free food each year at the expense of the more
affluent members of society. The story of Ruth gives a glimpse of
how this law was put into practice (Ruth 2).

The Structure of 19:11–18

The four paragraphs in this section each close with the motive clause

---

5. See *'ĕlîl* in *TDOT* I, pp. 285–87.
6. Exod. 22:20ff. [Eng. 21ff.]; 23:6, 11; Lev. 19:13; Deut. 14:28–29; 15:1ff.; 23:20–21
[19–20], 25–26 [24–25]; 24:6, 10–22; cf. Isa. 3:14–15; Amos 2:6ff.

"I am the Lord" (vv. 12, 14, 16, 18). Different words for "neighbor" are used within this section, so that v. 18 forms a literary as well as a theological climax to the whole passage.

11–12		fellow citizen,			I am the Lord
13–14				neighbor,	I am the Lord
15–16		fellow citizen,	people,	neighbor,	I am the Lord
17–18	brother,	fellow citizen,	people,	neighbor,	I am the Lord

Three times the sequence "fellow citizen . . . neighbor" occurs. First it is in simple form (vv. 11–14), then it is expanded by the insertion of "people" (vv. 15–16), and finally in vv. 17–18 the sequence becomes "brother . . . fellow citizen . . . people . . . neighbor." Someone listening to the laws would hear the repeating sequence. The slight delay in mentioning "neighbor" for the third time should make the listener specially alert for the great command to love his neighbor as himself (v. 18).

Good Neighborliness (11–18)

Honesty (11–12)

Do not steal (v. 11), a quotation of the eighth commandment (Exod. 20:15), is followed by a paraphrase of the ninth and fourth (Exod. 20:16, 7), *do not swear falsely in my name and profane the name of your God* (v. 12). False claims about property can be tantamount to theft, and may lead to a court case in which oaths will be sworn by God's name. One party may use it falsely and thereby *profane the name*[7] (cf. Exod. 22:6ff. [Eng. 7ff.]; Lev. 5:20ff. [6:1ff.]; Josh. 7:11; Hos. 4:2).

Fellow citizen (v. 11), Heb. *'ᵃmiṯ:* apart from Zech. 13:7 this term occurs only in Leviticus (5:21 [6:2]; 18:20; 19:11, 15, 17; 24:19; 25:14ff.). Its exact meaning is uncertain, but 24:19ff. suggests it includes both Israelites and resident aliens.

No exploitation of the weak (13–14)

Whereas vv. 11–12 forbid crooked dealings between equals, or at least between those capable of taking one another to law if they have a grievance, these verses deal with exploitation of the weak who would not be able to seek such redress. Sharp practice against them is called oppression and robbery[8] (v. 13).

---

7. On profaning God's name cf. 18:21 and commentary.
8. On *oppress* see Lev. 5:21 (Eng. 6:2); Deut. 28:29–33; Prov. 14:31; Eccl. 4:1; *rob:* Gen. 21:25; Judg. 9:25; Mic. 2:2; Ps. 35:10.

Do not keep a hired man's wages by you until the morning (v. 13). Day laborers could expect to be paid in the evening (Matt. 20:8). To delay payment till the following morning might not be illegal, but it could cause great hardship to a poor man and his family. Deut. 24:15 pictures him crying to God against his employer. The deaf and the blind (v. 14) also have no comeback against those who take advantage of their disabilities. The Israelites must fear God: malpractices will not escape his notice (cf. Deut. 27:18).

Justice in court (15–16)

Do not practice injustice in court (v. 15) is the theme of this paragraph. The judges must administer justice impartially without regard to the status of those being judged (v. 15), and those who are called on as witnesses must be fair. They must not spread gossip that would bring a man into court, or worse still accuse him falsely of crimes which bring the death penalty (v. 16). This insistence on fair treatment at law is a regular theme of the biblical literature (Exod. 23:1–3, 6–8; Deut. 16:19–20; 19:15–21; 27:25; Ps. 72:2; Prov. 16:13, cf. LH 1–5).

To our way of thinking it is hard to see a connection between v. 15 and v. 16. For the most part, justice in our society is administered by professional lawyers, but if one went to court in ancient Israel one's judges would be the elders of the village.[9] In the intimate atmosphere of a local trial it would be particularly easy for neighbors to let their feuds and personal animosities distort the proceedings. *I am the Lord* reminds all the participants that God is the ultimate judge: let their decisions reflect what he would do.

Love your neighbor (17–18)

It is much better to avoid taking your brother to court at all. These verses give some alternative remedies. First *do not hate your brother in your heart* (v. 17; cf. Matt. 5:21ff.; 1 John 2:9; 3:15). If you have a real reason to be annoyed with him, discuss the matter with him, *rebuke* him, as Abraham did with Abimelech (Gen. 21:25). The value of having things out with people rather than brooding on them is mentioned more than once in the Bible. "Better is open rebuke than hidden love" (Prov. 27:5). A mark of the wise man is that he learns from such rebuke, whereas the fool rejects it (Prov. 9:8; 15:12; 19:25). The NT also recommends that people be open with each other in giving and taking advice (Matt. 18:15–22; Gal. 6:1).

9. Cf. Excursus II: "Law Enforcement in Israel."

Hertz aptly comments on this verse: "A precept extremely difficult of fulfilment; it is as difficult to administer reproof with delicacy and tact, as it is to receive reproof. Reproof must, of course, be offered in all kindness, otherwise it fails of its purpose."[10]

So that you do not incur sin because of him. Elsewhere in the law this phrase refers to bearing the penalty of sin (Lev. 20:20; 22:9; 24:15). Here its sense is not so obvious. The most probable suggestion[11] is that whoever rebukes a man and stops him from sinning is freed from the guilt of that man's sin (cf. Ezek. 33). At the same time, by open rebuke the aggrieved party may save his own feelings from overflowing into a sinful action as Cain's did (Gen. 4).[12]

After two more "Don'ts", "Do not take revenge or harbor a grudge," comes the most positive command of all, "Love your neighbor as yourself." *Love*[13] and *neighbor*[14] are as wide-ranging in their scope and meaning in Hebrew as the corresponding English terms. Jesus and Paul were not stretching the meaning of these verses in claiming that all our other duties toward our fellow men were summed up in this command (Matt. 22:39–40; Rom. 13:9). "What every man's mind ought to be towards his neighbor could not be better expressed in many pages than in this one sentence."[15]

No Mixed Breeding (19–25)

This section proceeds from the sublime to the ridiculous! At least that is how the transition from love of neighbor (v. 18) to prohibitions on mixed breeding (v. 19; cf. Deut. 22:9–11) strikes the modern reader. But in Israel both were aspects of holiness. Lev. 11 pronounces unclean those animals that do not fit the normal categories. The divisions within the animal kingdom mirrored those within the human world, between clean and unclean men, between Israel and the nations. In creation God separated between light and darkness, waters and waters. This ban on all mixtures, especially mixed breeding, shows man following in God's steps. He must keep separate what God created separate. As God separated Israel from among the nations to be his own possession, so they must maintain their holy identity by not intermarrying with the nations (Deut.

10. Hertz, p. 200.
11. Cf. Hoffmann II, pp. 42f.
12. See Gispen, p. 279.
13. "Love" (Heb. *'āhēḇ*). See *TDOT* I, pp. 99–118; *THWAT*, pp. 60–73.
14. "Neighbor" (Heb. *rēᵃ'*). See *THWAT* II, pp. 786–791.
15. Calvin III, p. 195.

7:3–6). Thus in the major and minor decisions of life, Israel was constantly reminded that she was different; that she was holy, set apart for God's service.

Verses 20–22 deal with the case of the betrothed slave girl. It is not obvious why it should be grouped with regulations dealing with agriculture. Often slave-girls would be foreigners (Deut. 21:10–14), and this might explain why it was inserted after the ban on mixtures in v. 19. It is not marriage with a slave, however, that is the issue here, but adultery with *a slave-girl assigned to another man* (v. 20). In OT times sexual intercourse with a betrothed girl by someone who was not her fiancé was regarded as tantamount to adultery. Consequently both parties were liable to the death penalty.[16] This law states an exception to the general principle of capital punishment; in such cases *they must not be put to death* (v. 20).

The reason given for this exemption is *because she was not free*. Because she is a slave the death penalty applies neither to the girl nor to her seducer. If she had been a free girl and the circumstances of the offense suggested the girl had been an unwilling victim, she would have escaped while her partner would have been put to death.[17] In this case neither faces the death penalty but a completely different penalty is imposed on the man. *He must bring . . . a ram as a reparation offering* (v. 21).[18] This shows that adultery was regarded not just as an offense against the girl's fiancé and her parents, but as a grave sin demanding the dearest kind of sacrificial atonement.

In addition *damages must be paid* (v. 20). This is the most problematic phrase in this law: literally, "there will be a *biqqōret*." The word *biqqōret* occurs only here in the OT and its meaning is therefore quite uncertain. In the translation I have tentatively adopted Speiser's interpretation of the term.[19] He associates Heb. *biqqōret* with an Akkadian term (*baqrum/pirqum*),[20] and points out that in other cases of premarital intercourse the man was expected to pay the bride-money (engagement present) to the girl's father.[21] So in this case the girl's owner would demand compensation for the fact that following this episode he could not ask as much money from

16. E.g., Deut. 22:23–24.
17. E.g., Deut. 22:25–27; LE 26; LH 130; HL 197.
18. On the reparation offering see commentary on ch. 5. Also discussion in Milgrom, *Cult and Conscience*, pp. 129ff.
19. E. A. Speiser, *Oriental and Biblical Studies*, pp. 128–131.
20. Used in LH 279 of claims about slaves.
21. See Exod. 22:15–16 [Eng. 16–17]; Deut. 22:28–29; LE 31; HL 35.

any other would-be marriage partner. Speiser supposes that *assigned to another man* does not indicate betrothal, hence the injured party who receives the damages is her owner. In the light of remarks about the death penalty in v. 20, it seems more probable that the girl was reckoned to be betrothed, and therefore that the damages went to her fiancé, who had already paid over the bride-money to her owner. In other cases of adultery, the aggrieved husband might pardon his wife and insist that her partner pay ransom-money to save his life.[22] So in this case the slave-girl's fiancé receives damages for the broken engagement[23] and a reparation offering is offered in the sanctuary.

Other renderings of *biqqōreṯ* have less to commend them. "An inquiry shall be held" (RSV; cf. NEB) is vacuous: every legal dispute would have involved inquiry. "She shall be scourged" (AV) goes back to an old Jewish interpretation, probably based on the dubious derivation of *biqqōreṯ* from *bāqār,* "ox," i.e., an oxhide scourge.

After dealing with slave-girls, the law goes on to discuss problems associated with planting orchards (vv. 23–25). Holiness involves the total consecration of a man's life and labor to God's service. This was symbolized in the giving of one day in seven, and a tithe of all produce, and also in the dedication of the firstfruits of agriculture. This principle covers not only crops (Exod. 23:19; Lev. 23:10; Deut. 26:1ff.) but also animals (Exod. 34:19–20; Deut. 15:19) and even children (Exod. 13:2; Num. 8:16ff.). By dedicating the first of everything to God, the man of the Old Covenant publicly acknowledged that all he had was from God, and he thanked him for his blessings (1 Chr. 29:14).

In the case of fruit trees, however, little fruit is borne in the early years, and this law specifies that it is the fourth year's crop that counts as the firstfruits and must be dedicated to God. Old Babylonian law (LH 60) also reckons it takes four years for an orchard to develop its potential. Similarly sacrificial animals may not be offered till they are at least eight days old (Exod. 22:29 [Eng. 30]) and boys are not circumcised till the eighth day (Gen. 17:12).

So increase its produce for yourselves (v. 25). Faithfulness in dedicating the firstfruits will be rewarded by good crops in subsequent years. "Honor the Lord with your substance and with the firstfruits of all your produce; then your barns will be filled with plenty and your vats will be bursting with wine" (Prov. 3:9–10).

22. See HL 198; LH 129; MAL A15; Prov. 6:20–35; cf. G. J. Wenham, *VT* 22 (1972), p. 333.
23. Porter, p. 157, thinks the money went either to her owner or her fiancé.

Pagan Customs to be Avoided (26–28)

26 *Do not eat flesh with blood in it:* cf. 17:10ff. *Do not practice divination or soothsaying.* Joseph divined with his cup according to Gen. 44:5, 15. Apart from this reference we do not know exactly what magical devices are covered by this ban on divination and soothsaying. The surrounding nations made abundant use of magic in attempts to predict the future (cf. Isa. 2:6; Ezek. 21:26ff. [Eng. 21ff.]). Israel was forbidden to employ such devices, because she was in a special relationship with God and he made his will known through the prophets, or indirectly through the priestly Urim and Thummim (Exod. 28:30; Lev. 8:8). When God was silent, the people were expected to walk by faith and live in accordance with God's general will declared in the law.

27–28 No bodily disfigurement: cf. 21:5; Deut. 14:1; cf. Job 1:20; Isa. 22:12, etc. This is usually taken to be simply a prohibition of pagan mourning rites, but there is more to it than this. Mourning was not discouraged, only those customs which involved physical disfigurement. This law conforms to other holiness rules which seek to uphold the natural order of creation and preserve it from corruption (cf. v. 19; 18:22–23; 21:17ff.). God created man in his image and pronounced all creation very good (Gen. 1). Man is not to disfigure the divine likeness implanted in him by scarring his body. The external appearance of the people should reflect their internal status as the chosen and holy people of God (Deut. 14:1–2). Paul uses a similar line of argument in 1 Cor. 6. The body of the believer belongs to Christ, therefore "glorify God in your body" (1 Cor. 6:20).

No Sacred Prostitution (29–30)

Temple-prostitutes were a well-known feature of ancient religion. Indeed Hebrew often calls them "holy-girls."[24] To dispel any lingering doubts about the true nature of holiness, cult-prostitution is here declared to *profane* the girl, i.e., make her unholy, and fill the land *with wickedness.* Instead God is honored when men observe the sabbath, and reverence his sanctuary. Ezek. 23:37ff. condemns Israel for doing precisely the opposite of Lev. 19:29–30.

No Necromancy (31)

Whereas v. 26 was concerned with mechanical kinds of divination,

24. *Qᵉdēshāh*, "cult prostitute"; cf. *qādōsh*, "holy" (Gen. 38:21–22; Deut. 23:18 [Eng. 17]; Hos. 4:14).

this verse outlaws any resort to those who claim to be in contact with the spirits of the dead. *Spirits ('ôḇôṯ)* has been taken to refer to the woman who summoned up the spirits of the dead, usually by digging a pit and placing various offerings in it to entice the spirit. The method used in Israel is described in 1 Sam. 28:7ff. (cf. Isa. 29:4).[25] More probably *'ôḇôṯ* is a derogatory spelling of *'āḇôṯ* ("fathers") and means "spirits of the ancestors" who live on in the underworld.[26] *Mediums (yiddeʿōnî)* are usually associated with nec-romancy (Lev. 20:6; Deut. 18:11; 1 Sam. 28:3, etc.). Literally the word means "knower" and refers either to the knowledgeable prac-titioners of black magic or the knowing spirits they call up.[27] The latter sense is preferred in 20:27, where *yiddeʿōnî* is translated "ghost."

Respect the Old (32)

According to Isa. 3:5 a society which fails to honor the old is on the brink of destruction.

Love the Resident Alien (33–34)

The great command to love one's neighbor as oneself is specifically extended here to cover the foreign residents. Almost identical phraseology is used in vv. 18 and 34. Israel should be particularly sensitive to the resident aliens' problems since they were once themselves in that situation in Egypt; cf. Deut. 10:19.

Justice in Court and Fair Trading (35–36)

For fairness in court cf. vv. 15ff.; Deut. 16:18ff.

On fair trading cf. Deut. 25:13ff. Law and prophets alike condemn those who give short measure (Amos 8:5; Mic. 6:10ff.). "All who act dishonestly are an abomination to the Lord" (Deut. 25:16; cf. Prov. 20:10).

A hin was a sixth of an ephah. The exact modern equivalents are uncertain. An ephah may have been roughly 4 gallons (15 liters) and a hin 6 pints (3 liters).[28]

25. See *TDOT* I, pp. 130–34; H. A. Hoffner, "2nd Millennium Antecedents to the Hebrew *'ob*," *JBL* 86 (1967), pp. 385–401.
26. So J. Lust, "On Wizards and Prophets," *SVT* 26 (1974), pp. 133–142; M. Die-trich, O. Loretz, and J. Sanmartin, *UF* 6 (1974), pp. 450f.
27. See H. A. Hoffner, *JBL* 86, p. 396.
28. See de Vaux, *Ancient Israel*, pp. 200ff.

Leviticus 19 and the NT

Verse 18, "love your neighbor as yourself," is quoted frequently in the NT (Matt. 5:43; 19:19; 22:39; Mark 12:31, 33; Luke 10:27; Rom. 13:9; Gal. 5:14; James 2:8) and ever since has been regarded as the quintessence of Christian ethics.

It is, however, more than a summary of Christian principles. In its original context Lev. 19:18 epitomizes and expresses the principles governing all the laws that surround it. Love for one's neighbor comes out in not stealing from him, or lying to him, or cheating him in business. The other precepts about neighborly conduct in this chapter are applications of the principle of love in specific situations.

For the Christian it is self-evident that love for God and neighbor must still govern his actions. Insofar as the detailed laws of Lev. 19 exemplify the principle of love in action in Israelite society, we must ask ourselves whether similar situations still exist in our society, and if so how love would act today.

Many of the more general precepts are just as pertinent today as they ever were in ancient Israel. Corruption (vv. 15–16), prostitution (v. 29), divination (v. 26) and the occult (v. 31), exploitation of foreigners (vv. 33–34), and deceitful marketing methods (vv. 35–36) all flourish where man does not make love of his neighbor his guiding principle.

Slavery, for example, no longer exists, so the laws in vv. 20–22 are hardly relevant to us. As for leaving the edge of the field unharvested, there is nothing to prevent a Christian farmer from so doing (vv. 9–10); but if he did, he would not help the poor of society, which is the real purpose of this law. Giving to charity or supporting government welfare schemes would come closer to fulfilling the spirit of this law.

While some of these laws are inapplicable nowadays because our society is so different from ancient Israel's, others are no longer relevant to us because of the changed theological situation under the New Covenant. This is clear in the case of the sacrificial laws (vv. 5–8), because animal sacrifice has no further role after Christ's death. The law on mixtures (v. 19) is also theologically irrelevant in the Church situation. It is a law like that on unclean animals (ch. 11), which symbolized Israel's separateness from the nations. God's Church includes men of every nation and tongue and it is no longer necessary, therefore, to preserve those laws which typified the uniqueness and purity of Israel. But man is still called to imitate God

(Matt. 5:48; 1 Cor. 11:1), to "be holy, for I am holy" (Lev. 19:2; cf. 1 Pet. 1:16). The detailed application of these imperatives may change from age to age, but the fundamental principles of holy living remain unaltered.

D. CAPITAL AND OTHER GRAVE CRIMES (CH. 20)

1 *The Lord spoke to Moses as follows:*

2 *"Say to the Israelites, If a man, an Israelite or alien resident in Israel, gives any of his offspring to Molech, he must be put to death: the people of the land must stone him with stones.*

3 *I myself shall set my face against that man and cut him off from among his people, because he has given one of his offspring to Molech to pollute my sanctuary and profane my holy name.*

4 *If the people of the land close their eyes to that man when he gives one of his offspring to Molech, and do not execute him,*

5 *I myself shall set my face against that man and his family, and cut off from his people him and all those who follow him to prostitute themselves to Molech.*

6 *If anyone turns to spirits and mediums to prostitute himself to them, I shall set my face against that person, and cut him off from among his people.*

7 *You must sanctify yourselves and be holy, for I am the Lord your God.*

8 *You must keep my rules and do them. I am the Lord your sanctifier.*

9 *For if a man curses his father or mother, he must be put to death; since he has cursed his father and mother, his guilt is his own.*

10 *If a man commits adultery with his neighbor's wife,*[1] *the adulterer and adulteress must be put to death.*

11 *If a man lies with his father's wife, uncovering his father's nakedness, both of them must be put to death. Their guilt is their own.*

12 *If a man lies with his daughter-in-law, both of them must be put to death. They have made confusion, and their guilt is their own.*

13 *If a man lies with a male as with a woman (both of them have done an abomination), they must be put to death; their guilt is their own.*

14 *If a man cohabits with a woman and her mother, that is wickedness; they must burn him and them in the fire so that there will not be wickedness among you.*

15 *If a man copulates with an animal, he must be put to death: you must also kill the animal.*

---

1. There appears to be a dittography in the text here. Literally translated this verse reads, "If a man commits adultery with the wife of, if a man commits adultery with the wife of his neighbor. . . ." Since the versions have the same reading, the corruption must have occurred at an early stage in the transmission of the text. On the phenomenon of double readings see S. Talmon, "Conflate Readings," *IDBS*, pp. 170–73.

16 *If a woman approaches an animal to couple with it, you must kill the woman and the animal: they must die; their guilt is their own.*

17 *If a man cohabits with his sister, his mother's or father's daughter, and sees her nakedness, and she sees his, it is a disgrace. They will be cut off publicly before their people; he has had intercourse with his sister and will bear his guilt.*

18 *If a man lies with a woman who is unwell and has intercourse with her, he bares her flow, that is, he uncovers her flow of blood; both of them will be cut off from their people.*

19 *You must not have intercourse with your mother's or father's sister, because he has bared his close relative; they will bear their guilt.*

20 *If a man lies with his aunt, uncovering his uncle's nakedness, they will bear their guilt and die childless.*

21 *If a man cohabits with his brother's wife, this is uncleanness; he has uncovered his brother's nakedness; they will be childless.*

22 *You must keep all my rules and carry out all my laws, so that the land I am bringing you to live in does not vomit you out.*

23 *You must not follow the rules of the nation which I am expelling before you, because they have done all these things and I loathed them.*

24 *I told you, You will take possession of their land, and I shall give it to you to possess it, a land flowing with milk and honey. I am the Lord your God who separated you from the peoples.*

25 *So you must separate between clean and unclean animals, between clean and unclean birds so that you do not make yourselves abominable through the animals, birds, or anything that creeps on the earth which I separated for you as unclean.*

26 *You must be holy for me, because I the Lord am holy, and I separated you from the peoples to be mine.*

27 *If a man or a woman is possessed by a spirit or ghost, they must be put to death. They must be stoned. Their guilt is their own."*

The Structure of Leviticus 20

Phrases such as "I am the Lord your God" and "Keep my rules," which mark separate sections in ch. 19, serve the same function here. The chapter divides as follows:

1–2a   Introduction
2b–6   Sins against Religion
7–8   Exhortation to Holiness
9–21   Sins against Family
22–26 Exhortation to Holiness
27   Sins against Religion

Both main sections open with the same formula, "if a man" (vv. 2, 9, Heb. *'îsh kî*), and both close with exhortations to holiness (vv. 7–8, 22ff.). The first section divides into three paragraphs each concluding with the threat, "I shall set my face against that

276

man and cut him off . . ." (vv. 3, 5, 6). The repetition of the ban on necromancy in v. 27 (cf. v. 6) is strange.[2]

Most of the subjects dealt with in this chapter have already been discussed earlier in chs. 18 and 19 (cf. 20:2–5//18:21; 20:6, 27//19:31; 20:9//19:3; 20:10–21//18:6–20, 22–23). The exhortations to holiness (vv. 7–8, 22–26) are similar to those found in 11:44–45 18:2–5, 24–30; 19:36–37.

The difference between the laws in this chapter and previous ones lies in their form. Those in chs. 18–19 are apodictic in form; that is, they forbid or command certain types of behavior but they rarely indicate what the consequences of disregarding these rules would be. In contrast, the laws in this chapter are casuistic; that is, they state what must be done should one of the apodictic rules be broken. They set out what will befall a law-breaker in such a case. In this way they supplement and reinforce what is found in earlier chapters.

Introduction (1–2a)

Cf. 4:1; 6:1, etc.

Sins against Religion (2–6)

  Molech worship (2–5)

The nature of Molech worship has already been discussed in 18:21. Ch. 18 simply outlawed Molech worship. Ch. 20 prescribes the death penalty for those who ignore the ban. The death penalty is laid down for a variety of religious and sexual offenses, many of them listed in this chapter, but rarely is the mode of execution specified. Death by stoning was required for goring oxen (Exod. 21:28ff.), necromancers (Lev. 20:27), blasphemers (Lev. 24:16ff.; 1 K. 21:10ff.), sabbath breakers (Num. 15:35–36), idolaters (Deut. 13:11 [Eng. 10]; 17:5), intransigent children (Deut. 21:21), and adulterous brides (Deut. 22:21, 24). It is never precisely explained why stoning was regarded as appropriate in these particular cases, though there are hints that it expresses the community's rejection of these sins (Deut. 17:7) and that it was designed to serve as a deterrent to others (Deut. 13:12 [11]).

2. Hoffmann II, p. 80, offers a possible explanation. He suggests that the chapter is arranged symmetrically around the main list of offenses against decency (vv. 9–21). This is preceded and followed by exhortations (vv. 7–8, 22–26), which in turn are flanked by two crimes punishable by stoning (vv. 2, 27). Verses 3–6 are parenthetic.

2 The stoning was carried out by *the people of the land,*[3] that is, ordinary citizens (cf. Lev. 4:27) as opposed to just the elders and judges. In similar contexts Deuteronomy prescribes that it be done by "all the people" (13:10 [9]; 17:7) or "the men of the city" (21:21; 22:21).

3 *I myself shall set my face against that man and cut him off.* This threat seems to be additional to the judicial execution prescribed in v. 2, which suggests that "cutting off" may involve more than premature death.[4]

4 *If the people . . . close their eyes.* Prosecution was left to individual initiative,[5] and it was always easiest to ignore an offense and let sleeping dogs lie. Indeed, those most likely to know about someone's apostasy to Molech would be close neighbors and members of the family, who would naturally be most loath to prosecute. But loyalty to God must override ties of blood and friendship (cf. Deut. 13:7–12 [6–11]; Luke 14:26). If a man puts family loyalty before devotion to God, "I myself shall set my face against that man and his family" (v. 5).

5 *Prostitute themselves.* Infidelity to Yahweh, who had entered into a covenant with Israel, is often compared to sexual license (e.g., Exod. 34:15–16; Lev. 17:7; Judg. 2:17; Hos. 4:12, etc.). The NT uses the same imagery to describe the relationship between Christ and the Church (2 Cor. 11:2; Eph. 5:32–33; 1 Cor. 6:15ff.; Rev. 2:20–21).

6 Necromancy: cf. v. 27 and 19:31. 1 Sam. 28:9 states that Saul did attempt to purge the land of necromancy early in his reign.

7–8 Exhortation to holiness: cf. vv. 22–26; 11:44–45; 18:2–5, 24–30; Exod. 19:4–6; Deut. 7:6–11, etc.

Sins against Family Life (9–21)

If a man curses his father and mother, he must be put to death (v. 9). In the Decalog the command to honor one's parents comes after religious duties and before responsibilities to neighbors. Here the penal law follows the same order: cursing father and mother is sandwiched between necromancy (v. 6) and adultery (v. 10). All these sins are regarded as meriting the death penalty.

"To curse" means more than uttering the occasional angry word. 2 Sam. 16:5ff.; Job 3:1ff. give some idea of the venom and

---

3. On this term see de Vaux, *Ancient Israel,* p. 71.
4. See comments on 17:4.
5. See Excursus II on "Law Enforcement in Israel."

bitter feelings that cursing could entail. It is the very antithesis of "honoring." To honor in Hebrew literally means "to make heavy or glorious," whereas to curse literally means "to make light of, despicable."[6] That such cursing deserves the death penalty is reiterated elsewhere in Scripture (Exod. 21:17; Prov. 20:20; Matt. 15:4; Mark 7:10; cf. Deut. 21:18ff.). This point is underlined here by the phrase *his guilt is his own,* literally "his blood is in him." The phrase occurs only in Ezek. 18:13; 33:5 and in this chapter as a coda to several of the laws (vv. 11, 12, 13, 16, 27), apparently in justification of the death penalty in these cases. It seems to be equivalent to the commoner phrase "his blood shall be on his head" (e.g., Josh. 2:19; 2 Sam. 1:16). If a man breaks such a law, he does so knowing the consequences, and therefore cannot object to the penalty imposed.[7]

The sanctity of parental authority implied by this law is striking. Whereas in certain respects OT penal law was much more lenient than that of neighboring contemporary cultures, it was more strict with regard to offenses against religion and family life.[8] Cursing father or mother is singled out for special censure, partly out of a determination to maintain the structure of the family, and partly because the parents represent God's authority to the child: to curse them is almost tantamount to blasphemy. Nevertheless, rarely if ever can the death penalty have been invoked for this offense. Like other punishments laid down in the law, it represents a maximum not a minimum.[9]

Other capital crimes listed in vv. 10–16 cover adultery (v. 10; cf. 18:20; Deut. 22:22), incest with close relatives (vv. 11, 12, 14; cf. 18:7–8, 15, 17), homosexuality (v. 13; cf. 18:22), and bestiality (vv. 15–16; cf. 18:23; Exod. 22:18 [Eng. 19]). Then follow crimes for which no human penalty is laid down, but instead divine punishment is promised. Cohabitation with a sister (v. 17; cf. 18:9, 11) and intercourse with a woman during her menstrual period (v. 18; cf. 18:19) are punished by "cutting off" (cf. vv. 3, 5, 6 and 17:4). Childlessness will result from cohabitation with an aunt by marriage (v. 20) or sister-in-law (v. 21; cf. 18:16). An alternative penalty, apparently intermediate between cutting-off and childlessness, is

---

6. *THWAT* II, pp. 641–47.
7. Saalschütz, p. 462, suggests the use of this phrase means that the man must be executed by stoning. This interpretation would make the more explicit reference to stoning in v. 27 redundant.
8. See Excursus I: "Principles of Punishment in the Pentateuch."
9. See Excursus I below: "Principles of Punishment in the Pentateuch."

prescribed for intercourse with a blood aunt: *they will bear their guilt* (v. 19; cf. 18:12–13).

A few detailed points deserve note. *Cohabits with* (vv. 14, 17, 21)—literally "takes"; for a similar sense see Deut. 20:7. Generally the word "to take" *(lāqaḥ)* is used of a full and proper marriage (e.g., Gen. 11:29; Exod. 21:10); but since these unions are banned, the law can hardly envisage a public wedding of these people. Rather, they live together without the usual public ceremony to mark them as married.[10]

It is a disgrace (v. 17). The only other passage where the Hebrew word *(ḥeseḏ)* has this sense is Prov. 14:34, "sin is a disgrace to any people." Normally the word means "steadfast love," "goodness." Saalschütz[11] argues that the word is deliberately chosen to express the distortion of brotherly love into sheer sexual passion.

Childless (vv. 20–21). In biblical times, and even today in poor countries, childlessness was regarded as a great calamity (e.g., Gen. 30:1–2; 1 Sam. 1:8ff.; cf. Ps. 127:3ff.).

He has uncovered his brother's nakedness (v. 21), because a woman's nakedness is her husband's and vice versa; cf. v. 20: *his uncle's nakedness*. Through intercourse, man and wife become one flesh. See above on 18:6–18.

Exhortation to Holiness (22–26)

Cf. vv. 7–9; 18:24–30; 11:44–45.

In this short paragraph Israel is reminded of the basis of her whole existence. It is through the divine promises (v. 24; cf. Gen. 15:7–8; 28:4) that she now stands poised to enter Canaan and to expel its inhabitants (v. 23). God has chosen Israel to be his holy people. He has *separated* them from the nations (vv. 24, 26); therefore they must distinguish between the clean and unclean animals, as set out in ch. 11. In distinguishing between the different kinds of creatures they are imitating God, who chose Israel from all the nations to be a people for his own possession (vv. 25–26).

Leviticus 20 and the NT

In the discussion of ch. 18 it was argued that the NT endorsed the moral principles enshrined in that chapter. Adultery, incest,

---

10. The equivalent Akkadian term *aḫāzum* is used in a similar way to denote a common-law marriage in LH 128.

11. Saalschütz, pp. 792f.

homosexuality and the like are just as sinful under the New Covenant as they were under the old. This chapter, however, goes further: it insists that those who disregard these moral laws should be put to death.

The position of the NT on these penalties is not clear-cut. On the one hand Christ appears to endorse the death penalty for dishonoring parents (Matt. 15:4; Mark 7:10). Paul sums up the list of grievous sins in Rom. 1:18–32 with the words "those who do such things deserve to die" (v. 32). On the other hand Christ did not insist on the death penalty for the woman taken in adultery (John 8:1ff.).

How to reconcile these conflicting attitudes in the NT has perplexed many. Calvin[12] may be right in arguing that the reason why Christ did not insist on the execution of the adulteress was that he had come to save men rather than to judge.[13] But this is not to say that those whose job it is to uphold justice and morals, i.e., the judges and magistrates, should be inhibited from imposing penalties for adultery.

Such a position was defensible in the sixteenth century when nearly everyone professed Christian standards. Today in most countries the Church finds itself a minority in an alien culture, indeed in a situation closely resembling that of the early Church. As NT Christians acknowledged the divine authority of this legislation, but recognized that it was impossible to enforce in their time, so must the modern Church. Yet we may still profit from studying these laws. They remind us that however lightly modern man regards such conduct, in God's sight it constitutes grave and serious sin meriting the severest censure.

EXCURSUS I

PRINCIPLES OF PUNISHMENT IN THE PENTATEUCH

Collections of law,[1] often inaccurately termed law codes, from Mesopotamia and Asia Minor have helped to set biblical laws in a historical perspective and enable the modern commentator to perceive more clearly both the uniqueness of Israel's law and the points it had in common with the

---

12. Calvin III, p. 78.
13. See also J. D. M. Derrett, *Law in the NT* (London: DLT, 1970), pp. 156–188, who suggests that the woman escaped because of a legal technicality.

1. The principal collections of law are to be found in English translation in *ANET*, pp. 159–198. S. Greengus in *IDBS*, pp. 533ff., lists the main parallels.

legal codes of surrounding nations. In this excursus I shall draw attention to some contrasts between biblical law and that of other Oriental peoples, then look at what the Pentateuch itself has to say about the purpose of punishment, and finally outline the main types of penalty which it prescribes. This procedure will enable us to see what offenses the OT regarded as most serious.

An outstanding feature of biblical law is the preeminence it accords to human values, as opposed to the economic considerations of much cuneiform law. This emerges with particular clarity in Hebrew penal law.[2] In Israel, religious offenses, and offenses against life and the structure of the family, tended to be punished more severely than elsewhere, whereas cuneiform law tended to rate financial loss as more serious than loss of life, or at least see loss of life in economic terms. For instance Babylonian law punished by death breaking and entering, looting at a fire, and theft;[3] but in Israel no offenses against ordinary property attracted the death penalty.[4] By contrast, in Israel the death penalty was mandatory for murder, because man is made in the image of God (Gen. 9:5-6), whereas other legal systems permitted monetary compensation.[5]

The humanitarian outlook of the biblical law is also illustrated by its abolition of substitutionary punishment. Substitution was often allowed in cuneiform law; e.g., if through faulty construction a house collapses killing the householder's son, the son of the builder who built the house must be put to death (LH 230). But Deuteronomy explicitly forbids this kind of substitutionary punishment. "The fathers shall not be put to death for the children, nor shall the children be put to death for the fathers; every man shall be put to death for his own sin" (24:16). It is only in specifically religious matters that the principle of corporate guilt comes into play. Though Deuteronomy insists that sons shall not be put to death for the fathers, it also insists that a village should be wiped out if some of its inhabitants commit idolatry (Deut. 13:13ff. [Eng. 12ff.]), while the Decalog mentions that God will visit the sins of the fathers upon the children (Exod. 20:5; Deut. 5:9).

The Purpose of Punishment

The principles underlying the biblical laws on punishment are summarized

---

2. M. Greenberg, "Some Postulates of Biblical Criminal Law," *Yehezkel Kaufmann Jubilee Volume* (ed. M. Haran, Jerusalem, 1960), pp. 5–28; E. M. Good, "Capital Punishment and its Alternatives in Ancient Near Eastern Law," *Stanford Law Review* 19 (1967), pp. 947–977; S. M. Paul, *Studies in the Book of the Covenant in the Light of Cuneiform and Biblical Law* (Leiden: Brill, 1970); J. J. Finkelstein, "The Goring Ox," *Temple Law Quarterly* 46 (1973), pp. 169–290, and B. S. Jackson, *Essays in Jewish and Comparative Legal History*, pp. 25–63.
3. LH 6–11, 21f., 25.
4. Theft of booty dedicated to God in holy war was punishable by death (Josh. 7).
5. Cf. HL 1–6.

in Deut. 19:19–20, a passage dealing with the punishment of a false witness: "You shall do to him as he meant to do to his brother; so you shall purge the evil from the midst of you. And the rest shall hear, and fear, and never again commit any such evil among you." Five principles are alluded to in this passage and may be illustrated from other parts of the Pentateuch.[6]

(1) The offender must receive his legal desert, which is not simply to be equated with revenge. The penalty must correspond with the crime. This is perhaps most clearly seen in Gen. 9:6, "Whoever sheds the blood of man, by man shall his blood be shed," and in the general principle of talion enunciated in various places: "Life for life, eye for eye, tooth for tooth" (Deut. 19:21; Exod. 21:23–24; Lev. 24:18ff.). This talion formula is, however, just a formula; it is not to be taken literally except in the case of premeditated murder (Num. 35:31). Where the formula occurs, it is usually evident that the lawgiver is not demanding its literal fulfilment, but some payment to compensate for the offense (see Exod. 21:22ff.).[7]

(2) Punishment is designed to "purge the evil from the midst of you." What does this mean? "The evil" cannot refer to the offense itself, for it cannot be undone. Nor can it refer to the possible repetition of the offense. Rather it refers to the guilt that rests upon the land and its inhabitants. This concept, though foreign to our secular way of thinking, occupies an important place in the Bible. In Gen. 4:10–11 the blood of Abel cries out to God from the ground, which is therefore accursed for his sake. In Lev. 18:24–28 it is said that the offenses of the heathen cause them to be expelled from Canaan. Still clearer is Deut. 21:1–9, where a rite is prescribed to atone for the crime of an unknown murderer. The attempt to discover the murderer has proved futile, and therefore a calf is killed by a stream and various rites are performed. This series of actions does not undo the murder, nor does it ensure that no murders are committed in the future, but it does atone for the bloodguilt which rests upon those whose responsibility it is to execute punishment. The elders say: "Forgive, O Lord, thy people Israel, whom thou hast redeemed, and set not the guilt of innocent blood in the midst of thy people Israel" (v. 8).

(3) Punishment should deter others from committing the offense: "the rest shall hear and fear, and shall never commit any such evil among you" (Deut. 19:20; cf. 13:12 [Eng. 11]; 17:13; 21:21).

(4) Punishment allows the offender to make atonement and be reconciled with society. After he has paid the penalty, the offender suffers no loss of his civil rights. Degradation of the offender as a motive for punishment is specifically excluded by Deut. 25:3, where the number of strokes is limited to forty, "lest, if one should go on to beat him with more stripes than these, your brother be degraded in your sight." The degrading brutality of many punishments under Assyrian law is in marked contrast to the Hebrew

---

6. See J. L. Saalschütz, *Das Mosaische Recht*, pp. 493ff., for fuller exposition.
7. For a modern discussion see B. S. Jackson, *Essays*, pp. 75–107.

outlook. Mutilation is demanded only once in the Pentateuch, in an extreme case (Deut. 25:11–12), and there the penalty is mild compared with some of those in the Assyrian laws (e.g., MAL A4–5, 8–9, 40).

(5) Punishment allows the offender to recompense the injured party. Hebrew, like Mesopotamian law, had no system of fines. Instead it imposed damages, so that the one who suffered received benefits from the punishment, and not the state (e.g., Exod. 22; Lev. 5:20ff. [Eng. 6:1ff.]).

Civil and Criminal Law

The use of damages rather than fines highlights an aspect of the biblical legal system of which the layman is not usually conscious; it is basically a system of civil law on to which various criminal law features have been grafted. This means that many offenses are regarded as torts: wrongs against individual private citizens for which the injured party has to seek redress on his own initiative through the courts.

The number of offenses which can properly be called crimes, actions which the state itself forbids and seeks to stamp out, is very limited in Near Eastern law, though it is considerably augmented in the OT by the large number of religious crimes. It is somewhat artificial to attempt to distinguish civil and criminal law in the OT, since the whole of life is viewed as being lived under God and therefore all wrongdoing is sin. No sin can be viewed with equanimity by the community, since it is likely to provoke God's wrath. Nevertheless, if one wishes to distinguish the criminal and civil law elements, the type of penalty imposed may provide a criterion. Monetary compensation suggests that the offense should be regarded as falling within the realm of civil law, while the death penalty or corporal punishment suggests that the offense should be viewed as a crime. The prosecution of murderers, however, shows how foreign the civil/criminal law distinction is in biblical thinking. Though murder is viewed as a crime, in that the payment of damages to the victim's family is prohibited, the state does not take a hand in prosecuting the criminal. It is left to a relative, the avenger of blood, to kill the murderer if he can, or if he cannot, to chase him to the city of refuge and there convince the city authorities that the one who has committed homicide is a murderer. The avenger of blood must then execute him (Exod. 21:12–14; Num. 35:10ff.; Deut. 19).

Types of Punishment

The Pentateuch lays down three main types of punishment: the death penalty for the gravest public sins against life, religion, and the family, "cutting off" for grave private sins, and restitution for property offenses.

1. The death penalty

The death penalty is prescribed for a wide range of crimes: premeditated murder (Exod. 21:12ff.; Num. 35; Deut. 19), man-stealing (Exod. 21:16;

Deut. 24:7), persistent disobedience of authorities and parents (Deut. 17:12; 21:18ff.), adultery (Lev. 20:10; Deut. 22:22), homosexuality (Lev. 20:13), the worst forms of incest (Lev. 20:11–12), false prophecy (Deut. 13:2ff.), profanation of the sabbath (Num. 15:32ff.), blasphemy (Lev. 24:13ff.), idolatry (Lev. 20:2ff.), magic and divination (Exod. 22:17 [Eng. 18]). Some of these crimes were also punishable by death under Babylonian law.[8]

It is not clear in how many cases the death penalty was actually exacted and how often compensation was permitted. Compensation is explicitly prohibited in the case of murder (Num. 35:31), and this seems to be the force of the Deuteronomic phrase, "your eye shall not pity," in Deut. 19:13, and by analogy in 13:9 (8) (idolatry); 19:21 (false witness); and 25:12. It would seem unlikely that compensation was permissible in those cases where the mode of execution is prescribed (Deut. 21:21; 22:21). In the case of blasphemy and profanation of the sabbath, it evidently depended on the gravity of the particular offense whether the ultimate penalty was exacted (Exod. 31:13–17; Num. 15:32–36; Lev. 24:11–22). It was only profaning the sabbath by actual work, or blaspheming the name of Yahweh as opposed to God, that merited death. This shows that *the penalties prescribed in the law were the maximum penalties.* Where there were mitigating circumstances, lesser penalties would have been enforced. These were cases in which the evidence was clear. In practice, the demand for at least two witnesses (Deut. 19:15) would have limited the application of these penalties to flagrant violations of the law. Many secret offenders would inevitably have escaped punishment.

2. *"Cutting off"*

The law refers a number of times to God cutting off an offender, or the guilty person being cut off from among his people (e.g., Exod. 12:15, 19; Lev. 7:20–21, 25, 27; 17:4, 9, 14; 18:29; 19:8; 20:3, 5–6, 17–18; Num. 15:30–31). It is a punishment generally reserved for religious and sexual offenses. Since some of these offenses may also attract the death penalty, "cutting off" could conceivably be an alternative way of describing capital punishment (e.g., Lev. 20:6 and 27). However, since cutting off is contrasted with judicial execution in Lev. 20:2ff. (the man who escapes stoning must still face the possibility of being cut off), something different must be meant. For one case of incest Babylonian law demands expulsion from the community, whereas biblical law speaks of the guilty man being "cut off" (LH 154; cf. Lev. 20:17–18). It could be argued that "cutting off" means excommunication from the covenant community. But this treatment is reserved for the unclean rather than for criminals (Lev. 13:45–46; Num. 5:1–4). It seems best, therefore, to retain the traditional interpretation of "cutting off": it is a threat of direct punishment by God usually in the form of premature death. Insofar as many of the offenses punishable by "cutting

8. E.g., murder, LH 1; sorcery, LH 2; adultery, LH 129; incest, LH 157.

off" would easily escape human detection, a threat of divine judgment would have been the main deterrent to committing them.[9]

3. *Restitution*

In cases of theft or misappropriation of property, restitution of the stolen property was demanded. Additional penalties vary with the degree of penitence shown by the thief. If he is penitent, he restores what he has stolen plus a fifth (Lev. 5:24 [Eng. 6:5]).[10] If he is caught with the goods on him, he restores double. If he has already disposed of the goods by sale or other means, he must restore four- or five-fold. The penalty may have been increased in the latter case because of the greater difficulty of proving his guilt, and because the thief has made a deliberate attempt to cover his traces (Exod. 22).[11] If a thief cannot pay, he may be taken as a slave by the injured party until he has worked off the debt (22:2 [Eng. 3]). His slavery would usually be for a maximum of six years (Exod. 21:1ff.; Deut. 15:12ff.) or until the year of jubilee (Lev. 25:39ff.). Slavery in the ancient Orient was not as oppressive as it was in more modern times. There was little difference between a slave and a hired laborer (Lev. 25:39–55). Indeed, it could be argued that Hebrew slavery was more humane than its modern equivalent, namely, imprisonment. Neither in the laws of Hammurabi nor in the Pentateuch is imprisonment laid down as a punishment, though it was known in Egypt and under the later monarchy. To quote Driver and Miles: "This last punishment, which is expensive to the community, generally corrupting the prisoner and often bringing unmerited hardship to his dependents, is the invention of a later age."[12] Twice in the Pentateuch it is mentioned that someone was kept in custody while awaiting trial (Lev. 24:12; Num. 15:34). The nearest thing to imprisonment in ancient times was the restriction imposed on a manslaughterer, who is bound to live in a city of refuge until the death of the high priest (Num. 35:26ff.).

EXCURSUS II

LAW ENFORCEMENT IN ISRAEL

If ancient Israel had a most searching ethical code in the ten commandments and an elaborate penal system, did it also have means of enforcing the law? Did it just depend on public goodwill, or was there a recognized

9. See further discussion in commentary on Lev. 17.
10. This is the traditional view, and is to be preferred to B. S. Jackson's suggestion in *Theft in Early Jewish Law* (Oxford: Clarendon, 1972), pp. 172ff., that what Leviticus intends for secular offenses is restitution of two and a fifth times the amount stolen.
11. For other explanations see Jackson, *Theft*, pp. 154ff.
12. G. R. Driver and J. C. Miles, *The Babylonian Laws* I (Oxford: Clarendon, 1952), p. 501.

organization to maintain law and order? These are not easy questions to answer, for it was during those periods when law was not being enforced that the problem emerges in the OT. When the country lacked strong central government, injustice was most evident, and at that time most was said about the lack of good government. "In those days there was no king in Israel; every man did what was right in his own eyes" (Judg. 17:6; cf. 18:1; 19:1). Hence we are better informed about the failures of government than about its successes.

However, a good deal can be pieced together from the OT and neighboring cultures about how government worked.[1] But certain things must be borne in mind. First, the village culture of ancient Israel was very different from Western urban society, and the problems of law enforcement were trivial as compared with ours. They lived in small, closely knit communities in which everyone knew everyone else, and it would have been extremely difficult, therefore, for any local person to commit an offense without its becoming common knowledge. In the mass anonymity of modern society it is very much easier for criminals to remain undetected. Second, it was a conservative and authoritarian society, and therefore less likely to lead to social deviance. Finally, because society was so much more compact, there was inevitably less specialization. One man could easily play the role of city councillor, judge, and policeman in his spare time, and be a farmer the rest of the week. So we should not necessarily expect to find a professional police force, such as was later introduced into Imperial Rome by Augustus.

Though this means that the problem of law enforcement was much smaller than in our society, it does not mean it was nonexistent. We can distinguish various devices for encouraging observance of the law. First, knowledge of the law was promoted by a seven-yearly festival at which the law was read (Deut. 31:9ff.) by the Levites, who were sent out to instruct people in the law (2 Chr. 17:8–9). By this means the Hebrews would be thoroughly familiar with what the law demanded. In other words the Levites played a role equivalent to the mass media in modern society. Second, in the early period there was a system of tribal democracy. It seems likely that each tribe or village elected elders to govern its affairs and act as judges in legal disputes. In the period of the monarchy there was added to this older system a central court of appeal in Jerusalem to decide disputed cases (2 Chr. 19:8ff.).

Within this system, specific remedies were available against lawbreakers. When an offense was committed, it was up to the injured party or his family to bring the culprit before the court and prove his guilt. A man who suspected his wife of infidelity had to bring her before the court and prove it (Deut. 22:13ff.). Parents who had a stubborn and rebellious son had

1. R. de Vaux, *Ancient Israel*, pp. 150ff.; D. J. Wiseman, "Law and Order in OT Times," *Vox Evangelica* 8 (1973), pp. 5–21.

to report the case to the elders (Deut. 21:18ff.). In the case of murder, it was the responsibility of a relative, the avenger of blood, to execute the murderer (Num. 35). Essentially, then, the system was one of self-help regulated by the courts. Witnesses were publicly summoned to report crimes (Lev. 5:1; Judg. 17:2). Thus for most offenses the initiative for the prosecution rested in private hands.

In the majority of cases it seems as if the plaintiff was also responsible for enforcing the court's decision, but there is evidence that the plaintiff was sometimes aided by "officials" *(shōṭᵉrîm)*. The word literally means "scribe," so one of their functions may have been to record decisions. They also had the job of mustering the army and are mentioned alongside the judges in one or two cases (Deut. 20:5; 16:18; 1 Chr. 23:4), so they may also have had the job of bailiffs or constables deputed to ensure that the judgment was carried out; but this is not clear. As has already been explained, it is likely that an individual had several functions in society.

For the most part, then, law enforcement was a private matter for which the injured person was responsible. Religious offenses, however, were more serious, and public prosecutions could be instituted (e.g., Deut. 13:13ff. [Eng. 12ff.]). Furthermore, when the injured party was too weak to secure his legal rights by himself, he could appeal to the king (e.g., 1 K. 3:16ff.). One of the fundamental duties of the king was to promote justice in the land, to "defend the cause of the poor of the people, give deliverance to the needy, and crush the oppressor" (Ps. 72:4). David's failure to fulfil his duties in this regard gave Absalom an excuse for fomenting rebellion (2 Sam. 15).

E. RULES FOR PRIESTS (CH. 21)

1 *The Lord said to Moses: "Speak to the priests, the sons of Aaron, and say to them, Let no one pollute himself for the dead among his kinsfolk,*

2 *except for a near relative, his mother, his father, his son, his daughter, his brother,*

3 *or his unmarried teenage sister who is close to him, for her he may pollute himself.*

4 *He must not pollute himself in marriage among his kinsfolk so as to profane himself.*

5 *They must not shave their heads, trim their beards, or scar their bodies.*

6 *They must be holy to their God and not profane the name of their God, because they offer the food offerings of the Lord, the food of their God, and they must be holy.*

7 *They must not marry a prostitute or a woman who is not a virgin or a divorced woman, because he is holy to his God.*

8 *You must sanctify him, because he offers the bread of your God. He must be holy for you, because I, the Lord your sanctifier, am holy.*

9 *A priest's daughter who profanes herself in prostitution, thereby profaning her father, shall be burned in fire.*

10 *The priest, who is the highest among his brothers, on whose head anointing oil has been poured and who has been appointed to wear the garments, must not untidy his hair or tear his clothes.*

11 *And for the sake of any dead persons he may not go in, not even for his father or for his mother may he make himself unclean.*

12 *He must not leave the sanctuary, so that he does not profane the sanctuary of his God, because the consecration of the anointing oil of his God is on him: I am the Lord.*

13 *He must marry a girl in her teens.*

14 *A widow or divorcee, a girl who is not a virgin, or a prostitute, these he may not marry. But he must marry a young marriageable girl from his kinsfolk,*

15 *so that he does not profane his children among his kinsfolk, because I the Lord am his sanctifier."*

16 *The Lord spoke to Moses as follows:*

17 *"Speak to Aaron as follows, If any of your descendants has a physical defect, he must not draw near to offer the food of his God.*

18 *Indeed no man who has a physical defect may draw near, whether he be blind, or lame, or has a split nose or a limb that is too long,*

19 *or if he has a broken foot or hand,*

20 *is a hunchback, a dwarf, or has defective sight, or sores, or scabs, or crushed testicles.*

21 *No man from among the descendants of Aaron the priest with a physical defect may come near to present the food offerings of the Lord. If he has a defect, he may not present the food of his God.*

22 *He may eat the food of his God, that is, of the holiest things and the holy things.*

23 *Only he may not go into the curtain or draw near the altar, because he has a defect, so that he does not profane my sanctuaries, for I am the Lord their sanctifier."*

24 *And Moses spoke to Aaron and his sons and to all the Israelites.*

The Structure of Leviticus 21–22

The previous chapters have dealt with the holiness of ordinary Israelites. Chs. 21 and 22 now move on to consider the holiness of the religious leaders, the priests. Higher standards are expected of them.

These chapters divide into six sections, each of which closes with the formula "I am the Lord your (their) sanctifier" (21:8, 15, 23; 22:9, 16, 32). The only other place in Leviticus where this phrase is used is 20:8.

21:1–9   Restrictions on mourning and marriage for ordinary priests

10–15 Restrictions on mourning and marriage for the high priest
16–24 Physical impediments to exercise of priestly office
22:1–9 Impediments to eating priestly food
10–16 Relatives' right to priestly food
17–33 Physical impediments to sacrificial use of animals

The inclusion of rules about the requirements for sacrificial animals in a section principally concerned with priests is striking. If, as has been argued above (ch. 11), the sacrificial animals are the priests of the animal world,[1] this arrangement is quite logical. The phraseology of the law draws attention to this parallelism: many of the deformities that bar a priest from offering sacrifice (21:18–20) are the same as those that preclude animals from being offered in sacrifice (22:20–24).

Characteristically, the section ends with an exhortation to holiness stressing the importance of obeying the law (22:31–33; cf. 18:24–30; 19:36–37; 20:22–26).

Restrictions on Mourning and Marriage for Ordinary Priests (1–9)

Dead bodies were unclean, and anyone who came in contact with them became unclean (Num. 19:11ff.). For this reason priests were forbidden to take part in funeral ceremonies for anyone who was not a very close relative (vv. 2–3). *His unmarried teenage sister* (v. 3): if she was married, it would be her husband's duty to arrange her burial; if she was younger,[2] her parents would still be likely to be alive and well enough to bury her. The priest's wife is not explicitly mentioned in this list of people. Since she is "one flesh" with him, the law simply takes it for granted that he would defile himself for her. As a way of shocking his listeners, Ezekiel, a priest, was told not to go into mourning even when his wife died (Ezek. 24:15ff.).

4 *He must not pollute himself in marriage* is somewhat obscure. Perhaps the most plausible interpretation[3] is to regard it as anticipating v. 7. It warns the priest to avoid pollution by joining himself in marriage to a woman of doubtful character. Most commentators, however, think that the verse refers to defilement through the death of an "in-law," i.e., someone related to the priest through marriage rather than by blood.[4]

1. Priests = sacrificial animals. Israel = clean animals. Gentiles = unclean animals.
2. For a justification of the translation *teenage* for *bᵉṭulāh,* usually rendered "virgin," see G. J. Wenham in *VT* 22 (1972), pp. 326–348; cf. *TDOT* II, pp. 338–343.
3. See Keil, p. 430.
4. For these suggestions see Hoffmann II, pp. 85f.; Gispen, pp. 301f.; Porter, p. 168.

5–6 *They must not shave their heads:*[5] cf. 19:27–28; Deut. 14:1. Defacement of the human body is incompatible with holiness, which is symbolized in physical perfection; cf. vv. 18–21. If this rule applied to laymen (19:27–28), how much more to the priests who had been set apart for divine service, to offer *the food of their God* (v. 6). On this expression cf. 3:11, 16; 21:21.

7–8 The priests are consecrated to God and their wives must be of good character. They may not marry those known to be wayward in sexual behavior. That the law is more interested in the woman's character and reputation than her previous sexual experience is indicated by the fact that the ordinary priest was allowed to marry a widow (see v. 14, where widows are added to those debarred from marrying the high priest) but not a divorcee. However innocent the divorced woman was in fact, her reputation was likely to have been affected by the divorce.

9 Just as the wife's character reflects on her husband, so can the children's. Therefore a priest's daughter who turns to prostitution (frequent enough in a world where cultic prostitution was commonplace) profanes her father. An exemplary punishment, burning, is prescribed for this offense to demonstrate that the worship of the Lord has no place for such pagan practices.

Restrictions on Mourning and Marriage for the High Priest (10–15)

10 Even tighter restrictions are imposed on the high priest. His holy station of supreme mediator between God and Israel is symbolized by his anointing and his magnificent ceremonial robes (cf. Exod. 28–29; Lev. 8). He is forbidden even to exhibit the normal marks of grief, dishevelling the hair and tearing his clothes (cf. Josh. 7:6; Job 2:12; Gen. 37:29, 34). His hair had been anointed and his clothes specially designed for him. If he disturbed them, it could serve to nullify his consecration.

11–12 He is not even allowed to take part in the burial of his closest relatives, his father and mother, so total is his dedication to the service of God. Verse 12 does not mean that the high priest lived in the sanctuary, only that his duties there took precedence over family ties, even when his parents died. 10:3–7 tells how Aaron's two sons died and how the priests had to behave then. On that occasion they were restrained from mourning because the deaths were divine judgment, and to mourn would imply criticism of God.

5. Lit. "make bald patches."

In this law the high priest is directed always to put his official duties above family ones (cf. Matt. 8:21–22).

13–15 Finally his wife must be of spotless character. Not even a widow is good enough for the high priest. She must be a young Israelite girl *from his kinsfolk,* ready for marriage (v. 14). Verse 15 gives the reason, *so that he does not profane his children among his kinsfolk.* This is usually supposed to be an insistence that his wife should be suitable for a man of his standing. But it may mean that by marrying such a girl he will ensure her children are really his own. If he married a woman who was not a virgin, there would always be a possibility that the first child (and therefore potential high priest) would not be of priestly stock.[6]

Physical Impediments to the Exercise of Priestly Office (17–24)

Various bodily deformities, not all of which can be identified with certainty,[7] preclude a priest from officiating in the sanctuary. The idea emerges clearly that holiness finds physical expression in wholeness and normality. The unclean animals (ch. 11) are unclean because they fail to travel in the normal way appropriate to their type. Various offenses listed in ch. 19 were unholy in that they do not express moral integrity.[8]

Although a blemished priest may not offer sacrifice himself, he may still enjoy the priestly perquisites, those parts of the sacrifices reserved for the priests (see Lev. 2:3, 10; 6:10–11, 22 [Eng. 17–18, 29]; 7:6), as long as he is in a state of ritual purity (see 22:1–9).

F. RULES ABOUT EATING SACRIFICES (CH. 22)

1 *The Lord spoke to Moses as follows:*
2 *"Tell Aaron and his sons to separate themselves from the holy things*

---

6. G. J. Wenham, *VT* 22 (1972), p. 338.
7. *Ḥārūm (split nose),* only in v. 18, is formally a passive participle possibly meaning "split"; cf. Isa. 11:15. The versions and Jewish commentators think damage to the nose is meant.
   Gibbēn, only in v. 20. LXX, Vulgate, and most modern translators think it means "hunchbacked." The NEB tentatively revives an old Jewish tradition that it refers to "misshapen eyebrows."
   Daq means "thin, small," e.g., of incense (16:12) or cows (Gen. 41:3–4). Only here is the meaning "dwarf" proposed. Another possibility is that it refers to an eye complaint; so NEB and apparently LXX and Vulgate.
   Gārāḇ (sore) and *yallepet (scab)* are found in v. 20 and 22:22 (*gārāḇ;* also in Deut. 28:27), and denote some kind of skin complaint. Akk. *garābu* means "scab" or "leprosy" according to *CAD* G, p. 46.
8. See Introduction, VI.2: "Holiness."

of the Israelites which they dedicate to me so that they do not profane my holy name: I am the Lord.

3 *Say to them, If any man among any of your descendants throughout your generations approaches the holy things which the Israelities dedicate to the Lord, while he is unclean, that person will be cut off from before me: I am the Lord.*

4 *No descendant of Aaron who suffers from a severe skin disease or bodily discharge may eat of the holy things until he is clean. This applies to the man who touches a corpse or suffers a flow of semen,*

5 *or the man who touches any swarming thing which makes him unclean or who touches a man who suffers from any contagious uncleanness,*

6 *the person who touches him becomes unclean until the evening, and he may not eat of the holy things unless he washes his body in water.*

7 *When the sun goes down, he will be clean, and afterward he may eat of the holy things, for that is his food.*

8 *He must not eat any animal that dies naturally or is killed by animals to make himself unclean by it: I am the Lord.*

9 *They must keep my charge and not incur sin through it and die as a result when they profane it; I am the Lord their sanctifier.*

10 *No outsider may eat holy things, whether he lives with the priest or is employed by him.*

11 *But if a priest buys anyone as a slave, he may eat, and anyone born in his house may eat his food.*

12 *The daughter of a priest who marries an outsider may not eat of the contributed holy things.*

13 *But if a priest's daughter is widowed or divorced, has no children and returns to her father's house as in her childhood, she may eat of her father's food. But no outsider may eat it.*

14 *If anyone eats holy food inadvertently, he must add a fifth to it and give it to the priest,*

15 *so that the holy things of the Israelites that they contribute to the Lord are not profaned.*

16 *And they must make them bear the penalty of reparation, if they eat their holy things, because I am the Lord their sanctifier."*

17 *The Lord spoke to Moses as follows:*

18 *"Speak to Aaron and his sons and all the Israelites and say to them, If anyone from the house of Israel or from the resident aliens in Israel offers an offering as a burnt offering for their vows or free-will offerings which they present to the Lord,*

19 *if it is to be accepted for you, it must be a perfect male from the cattle, the sheep or the goats.*

20 *You must not offer anything that is blemished, because it will not be accepted for you.*

21 *If anyone offers a peace offering in fulfillment of a vow or for a free-will offering, of cattle or sheep, it must be perfect to be acceptable, there must be no blemish in it.*

22 *You must not offer these to the Lord: the blind, those with broken bones or cuts, discharges or sores or scabs. You must not give any of them as a food offering on the altar for the Lord.*

23 *You may make a free-will offering of an ox or sheep with overgrown or stunted limbs, but it will not be acceptable for a vow.*

24 *You must not offer to the Lord an animal that has been castrated in any way: you must not do it in your land.*

25 *Nor may you offer as the food of your God any animals like these acquired from foreigners, because they are damaged, there is a blemish in them, they would not be accepted for you."*

26 *The Lord spoke to Moses as follows:*

27 *"When a calf, or a lamb, or a kid is born it must remain with its mother for seven days; from the eighth day onward it is acceptable as an offering, a food offering to the Lord.*

28 *You must not slaughter an ox or a sheep and its young on the same day.*

29 *When you offer a confession sacrifice to the Lord, sacrifice it so that you are accepted.*

30 *On that day it must be eaten. Do not leave any of it over until the morning: I am the Lord.*

31 *You must keep my commandments and do them: I am the Lord.*

32 *You must not profane my holy name and I must be hallowed among the Israelites. I am the Lord, your sanctifier,*

33 *who brought you out of the land of Egypt to be your God: I am the Lord."*

Impediments to Eating Priestly Food (1–9)

The previous paragraph dealt with permanent physical impediments to priestly office. These nonfunctioning priests were still allowed to eat priestly food. But this paragraph sets out under what circumstances priests may neither officiate at the sacrifices nor eat priestly food. Whenever they are unclean, whether through skin disease (cf. chs. 13–14), discharges (ch. 15), or contact with dead men or animals (11:39), they may not eat priestly food on pain of being cut off, because it is holy (vv. 2–3). The holy and the unclean must be kept apart.[9]

Relatives' Rights to Priestly Food (10–16)

The parts of the sacrifices assigned to them and the tithes (see chs. 6–7) constituted the income of the priests, who had no land of their own to work. As a matter of course, the priests' families also ate the holy things. But who counted as belonging to the priest's family? This paragraph explains. No one who is an *outsider* (v. 10)—i.e., not of priestly stock—may eat the holy food, unless he has been incorporated into the priest's family. Simply to live with the priest or to work for him (v. 11) is insufficient. Slaves, however, and their

9. See Introduction, VI.2: "Holiness."

children did count as members of the family (v. 11). The priest's own children, of course, were entitled to eat priestly food. His sons are not mentioned, since they would have been entitled automatically to priestly dues when they became priests in their own right. A priest's daughter was also entitled to priestly food, until she married (v. 12). Then she was regarded as belonging to her husband's family. If he was an "outsider," she would no longer enjoy priestly food. But if this man subsequently died or divorced her, and the woman had no children who could support her, she could return to her parental home and enjoy priestly food again (v. 13).

Sometimes an outsider might unwittingly eat the holy things, and in effect rob the priest. In this case he had to replace it and add 20 percent (v. 14). Verse 16 is somewhat obscure. It may be a reference back to 5:14ff., which insists that anyone who sins unwittingly with regard to the holy things must also bring a ram as a reparation offering, or another reminder of the compensation mentioned in verse 14.[10]

Blemishes in Sacrificial Animals (17–30)

As physical defects debarred the priests (21:17–23) from service in the tabernacle, so any kind of blemish in an animal precluded its use in sacrifice. Both priests and victim must be perfect. The need for blemish-free animals was repeatedly emphasized in chs. 1–4. Here some of the faults that count as blemishes are listed (vv. 19–24), in terms that clearly echo the blemishes in priests in ch. 21 (vv. 17–21). These linguistic parallels are unlikely to be coincidental in view of the close relationship between priests and sacrificial animals in Israelite thinking (see ch. 11).

In totally optional sacrifices such as free-will offerings, minor blemishes did not matter (v. 23), but no castrated animals were to be offered under any circumstances. Castration of animals was not to be practiced in Israel. *You must not do it in your land* (v. 24).[11] Not

---

10. Keil, p. 435. Milgrom, *Cult and Conscience*, pp. 63–66, thinks it unlikely that a ram was required in this case. The ambiguity of the third person suffixes complicates the interpretation. *Are not profaned* (v. 15) (lit. "they shall not profane"). According to Keil the third plural has indefinite force: hence the passive translation adopted here. According to Milgrom "they" = the priests. Verse 16a can be expanded: *"They* (the priests) *must make them* (the Israelites) *bear the penalty of reparation, if they* (the Israelites) *eat their holy things."*

11. Here we follow the opinion of the early translators (Vulgate, Targums, Pseudo-Jonathan and Neofiti), Josephus *Antiquities* 4:8:40, and some modern commentators (e.g., Elliger, p. 300; Hoffmann II, p. 113; Porter, p. 176) that this verse is outlawing castration as such, and not just the sacrifice of castrated animals (RSV; NEB; Gispen, p. 317).

even castrated animals bought from foreigners were to be used in sacrifice (v. 25). Men in similar condition were forbidden even to worship in ancient Israel (Deut. 23:2 [Eng. 1]). Underlying this prohibition is the idea that castration damages God's good creation. Holiness is symbolized in wholeness. Moreover, God's blessing upon all living creatures was that they should "be fruitful and multiply" (Gen. 1:22, 28; 8:17).

26–30 The same theme reappears here. A calf or lamb may not be sacrificed on the same day as its mother (v. 28). More than mere sentimentality seems to underlie this law. It is in conformity with other laws such as that forbidding men to take a bird and its eggs (Deut. 22:6–7), or to cook a kid in its mother's milk (Exod. 23:19; 34:26; Deut. 14:21), or wantonly to destroy trees (Deut. 20:19–20). Noah was commissioned to gather a pair of each kind of animal to preserve life from the all-destroying flood (Gen. 6:19–20; 7:2–3). Every Israelite was expected to do his part in conservation by avoiding wanton destruction of the God-given creation.

That animals must be at least eight days old before being sacrificed (v. 27) is also stated in Exod. 22:29 (Eng. 30). Sacrificial animals had to be eaten up promptly (cf. Exod. 23:18). More precise rules governing the consumption of peace offerings are found in Lev. 7:15–18.

31–33 An exhortation typical of this part of Leviticus (cf. 18:24ff.; 19:36–37; 20:26) concludes chs. 21–22. For the sixth time the key phrase *I am the Lord your* (their) *sanctifier* (v. 32) marks the end of a section (21:8, 15, 23; 22:9, 16). The holiness of God and his redemptive grace, *who brought you out of the land of Egypt*, should inspire God's people to keep his laws (v. 31).

Leviticus 21–22 and the NT

These chapters like many others in this book form the background to much NT teaching. Christ is both perfect priest (21:17–23; Heb. 7:26) and perfect victim (22:18–30; Heb. 9:14; 1 Pet. 1:19; 2:22). His bride (cf. 21:7–15) is the Church, whom he is sanctifying to make her "without spot or wrinkle or any such thing, that she might be holy and without blemish" (Eph. 5:27; cf. Rev. 19:7–8; 21:2).

We see here that the demand for holiness is common to both testaments. The NT sees it primarily in moral terms, however, and insists that true holiness can be achieved only through redemption, not by nature. This redemption includes those with physical deformities; to Christ's marriage feast are invited the maimed, the lame, and the blind (Luke 14:13, 21; cf. John 5:3). The extension of God's grace to eunuchs and foreigners had already been anticipated in Isa. 56:4–8.

There are indications within Lev. 21 that physical integrity was viewed as symbolic of moral integrity. Certainly the OT expected its priests to behave uprightly and with dignity (cf. 1 Sam. 2:12ff.; Hos. 4:4–10; 5:1). Similarly the religious leaders of the Church should be seen to be of good character (Acts 6:3; 1 Tim. 3; Tit. 1:5–11). Their wives (1 Tim. 3:11; cf. Lev. 21:7, 13–15) and their children (1 Tim. 3:4; Tit. 1:6; cf. Lev. 21:9) should be well-behaved. Their children must not be accused of profligacy (*asōtia*, Tit. 1:6), a term that could well describe the behavior of the priest's daughter mentioned in 21:9.

Addressing his fellow ministers on this subject, Bonar writes on the choice of a wife: "Very awful is your responsibility if you diminish your zeal, love, spirituality, by marrying one who has more of earth and a present world in her person and spirit, than of heaven and a coming eternity."[12] And on the behavior of ministers' children he remarks: "The conduct of the family is noticed by the world, and they lay the blame of their misdeeds at the door of their parents. . . . They [the children] hinder the usefulness of their father, who loses influence in the eyes of the world if his counsels and walk have not succeeded in drawing his own family to God."[13]

Finally, all Christians are called to be priests in a figurative sense (1 Pet. 2:5, 9). They are to put love of God above love for family (Luke 14:26). The high priest was not allowed to defile himself by burying his father and mother (21:11). In similar vein Jesus challenged a reluctant disciple with the words, "follow me, and leave the dead to bury their own dead" (Matt. 8:21–22; Luke 9:59–60.

G. RELIGIOUS FESTIVALS (CH. 23)

1 *The Lord spoke to Moses as follows:*
2 *"Speak to the Israelites and say to them, When you summon the Lord's appointed meetings, they are holy conventions; these are my meetings.*
3 *For six days work may be done, but on the seventh day, the sabbath of solemn rest, there shall be a holy convention: do not do any work. It is a sabbath to the Lord in all your dwellings.*

12. Bonar, p. 375.
13. Bonar, p. 376.

4 *These are the Lord's meetings, the holy conventions which you must announce at the appropriate time.*

5 *On the fourteenth day of the first month at twilight there is the Lord's passover.*

6 *On the fifteenth day of this month the Lord's feast of unleavened bread begins: for seven days you must eat unleavened bread.*

7 *On the first day you must have a holy convention. You must not do any heavy work.*

8 *You must offer to the Lord a food offering for seven days. On the seventh day there must be a holy convention. You must not do any heavy work."*

9 *The Lord spoke to Moses as follows:*

10 *"Speak to the Israelites and say to them, When you enter the land which I am giving to you and you reap your harvest, you must bring a sheaf, the firstfruits of your harvest to the priest.*

11 *Then he must dedicate the sheaf before the Lord, so that you may be accepted: on the day after the sabbath the priest must dedicate it.*

12 *On the day you dedicate the sheaf you must make a burnt offering to the Lord of a perfect one-year-old male lamb,*

13 *and a cereal offering of one fifth of an ephah of fine flour mixed with oil, as a food offering with a soothing aroma for the Lord, and a drink offering of a quarter hin of wine.*

14 *You must not eat bread, roasted grain, or fresh grain until this very day, when you bring the offering of your God. This is a permanent rule for your descendants wherever you dwell.*

15 *You must count seven full weeks from the day after the sabbath, from the day you bring the dedication sheaf*

16 *until the day after the seventh sabbath. (In other words) you must count fifty days and then offer a new cereal offering to the Lord.*

17 *From your homes you must bring as a dedication offering two loaves made of one fifth of an ephah of fine flour baked with yeast as the Lord's firstfruits.*

18 *With the bread you must offer seven perfect one-year-old lambs, one young bull, and two rams, as a burnt offering, as well as their cereal offering and drink offerings, as a food offering with a soothing aroma for the Lord.*

19 *You must make a purification offering with one male goat and a peace offering with two one-year-old male lambs.*

20 *The priest must dedicate them as a dedication offering before the Lord together with the bread of the firstfruits, and the two lambs. They are holy to the Lord, that is, to the priest.*

21 *You must issue a proclamation on that same day. You must hold a holy convention. You must not do any heavy work. This is a permanent rule for your descendants wherever you dwell.*

22 *When you reap the harvest of your land, do not go right up to the corner of your field in your reaping and do not gather up the gleanings of your harvest. Leave them for the poor and the resident alien: I am the Lord your God."*

23 *The Lord spoke to Moses as follows:*

24 *"Speak to the Israelites as follows: On the first day of the seventh*

month you must have a day of solemn rest and remembrance announced with a trumpet, a holy convention.

25 *Do not do any heavy work, and offer a food offering to the Lord."*

26 *The Lord spoke to Moses as follows:*

27 *"But on the tenth day of this seventh month is the day of atonement. You must hold a holy convention, afflict yourselves, and offer a food offering to the Lord.*

28 *Do not do any work on that particular day, for it is the day of atonement to make atonement for you before the Lord your God.*

29 *For if anyone does not afflict himself on that particular day, he will be cut off from his people.*

30 *And if anyone does any work on that particular day, I shall destroy him from among his people.*

31 *You must not do any work. This is a permanent rule for your descendants wherever you live.*

32 *You must keep it as a sabbath of solemn rest and afflict yourselves: from the evening of the ninth day till the following evening you must observe it as your sabbath."*

33 *The Lord spoke to Moses as follows:*

34 *"Speak to the Israelites as follows: From the fifteenth day of the seventh month, for seven days you must keep the feast of booths to the Lord.*

35 *On the first day there must be a holy convention: you must not do any heavy work.*

36 *For seven days you must present a food offering to the Lord. On the eighth day you must hold a holy convention and offer a food offering to the Lord: it is a sacred assembly. You must not do any heavy work.*

37 *These are the appointed seasons of the Lord, when you must summon holy conventions to offer the Lord's food offerings, burnt offerings, cereal offerings, and drink offerings corresponding to each day.*

38 *These are in addition to the Lord's sabbaths, and your gifts, votive offerings, and free-will offerings that you give to the Lord.*

39 *But on the fifteenth day of the seventh month, when you have gathered in the produce of your land, you must celebrate the Lord's feast for seven days. On the first day and on the eighth day there shall be a solemn rest.*

40 *On the first day you must take for yourselves the fruit of splendid trees, palm branches, boughs of leafy trees, willows from the river banks, and rejoice before the Lord your God for seven days.*

41 *You must celebrate it as a feast to the Lord for seven days in the year. It is a permanent rule for your descendants. You must celebrate it in the seventh month.*

42 *You must live in booths for seven days, that is, every native Israelite must dwell in booths,*

43 *so that your descendants may know that I made the Israelites live in booths when I brought them out of the land of Egypt: I am the Lord your God."*

44 *And Moses told the Israelites about the Lord's meetings.*

The Structure of Leviticus 23

In the preceding chapters "I am the Lord (your God)" often served to highlight the structure of the material. It does so again in this chapter (vv. 22, 43), dividing the chapter into two main sections— the spring festivals (vv. 5–22) and the autumn festivals (vv. 26–43). These are further subdivided by another phrase that is infrequent outside this chapter, "This is a permanent rule for your descendants wherever you dwell" (vv. 14, 21, 31, 41).

Other key words and phrases in this chapter are "the Lord's meetings (appointed seasons)" (vv. 2, 4, 37, 44), "holy conventions" (vv. 2, 4, 7, 8, 21, 24, 27, 35, 37), and "do not do any (heavy) work" (vv. 7, 8, 21, 25, 28, 30–31, 36).

Using these phrases as markers we divide the chapter as follows.

1–4   Introduction: the sabbath
5–22   Spring festivals
        5–14 Passover and unleavened bread
        15–22 Feast of weeks
23–43   Fall festivals
        23–32 Solemn rest day and day of atonement
        33–43 Feast of booths
44   Concluding summary

The recurring refrains in this chapter about "holy conventions" and "rest days" show that this chapter is dealing with how the laity should celebrate these "holy days." This is a calendar for laymen, not for priests. A comparison with Num. 28–29 confirms this. Num. 28–29 specifies in detail which animals are to be offered on each day. By contrast this chapter is usually content with a brief reference to "food offerings" (vv. 8, 13, 18, 25, 27, 36–37), a phrase which covers all sacrifices except the purification offering.[1] It was the priest's task to know what kind of sacrifice must be offered on which occasion. It was enough for the layman to remember that he had to attend the holy convention, at which sacrifices would be offered on his behalf, and to observe the extra rest days.

Introduction: the Lord's Meetings and the Sabbath (1–4)

These verses introduce the subject of the Lord's meetings (vv. 2, 4, 44) or "appointed seasons" (v. 37) (*mô'ēḏ*). The word is derived from a verb meaning "to appoint or fix" (e.g., 2 Sam. 20:5). The

1. See above on 1:9.

noun most commonly occurs in the phrase "tent of meeting," i.e., the tented part of the tabernacle which God had appointed as the place to meet his people. God also fixed seasons when his people could come to meet him, at a holy convention.

Holy convention (vv. 2, 3, 4, 7, 8, 21, 24, 27, 35, 36, 37)—this phrase occurs eleven times in this chapter, six times in Num. 28–29, twice in Exod. 12:16, and nowhere else. From these passages we discover that sacrifices were offered at holy conventions. The word *convention (miqrā')* literally means a "call," "summons," or "reading." "Convention" is used on its own in Num. 10:2, of occasions when all the people are to be summoned to the tabernacle by sounding a trumpet. In Isa. 1:13; 4:5 it refers to the great services held in the temple courts. Putting these scraps of information together we may suggest that a "holy convention" was a national gathering for public worship. Primarily it was an occasion for the offering of sacrifice, but in later times it may also have included the reading and exposition of Scripture (cf. Deut. 31:10ff.; Neh. 8–9).

This chapter details these annual festivals. But before these are set out the people are reminded of the weekly festival, *the sabbath*. Like the other festivals listed here, it was a time of rest from work and an occasion for "a holy convention" (vv. 2–3). On the sabbath, man had to imitate his Creator, who rested from his work of creation on the seventh day (Gen. 2:1–3; Exod. 20:11), and recall his redemption from Egyptian slavery (Deut. 5:15; cf. Lev. 23:43).

Keil[2] points out that the sabbatical principle informs all the pentateuchal laws about the festivals. There are seven festivals in the year: passover, unleavened bread, weeks, solemn rest day, day of atonement, booths, day after booths. During these festivals there were seven days of rest, first and seventh unleavened bread, weeks, solemn rest day, day of atonement, first of booths, first day after booths. The majority of these festivals occur in the seventh month of the year. Every seventh year is a sabbatical year (Exod. 21:2ff.; Lev. 25:2ff.; Deut. 15:1ff.). After forty-nine (7 x 7) years there was a super-sabbatical year, the year of jubilee (Lev. 25:8ff.). Through this elaborate system of feasts and sabbatical years the importance of the sabbath was underlined. Through sheer familiarity the weekly sabbath could come to be taken for granted. But these festivals and sabbatical years constituted major interruptions to daily living and introduced an element of variety into the rhythm of life. In this way

2. *Biblical Archaeology* I, pp. 469ff.

they constantly reminded the Israelite what God had done for him, and that in observing the sabbath he was imitating his Creator, who rested on the seventh day.

The Spring Festivals (5–22)

Passover and unleavened bread (5–14)

5 Nothing more than a brief reminder about the passover is given here. Evidently the more detailed law in Exod. 12–13 is presupposed, and those chapters are the best commentary on this verse.[3]

6 The following day, the fifteenth of the first month,[4] was

3. Cf. also Deut. 16:1–8; J. B. Segal, *The Hebrew Passover* (London: 1963); de Vaux, *Ancient Israel*, pp. 484ff.; H. J. Kraus, "Zur Geschichte des Passah-Mazzot-Festes," *Evangelische Theologie* 18 (1958), pp. 47–67; M. Haran, "The Passover Sacrifice," *VTS* 23 (1972), pp. 86–116. *Twilight* (v. 5) (lit. "between the evenings"); cf. Exod. 12:6; 29:4; 30:8, etc. The meaning of the phrase is much discussed. Most commentators think it means "in the evening" (cf. Deut. 16:6, "at sunset"), or more precisely the period between sunset and complete darkness. The orthodox Jewish view is that it means "between midday and sunset," and this is supported by Gispen, pp. 323f., on the grounds that it would have been impossible to kill all the passover lambs in the temple between sunset and darkness. In NT times the passover sacrifice began about 3 p.m.

4. The first month of the year Nisan began in about mid-March. By NT times most Jews followed a lunar calendar, with 29 or 30 days in each month. About once every three years an extra month had to be intercalated to keep the lunar year in step with the sun. Under this calendar the Jewish festivals fall on different days of the solar year each year (e.g., in 1976 passover fell on April 15 and in 1977 on April 3) and on different days of the week (1976, Thursday; 1977, Sunday). It is generally supposed in most textbooks that a more primitive version of this system was followed in OT times (see de Vaux, *Ancient Israel*, pp. 178ff.).

More recently, however, it has been argued that in fact the OT follows the calendar mentioned in the book of Jubilees and used by the Essenes at Qumran, the so-called Jubilees calendar. This employs a year of exactly 52 weeks (364 days). Each year began on a Wednesday, and the major festivals of unleavened bread (Lev. 23:6), the solemn rest day (Lev. 23:24), and the feast of booths (Lev. 23:34) all began on Wednesday. In support of this theory it has been pointed out that according to Gen. 1:14 the sun and moon were created on Wednesday (the fourth day of the week) to be for "signs and seasons" (lit. "meetings," Heb. *mōʿēḏ*) (so P. Beauchamp, *Création and Séparation* [Paris, 1969], p. 113f.). If we suppose a Jubilees calendar to underlie the flood story, the turning points in that narrative all occur on appropriate days of the week; see G. J. Wenham, "The Coherence of the Flood Narrative," *VT* 28 (1978), pp. 342–45. Finally, S. B. Hoenig has suggested that the jubilee year mentioned in Lev. 25:8ff. also served to bring the calendar into line with the solar year by adding an extra 49 days every 49 years (*Tradition* 7 [1964], p. 23; "Sabbatical Years and the Year of Jubilee," *JQR* 59 [1969], pp. 222–236).

The simplicity of the Jubilees calendar is obvious. If the major festivals did always begin on Wednesdays, it would have been a great boon to ordinary people, who would not have possessed calendars. If the festivals began on Wednesday, those who lived a long way from Jerusalem would not have needed to journey on the sabbath to go up to the temple. But whatever calendar was used, it makes no difference to the religious significance of the festivals.

the opening day of the week-long *feast of unleavened bread*. It is called by this name because no ordinary leavened bread could be eaten during the week, recalling the exodus from Egypt, when the Israelites had to leave so suddenly that there was no time to leaven the bread (Exod. 12:14ff.).

The Hebrew word here translated *feast (ḥag)* may literally mean "pilgrimage" (cf. Arab. *ḥaj* of the pilgrimage to Mecca). The word is used of the festivals of unleavened bread (v. 6), tabernacles (v. 39), and weeks (Exod. 34:22; Deut. 16:16). If this is the correct etymology, it may reflect the fact that in later times these feasts were always celebrated in the central sanctuary in Jerusalem and involved a pilgrimage for those outside the town who wished to participate (cf. 1 K. 12:26–32).

The first and the last days of this feast were, like the first and last days of the main autumn festival, the feast of booths, rest days when "no heavy work" could be done (vv. 7, 8, 35, 36). The phrase *no heavy work* (lit. "work of labor or service," *mᵉleʾḵeṯ ʿᵃḇōḏāh*) is not precisely defined, and seems to be an allusion to the fourth commandment. "Six days shalt thou labor *(taʿᵃḇōḏ)* and do all thy work *(mᵉlaʾḵᵗᵉḵā)*" (Exod. 20:9). The opening and closing days of the festivals were days, like the sabbath, when ordinary work like farming or trading stopped and a holy convention was held. The adjective *heavy* is not applied to work forbidden on the sabbath or the day of atonement. There another phrase occurs, *a sabbath of solemn rest* (vv. 3, 32). Many commentators suggest that *solemn rest* covers not only heavy work but minor household chores, such as cooking or fire-lighting (cf. Exod. 16:23–30; Num. 15:32–36).

Food offerings (vv. 8, 13, 18, 25, 27, 36)—this is probably a shorthand for "all the appropriate sacrifices."[5] Num. 28–29 sets out the number and type of sacrifice required on each day of the feasts.

Leviticus introduces a new element into the older ceremonies customary at the feasts of passover and unleavened bread (see Exod. 12–13). Both Exod. 23:15 and 34:18–20 hint that an offering of firstfruits should be brought on this occasion. Lev. 23:10–13 is more specific. After the people have entered the promised land, they are to bring *a sheaf* (probably of barley, because it ripened before the wheat) as a dedication offering,[6] and a lamb as a burnt offering, with the prescribed accompaniments of cereal and drink offerings. The cereal offering on this occasion was twice as large as usual (cf.

5. See above on 1:9 (p. 56).
6. On this term see 7:30 (pp. 126f.).

Num. 28:13), probably because it was the start of the harvest. Only after these offerings had been made to God could the worshipper eat of the new season's produce himself (v. 14).

On the day after the sabbath (vv. 11, 15, cf. v. 16)—the meaning of this phrase has been the subject of much controversy. Is the sabbath in question the ordinary sabbath, i.e., the first Saturday after the beginning of the festival of unleavened bread? Or is the sabbath the first day of unleavened bread when heavy work was forbidden? According to the first interpretation "the day after the sabbath" means Sunday; according to the second it means the sixteenth day of the month.

Orthodox Judaism and most modern commentators favor the second suggestion. Some Jewish sects, however, and a few modern writers favor the first suggestion.[7] The exegetical arguments are finely balanced. It seems slightly more natural to equate "the sabbath" with Saturday than with the first day of the feast. Furthermore, if one accepts that Leviticus is based on the Jubilees Calendar,[8] it would seem more likely that the first sheaf was offered on Sunday (the day after the sabbath) than on Thursday (second day of the feast).

The feast of weeks (Pentecost) (15–22)

Fifty days (seven weeks) after the first sheaf had been offered, a feast to mark the end of the grain harvest was held (vv. 15–16). It is also called the feast of harvest (Exod. 23:16). Its NT name, Pentecost (Acts 2:1), comes from the Greek word meaning "fiftieth" *(pentēkostos)*.

Like the other major festivals it was a day of rest on which a holy convention was held and appropriate sacrifices were offered, including fresh loaves of bread (v. 17). This was the one occasion in the year when leavened bread had to be brought as an offering (Lev. 2:11; cf. 7:13).

The sacrifices at the feast of weeks are on a much more generous scale than those for the feast of unleavened bread (cf. vv. 12, 18–19). After the blessings of harvest had been gathered in, it was right and fitting to express in worship gratitude for God's goodness and to remember the needs of the poor (v. 22).

Verse 22 is a slight abridgement of the law in 19:9–10. It omits the reference to the grape harvest, which would be inappropriate at

---

7. Elliger, p. 315; Heinisch, p. 104; Bertholet, p. 80.
8. See above on v. 6.

this time of year, since grapes ripen much later. It is often suggested[9] that it is an inept insertion derived from 19:9–10. But in both chapters the verses are in fact carefully integrated into the total structure with the formula "I am the Lord your God." It may be that there is the same train of thought in both chapters. The sacrifices provide for the material needs of the priests (Lev. 19:5–8; 23:17–21), then the other weak members of society must be provided for, namely, the poor and the resident aliens. Deuteronomy regularly couples the needs of the Levites with those of the poor and sojourner (e.g., Deut. 14:27–29; 16:11).

The Fall Festivals (23–43)

The other main group of festivals falls in the seventh month of the year (September-October). In this month the dry hot summer draws to an end, the grapes and olives are picked, and the Israelite starts to look forward to the coming of the rains. In a good year these would begin in October and last until March. The seventh month, then, marked the end of the agricultural year and the beginning of a new one. Farm work was at a minimum and there was time to take stock spiritually and materially. The festivals in this month have a more solemn flavor than those in spring. Four extra sabbaths are prescribed in the space of one month including the most holy day of atonement (vv. 25, 28, 35, 36).

The special sacrifices for these festivals are listed in Num. 29. This list shows that the feast of booths was regarded as the most important of the year.

Verses 26–32 summarize how laymen had to observe the day of atonement, abstaining from all kinds of work and afflicting themselves (i.e., by fasting and other penitential exercises). If they did not observe the day, they were *cut off*[10] (cf. 16:29–30).

Verses 33–43 again emphasize the important features of the feast of booths as far as laymen are concerned. They are to live for the week in shelters made of branches. This was to remind them how they once had to live in tents when they came out of Egypt and make them appreciate the good housing they now enjoyed (cf. Deut. 6:10–11). It is only when we are deprived of our daily blessings, health, food, clothes, or housing, that we realize just how much we ought to be thankful for. Deuteronomy makes the point most

9. So Gispen, pp. 329f.; Elliger, p. 317; Noth, p. 172.
10. On this phrase see commentary on 17:4.

eloquently in 7:12–8:20: "Take heed lest you forget the Lord your God . . . when you have eaten and are full . . ." (8:11–12).

Leviticus 23 and the NT

Nowhere is the continuity between the testaments so clear as in the calendar. Three of the principal OT feasts were taken over directly by the Christian Church: passover = Good Friday, unleavened bread = Easter, weeks = Pentecost. The three most significant events in Christ's redemptive ministry coincided with these festivals. That they no longer always coincide today is because of various modifications to the calendar introduced since the first century.

The last supper seems to have been a passover meal (cf. Matt. 26:17), and John implies that our Lord was the true passover lamb whose bones were not to be broken (John 19:36 quoting Exod. 12:46; cf. John 19:14). Easter Sunday was probably[11] the day the first sheaf was offered as a dedication offering. It is this ceremony of offering the firstfruits which led Paul to speak of Christ in his resurrection as the firstfruits (1 Cor. 15:23). Elsewhere he uses another aspect of the festival of unleavened bread as an incentive for holiness: as all yeast had to be cleared out of the home in preparation for the feast of unleavened bread, so sin must be put out of the Christian community.

"Cleanse out the old leaven that you may be a new lump. . . . For Christ, our paschal lamb, has been sacrificed. Let us, therefore, celebrate the festival, not with the old leaven, the leaven of malice and evil, but with the unleavened bread of sincerity and truth" (1 Cor. 5:7–8).

Finally, the sending of the Holy Spirit to the Church fell on the feast of weeks, Pentecost, the fiftieth day after Easter (Acts 2:1).

Recognition of the OT background to these Christian festivals could perhaps give greater depth to Christian worship. When we celebrate Good Friday we should think not only of Christ's death on the cross for us, but of the first exodus from Egypt which anticipated our deliverance from the slavery of sin. At Easter we recall Christ's resurrection and see in it a pledge of our own resurrection at the last day, just as the firstfruits of harvest guarantee a full crop later on (1 Cor. 15:20, 23). At Whitsun (Pentecost) we praise God for the gift of the Spirit and all our spiritual blessings; the OT reminds us to praise God for our material benefits as well.

---

11. See above on the question of the meaning of the day after the sabbath.

In OT times these festivals were occasions for rest from everyday work and for a coming together of the people of God in holy conventions. The feasts were also a time for rejoicing before the Lord (23:40). How much more reason has the Church to rejoice today, in view of all the spiritual benefits that are ours in our Lord Jesus.

H. RULES FOR THE TABERNACLE (24:1–9)

1 *The Lord spoke to Moses as follows:*

2 *"Command the Israelites to take for you pure refined olive oil for the light to keep a lamp always alight.*

3 *Outside the curtain of testimony in the tent of meeting Aaron must arrange it before the Lord regularly from evening till morning. This is a permanent rule for your descendants.*

4 *On the pure lampstand he must regularly arrange the lamps before the Lord.*

5 *You must take fine flour and bake twelve loaves from it; two tenths of an ephah of flour shall go into each loaf.*

6 *You must put them in two piles: six in each pile on the pure table before the Lord.*

7 *On top of each pile you must place pure incense so that it may be used for the bread as a memorial portion, a food offering to the Lord.*

8 *Every sabbath day he must regularly arrange it before the Lord: it is from the Israelites as an eternal covenant.*

9 *It is for Aaron and his sons, and they must eat it in a holy place, for it is one of the most holy things, a permanent due for him from the Lord's food offerings."*

I. A CASE OF BLASPHEMY (24:10–23)

10 *A man with an Israelite mother and an Egyptian father, who lived among the Israelites, started fighting with a pure-blooded Israelite.*

11 *The man of mixed parentage uttered the Name and cursed. So they brought him to Moses. Now his mother's name was Shelomith, daughter of Divri from the tribe of Dan.*

12 *They put him in custody while they sought guidance from the Lord.*

13 *The Lord spoke to Moses as follows:*

14 *"Bring the blasphemer out of the camp and then let those who heard him lay their hands on his head and let the whole congregation stone him.*

15 *You must say to the Israelites: If a man curses his God, he will bear his punishment.*

16 *But whoever utters the name of the Lord as a curse must certainly be put to death. All the congregation must stone him. This applies*

equally to resident aliens and to native Israelites. When he utters the Name as a curse, he must be put to death.

17 *If a man takes a man's life, he must certainly be put to death.*

18 *Whoever takes an animal's life must pay it back, life for life.*

19 *If a man injures his fellow citizen, whatever he did must be done to him,*

20 *injury for injury, eye for eye, tooth for tooth. Whatever injury he inflicts on a person, the same must be done to him.*

21 *Whoever kills an animal must pay it back, and whoever kills a man must be put to death.*

22 *You must have one law for the resident alien and for the native Israelite, because I am the Lord your God."*

23 *So Moses spoke to the Israelites, and they brought the blasphemer outside the camp and stoned him. Thus the Israelites did as the Lord had commanded Moses.*

The Structure of Leviticus 24

The material in this chapter divides as follows:

  1   Introduction
  2–9   Laws about the Holy Place
       2–4   The lampstand
       5–9   The bread of the Presence
  10–23 A Case of Blasphemy
       10–12 The offense
       13–22 The judgment of God
       23   Execution by the people

This chapter lacks the clear structural markers characteristic of many sections of Leviticus. Points of contact with surrounding chapters include "I am the Lord your God" (v. 22), "This is a permanent rule for your descendants" (v. 3; cf. 3:17; 10:9; 16:29; 17:7; 23:14, 21, 31, 41), and "a permanent due" (v. 9; cf. 6:11 [Eng. 18]; 7:34; 10:15).

Despite these familiar phrases, commentators have been unable to discern any obvious connection between the material in this chapter and what precedes and follows it. Gispen[1] suggests that the laws about the holy place (vv. 2–9) may be included to remind the people that they were obliged to provide for the worship of God at all times and not only at the festivals listed in ch. 23.

The only reason that commentators can find for the present position of the story of the blasphemer (vv. 10–23) is that it took place soon after Moses had been given the instructions about the

1. Gispen, p. 337.

lampstand and bread of the Presence (vv. 2–9). If this explanation is correct, it underlines that Leviticus is essentially a narrative work (cf. chs. 8–10). The laws were given at specific times and places to meet particular situations.

Within each section signs of careful organization may be noted. The law about the bread of the Presence echoes that dealing with the lampstand: "take" (vv. 2, 5), "arrange" (vv. 3–4, 8), "regularly" (vv. 3–4, 8), "before the Lord" (vv. 3–4, 6, 8). In the case of the blasphemer the description of his execution (v. 23) follows closely the divine judgment (v. 14). This is an example of the command-fulfilment pattern also found in chs. 8–10, used to emphasize the people's obedience to God's word. The explanation of the judgment (vv. 15–22) is also carefully arranged.[2]

The Lampstand (2–4)

Verses 2–3 repeat with slight abbreviation the instructions given in Exod. 27:20–21. The design of the lampstand is described in Exod. 25:31–39, its construction in Exod. 37:17–24, and its erection in Exod. 40:25–26. Various features of its design and decoration are entirely appropriate to the Late Bronze Age (15-13th centuries B.C. and went out of fashion later.[3] The antiquity of the lampstand is further confirmed by 1 Sam. 3:3.

The Bread of the Presence (5–9)

Like the lampstand and the altar of incense, the bread of the Presence[4] was kept in the holy place, the outer part of the tent of meeting.

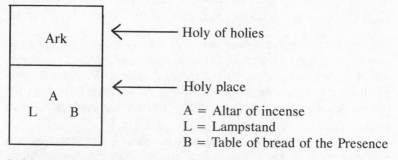

Holy of holies

Holy place

A = Altar of incense
L = Lampstand
B = Table of bread of the Presence

2. See commentary on these verses.
3. C. L. Meyers, *The Tabernacle Menorah* (1976), esp. pp. 182ff.
4. The "bread of the Presence" (Exod. 25:30), probably so called because it was put before the Lord (vv. 6, 8), is in the AV called "shewbread."

The bread was placed on a fairly small low table covered in gold plate (see Exod. 25:23–30//37:10–16). Along with the bread, various small dishes had to be placed on the table. Josephus says the loaves of bread were piled up (*Antiquities* 3:6:6). Despite the usual English translation,[5] this seems the only way that twelve huge loaves[6] could have been arranged on a table of this size (3' x 1'6" = 90 x 45 cm).

6 *You must put them in two piles: six in each pile.* It seems likely that the two piles of six loaves represented the twelve tribes of Israel, in the same way as the two onyx stones each engraved with six names served as "stones of remembrance for the sons of Israel" (Exod. 28:9–12). Like circumcision (Gen. 17:13, 19) and the sabbath (Exod. 31:16), the bread of the Presence symbolized the "eternal covenant" (v. 8) between God and Israel (cf. Ps. 105:10; Rom. 11:28–29). Alternatively this phrase could refer to the everlasting covenant announced to Noah that God would never again destroy the earth and its crops in a flood. But this seems less likely (Gen. 9:16).

7–9 *Memorial portion* (v. 7)—the term used to describe the cereal offerings in 2:2, 9, 16; 5:12; 6:8 (Eng. 15). See commentary on 2:2. In the case of the bread of the Presence, though, the incense was burned instead of the bread.

It is one of the most holy things (v. 9). This meant that the bread could be eaten only by the priests in a holy place (cf. 6:9ff. [Eng. 16ff.]). Ahimelech priest of Nob was therefore deviating from the rules somewhat in allowing David and his men to eat the bread. He did, however, insist that the men must not be unclean as a result of recent sexual intercourse (1 Sam. 21:4–7 [Eng. 3–6]; cf. Lev. 15:16ff.).

The Case of a Blasphemer (10–23)

This episode illustrates how many of the case laws[7] in the Pentateuch may have originated. They arose out of specific situations which were brought to court for a legal judgment. The penalty in a given case is recorded as a guide for judges in the future should similar cases occur again. It should be noticed that the judge whose

---

5. *Ma'areket*, generally translated "row," literally means "arrangement" and is used only of the bread of the Presence. Both Gispen, p. 340, and Elliger, p. 324, translate it "staple," i.e., *pile*.

6. Verse 5 says that one fifth of an ephah of flour went into each loaf. The exact volume in an ephah is uncertain (see de Vaux, *Ancient Israel*, p. 202), but the figures suggest that about 3 liters of 3½ lbs. of flour went into each loaf.

7. Those that begin "If a man does so and so," and then set out the penalty.

decision is here recorded is not Moses, but God. God himself was the author of law in Israel,[8] not the king or some human authority as in Mesopotamian law.

Uttered the Name and cursed (v. 11). It was not simply uttering the holy name of Yahweh (the Lord) that constituted the offense, as Jews often hold, or cursing by itself. It was using the Lord's name in a curse that merited the death penalty (see vv. 14ff.).[9]

Misuse of God's name is condemned in the third commandment (Exod. 20:7). Cursing God is forbidden in Exod. 22:27 (Eng. 28). (The same verb *qillēl* is used in Exod. 22 and this verse, also of cursing parents in Lev. 20:9.) The story of Naboth shows that the death penalty for blasphemy was no dead letter in OT times (1 K. 21:10, 13). Blasphemy was one of the charges for which our Lord and Stephen were condemned to death (Matt. 26:65–66; Acts 6:11ff.).

Blasphemy brings guilt on those who hear it as well as on the blasphemer himself. To rid themselves of this guilt the hearers had to lay their hands on the blasphemer's head (v. 14). His subsequent death then atoned for his own and his hearers' sin.[10]

Throughout the ancient Orient the death penalty was imposed for a wider variety of crimes than currently in western society. This applies to the OT as much as the Mesopotamian systems, but whereas the laws of Hammurabi regard property offenses and similar crimes as capital, the OT does not. In its eyes, sins against the family and religion are the most serious, and hence often attract the death penalty, whereas economic matters are treated more lightly.

This applies equally to resident aliens and to native Israelites (vv. 16, 22). Foreigners resident in Israel were expected to show respect for God. Other laws that also applied to foreign residents are mentioned in Exod. 12:19, 49; Lev. 16:29; 17:15; 18:26; Num. 9:14; 15:30. Non-Israelites were among those who came out of Egypt according to Exod. 12:38.

This incident of blasphemy provided an occasion to spell out some of the cardinal principles of biblical law in a short digression, vv. 16–22. These verses are carefully arranged in a concentric pattern called a palistrophe.

8. Cf. the ten commandments being written with the finger of God (Exod. 31:18). For a useful comparison of biblical and Mesopotamian thought on law see S. M. Paul, *Studies in the Book of the Covenant* (Leiden: Brill, 1970).
9. Saalschütz, p. 495.
10. Hoffmann I, pp. 121f.; Gispen, p. 38.

A	resident alien and native Israelite (v. 16)
B	take a man's life (v. 17)
C	take an animal's life (v. 18)
D	whatever he did, must be done to him (v. 19)
D'	whatever . . . , must be done to him (v. 20)
C'	kill an animal (v. 21a)
B'	kill a man (v. 21b)
A'	resident alien and native Israelite (v. 22)

The symmetry and balance of this structure reinforces the points made explicitly in the text, namely, that in these cases the same penalty must be applied to both resident alien and native Israelite (vv. 16, 22) and that in all cases the punishment must match the offense: *If a man injures his fellow citizen, whatever he did must be done to him* (v. 19).

Eye for eye, tooth for tooth (v. 20)—this is one of three passages in the OT setting out the so-called *lex talionis* (cf. Exod. 21:23–25; Deut. 19:21), a fundamental principle of biblical and Near Eastern law, namely, that punishment must be proportionate to the offense. Retribution is a principal goal of the penal system in the Bible.[11]

It seems likely that this phrase *eye for eye*, etc. was just a formula. In most cases in Israel it was not applied literally. It meant that compensation appropriate to the loss incurred must be paid out. Thus if a slave lost an eye, he was given his freedom (Exod. 21:26). The man who killed an ox had to pay its owner enough for him to buy another (Lev. 24:18). Only in the case of premeditated murder was such compensation forbidden (Num. 35:16ff.). Then the principle of *life for life* must be literally enforced, because man is made in the image of God (Gen. 9:5–6).[12]

Leviticus 24 and the NT

The golden lampstand and the table of the bread of the Presence are mentioned in Heb. 9:2. Jesus refers to the bread of the Presence in Matt. 12:1ff.//Mark 2:23ff.//Luke 6:1ff. The Pharisees criticized Jesus for allowing his disciples to pick and eat corn on the sabbath. According to their tradition this action was tantamount to harvesting, and the disciples were therefore working on the sabbath. Jesus

11. See further Excursus I: "Principles of Punishment in the Pentateuch"; also de Vaux, *Ancient Israel*, pp. 149f.
12. B. S. Jackson, *Essays in Jewish and Comparative Legal History* (Leiden: Brill, 1975), pp. 75–107.

points out that when David was hungry he broke the law (that of Lev. 24:9) much more blatantly by eating the bread of the Presence (see 1 Sam. 21). The Pharisaic rules about the sabbath, Jesus says, miss the point of the sabbath. The rules were made for man's good, not to make him starve on the sabbath.

The law on blasphemy (Lev. 24:14ff.) was part of the justification of the death sentences passed on Christ and Stephen (Matt. 26:65ff.; Acts 6:11ff.), though clearly in these cases blasphemy had a broader meaning than in Lev. 24. Nevertheless the NT is certainly at one with the OT in discouraging profane use of God's name (e.g., Matt. 5:34ff.; Jas. 3:9).

Jesus discusses the *lex talionis* in the Sermon on the Mount. "You have heard that it was said, 'An eye for an eye and a tooth for a tooth.' But I say to you, Do not resist one who is evil" (Matt. 5:38–39). In context Jesus' remarks are a criticism of interpretations of the OT current in his day. These interpretations aimed to take the sting out of OT ethics. For instance it was said, "Murder was forbidden, but it does not matter being angry." Jesus said that while murder may be the worst consequence of anger, even anger is sinful (5:21ff.). Further it was said, "adultery was wrong, but divorce was all right." Jesus said that remarriage after divorce could be adultery by another name (Matt. 5:27–32). The context of vv. 38–42, therefore, makes it improbable that Jesus was rejecting the *lex talionis* as such. What seems more probable is that Jesus is attacking those who turn this legal principle into a maxim for personal conduct. Christ's followers are not to live on a tit-for-tat basis. Total selfless love like that of Christ must characterize their attitude to others. "Give to him who begs from you, and do not refuse him who would borrow from you" (v. 42). It is unlikely that our Lord's remarks were intended to encourage judges to let offenders off scot-free. The NT recognizes that human judges must mete out punishments appropriate to the offense (Acts 25:11; Rom. 13:4; 1 Pet. 2:14, 20) and declares that it is on this basis that God will judge mankind (Luke 12:47–48; 1 Cor. 3:8ff.).

J. SABBATICAL AND JUBILEE YEARS (CH. 25)

1 *The Lord spoke to Moses on Mount Sinai as follows:*
2 *"Speak to the Israelites and say to them: When you enter the land which I am giving you, the land must rest as a sabbath for the Lord.*
3 *For six years you must sow your field, prune your vineyard, and gather in its produce,*

4 *but in the seventh year there must be a sabbath of solemn rest for the land, a sabbath for the Lord. You must not sow your field or prune your vineyard.*

5 *You must not reap what grows of itself or gather the grapes of your unpruned vines: it shall be a year of solemn rest for the land.*

6 *The sabbatical growth of the land will be food for you, your slave and your slave-girl, your employee, and your settler who lives with you,*

7 *for your cattle and for the wild animals that are in your land. All its produce may be eaten.*

8 *You must count seven cycles of sabbatical years, that is, seven years seven times, and the forty-nine days of the seven cycles of sabbatical years shall be for you a year (or: the days of the seven cycles of sabbatical years shall be for you forty-nine years).*

9 *Then you must sound the trumpet throughout your land on the tenth day of the seventh month, the day of atonement.*

10 *You must sanctify the year of the fiftieth year and proclaim a release in the land. It is a jubilee for you: you must all return to your property and to your families.*

11 *The fiftieth year shall be a jubilee for you: do not sow or reap what grows by itself and do not pick your unpruned vines,*

12 *because the jubilee shall be holy for you: you may eat of the produce of the open country.*

13 *In this year of jubilee each of you must return to your inheritance.*

14 *If you sell something to your fellow citizen or buy something from your fellow citizen, do not exploit your brother.*

15 *But at a price proportionate to the number of years after the jubilee you must buy it from your fellow citizen: he must sell it to you at a price proportionate to the number of years of production.*

16 *If there are many years (to the jubilee), you may increase the price proportionately; but if there are few years, you must reduce the price proportionately; because he is selling you a number of crops.*

17 *Let none of you exploit his fellow citizen, but fear your God, for I am the Lord your God.*

18 *You must do my rules and keep my judgments to do them and then you will dwell in the land securely.*

19 *The land will give its fruits and you will eat to the full and live in it securely.*

20 *If you ask, "What shall we eat in the seventh year if we do not sow and do not gather in its produce?"*

21 *I shall command my blessing for you in the sixth year and it shall produce enough crops for three years.*

22 *You shall sow again in the eighth year, and eat the old produce until the ninth year when the new crops arrive; until then you shall eat the old produce.*

23 *The land must not be sold off permanently, for the land is mine, for you are resident aliens and settlers with me,*

24 *and you must allow redemption for every part of the land you own.*

25 *If your brother becomes poor and sells part of the land he owns, his*

redeemer who is most closely related to him must come and redeem what his brother has sold.

26 *If the man has no redeemer but later can find enough for his own redemption,*

27 *he must calculate the number of years from the sale, and return the balance to the man to whom he sold his property, and then return to his property.*

28 *But if he cannot find enough to pay him back, the property that he sold must remain in the purchaser's possession until the year of the jubilee. Then it will be released in the jubilee and he may return to his property.*

29 *If a man sells a dwelling house in a walled town, it may be bought back within a year of its sale. The redemption period for it shall be a year.*

30 *If it is not redeemed within a full year, a house in a walled city becomes the inalienable property of the purchaser for his descendants; it shall not be released in the jubilee.*

31 *But houses in open, unwalled villages shall count with fields of the land: redemption is possible for them and they will be released in the jubilee.*

32 *As for the levitical cities, the houses in the cities that belong to them, the Levites may always redeem them.*

33 *If one of the Levites redeems, the purchased house in the city that they own shall be released in the jubilee, because the houses of the levitical cities are their property among the Israelites.*

34 *But the fields and pasture land attached to their cities may never be sold, because it is their property for ever.*

35 *If your brother becomes poor and cannot support himself, you must maintain him as if he were a resident alien or settler and let him live with you.*

36 *Do not take any kind of interest from him, but fear God and let him live with you.*

37 *Do not charge him interest on any loans of money or food that you make to him.*

38 *I am the Lord your God, who brought you out of the land of Egypt to give you the land of Canaan to be your God.*

39 *If your brother who lives with you becomes poor and sells himself to you, you must not make him work for you like a slave.*

40 *He must be with you like an employee or a settler; until the year of jubilee he must work with you.*

41 *Then he must be released from you, he and his sons as well, and return to his family and go back to his father's property.*

42 *For they are my slaves, whom I brought out of the land of Egypt; they must not be resold as slaves.*

43 *Do not boss him around harshly but fear your God.*

44 *But if you have any slaves or slave-girls from among the nations round about you (you may obtain slaves or slave-girls from them,*

45 *and also from the settlers who live among you and their families who*

315

are with them, if they bear children in your land), you may own them as property.

46 *You may bequeath them to your children as an inheritance. You may make them work for you for ever. But you must not harshly boss around your brothers, the Israelites.*

47 *If a resident alien or settler does well for himself, and your brother living with him becomes poor and sells himself to the resident alien or settler[1] who lives with you, or to a member of the resident alien's family,*

48 *there remains the right of redemption for him after he has sold himself. One of his brothers may redeem him;*

49 *or his uncle or cousin may redeem him; or one of his blood relations from his family may redeem him; or if he does well, he may redeem himself.*

50 *He must calculate with his purchaser the number of years from his sale (into slavery) until the year of jubilee, and his sale price must be fixed by the number of years he will have been with him, as if he were an employee.*

51 *If there are still many years to run he must pay back as his redemption price an appropriate proportion of the purchase price.*

52 *If there are just a few years left to the jubilee, he shall calculate it and in proportion to the number of years pay back the redemption money.*

53 *He must treat him like an employee during the years that he is with him. Do not let him boss him around harshly.*

54 *If he does not redeem himself during these (years), he must be released in the year of jubilee, he and his children.*

55 *For the children of Israel belong to me as slaves; they are my slaves whom I brought out of the land of Egypt. I am the Lord your God."*

The Structure of Leviticus 25

As in the preceding chapters, the phrase "I am the Lord your God" signals the close of a section (vv. 17, 38, 55). The chapter thus divides into three main sections:

1 Introduction
2–22 The Jubilee—a sabbath for the land
23–38 The Jubilee—and the redemption of property
39–55 The Jubilee—and the redemption of slaves.

Each section closes with an exhortation giving theological reasons for observing the law (vv. 17–22, 35–38, 55). Certain words and phrases distributed fairly evenly throughout the three sections indicate the main concerns of the chapter: e.g., "jubilee," "return to his property," "your brother becomes poor," and "fear your God."

---

1. Following the versions "and settler" rather than MT "settler."

The Jubilee

The main purpose of these laws is to prevent the utter ruin of debtors. In biblical times a man who incurred a debt that he could not repay could be forced to sell off his land or even his personal freedom by becoming a slave. When left unchecked this process led to great social division, with a class of rich landowners exploiting a mass of landless serfs. This sort of situation has arisen in many societies, and even Israel was not immune to it, despite this legislation. Standards of house-building have led archeologists to conclude that early Israel was a relatively egalitarian society, but that by the later monarchy period the gap between rich and poor had widened. "The rich houses are bigger and better built and in a different quarter from that where the poor houses are huddled together."[2] Isaiah denounces "those who join house to house, who add field to field, until there is no more room" (Isa. 5:8), while Amos angrily decries those who "sell the righteous for silver, and the needy for a pair of shoes" (Amos 2:6). Had the jubilee been observed, such unbridled exploitation of the poor would have been checked. Lev. 25 prohibits anyone from selling himself or his land off permanently. In effect he may only rent out his land or his labor for a maximum of forty-nine years. The rent is payable in one lump sum in advance, as if there were a sale, but in the jubilee year the land reverts to its original owner and the slave is given his freedom.

This jubilee year occurred every forty-nine years. If a man went bankrupt the year after the jubilee, he would be enslaved for up to forty-eight years unless a relative was able to redeem him; but if it happened at a later stage in the cycle, he would have had a shorter time to wait for release. Thus, about once in any man's lifetime the slate was wiped clean. Everyone had the chance to make a fresh start. The rich had to part with the land and slaves they had acquired in the previous forty-nine years, while the poor recovered their land and freedom. The jubilee would have restored some semblance of equality between men, thereby recapturing something of the relationship that existed between men at their creation. Other laws in the pentateuch have a similar aim. Exod. 23 prescribes that every seven years the ground is to be left untilled, so that it may enjoy a sabbatical year. The ground is allowed to run wild and return at least partially to its state prior to human cultivation. Because of the

---

2. De Vaux, *Ancient Israel*, p. 73; cf. W. F. Albright, *The Archaeology of Palestine*[4] (Harmondsworth: Penguin, 1960), p. 119.

similar notion underlying the sabbatical year it is mentioned in Lev. 25.

But as a social institution the jubilee year remained an ideal, which was rarely, if ever, realized. Rabbinic literature says that it was reckoned to be obsolete in postexilic times. Chronicles may imply that not even the sabbatical year was observed in preexilic times (2 Chr. 36:21). But failure to implement an ideal does not mean it could not have been realized had the will been present. Evidence from Mesopotamia indicates that in old Babylonian times (19th/17th centuries B.C.) some kings did make administrative decrees whose effects were similar to the jubilee laws.[3] It has been suggested that the jubilee was the invention of Nehemiah's day,[4] but North has made a strong case for supposing that the followers of Moses were more likely to have embraced such idealism than the dispirited men who returned from exile.[5]

The Jubilee—A Sabbath for the Land (2–22)

The land must rest as a sabbath for the Lord (v. 2). The jubilee laws begin with a reminder of the sabbatical year (vv. 2–5) (cf. Exod. 23:10–11). As man works for six days and rests every seventh day,[6] so the land must be tilled for six years and then allowed to rest by lying fallow in the seventh year. During that year there is to be no organized farming, sowing, pruning or reaping (vv. 4–5). The children of Israel are to behave like the nomads they were before the conquest. Anyone can pick and gather whatever he finds, wherever it is. This should be of special benefit to slaves and other landless persons (v. 6; cf. Exod. 23:11).[7]

The year of rest proclaimed to the Israelites that the decisive factor is not daily work in the field or vineyard, but Yahweh the giver of the land. In this way the sabbatical year speaks even more clearly

3. See J. J. Finkelstein, *JCS* 15 (1961), pp. 91–104; *idem*, "Some New *Misharum* Material and Its Implications," in *Studies in Honor of B. Landsberger* (Chicago: University Press, 1965), pp. 223–246; D. J. Wiseman, *JSS* 7 (1962), pp. 161–172.
4. R. Westbrook, "Jubilee Laws," *Israel Law Review* 6 (1971), pp. 209–226, argues that the only feature of the jubilee law that is late and impracticable is the idea of a *regular* 50-year cycle of releases.
5. R. North, *Sociology of the Biblical Jubilee* (Rome: Pontifical Biblical Institute, 1954), pp. 204ff. A. van Selms, *IDBS*, pp. 496–98 argues that the jubilee was occasionally implemented in the pre-exilic times. B. Z. Wacholder, *IDBS*, pp. 762f. thinks the sabbatical year was also observed before the exile.
6. Note the echoes of the fourth commandment (Exod. 20:9–10) in vv. 3 and 4.
7. *Sabbatical growth* (v. 6) (lit. "sabbath"). Used only with the meaning "what grows in the sabbatical year" in this verse.

than the weekly sabbath of the relativity of all work. The goal of all work, its crown, is rest, the sabbath before the Lord.[8]

While the sabbatical year alleviated the plight of the poor, every seventh sabbatical year an attempt was made to give them a new start. Land was returned to those who had sold it (*you must all return to your property*), and those who had been enslaved returned to their families (v. 10). This was the *jubilee*. This word is a rough transliteration of the Hebrew term (*yôḇēl*), which is usually supposed to mean "ram" or "ram's horn." The year of jubilee would then take its name from the blowing of the ram's horn at the beginning of the year (v. 9). If this is the basic meaning of the word, one must suppose it was soon forgotten, because Josh. 6:6, 8 needs to explain it with another word for ram's horn (*shôpār*). Alternatively the LXX may be correct to translate it as "release" (*aphesis*).[9]

The fiftieth year shall be a jubilee for you (v. 11). Taken in conjunction with v. 8 which speaks of *seven cycles of sabbatical years*, it would appear that the jubilee year (year 50) immediately followed a sabbatical year (year 49), i.e., that there were *two* fallow years succeeding each other. Though this is the view of the majority of commentators, North rejects this on the grounds that it would have been impossible to forgo two harvests in a row. Verses 20–22 envisage enough problems in the celebration of one sabbatical year, let alone two in succession. North suggests, therefore, that by the fiftieth year (v. 11) the forty-ninth year is meant. This would be a case of inclusive reckoning.[10]

Another possibility, suggested by Hoenig[11] and tentatively adopted in my translation of v. 8, *the forty-nine days of the seven cycles of sabbatical years shall be for you a year,* is that the jubilee year was a very short "year" only forty-nine days long, intercalated in the seventh month of the forty-ninth year. This short "year" would function like February 29 in our leap years, and serve to keep the religious festivals, many of which were connected with harvesting, in step with the seasons.

Since the jubilee requires any purchaser of land to return it to

8. Gispen, p. 350.
9. This is the meaning favored by North, *Biblical Jubilee*, pp. 96ff., where a full discussion of the etymologies that have been proposed will be found.
10. North, *Biblical Jubilee*, pp. 109ff.; cf. John 20:26, where "eight days later" means a week later.
11. S. B. Hoenig, "Sabbatical Years and the Year of Jubilee," *JQR* 59 (1969), pp. 222–236. For further discussion see above, footnote on Lev. 23:6.

the original owner, the purchase price must be proportional to the number of years to the next jubilee (vv. 13–17).

Those who obey the law are promised a rich blessing (vv. 18ff.). They will enjoy peace *(dwell securely)* and heavy crops. These promises recur throughout the OT but they are most fully elaborated in Lev. 26:3–13 and Deut. 28:1–14. The institution of the sabbatical year provided a real test of Israel's faith in these promises. In that period they were asked deliberately to forgo one year's harvest, trusting that God would supply enough in the previous years to tide them over. Some of the questions that inevitably arise about the wisdom of such a law are answered in vv. 20ff. The idea of a bumper crop to last three years[12] in the sixth year may strike the Westerner as fanciful. But if the timing is miraculous, the notion of large variations in yield is not. The size of the harvest is determined by the timing and quantity of the rain during the growing season. Both factors can change dramatically from one year to the next in Israel.[13]

The Jubilee and the Redemption of Property (23–38)

23 The theological principle underlying the jubilee is enunciated: *The land must not be sold off permanently, for the land is mine.* Time and again the Pentateuch reiterates that it is God who gives Israel the land (e.g., Gen. 15:7; 17:8; 24:7; Exod. 6:4; Lev. 20:24; 25:2, 38; Deut. 5:16). Every tribe and every family within each tribe is allotted a portion of the land by divine decree (Num. 32; Josh. 13ff.). By insisting that the land could not be alienated from the family to whom God has assigned it (cf. 1 K. 21:3), this law aims to preserve the idea that the land ultimately belongs to God. His people are but *resident aliens and settlers* in the land. In other words it does not really belong to them; they inhabit it thanks solely to the mercy and favor of their God, the great landowner (cf. 1 Chr. 29:15; Ps. 39:13 [Eng. 12]; Heb. 11:13; 1 Pet. 2:11).

25 The law's immediate concern is with the redemption of land and property. If a man is forced to sell off some of his family property, ideally another member of the family should come and buy it back for the family. Examples of this are recorded in Ruth 4 and Jer. 32:7ff. The closer the relationship, the greater the moral duty to act as redeemer (see vv. 48–49).

12. By the three years probably part of the 6th, all of the 7th, and part of the 8th year is meant. So Rashi, p. 116, followed by Hoffmann II, p. 336.
13. See D. Baly, *The Geography of the Bible*[2] (London: Lutterworth, 1974), pp. 43ff.

26 If a relative fails to redeem the property, and the man's fortunes recover, he may buy it back himself.

27 The price of redemption has to be calculated by reference to the date of the jubilee (cf. vv. 16, 50ff.).

28 The release in the year of jubilee is a last resort.

29-34 Various special cases are dealt with here. Houses in towns are not subject to jubilee release, perhaps because even in those days redevelopment was fairly rapid in towns. If they are to be redeemed, it must be done within a year[14] (vv. 29-30). Levitical cities must be treated differently, though. All the tribes apart from the Levites were granted land. The Levites were not given any land, only forty-eight cities and the pasture lands immediately surrounding them (Num. 35:1-8; Josh. 21; 1 Chr. 6:54-81). Had the Levites been allowed to sell off their town houses with no guarantee of ultimate redemption in the jubilee, the Levites could have found themselves with no homes of their own at all. The purpose of the laws in vv. 32-34 is to prevent this occurring.

The case discussed in v. 33 is a little obscure. Some modern translations follow the Vulgate and insert "not" in the first clause, *If one of the Levites redeems*. But this is unnecessary, for the law makes good sense as it stands. If one Levite sells his property, and another Levite redeems it, the property still reverts to the original owner in the year of jubilee.[15]

35 *You must maintain him as if he were a resident alien.* Family pride may sometimes make for vindictiveness when one member of the family falls on hard times. For disgracing the family name he may be shunned instead of helped. The Israelites are not to let such feelings determine their behavior. They must be as generous to members of their own family who are in need as they would be to aliens. Biblical law is most insistent that aliens should be well treated. If the family steps in to help in this way, the man who has sold his land may not have the further disgrace of slavery imposed on him (see vv. 39ff.).

36-37 *Do not take any kind of interest from him.* Interest-free loans are well attested in ancient financial records, and laws against taking excessive interest are also known,[16] but Israel is alone

14. In v. 30 *in a walled city* follows the I ᵛX rather than the MT, reading *lāh* for *lō'*.
15. So Saalschütz, p. 150; Hoffmanr ᵛ, pp. 341f.; Gispen, pp. 362f. Keil. p. 463, suggests that the law covers not only redemption by Levites of levitical property, but sales to non-Levites, which could be described as redemption in that all Levitical homes had originally been ceded to them by the other tribes.
16. LE 18A-21; LH 48-51, 88ff.

in totally prohibiting interest payments on loans to the poor.[17] These loans were essentially charitable: they enabled a poor farmer to buy enough seed corn for the next season. Both here and in Exod. 22:24 (Eng. 25) interest is prohibited on loans to the poor, while Deut. 23:21 (20) explicitly allows foreigners to be charged interest.

38 *I am the Lord your God . . . to give you the land.* God's generosity to his people is an example to them how they should treat each other (cf. Matt. 18:23–35). "If God so loved us, we also ought to love one another" (1 John 4:11).

Redemption from Slavery (39–55)

As a last resort in cases of serious debt (e.g., Exod. 22:2 [Eng. 3]; 2 K. 4:1–7), the debtor could sell himself into slavery. These laws are designed to make the slavery as humane as possible. *Do not boss him around harshly* (vv. 43, 46, 53). *Boss around* (lit. "rule"; see Ps. 72:8) sometimes has a bad sense (e.g., Neh. 9:28). Harshness characterized slavery in Egypt (Exod. 1:13–14).

In our minds slavery conjures up pictures of slave-ships from Africa and oppression on plantations. Slavery in Israel was intended to be very different, as these laws make clear. It was somewhat akin to imprisonment in the modern world, and served a roughly similar purpose of enabling a man who could not pay a fine to work off his debt directly. In some respects it was less degrading and demoralizing than the modern penitentiary; for one thing the man was not cut off from society as he would be in prison. Ideally one of his relatives should buy the debtor and so pay off the debt (vv. 39–43). If this is not possible, because none of his relatives has enough money at that moment, they should still try to redeem him later if their funds permit (vv. 48–53). If this proves impossible he is to be freed in the year of jubilee (vv. 40–41, 54).[18]

The jubilee release does not apply to foreign slaves (vv. 44–46). A theological reason underlies this discrimination: God redeemed his people from Egyptian slavery, to become his slaves (vv. 42, 55). It is unfitting, therefore, that an Israelite should be resold

17. See R. P. Maloney, "Usury and Restrictions on Interest-Taking in the Ancient Near East," *CBQ* 36 (1974), pp. 1–20; also S. E. Loewenstamm, *JBL* 88 (1969), pp. 78–80, and H. Gamoran, *JNES* 30 (1971), pp. 127–134.
18. Exod. 21:1ff. and Deut. 15:12ff. allow the slave to be released after seven years' service, though he has the option of continuing in service if he wants. It is uncertain how the jubilee release relates to this seven-year release. If the jubilee was never actually enforced, the question of reconciling the two provisions would never have occurred in practice.

into slavery, especially to a foreigner (cf. Rom. 6:15–22; Gal. 4:8–9; 5:1). The jubilee law is thus a guarantee that no Israelite will be reduced to that status again, and it is a celebration of the great redemption when God brought Israel out of Egypt, so that he might be their God and they should be his people (vv. 38, 42, 55; cf. Exod. 19:4–6).

Leviticus 25 and the NT

Robert North discusses the lessons a Christian may learn from this chapter under four heads: social justice, social worship, personal values, and messianic typology.[19] His discussion is difficult to improve on, and here some of his main points are summarized.

Social justice

The jubilee was intended to prevent the accumulation of the wealth of the nation in the hands of a very few. Every Israelite had an inalienable right to his family land and to his freedom. If he lost them through falling into debt he recovered them in the jubilee. The biblical law is opposed equally to the monopolistic tendencies of unbridled capitalism and thorough-going communism, where all property is in state hands. By keeping land within a particular family, the jubilee also promoted family unity.

Social worship

The jubilee is presented in this chapter as an extension of the sabbath day and sabbatical year (vv. 3ff.). True religion is not opposed to a just society. Concern for the one should go hand in hand with concern for the other. The prophetic word "I desire mercy and not sacrifice" (Hos. 6:6; Matt. 9:13; 12:7) was a word to a society who thought God would be satisfied with sacrifice by itself. Had they paid attention to Leviticus, the men of Hosea's day might not have made that mistake.

Personal virtues

"Love your neighbor as yourself" (Lev. 19:18) is the all-embracing moral principle that inspires the jubilee legislation. The NT too recognizes that the rich have an obligation to give to the poor (e.g., 1 John 3:17; Jas. 2:15ff.). The jubilee also draws attention to the fleeting nature of man's earthly abode: *you are resident aliens and settlers with me* (v. 23). Equally Christians must recognize that

19. R. North, *Biblical Jubilee*, pp. 213–231.

they are but pilgrims and sojourners here and look for another city "whose builder and maker is God" (Heb. 11:10). Finally believers in both covenants are assured that those who put God's will first will have all their physical needs provided (Lev. 25:18ff.; cf. Matt. 6:25ff.).

Messianic typology

At Nazareth Jesus declared (Luke 4:18–19):

> *"He has sent me to proclaim release to the captives*
> *and recovering of sight to the blind,*
> *to set at liberty those who are oppressed,*
> *to proclaim the acceptable year of the Lord."*

In Isa. 61:1, from which Jesus was quoting, the word used for "release" *(derôr)* is the same as that found in Lev. 25:10. It seems quite likely, therefore, that the prophetic description of the "acceptable year of the Lord" was partly inspired by the idea of the jubilee year. The messianic age brings liberty to the oppressed and release to the captives.

This age was inaugurated with Christ's first coming (Luke 4:21). It will be completed by his second coming (Jas. 5:1–8; cf. Luke 16:19–31). The jubilee, then, not only looks back to God's first redemption of his people from Egypt (Lev. 25:38, 55), but forward to the "restitution of all things,"[20] "for new heavens and a new earth in which righteousness dwells" (Acts 3:21; 2 Pet. 3:13).

K. EXHORTATION TO OBEY THE LAW: BLESSING AND CURSE (CH. 26)

1 *"Do not make idols for yourselves, or erect carved sacred pillars or put decorated stones in your land for worship, for I am the Lord your God.*

2 *You shall keep my sabbaths and reverence my sanctuary. I am the Lord.*

3 *If you follow my rules and keep my commandments and do them,*

4 *I shall give your rains at the right time, and the land will give its produce and the trees will give their fruit.*

5 *The threshing will last until grape-harvest, and the grape-harvest will last until the sowing, and you will eat your food in plenty and dwell in your land securely.*

6 *I shall give peace in the land and you will lie down without anyone frightening you. I shall exterminate the dangerous wild animals from your land and no army will pass through your land.*

---

20. "Restitution" *(apokatastasis)* is used by Philo to designate the jubilee in *Decalogue* 164.

7 *You will pursue your enemies and they shall fall by the sword before you.*

8 *Five of you will chase a hundred and a hundred of you will chase ten thousand, and your enemies will fall by the sword before you.*

9 *I shall be gracious to you, make you fruitful, multiply you and establish my covenant with you.*

10 *You will eat old harvest until it is stale, and then clear out the old to make way for the new harvest.*

11 *I shall make my dwelling among you and not loathe you.*

12 *I shall walk among you and become your God, and you will become my people.*

13 *I am the Lord your God who brought you out of the land of Egypt from being slaves to them, and I broke the bars of your yoke and enabled you to walk unbowed.*

14 *But if you will not listen to me and will not do all these commandments,*

15 *if you reject my rules and loathe my judgments so as not to do all my commandments and break my covenant,*

16 *I myself shall do this to you: I shall punish you with panic, with disease, and with fever, making your sight fail and your heart ache. You will sow your seed in vain and your enemies will eat it.*

17 *I shall set my face against you and you will be defeated before your enemies; those who hate you will rule you, and you will flee even when no one is chasing you.*

18 *If even then you will not listen to me, I shall discipline you seven times more for your sins.*

19 *I shall smash your strong pride. I shall make your sky like iron and your earth like bronze.*

20 *Your strength will be used up pointlessly, so that the earth will not produce its crops and the trees will not produce their fruit.*

21 *And if you defy me and are not willing to listen to me, I shall smite you another seven times for your sins.*

22 *I shall send the wild beasts of the countryside against you and they will kill your children, destroy your cattle and reduce your population and make all your paths desolate.*

23 *If you are not turned to me by these things and still defy me,*

24 *then I personally shall defy you and shall strike you seven times for your sins.*

25 *I shall bring upon you an avenging sword of covenant vengeance: you will gather in your cities and I shall send a plague in your midst, and you will be given into the power of an enemy.*

26 *When I break your bread supply, ten women will bake your bread in a single oven, they will weigh it again before giving it back, and you will eat but not be satisfied.*

27 *If in spite of this you will not listen to me but defy me,*

28 *I shall defy you in anger and I shall personally discipline you seven times for your sins.*

29 *You will eat the flesh of your sons and daughters.*

30 *I shall destroy your high places, cut down your incense altars, and*

throw your corpses on the wrecks of your idols, and I shall loathe you.

31 *I shall turn your cities into ruins and lay waste your sanctuaries, and shall not smell your soothing aromas.*

32 *I myself shall so desolate the land that your enemies who settle in it will be shocked by it.*

33 *As for you, when I scatter you among the nations, I shall unsheathe the sword after you and your land will become desolate and your cities ruins.*

34 *Then the land will enjoy its sabbaths all the period of its desolation, while you are in the land of your enemies; then the land will rest and enjoy its sabbaths.*

35 *For all the days of desolation it will rest, the rest it did not have during your sabbaths when you dwelt in it.*

36 *I shall bring softness into the hearts of those of you who are left in the lands of their enemies: the sound of a blown leaf will start them running. They will flee as if they were fleeing from the sword. They will fall, even though no one is chasing them.*

37 *They will stumble into each other as in battle, though there is no one chasing them, and you will not be able to stand up to your enemies.*

38 *And you will perish among the nations and the land of your enemies will eat you up.*

39 *Those of you who are left will rot away in your guilt in the lands of your enemies, and they will rot away in the guilt of their fathers as they did.*

40 *If they then confess their guilt and the guilt of their fathers that they dealt treacherously with me and even defied me,*

41 *so that I even defied them and brought them into the land of their enemies, or if then their uncircumcised heart is humbled and they accept their guilt.*

42 *I shall remember my covenant with Jacob and also my covenant with Isaac, and shall also remember my covenant with Abraham, and I shall remember the land.*

43 *The land must be forsaken by them and enjoy its sabbaths, when it lies waste without them, and they must accept the punishment for their guilt, because they have rejected my judgments and loathed my rules.*

44 *But even in spite of this, when they are in the land of their enemies, I shall not reject them or loathe them, so as to destroy them utterly and break my covenant with them, for I am the Lord their God.*

45 *But I shall remember for their benefit the covenant with the men of the first generation, whom I brought out of the land of Egypt in the sight of the nations in order that I might become their God: I am the Lord.''*

46 *These are the rules, judgments, and laws which the Lord put between himself and the Israelites in Mount Sinai by the hand of Moses.*

The Structure of Leviticus 26

Leviticus 26 is a collection of blessings on those who keep the law and curses on those who do not. A collection of such blessings and curses was the usual way to close a major legal text in biblical times. The main section of Deuteronomy ends with a similar series of blessings and curses (Deut. 28). We also find this pattern in Exod. 23:25ff. and Josh. 24:20.

It is a pattern that occurs outside the Bible in literature spanning the first three millennia B.C. Legal collections such as the laws of Ur-Nammu, Lipit-Ishtar, and Hammurabi, Babylonian boundary stones, and Hittite, Aramean, and Assyrian treaties typically conclude with a section of blessings and curses.[1]

The resemblance between the biblical and legal texts is more than formal, however; it often extends to content. Many of the biblical curses find parallels in extrabiblical texts.[2] There is nevertheless an important and significant difference in outlook. Whereas the biblical texts are straightforward promises about how God will respond to his people's behavior, in blessings on the obedient and judgment on the careless, the nonbiblical texts are prayers to the gods to act. Furthermore, the Bible only acknowledges one God as creator and judge who will carry out these threats. Other writings appeal to a plurality of deities, requesting each god responsible for a particular sphere of natural effects, rain, disease, war, and the like, to act in his own way if the treaty or law was not obeyed.

Internally, the chapter is quite clearly structured. Phrases that were keys to the division of the material in previous chapters reappear in this one, "I am the Lord (your God)" (vv. 1, 2, 13, 44, 45). As in ch. 19 we have a double formula at the beginning and end of the chapter. These phrases suggest the following division of the material.

1–2   The fundamentals of the law
3–13 Blessings
14–45 Curses
46   Summary

1. For more detailed discussion of the covenant treaty form see K. Baltzer, *The Covenant Formulary* (Oxford: Blackwell, 1971); D. J. McCarthy, *Treaty and Covenant* (Rome: Pontifical Biblical Institute, 1963) and *OT Covenant* (Oxford: Blackwell, 1972).
2. See D. R. Hillers, *Treaty-Curses and the OT Prophets* (Rome: Pontifical Biblical Institute, 1964).

The curses are further divided into six subsections by the introductory clauses, "If you will not listen to me (vv. 14, 18, 21, 23, 27), I shall punish you (seven times for your sins)" (vv. 16, 18, 21, 24, 28). Verse 40 states the converse and offers a promise of restoration when the people repent.

14–17 General curses—illness, famine, defeat
18–20 Drought and bad harvest
21–22 Wild animals
23–26 War, leading to plague and famine
27–39 War, leading to cannibalism, devastation and deportation from land
40–45 Promise of restoration

Hoffmann[3] has suggested that the blessings can also be divided into five subsections (viz., vv. 4–5, 6, 7–8, 9–10, 11–12). But he does not base this on content or form. The five blessings do not match the five curses in subject matter, and he does not draw attention to any phrases that recur. Using the last criterion as our guide the blessings fall into three groups each beginning with "I shall give" (w^{e}naṭaṭtî, vv. 4, 6, 11).

The blessings are then divided as follows:

4–5   the gift of rain and good harvests
6–10   the gift of peace, no wild animals, defeats, or famine
11–13 the gift of God's presence

Though the blessings do not exactly match the curses in length[4] or number, the subject matter of both is similar and there are a number of clear echoes of the blessings in the curses.[5]

The Fundamentals of the Law (1–2)

It is characteristic of the biblical collections of law to include a reminder of some of the most important points just before the end (cf. Exod. 23:20–24; Deut. 29). There are brief allusions here to some of the commandments (Exod. 20:3ff.), especially as they apply in the land of Canaan, though Lev. 19:3–4, 30 provide the closest verbal parallels. It is striking to find reverence for the sanctuary singled out for special mention, but the purity of the tabernacle does

3. Hoffmann II, pp. 363ff.
4. It is usual for the number and length of curses greatly to exceed the number of blessings, e.g., Deut. 28, laws of Hammurabi, and most of the extrabiblical treaties.
5. "Covenant" (vv. 9, 15, 25, 42, 44); rules, commandments (vv. 3, 14–15); become their (your) God (vv. 12, 45); brought out of the land of Egypt (vv. 13, 45); loathe (vv. 11, 15, 30, 43, 44); "and I shall give" (vv. 4, 6, 11, 17, 19, 30–31).

occupy a very important place in the Levitical law. Bonar comments, "All declension and decay may be said to be begun wherever we see these two ordinances despised—the *sabbath* and the *sanctuary*. They are the *outward* fence around the *inward love* commanded by v. 1."[6]

The Blessings of Obedience (3–13)

The gift of rain and good harvests (4–5)

For maximum effect the rains must come at the right season. Verse 4 promises this, and the consequence is described in v. 5; the farmers will have to work non-stop to gather in all the crops. The grain was usually gathered in early summer, then there was a gap of two months until the grapes and olives were ready to pick. Once the rains began in late fall or early winter, sowing would commence.[7] The magnificent harvests will mean that there will be no worry about food supplies. "You will eat your food in plenty and dwell in your land securely" (v. 5) (cf. Judg. 6:11; 18:7; Isa. 47:8). Jesus also promised that those who put God's kingdom first need not worry about food and clothing (Matt. 6:25–33).

The gift of peace (6–10)

Food without security is of limited value. If enemies invade, they may deprive the country of much of its produce, as happened in Gideon's day (Judg. 6:3–4, 11). The next blessing on the obedient assures them of peace, or if their enemies do attack, of easy and convincing victories (vv. 7–8; cf. Judg. 7). Even the wild animals will not harm them. In biblical times lions and bears still inhabited Canaan (Judg. 14:5; 2 K. 2:24; Isa. 11:6–9). Safe from the attack of human and animal foe, the people would grow in numbers and see the promise to Abraham fulfilled (v. 9; Gen. 17:6; cf. Gen. 1:28; 9:1, 7; 35:11).

The gift of God's presence (11–13)

I shall make my dwelling among you (v. 11). A more literal translation would be, "I shall give my tabernacle among you." The tabernacle was designed to be the place where God dwelt among his people (Exod. 25:8), but Israel's sins could make it an empty shrine (Exod. 33:14ff.; cf. Lev. 16:16). The blessings reach a great climax in reassuring the people that if they are faithful, all the promises

6. Bonar, p. 473.
7. Details of the agricultural calendar in 10th-century Canaan are recorded in the Gezer calendar; see de Vaux, *Ancient Israel*, p. 184; translation in *ANET*, p. 320.

included in the covenant will be fulfilled. God will *walk*[8] with his people, as he did in the garden of Eden before the fall (Gen. 3:8; cf. Deut. 23:15 [Eng. 14]). What God had repeatedly promised as the goal of the covenant, "I shall become your God," will then be seen to be true (Gen. 17:8; Exod. 6:7; 29:45–46; Lev. 11:45; cf. Exod. 19:5–6).

The psalmists (e.g., Ps. 72) and the prophets (e.g., Isa. 11) look forward to a time when the promised blessings would become a reality. But it is Ezekiel who makes most use of Leviticus as a direct inspiration for his prophecies. He looks forward to a new age when God would send a faithful shepherd, like David, to save the people from wild beasts (Ezek. 34:25; cf. Lev. 26:6). In the New Covenant there will be abundant rain and harvests (Ezek. 34:26–27; cf. Lev. 26:4–5, 13). The people will not be oppressed by the nations (Ezek. 34:28; cf. Lev. 26:7–8). They will be multiplied and fruitful (Ezek. 36:10–11; cf. Lev. 26:9). They shall become God's people, and his dwelling shall be with them (Ezek. 36:28; 37:24–27; cf. Lev. 26:2, 11–12).

The Curses for Disobedience (14–45)

First curse: general warnings (14–17)

In the curses the converse of the blessings is spelled out. It was usual in legal texts for the curses to be much fuller and longer than the blessings section (cf. Deut. 28 and introduction above). But this disproportion has a positive didactic purpose as well. It is very easy to take the blessings of rain, peace, and even God's presence for granted. It is salutary to be reminded in detail of what life is like when his providential gifts are removed.

If they *reject my rules* they thereby *break my covenant* (v. 15; cf. v. 44). In every sphere Israel will face failure. Physical and mental disease will be accompanied by defeat in battle. For similar threats against covenant-breakers see Deut. 28 (cf. v. 16 with Deut. 28:22, 33, 65; 1 Sam. 2:33; cf. v. 17 with Deut. 28:25).

Second curse: drought and poor harvests (18–20)

I shall discipline you seven times more (v. 18). These judgments are described as *discipline*. Throughout the Bible divine discipline is referred to: God punishes his people not merely because they de-

---

8. An unusual form (Hithpael) of the common verb "to go" is used here; it often has the meaning "to walk to and fro." This word is also used of the patriarchs' walk with God in Gen. 5:22, 24; 6:9; 17:1; 24:40; 48:15.

serve it, but because he loves them and wants to correct their foolish ways (Deut. 8:5; Jer. 30:11; 31:18; Ps. 38:2 [Eng. 1]; 94:12; Prov. 3:11-12; Heb. 12:5-11). Amos laments that, despite judgments of famine and drought, disease and defeat, "yet you did not return to me" (Amos 4:6, 8, 9, 10, 11).

Seven times more for your sins (vv. 18, 21, 24, 28). Seven seems to be a round number for repeated punishments (cf. Ps. 79:12; Prov. 24:16; Isa. 4:1). It is an appropriate and evocative number in view of the importance of the seventh in Israelite religion,[9] and it serves as a reminder that these punishments are for breach of the heart of this religion, the covenant (cf. v. 25). The book of Revelation portrays a series of sevenfold judgments overtaking the world in the last days (Rev. 5-16).

I shall smash your strong pride (v. 19). Prosperity often leads to pride and self-confidence (Deut. 8:11-19; 32:15). Judgment cuts a man down to size and reminds him on whom he really depends (cf. Prov. 8:13; 16:18; Isa. 2:9-22; 13:11; Luke 1:51; Jas. 4:6).

I shall make your sky like iron (v. 19)—more literally, "I shall give your sky like iron and your earth like bronze." Here the phraseology of v. 4 is ironically echoed. God does not forsake his rebellious people: his gifts to them are just different. Instead of rain he gives drought and crop failure. This vivid image, describing the effect of a merciless sun which makes the ground too hard for ploughing, is found in slightly different forms in Deut. 28:23 and VTE 528-532.

Third curse: wild animals (21-22)
This is the reverse of vv. 6 and 9. The early "Samaritans" were afflicted in this way according to 2 K. 17:25-26. Ezekiel repeats this curse in his preaching (Ezek. 5:17; 14:15, 21). *If you defy me* (v. 21) (lit. "walk obstinately with me") is a phrase peculiar to this chapter (cf. vv. 23-24, 27-28, 40-41).

Fourth curse: war (23-26)
Whenever God has not given peace (v. 6) mankind has suffered the horrors of war listed in vv. 23-26. For the biblical writers wars against Israel were not capricious; they were sent by God as a *sword of covenant vengeance* (v. 25) to punish his people for their infractions of the covenant (Judg. 2:11-15; 2 K. 17:7ff.; Isa. 10:5ff.; Luke 19:42-44). Frequently the prophets Jeremiah and Ezekiel refer to

9. Seventh day, month, year, etc. See above, p. 301.

sword and plague as heaven-sent judgments, on occasions clearly quoting from Leviticus.[10]

Fifth curse: war and exile (27–39)

In ghastly detail some other aspects of war are now mentioned, including cannibalism (v. 29; cf. Deut. 28:53–57; 2 K. 6:28–29; Lam. 2:20), wholesale slaughter (v. 30; cf. Amos 8:3; Ezek. 6:5), destruction of cities and sanctuaries (vv. 30–31; cf. Ezek. 6:3ff.), and dispersion among the nations (v. 33; cf. Jer. 31:10; 49:32; Ezek. 5:10, 12; 12:14, etc.).

While we may look on these events merely as the unhappy side-effects of war, there is much more to them than that. They are a denial of all the hopes enshrined in the covenant with Abraham, that his descendants would become a great nation, inherit the land of Canaan, and so on (cf. Gen. 15, 17). They represent a reversal of the blessing in vv. 11–13 that God would be present with his people. Even the symbols of God's presence with his people, *high places*,[11] *incense altars, sanctuaries,* and sacrifices producing *soothing aromas* will be destroyed (vv. 30–31).

Promise of restoration (40–46)

Yet the judgments are still described as "discipline" (v. 28, cf. v. 18 above). They are not God's last word to his erring people. Judgment does not prove that God has rejected his people. Rather he punishes them because they are his own (Amos 3:2). So if they confess their sin and humble their hearts,[12] God will remember his covenant with the patriarchs (vv. 42–45). What this remembering will mean in practice is not spelled out here, but Deut. 30, a similar passage in a similar context, explains that it will mean restoration to the land of promise and prosperity there. This would seem to be implicit in this Leviticus passage too.

---

10. See the concordances. Ezekiel three times refers to breaking the food supply, 4:16; 5:16; 14:13; cf. Lev. 26:26.

11. *High places* (v. 30) generally refers to Canaanite places of worship. On this term see P. H. Vaughan, *The Meaning of Bāmâ in the OT* (London: Cambridge UP, 1974). Upon entry into the land, Israel was to destroy such shrines (Num. 33:52). Those kings who did not were viewed as law-breakers (2 K. 16:4). Here, however, they seem to be regarded as legitimate, perhaps an indicator of the early date of the material. The reference to *sanctuaries* (v. 31, plural) also seems to be early.

12. *Accept (the punishment for) the guilt* (vv. 41, 43). *'Āwōn* means both "guilt" and "punishment for guilt" (BDB 730b). *Accept (rātsāh)* is the word used of God accepting a sacrifice (see 1:4 for further discussion).

Leviticus 26 and the NT

The blessings and curses of this chapter are addressed to the elect nation of Israel. The prophets saw the curses fulfilled in the tribulations that culminated in the exile, while Ezekiel (Ezek. 34–37) looked forward to the fulfilment of the blessings in the messianic age. But the dawning of that age brings new complications to the interpretation of this chapter. The elect are not to be found now in Israel alone, but among all nations. The kingdom promised to the Church is a spiritual one, not an earthly one (cf. John 18:36). How does the NT see the relevance of this chapter? Does it apply only to Israel, to the Church, or to the whole world? Are the blessings and curses to be understood entirely spiritually or are they experienced in this life as well? Some of these questions seem to receive no clear answer, but in some cases we can be more definite.

First the NT does consider that the nation of Israel is still God's covenant people and subject, therefore, to the blessings and curses entailed in this chapter. Christ's warnings to his fellow countrymen presuppose that they are God's covenant people, liable to God's judgment if they do not listen to his word. Some of the curses in Lev. 26 have their counterparts in Christ's teaching about wars and famines and the destruction of the temple (Mark 13//Luke 19–21).

Paul categorically asserts that the covenant with the Israelites has not been invalidated by their unbelief. "The gifts and call of God are irrevocable" (Rom. 11:29)[13] simply means that they must suffer the covenant curses rather than enjoy its blessings. But one day he expects them to be saved (Rom. 11:26), just as Lev. 26 and Deut. 30 do. There seems to be a hint of this in Jesus' own teaching as well, when he speaks of Jerusalem being "trodden down by the Gentiles until the times of the Gentiles are fulfilled" (Luke 21:24; cf. Rom. 11:25).

The NT also seems to regard the principle of blessing and curse as applying to the Church, individually and corporately.[14] In both testaments salvation is brought by the grace of God, whether that grace is to be seen in the promises to Abraham or in the death of Christ; but those who accept that grace will enjoy its privileges in doing God's will but will suffer if they do not. Thus Jesus speaks of

13. Paul's views are presented most fully in Rom. 9:27–11:32.
14. See Rev. 2–3.

rewards for the faithful disciples and warns shirkers that their laxity will not pass unnoticed in the last judgment (e.g., Matt. 5:19; 6:25ff.; Luke 11:41ff.). Paul expects all to appear before God's judgment seat to receive the reward for the things done on earth (1 Cor. 3:10–15; 2 Cor. 5:10).

Though the NT seems to expect that it will only be at the last judgment that the blessings and curses will finally be seen to be fairly distributed, the Gospels and Epistles also envisage a partial and provisional fulfilment in this life. Jesus promised, "seek first his kingdom and his righteousness, and all these things (i.e., food and clothing) shall be yours as well" (Matt. 6:33). Paul ascribed the illness and death of Corinthian believers to their misbehavior at the Lord's supper (1 Cor. 11:30; cf. Lev. 26:16). But the NT does not look for an exact correspondence between the present lot of the believer and his final glory.[15] In some societies indeed "all who desire to live a godly life in Christ Jesus will be persecuted" (2 Tim. 3:12).

Finally, the NT points out that as the whole world enjoys God's bounty (Matt. 5:45; Acts 17:25) and should believe in the gospel, so all men should fear his curse (Acts 17:30–31). What this means in detail is spelled out in the book of Revelation: many of the horrifying judgments described in Rev. 6ff. find their original setting in the covenant curses of Lev. 26 and Deut. 28.

L. REDEMPTION OF VOTIVE GIFTS (CH. 27)

1 *The Lord spoke to Moses as follows:*

2 *"Speak to the Israelites and say to them: If a man makes an unusual vow to the Lord involving the valuation of persons,*

3 *the valuation of a male between twenty and sixty years of age shall be fifty silver shekels, that is, sacred shekels,*

4 *but a female's valuation shall be thirty shekels.*

5 *For a male aged between five and twenty years the valuation shall be twenty shekels, but for a female ten shekels.*

6 *Between a month and five years old the valuation shall be five shekels for a male and three shekels for a female.*

7 *For sixty years and over the valuation shall be fifteen shekels for a male and ten shekels for a female.*

8 *If a man is poorer than the valuation, he must be stood before the priest and the priest must value him; according to what the man who vows can afford, the priest must value him.*

15. Nor does the OT; see, for example, Ps. 73 or the book of Job.

9 *If (anyone makes a vow involving) an animal that may be offered in sacrifice to the Lord, all he gives to the Lord shall be holy.*

10 *He may not change it or substitute good for bad or bad for good. If he does in fact substitute one animal for another, both it and the substitute become holy.*

11 *If (anyone makes a vow involving) any unclean animal that may not be offered in sacrifice to the Lord, he must stand the animal before the priest.*

12 *The priest must assess how good or bad it is: his valuation shall be binding.*

13 *If he really wants to redeem it, he must add a fifth to the valuation.*

14 *If a man dedicates his house as a holy gift for the Lord, the priest shall assess how good or bad it is: whatever the priest values it at shall stand.*

15 *If the dedicator wants to redeem his house, he must add a fifth to the valuation price and then he may have it.*

16 *If a man dedicates to the Lord part of the land that he owns, its valuation shall be proportionate to its seed: a field yielding a homer of barley seed is valued at fifty shekels of silver.*

17 *That valuation shall stand if he dedicates his field from the year of jubilee.*

18 *But if he dedicates his field after the jubilee, the priest must calculate for him the money according to the number of years left until the (next) jubilee, and it shall be deducted from the (full) valuation.*

19 *If the dedicator really wants to redeem the field, he must add a fifth to the valuation price and then it shall remain his.*

20 *But if he does not redeem the field or if he has sold the field to another man, it may not be redeemed again.*

21 *When the field is released in the jubilee year, it becomes a holy gift for the Lord like a devoted field: it becomes priestly property.*

22 *If a man dedicates to the Lord a field he has purchased which is not part of his (family) property,*

23 *the priest must calculate for him the amount of the valuation until the year of jubilee, and he must give the valuation the same day as a holy gift to the Lord.*

24 *In the jubilee year the field shall return to the man from whom it was bought, i.e., the man whose family property it is.*

25 *Every valuation shall be fixed on the basis of the holy shekel, at twenty gerahs to the shekel.*

26 *No man may dedicate to the Lord a firstling animal whose firstlings are normally offered, such as an ox or a sheep. It is (already) the Lord's.*

27 *But if it is an unclean animal, he may ransom it at its valuation and add a fifth to it; and if he does not want to redeem it, it must be sold for its valuation.*

28 *But every devoted thing which a man may devote to the Lord from all that are his, whether it is human, animal, or part of the land he owns, may not be sold or redeemed. Every devoted thing is holy: it is the Lord's.*

335

29 *Any human being that is devoted may not be ransomed: he must be put to death.*

30 *Every tithe of the land, of the harvest of the land or the fruit trees, is the Lord's; it is a holy thing for the Lord.*

31 *If a man redeems part of his tithe, he must add a fifth to it.*

32 *Every tithe of cattle and sheep, i.e., all that are counted by passing under the shepherd's staff, the tenth one is a holy thing for the Lord.*

33 *One must not consider whether they are good or bad or make any substitution in them, and if one does make substitution, both it and the substitute animal shall be holy. It may not be redeemed."*

34 *These are the commandments which the Lord commanded Moses for the Israelites in Mount Sinai.*

Leviticus 27: Vows

It is a puzzle why ch. 27, which deals with vows, should appear in its present position, since ch. 26 with its blessings and curses would have made a fitting conclusion to the book. Generally commentators offer a historical explanation for the chapter's position: either that it comes here because this was the law that was revealed next at Sinai (the conservative view), or that it was a later addition to the holiness code in Lev. 17–26 (the liberal view).

Neither view, though, really explains why the law-giver or editor put the laws on vows here rather than somewhere else.[1] It could be an association of ideas. The blessings and curses (ch. 26) are in a sense God's vows to his people, his promises as to what he will do for them in the future. It could be that this prompts consideration of how men make vows to God (ch. 27). Alternatively, men frequently make vows in times of stress, and more rarely in times of great prosperity. Ch. 26 first deals briefly with times of blessing and then at length with times of cursing. The latter is followed immediately by a section (ch. 27) which shows how vows should be honored.

The Structure of Leviticus 27

1	Introduction
2–13	Vows Involving People and Animals
	2–8 Vows of persons
	9–10 Vows involving clean animals
	11–13 Vows involving unclean animals

1. Hertz, p. 305, suggests that as the book begins with laws dealing with the sanctuary it is appropriate that it should close with a similar topic.

336

14–24 Dedication of Houses and Land
    14–15 Houses
    16–24 Land
25–33 Miscellaneous Regulations about Vows
    25   Standard of payment
    26–27 Treatment of first-born
    28–29 The ban
    30–33 Tithes
34   Conclusion

The first two sections, dealing with vows (vv. 2–13) and dedications (vv. 14–24), are clearly structured. Both begin with a main case introduced by "if a man" (*'îsh kî*) (vv. 2, 14) and subsidiary cases are introduced by "and if" *(we'im)*. This pattern is more like that found in the early chapters of Leviticus than that of chs. 18–26.

The Use of Vows

Facing death, even hardened atheists are known to pray. Throughout human history, when men have found themselves in dire straits they have prayed for deliverance and made vows to God, promising to do something for God if he rescued them. The OT gives a number of examples of men making vows in such circumstances. Jacob, fleeing from his brother, offered to tithe his goods if God brought him home safely (Gen. 28:20ff.). Israel, after suffering defeat by the Canaanites, vowed the enemy cities to total destruction (Num. 21:2). Jonah made vows in the belly of the fish (Jon. 2:10 [Eng. 9]).

Vows are made in the heat of the moment. In retrospect, when the crisis is over, they may well seem foolish and unnecessary, and the person who made the vow may be tempted to forget it or only fulfil it partially. Scripture includes a number of warnings about such an attitude. Typical of the biblical view is Eccl. 5:3–4 (4–5), "When you vow a vow to God, do not delay paying it; for he has no pleasure in fools. Pay what you vow. It is better that you should not vow than that you should vow and not pay" (cf. Deut. 23:22–24 [21–23]; Prov. 20:25). It may well be part of the purpose of this chapter to discourage rash swearing by fixing a relatively high price for the discharge of the vows, and penalizing those who change their minds.[2] If a man tries to substitute a different animal for the one he has promised, he forfeits both animals (vv. 10, 33). If he wishes to

2. See Saalschütz, pp. 358ff.

redeem the property he vows, he must pay 20 percent extra (vv. 13, 15, 19, 27, 31).

Vows of Persons (2–8)

The most basic kind of vow is to dedicate oneself to the service of God, as Absalom did in exile (2 Sam. 15:8), or as the psalmist did (Ps. 116:14–18). Both use a word which often implies slavery, in which case the substance of their vow was to make themselves God's slaves. Had the regulations permitted, they could have worked as slaves in the temple; but that was a privilege reserved for the priests and Levites. To free themselves from the vow, they had instead to pay to the sanctuary the price they would have commanded in the slave market.[3] Fifty shekels was a reasonable price for a male adult slave[4] (v. 3; cf. 2 K. 15:20). Twenty shekels was paid for a boy (v. 5; cf. Gen. 37:2, 28). Women generally fetched less than men in the market, so if they vowed themselves to God they had to pay less: 50-67 percent of the male rate according to vv. 4–7. That children are included in this table suggests that a man might vow his family as well as his own person to God.

These figures are very large. The average wage of a worker in biblical times was about one shekel per month.[5] It is little wonder that few could afford the valuations set out here (v. 8).

Vows of Clean Animals (9–10)

In a culture where animal sacrifice was the normal form of worship, the vowing of a suitable sacrificial animal was frequent (see Lev. 7:16; 22:18ff.; Deut. 12:11, 17; Ps. 50:14; 56:13 [Eng. 12]; 66:13, etc.). When a man made a vow he would name a particular animal that he would offer (e.g., Judg. 11:30–31). When the time came for the sacrifice, he might well think he had been too generous, and seek to offer another less valuable beast. Verse 10 gives a stern warning against such a move: *both it and the substitute become holy,* i.e., are forfeit to the sanctuary.

---

3. G. J. Wenham, "Leviticus 27:2–8 and the Price of Slaves," *ZAW* 90 (1978), pp. 264–65. On the term *valuation ('erkᵉkā)* (vv. 2ff.) see above on 5:15, and E. A. Speiser, *Oriental and Biblical Studies,* pp. 124ff.
4. See I. Mendelsohn, *Slavery in the Ancient Near East* (New York: Oxford UP, 1949), pp. 117ff.
5. So Mendelsohn, *Slavery,* p. 118; cf. de Vaux, *Ancient Israel,* p. 76.

Vows of Unclean Animals (11–13)

Vows involving unclean animals were also permitted in Israel. This was not as anomalous as first appears. If ordinary laymen could vow themselves to divine slavery in the sanctuary (see vv. 2–7) even though they could not serve there, so unclean animals could be vowed even though they could not be sacrificed. They could be used by the priests, or if the priests had no need of them, sold for their profit. If, however, the man preferred to keep his animal, he could redeem it for 20 percent more than the priest's valuation (v. 13).

Dedications (14–24)

Houses (14–15)

A new section begins in v. 14. It is introduced by the word for *if (kî)* that indicates a major regulation. It marks a transition from vv. 2–13, which deal with people and living animals, to vv. 14–24 dealing with inanimate objects such as houses and land. Things such as these are "dedicated," literally "made or declared holy" (see vv. 14–19, 22, 26). This evidently has the same effect as vowing—they become *holy* (cf. vv. 9 and 14). As a result, the house or piece of land passes into the possession of the sanctuary and the priests may dispose of it as they wish. If the dedicator wishes to retain possession of his house, he may do so by paying 20 percent more than the priestly valuation (v. 15).

It seems likely that the houses referred to here are town houses, which did not count as part of a family's estate and therefore could be bought and sold freely (cf. 25:29ff.). Dedication of land was more complicated, as the following paragraph (vv. 16–24) explains, because in the jubilee it normally reverted to the original owner. Village houses and the land on which they were built belonged to the family estate, and therefore could not be given outright to the sanctuary.

Dedication of land (16–24)

If a man dedicates part of his estate to God, he is expected to redeem it before the year of jubilee by paying 20 percent more than the priestly valuation (vv. 19–20). This valuation is determined by the size of the field and the number of years to the next jubilee. *A field yielding a homer of barley seed*[6] is valued at a shekel for every year

6. A homer *(kōr)* varied between 29 and 53 gallons, or 134–241 liters; de Vaux, *Ancient Israel*, p. 202.

until the jubilee, giving a maximum of fifty shekels (vv. 16ff.). In Mesopotamia the standard price of barley was a shekel per homer,[7] so that an annual valuation of one shekel per year for a field of one homer seems quite appropriate here. The value of the field was thus equal to the value of the crops it would produce until the jubilee. We cannot be sure that barley was as cheap in Israel as in Mesopotamia, where grain yields were outstandingly good. The OT suggests that fifteen shekels per homer was cheap compared with famine prices (2 K. 7:1), but presumably normal prices were even lower. If barley did cost more than a shekel per homer in Israel, this would mean that an owner could redeem his field for less than the value of the crops. This would be reasonable, since once he had redeemed the field, he would have to work to produce any crops.

Most commentators, however, translate v. 16b differently, viz., "a field *requiring* a homer of barley seed."[8] Since yields of grain in Israel varied between thirty and one hundred fold (Matt. 13:8) this would put a very low value on the land. This might, of course, be deliberate policy in order to encourage redemption of the family estate (v. 19).

Certainly failure to redeem the land before the year of jubilee is penalized. Such land is forfeit to the priests (vv. 20–21). Verse 20 mentions another circumstance in which the land is forfeit, *if he has sold it to another man.* How can a man sell a piece of land that he had dedicated to the sanctuary? Some commentators see this as sharp practice by the owner, which explains the penalty. Keil[9] regards it as laziness. He thinks that if a man dedicated a field to the sanctuary, he still had to cultivate it, as the priests would not have time with their religious duties to work it themselves. The owner could pay the redemption money year by year and keep the produce himself. But if he decided to "sell," i.e., let[10] his field to another

7. For prices of barley see R. P. Maloney, *CBQ* 36 (1974), pp. 4ff.; P. Garelli and V. Nikiprowetsky, *Le Proche-Orient Asiatique: Les Empires mésopotamiens, Israel* (Paris: Presses universitaires de France, 1974), pp. 273f., 285f.
8. The ambiguity arises because the Hebrew does not make it clear whether *seed* = seed or crops. The latter meaning is clear in v. 30, "harvest (i.e., seed) of the land." The Hebrew would be more literally translated "seed (*zera'*) of a homer of barley is valued at fifty shekels." "Seed" is thus ambiguous. Does it refer to the seed sown or to the seed harvested? Most commentators suppose the former: that a field *requiring* a homer of seed is valued at one shekel for each year until the jubilee. Following de Vaux, *Ancient Israel*, p. 168, I prefer to think that a field *producing* a homer of seed is valued at this price. *Zera'* clearly has this sense in v. 30, "harvest of the land," and it makes for a more reasonable valuation of the land.
9. Keil, pp. 483f.
10. Every sale of land was in effect only a letting of the land until the year of jubilee. See 25:13ff.

man, then it did not revert to him in the jubilee but to the sanctuary (v. 21). *Like a devoted field* (v. 21)—see v. 28.

Verses 22–24 consider the slightly different case of land which has been bought but does not belong to the family estate. In the year of jubilee it will revert to the original owner (v. 24). It may, however, be dedicated to the Lord at any time prior to the jubilee, but in that case it must be immediately redeemed at the valuation fixed by the priest (v. 23).

Miscellaneous Regulations (25–33)

Standard of payment (25)

A shekel weighed about half an ounce (12 grams), but there was quite a lot of variation according to local standards.[11] Disputes about dedications to the sanctuary are to be determined by the sanctuary shekel.

The first-born (26–27)

First-born animals automatically belonged to God (Exod. 13:2; 34:19–20) and therefore could not be dedicated to the Lord in a vow. The old law (Exod. 34:20) prescribed that first-born unclean animals should be ransomed by a lamb or killed. In this section redemption is allowed on the usual terms, payment of the animal's value plus 20 percent to the sanctuary.

The ban (28–29)

Banning or devoting was a more solemn and irreversible vow than ordinary dedication. Anyone or anything that was devoted to the Lord could not be ransomed. It was usual to invoke the ban in wars against the native inhabitants of Canaan. In divine judgment all Israel's enemies and their property were devoted to the Lord (e.g., Num. 21:2; Deut. 7:2; 1 Sam. 15). It could also be used as a judicial sentence against idolaters (Exod. 22:19 [Eng. 20]; Deut. 13:16 [15]). It seems unlikely that ordinary Israelites could pronounce such vows; only the recognized leaders had authority to declare a death sentence.[12]

Tithes (30–33)

After God had appeared to Jacob at Bethel, Jacob made a vow saying, "If God will be with me . . . of all that thou givest me I will give the tenth to thee" (Gen. 28:20–22). This indicates that tithes are

11. See de Vaux, *Ancient Israel*, p. 205.
12. See Saalschütz, pp. 368ff.; *THWAT* I, pp. 635–39.

a kind of vow. Lev. 27, therefore, allows the rules governing ordinary vows to apply to tithes as well (cf. vv. 9–13 with 30–33).

Leviticus 27 and the NT

The custom of making vows and tithing is simply assumed in the NT (see Acts 18:18; 21:23; Matt. 23:23) as it is in Lev. 27. But underlying these Levitical laws, we noted a concern that a man should keep his vows; he should not rashly promise to give something to God in the heat of the moment and then later, when he had cooled down, retract his promise. Changes of mind are penalized by a 20 percent surcharge on the vow. The NT is similarly concerned that men should keep their word: "Let your yes be yes and your no be no" (Matt. 5:33–37; 23:16–22; 2 Cor. 1:17–20; Jas. 5:12). Only in the case of vows involving family property (Lev. 27:16–24) does the law appear to facilitate retraction of vows by valuing the land rather cheaply. This enabled the rash dedicator of land to recover the family estate without too much difficulty. If the land was lost for good, it would have led a man into poverty, unable to support his parents or children adequately. Jesus, too, saw this danger in vows. It was wrong, he said, to dedicate something to the temple if it left your parents without support. The Pharisees, who encouraged such irresponsible vows as a mark of piety, were in fact disregarding the commandment to honor one's father and mother (Matt. 15:3–9// Mark 7:9–13.

Epilogue

With these laws on vows and tithes Leviticus closes. On first reading it seems a strange point at which to end. But the theme of vowing is in fact closely related to the principal concerns of the whole book. Men who dedicate themselves to God become as it were God's slaves, holy to the Lord. Some men, the priests, can indeed serve God in the sanctuary. Chs. 8–10 tell of the ordination of Aaron and his sons to the priesthood. Chs. 21–22 expound the qualities looked for in priests, qualities which symbolize the perfection and holiness of God. Those not of priestly stock can still serve God, indeed they must be holy for God is holy (11:44–45; 19:2; 20:7, 26). This theme runs through chs. 11–20: the elect people of God must visibly embody the character of God. In their choice of food, in sickness and in health, in their family life, in their honest and upright dealing, and in their love of neighbor, they show the world what God is like.

Vowed animals are intended for sacrifice; they too become holy when vowed. Sacrifice was the heart of OT worship, and Leviticus gives more precise directions about sacrificial procedures than any other part of Scripture, and also lists the occasions when animals had to be offered (chs. 1–7, 12–17, 22–23). Finally a man can dedicate land or property to God, recalling the jubilee legislation (ch. 25).

Thus this chapter in effect recapitulates and reminds us of the great themes that have engaged our attention in the rest of the book. Lev. 27 points out that holiness is more than a matter of divine call and correct ritual. Its attainment requires the total consecration of a man's life to God's service. It involves giving yourself, your family, and all your possessions to God.

"Be holy, for I the Lord your God am holy."

I. INDEX OF CHIEF SUBJECTS

344

II. INDEX OF AUTHORS

INDEX OF AUTHORS

348

III. INDEX OF SCRIPTURE REFERENCES

MARK			22:37	111	ROMANS	
1:6	176		23:45	237	1:18–32	281
1:11	64				1:27	259, 260
2:23ff	312				2–3	145
5:25	221		JOHN		3:23	213
5:34	224		1:14	18, 151	5:8	33
5:41	224		1:17–18	145	6:5ff	142
7	225		2:11	151	6:15–22	323
7:9–13	342		3	27	6:17–19	25
7:10	34, 279, 281		3:16	64	6:23	65
7:11	50		4:9	182	8:20ff	213
7:14ff	162, 181		4:24	151	8:32	64
7:19	182		5:3	297	9:27–11:32	333
10:2–12	260		5:30ff	145	10:5	253, 260
10:45	64		6:54	248	10:16	111
12:30–31	33		8:1ff	281	11:25, 26	333
12:31	274		8:12	252	11:28–29	310
12:33	63, 274		8:51	253	11:29	333
13	333		10:28	32	12:1–2	72, 82
14:3	213		12:38	111	13:4	313
15:38	237		14:15	32	13:9	260, 269, 274
			17:24	151	13:13	252
LUKE			18:28	82	14:2–3	247
1:15	159		18:36	333	14:14–15	247
1:51	331		19:14	306	14:15	183
2:9	151		19:36	306	15:4	vii
2:22–24	189		20:26	319		
2:24	63				I CORINTHIANS	
3:22	64				2:8	151
4:18–19	324		ACTS		3:8ff	313
4:21	324		2:1	304	3:10–15	34, 334
6:1ff	312		2:11	151	5	247, 260
7:36ff	224		2:43	151	5:1–5	225
8:43	221		3–5	153	5:7–8	306
9:31	151		3:21	324	6	272
9:59–60	158, 297		3:22	145	6:9ff	225
10:7	73		6:3	297	6:9	259, 260
10:27	274		6:11ff	311, 313	6:15ff	225, 278
11:41ff	334		6:15	18	6:19–20	18
12:47–48	313		7:55–56	18	6:20	272
12:48	103, 160		10	162	8	247
14:13	297		10:11–16	182	9:4	73
14:21	297		10:28	182	9:5	73
14:26–27	158, 278, 297		13:1–3	145	9:7	73
16:13	246		15	162, 183	9:9	34
16:18	260		15:5	183	9:13–14	73
16:19–31	324		15:29	247	10:1–11:32	34
17:11–19	213		17:25	334	10:7ff	260
17:11–14	72		17:30–31	334	10:20–22	247
17:14	64		18:18	342	10:23ff	162
19–21	333		21:22–26	72, 82	10:25ff	247
19:8–9	112		21:23	342	10:26	183
19:42–44	331		21:26	64	11:1	25, 275
21:24	333		25:11	313	11:25	82

360

IV. INDEX OF NONBIBLICAL TEXTS